The World's First Underground Railway: Baker Street Station, Metropolitan Railway, 1863

A
HISTORY OF
LONDON
TRANSPORT

PASSENGER TRAVEL AND

THE DEVELOPMENT OF THE METROPOLIS

by

T. C. BARKER

and

MICHAEL ROBBINS

VOLUME I

The Nineteenth Century

LONDON

GEORGE ALLEN & UNWIN LTD

1975

First Published 1963
Paperback Edition, revised, 1975

ISBN 0 04 385066 9

PUBLISHED BY GEORGE ALLEN & UNWIN LTD
FOR THE LONDON TRANSPORT EXECUTIVE
PRINTED BY STAPLES PRINTERS LTD AT THE GEORGE PRESS
KETTERING NORTHAMPTONSHIRE

LIST OF ILLUSTRATIONS

CONTENTS

LIST OF MAPS

FOREWORD

BY THE CHAIRMAN OF LONDON TRANSPORT

The bus and the underground train are two of the most familiar features of everyday life in London today. Their existence is taken for granted by citizens and visitors alike; yet it is surprisingly difficult to find a comprehensive account of how London's public passenger transport came into being—still more to gain any clear notion of its influence on the life of the city at different periods.

How did London's transport system come into existence? Who were the people who built it up? What has it meant to the physical and social growth of the metropolis? The answers to these questions are of great interest in themselves; and furthermore they point, with broad indications, to important lessons for the future of city development, not only in London but also elsewhere. This first volume tells how the Victorians, when confronted with serious and growing traffic problems in the middle of the nineteenth century, held a number of Parliamentary enquiries and then managed to raise the capital to provide additional travelling facilities. The situation was eased for a time, but by the late nineteenth century, when this volume ends, another traffic crisis was developing and a further large outlay of capital was called for.

History never repeats itself exactly, for situations are never exactly the same; but the hard problems of today and tomorrow can surely be viewed with a steadier eye and a more informed judgement if we know what was done—both well and ill—in the past.

I hope that this book will be read by historians, administrators, and passengers alike; for, while it records the story of the different decades and the successive developments and changes, it also reveals the underlying characteristics which are always found in passenger transport in cities everywhere.

But I hope that this book will be read not only for that somewhat solemn reason. I hope it will also be read for more general interest. This is really the story of the efforts of thousands of men who devised, financed, built, and operated the means of public transport which made it possible for London to grow and in great measure determined the way it has grown. Few of them can be named; but we salute their memory. Without them the London that we know could not have been.

A B B Valentine

February 1963

PREFACE

[I]

Some ten years ago, the London Transport Executive decided that the story of the development of their undertaking should be put on record, the intention being to trace the *rôle* of public transport in London's development from the early nineteenth century onwards. In the first place, Mr. Harold Pollins was asked to carry out preliminary research, and this he did from 1954 to 1958. In 1960 we were invited to undertake further research and write this history, Dr. Barker being responsible for taking the story down to the early 1920s and Mr. Robbins for the remainder. Each was to criticize and, where desirable, supplement the work of the other; but the research for each section and the drafting of the chapters were to be according to this chronological division. While this volume appears as a work of joint authorship and there has been close collaboration between us throughout, these chapters have, therefore, all been written by Dr. Barker.

A number of readers, approaching this book as specialists —railway historians, for instance, or transport economists, or experts on some particular branch of London's history— may well find that, from their particular points of view, our history lacks depth. We hope, however, that its breadth provides adequate compensation. Our aim has been to look at all branches of passenger transport in the London area and to relate them and their interaction to the growth of London itself—the growth, that is, both of the whole built-up area and of business, shopping, and entertainment facilities in the centre. The extension of public transport was made possible by the growing wealth generated in London—and outside it as well, for this allowed an increasing number of people to visit, or pass through, the capital. The form these transport developments took was determined by a number of factors: by Parliamentary action, for instance, which was ultimately responsible in the nineteenth century both for linking the main-line termini by means of an underground railway and for keeping the horse tram out of central London; by high site values, greedy railway promoters, and financial crises which all helped to make railway building very costly, thereby keeping railway dividends low and hindering the raising of fresh capital; by reduced omnibus operating costs, made possible by tax reductions and cheaper horse feed, which helped to preserve the profitableness of horse traction in London even in the heyday of the steam locomotive; by able businessmen who were able to gain a growing share of the traffic at the expense of their less resourceful rivals. The subject clearly calls for treatment in breadth rather than in depth. Such a broad approach will, we hope, commend itself both to those who are interested in London's history and to many of the travelling public who may wonder how we have reached the present state of affairs in public transport.

An index will be included in volume II, which we hope to complete without undue delay. We also hope to include in volume II a list of *corrigenda* to this volume, and we shall, therefore, be glad to hear of errors in these pages as they are spotted.

T. C. BARKER
London School of Economics

R. M. ROBBINS
London Transport

February 1963

[II]

While this volume is primarily my concern, it owes very much to my co-author's remarkable knowledge about both railways and London's history. It has also been of great benefit to me to discuss nineteenth-century developments with someone who is engaged in the practical, day-to-day problems of London Transport. At the periodical meetings we have held, I have found him a most stimulating guide; his comments on the draft of my text have been most valuable and, in the chapters dealing with the Underground, the paragraphs on locomotives and railway operation are based almost wholly on his additions to the draft version. At the proof stage, the hawk eye of one well accustomed to much editorial proof correction spotted many slips which had eluded me.

I have also derived much help from Mr. Pollins's earlier researches. These quickly put me on to a number of sources. Although neither of us has been successful in discovering any notable privately-owned body of manuscripts for this volume, yet, as the reference notes will show, sources in various record offices have been tapped which have not, perhaps, been used in any previous study on this subject. I have relied on Mr. Pollins's work particularly in the part of chapter eight which deals with the later horse-tramway companies. In some aspects of the volume, notably on the financial and technical side, Mr. Pollins dug deeper than I have done. Specialists who are interested in such detail may care to consult Mr. Pollins's files, to which access can be had through London Transport.

The first selection of illustrations for this volume was undertaken by Mr. J. L. Howgego of the Guildhall Library, City of London, who provided Mr. Robbins and me with a range of pictures from which we made the final choice. The Institution of Civil Engineers allowed the photographing of certain of their portraits, and Mr. Reginald Tilling and Mr. John Birch those of Thomas Tilling and Samuel Birch. Mr. John Hayes of the London Museum helped me in tracking down some pictures there.

Advice and assistance have been received from many people, both inside and outside London Transport, and it is impossible to thank them all personally. But I should like to acknowledge particularly the generous help given by Mr. Charles E. Lee and Mr. Charles F. Klapper. Professor M. J. Wise made valuable comments and was good enough to arrange for the drafting of maps, the work of Miss Sheila Marshall. The final copies were drawn at 55 Broadway under the supervision of Mr. W. C. Hale. The text was much improved in draft as the result of comments by Professor William Ashworth, Mr. D. L. Munby, Dr. W. B. Price, and Mr. M. N. Leathwood. Some literary references were suggested by Mr. E. C. Blake and Mr. P. A. W. Collins. Miss E. M. Myatt-Price also helped me in searching for published diaries which might contain relevant entries. Lady Chorley assisted with information about her father and uncle, Edward and John Hopkinson (and supplied the photograph of the former), and Mr. W. L. Mather with details of Mather & Platt's early electrical interests. I am also grateful to my father for making calculations of the electrical efficiency of the City & South London Railway. Mr. G. F. A. Wilmot gave advice about Finchley and the development of the Great Northern's 'suburban incubus', and Mr. D. A. Reeder about property development in west London. Mr. K. Benest and Mr. J. E. D. Binney placed at my disposal the results of their researches into coaching stock on the Underground, and Mr. Desmond Heap, the Comptroller and City Solicitor, provided biographical information about Charles Pearson. Mr. R. C. Hider allowed me to consult some notes he made on the early history of the Metropolitan Railway. I also gained much from conversations on various aspects of the volume with

Dr. I. C. R. Byatt, Dr. H. J. Dyos and Mr. G. J. Ponsonby. Miss Jackson, Mr. Levey, and Mr. Wymer, all of London Transport, were concerned with the preparation of the book at various stages. M. Michel Linon of the Régie Autonome des Transports Parisiens was most helpful and hospitable during a visit to Paris to consult papers relating to the origins of the L.G.O.C.

Much of the research was done at the B.T.C. Historical Records and the House of Lords Record Office, and I am particularly grateful for the assistance given me by Mr. E. Atkinson and his staff at the former and by Miss Poyser and Mr. Cobb at the latter. My thanks are also due to the staff of Guildhall Library, whose kindness and efficiency are always a pleasure to experience. I also received help from Mr. R. C. Jarvis, Librarian of H.M. Customs & Excise, Mr. E. C. Baker, Archivist of the Post Office Records, Miss H. Wallis of the British Museum Map Room, and Mlle Labignette and M. Marquand of the *Archives Nationales*.

My final debt is to my wife for her patience and encouragement.

T. C. BARKER

The publication of a paperback edition gives me the opportunity to record with sadness the death, on 18 January 1974 at the age of 51, of Michel Linon, a great loss to Paris transport; and of my own father, N. H. Barker, whose help is also acknowledged in the introduction to Volume II. Although in his 88th year, he was keen to attend the launching of that volume at the Festival Hall on 24 September 1974. It was a most happy occasion and he was in fine form; but he collapsed and died while I was taking him to catch a train immediately afterwards. To me he is doubly associated with this work. He was equally devoted and encouraging in old age as he had been in my own childhood. I owe him more than I can express in words.

July 1975   T.C.B.

Such errors as could be corrected in the present reprint, without major consequential alterations to the text, have been corrected. The remaining corrigenda *will be found in Appendix 4. (page 413 in this Volume), and in Appendix 6, Volume II.*

THE NINETEENTH-CENTURY SCENE IN
LONDON

THE HISTORY of London's transport is an integral part of the history of London itself. Population began to increase rapidly towards the end of the eighteenth century and grew sixfold—from 1,110,000 to 6,580,000—during the nineteenth.[1] Accommodation for these many extra millions was provided by building outwards rather than upwards: London, unlike Paris, had long ceased to be confined within its city walls, and sites just beyond the existing urban perimeter beckoned invitingly to all those who had a vested interest in covering green fields and market gardens with bricks and mortar. As economic growth brought modest competencies to a small but increasing number of people, so these new recruits to the ranks of the middle classes—and others, longer established, who also developed a preference for less cramped quarters—moved out to occupy the tall, narrow, terraced houses of Camden Town or the superior semi-detached residences in the vicinity of Regent's Park. As distances between home and work became greater, everyone who could afford it chose to ride rather than to walk, and for all who could not keep their own carriage this meant a public conveyance. More potential passengers called into being more vehicles seeking their custom; and the more frequent the service, the greater was the attraction of the house or rented accommodation on the outskirts. In this way London's passenger transport came to expand, first using various types of horse-drawn carriage along the main roads and steamboats on the river; and then, as the suburban frontier became so remote that the journey by road took·too long or cost too much, also using the newly-built railways. In the first half of the nineteenth century, public transport, if not yet an essential element in London's life, was becoming a very important adjunct to it. Later, in the railway phase, it became a prerequisite of continued outward growth.

A home or lodgings in the suburbs and the daily ride to work were, however, comforts restricted to a small, though growing, minority; and many who were in a position to live outside central London could not afford to ride to work, at least as a general rule. 'Parties coming from Peckham and Camberwell', testified a witness at an inquiry in 1846, 'would be foot passengers'.[2] In the second half of the century, and particularly in the last quarter of it, real earnings rose and fares fell. The number of journeys per head rose quickly. Yet even in the 1890s a remarkably high proportion of people were still not using public transport as a means of getting to work. According to a count of nearly 160,000 south London members of trade unions carried out in 1897, for instance, fewer than a quarter used public transport regularly.[3] Some, of course, would have jobs locally and did not need to travel; and a few others may have been able to afford bicycles, although the bicycle was still an expensive machine; but many must still have walked quite long distances. And, at the end of the nineteenth century, such a sample of trade unionists would have contained a preponderance of better-paid, skilled men. Others, less fortunate, had to live much nearer in, so as to be close to their place of work. London then, as now, was the leading manufacturing centre in the country as well as the heart of its commercial and financial life. Industries such as clothing and furniture-making were carried on in tiny workshops both near the West End stores and in East London. They flourished on the vast pool of surplus labour which was at hand.[4] Jobs in these industries, as well as work at docks, markets and warehouses, rarely allowed the people employed to live far away, particularly if outwork was involved.

The comment of another witness in 1846 was still true fifty years later. 'A poor man', he declared, 'is chained to the spot. He has not leisure to walk and he has not money to ride to a distance from his work.'⁵ The witness's name was Charles Pearson, solicitor to the City of London; we shall hear more of him.

While many of the poorest people were confined to the central area so as to be close to their work, the amount of accommodation available for them was being steadily reduced. As industry and commerce developed, there was a growing need of central sites for use as offices, warehouses and shops, for road improvements, and for railway building. The commandeering of private dwellings for business sites removed some of the worst property; but it meant that the evicted occupants had no alternative but to crowd more and more into buildings in the immediate neighbourhood. In the first half of the nineteenth century, for instance, the resident population of districts such as Holborn and Finsbury rose rapidly. It was in areas such as these, just beyond the business quarters, that the worst rookeries were to be found. In the notorious St. Giles district there were, in 1836, 260 houses with an average of 20 people in each; in some instances there were 15 to a single room, 'in one corner of the room, lodgers, in another corner another set of lodgers, and besides a separate set of lodgers in the centre of the room, all distinct'.⁶ In the second half of the century the expulsive forces were intensified as more central sites were earmarked for business purposes. The residential population of the City fell sharply after 1850 and that of Westminster, Holborn, Finsbury and St. Marylebone followed suit a decade or two later. But there still remained, throughout the nineteenth century, the poorly-paid central nucleus and others, living in the inner suburbs, who were chained to their work. As the Royal Commission on Housing explained in the middle of the 1880s:

If regular work was to be had by all who want it without any

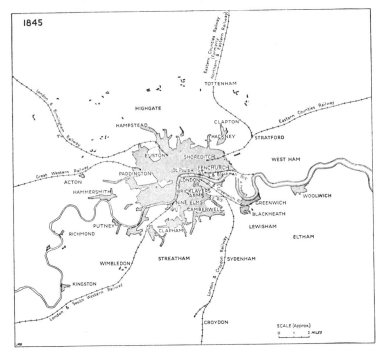

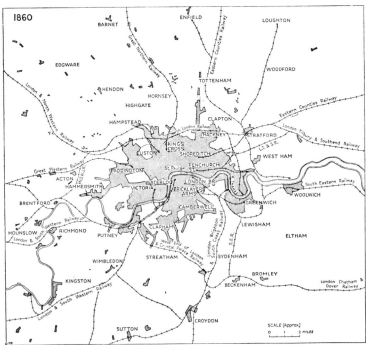

The growth of London 1845–1860

xxviii

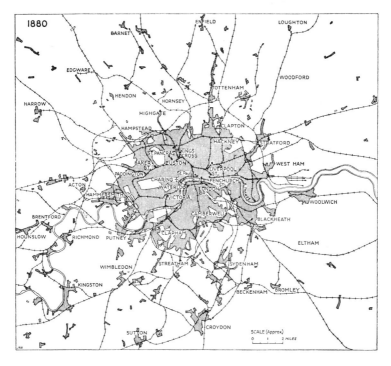

The growth of London 1880–1900

xxix

uncertainty, the poor might pick and choose the locality for their dwellings, but as it is, it has been noticed that when they have made an attempt to leave an overcrowded neighbourhood for some better locality at a little distance away, after a short sojourn many of them have often been compelled to come back to be near their work.[7]

Our subject has to be seen, therefore, not merely in terms of new, cost-reducing techniques in transport itself, but also in its broader economic context. As economic growth brought higher incomes to more people, so suburbia grew; and wage earners in regular employment also tended to move out beyond the more crowded districts. With population growing fast, more jobs being created in the heart of London and more people moving out, traffic kept on increasing. But it was not until working hours were shortened and earnings rose that the regular daily use of public transport could become available to all. And it was not until then that the most important cost-reducing innovations—the electric motor and the internal combustion engine—were developed to the point where they could be used commercially. All this had to await the twentieth century, however. Throughout the nineteenth, London's road transport had to rely on that most expensive form of traction, the horse; and its railways—with one or two minor exceptions in the 1890s—on the steam locomotive.

While the journey to work and the physical growth of London provide the central theme of this volume, they are by no means the whole story. If only a minority of Londoners travelled daily to work, a much higher proportion went off on excursions by steamboat or railway on Sundays or public holidays. Excursion trains also brought crowds into London, particularly in years when exhibitions were held. Between June and October 1851, for instance, more than 750,000 excursion travellers passed through Euston[8] and many others poured into London through the other main-line termini. Yet other visitors arrived to stay with relatives or friends, or to put up at one of the fine and spacious new hotels which had been opened to accommodate them. While the Season continued to bring the few great families to town for a few months in the year, the railways now also enabled large numbers of people in humbler walks of life to enjoy the sights of London, if not the glittering receptions and gay dinner parties. And, of course, there was a constant stream of men who came up to town on private or public business. According to a prominent city official, writing in 1866, there was 'scarcely a manufacturer of note or a merchant of celebrity in the whole nation' who did not have an office or agency in London which he had to visit personally.[9] Finally, there were other people—many of them—who needed to cross London to get from one part of the country to another or to reach the Continent. All these arrivals greatly supplemented the traffic generated by those who lived and worked in the metropolis.

Meanwhile, a considerable off-peak traffic was built up among Londoners themselves. Wives and children went visiting their friends or up to town shopping—particularly after the opening of the new department stores. Those who worked in central London took advantage of the cheap, short-distance fares to ride from one part of it to another. The spread of the Saturday half-holiday provided further opportunities for travel; and on weekday evenings an increasing number of theatres, music and concert halls drew audiences from all corners of the metropolis. Transport services not only enabled London to grow outwards: they also helped it to develop as a centre of amusement, pleasure and recreation.

This, then, is more than an account of how a number of transport undertakings were built up and operated; more than a description of when this railway line was opened or that type of bus came into operation. These events have their rightful place in the story. But they have all to be set against the many-sided development of London itself. No branch of history can exist in isolation: transport history least of all.

CHAPTER ONE

THE ORIGINS OF THE OMNIBUS

On 4 July 1829, an omnibus drawn by three horses was put into regular service at advertised times by George Shillibeer on a route between Paddington and the Bank by way of the Angel. This event has been recorded and commemorated as marking a new era in urban transport in Great Britain—as being, in fact, its real beginning. It was an important development, certainly, and its significance was considerable; but there are always dangers in attributing important developments to a single hero. In this case, vehicles closely resembling omnibuses had operated in the London area some time before Shillibeer came upon the scene; and Shillibeer was less successful than other men of the time in making a commercial success of the omnibus business.

Why were omnibus services not started in London before 1829? Was it merely because there had been no energetic pioneer at hand to do so? And why did Shillibeer choose as his route a road which ran round the perimeter of the metropolis instead of through the central streets where the traffic was heaviest? The answers to these questions involve, first of all, some consideration of the timing and direction of metropolitan growth.

THE NORTH-WESTERN THRUST

LONDON is Thames-orientated. The river was its main highway, and few people lived or worked far from it. Much of the south bank was, however, swampy and unattractive, and, in any case, could be reached by only one bridge. As the capital outgrew its city limits, therefore, it spread in a thin ribbon of habitation along the north side of the river, both eastwards and (particularly) westwards; and, when population started to grow more rapidly in the eighteenth century, it pushed out tentacles along all the main roads.

c

'There will soon be one street from London to Brentford;
ay, and from London to every village ten miles around,'
declared Horace Walpole in 1791.[1] Outlying villages such
as Kensington, Bow, Greenwich, Camberwell and Streatham increased quickly in size. The most extensive, concentrated growth, however, took place to the west and north-
west. There the limits of the central built-up area were
farthest removed from the heart of the City. This pattern
had already been set during the eighteenth century. What
has been called 'the early Georgian building boom'[2] had
covered the ground between Oxford Street and Piccadilly
as far west as Hyde Park. But, apart from one or two places,
there was little penetration beyond Oxford Street for some
years after that. In 1756, when the New Road was opened
from the Edgware Road at Paddington to the Angel at
Islington (the present-day Marylebone, Euston and Pentonville Roads), it ran through open country well to the north
of the built-up area. It was made by cutting down hedges
and filling in ditches, its course being marked by a couple
of neat post and rail fences.[3] By 1820, however, the builder
had reached this road along most of its length and in some
places had crossed it. Lord's had been removed in 1810 to
make way for Dorset Square, for instance,[4] and, farther to
the east, some of the buildings across the New Road must
by then have become quite weathered with age and covered
with London grime.

'The extensive chapelry of Pentonville', recalled a writer in
1820, 'was begun about the year 1780, and is now united with
Islington. Somers Town was commenced about 1786, and Camden
Town about 1791. Since that time almost the entire mass of
buildings which constitutes the upper part of Tottenham Court
Road has been built, together with its wide-spreading neighbourhood to the west. Even the distant village of Paddington, by the
increase of buildings in this direction, has now been completely
united with the metropolis and is itself in a state of very rapid
enlargement. The new buildings along the Hampstead Road and

on the east and west of [the newly laid out] Regent's Park are also rapidly augmenting.'[5]

John Luffman's map of 1820, while it makes clear that the 'very rapid enlargement' of Paddington was rather an exaggeration—there was as yet no growth to speak of to the west of the Edgware Road—does show that the extremity of the north-western thrust then lay just to the north of the New Road in a narrow salient bounded by Regent's Park on the east and Edgware Road on the west. There was also ribbon development along Edgware Road itself as far as Maida Vale, where the northern boundary was marked by ten villas built at a respectful distance from one another on the east of the road and known collectively as Pine Apple Place. St. John's Wood was still only the name of a farm on the north-western fringe of Regent's Park, but a little way round the edge of the Park and to the south-east of it there was a most significant development: the appearance of pairs of semi-detached houses, in Sir John Summerson's view 'the first part of London, and indeed of any other town, to abandon the terrace house for the semi-detached villa—a revolution of striking and far-reaching effect'.[6]

With a well-to-do population growing up on each side of it, the New Road came to carry an increasing passenger traffic bound for the City. It was here that London's busiest stage coach service was to develop.

The Short-Stage Coach

The romantic story of the long-distance stage coach—a triumph of organization and the most spectacular exhibition of natural horse power—has fired the imagination of many writers; but the more prosaic story of the short-stage, dragged slowly along the road and stopping frequently for passengers, has still to be told. The short-stage was to the *Wonder* or the *Tally-Ho* what, at a later time, the branch line train was to be to the *Cheltenham Flyer* or the *Flying*

Scotsman: undistinguished and made contemptible by familiarity, yet full of local colour and performing a most valuable function. And the short-stage, on occasion, offered Londoners a service which the later branch line train could not: it sometimes collected the half dozen or so inside passengers from their own homes.[7] Most of those who travelled by these short-stages had booked in advance and this involved calling at various booking offices (usually public houses) *en route*. But not everybody booked in advance and the journey was further prolonged by stops on the road to pick up these other passengers. A Frenchman who went from Richmond to London at the beginning of 1810, for instance, noted in his diary that the coach was

crammed inside and *hérissé* outside with passengers, of all sexes, ages, and conditions. We stopped more than twenty times on the road—the debates about the fare of way-passengers—the settling themselves—the getting up, and the getting down, and damsels shewing their legs in the operation and tearing and muddying their petticoats—complaining and swearing—took an immense time. I never saw anything so ill managed. In about two hours we reached Hyde Park corner . . .[8]

By the 1820s this short-stage traffic was reaching considerable proportions in the London area. Directories show hourly services from various inns in the City and West End to the growing suburbs and outlying villages. At the beginning of December 1825 the City Police Committee took a record of the number of short-stage coaches starting from several points within the City limits, together with their destinations and the number of return journeys made by each in a day.[9] In all, 418 vehicles were counted and these made a total of 1,190 journeys. If we may suppose that half as many short-stage coaches left from the West End as from the City—this, the directories suggest, would not lead to overestimation—that would produce a total of some 600 short-stages and about 1,800 daily journeys. This was probably about one-fifth of all the stage coaches in the whole country at that time,[10] a remarkable proof of the importance which this metropolitan short-stage traffic had then assumed. Of the journeys from the City, about 400 were south of the river, another 400 to the north and east, some 170 to the west and 240 to the north-west. Many more coaches ran to Paddington than to any other single destination.

TERMINI OF THE 12 MOST IMPORTANT SHORT-STAGE
ROUTES FROM THE CITY IN 1825

Destination	Number of Coaches	Number of Return Journeys Per Day
Paddington	54	158
Camberwell	23	104
*Blackwall	29	72
Clapham	21	57
Islington	11	53
Kentish Town	7	50
Clapton	12	44
Peckham	10	40
Edmonton	17	39
Hackney	7	39
Homerton	5	32
Hammersmith	12	30

*The large traffic to Blackwall is explained to some extent by coaches operated by the West India Dock Company to carry passengers and samples of goods.[11]

Source: A Statement of the Number of Short-Stage Coaches Standing in the Streets of the City of London (Corporation of London Records Office, B.12.V). For fuller details see Appendix 1.

The fares on these coaches were high, for example 1s. 6d. to 2s. single to the City or West End from Paddington, Peckham or Clapham for each of the four or six inside seats and sixpence less for those outside. Fares varied, however, 'according to the prices of hay and corn and other circumstances affecting the proprietors' interests'.[12] For safety, the number of outside passengers was limited to seven on coaches carrying no roof luggage and drawn by two or three horses, and to twelve on those drawn by four.[13] Operating costs were considerable: horses (£20 each) had a working life of only three or four years. Additional horses would be needed in case of illness or accident, and no doubt a succession of relief horses would be required to maintain services on the busier routes. The feeding and stabling of all these animals was expensive (perhaps over 15s. a week were needed per horse for feed alone[14]) and the upkeep of coaches (costing about £100 when new) was also considerable, for there was much wear and tear. Many of the vehicles employed on long-distance runs were hired from their builders, who contracted to maintain them for a fixed sum per mile,[15] but it is not clear whether this method of capital saving was employed by operators of short-stages. They certainly had to pay heavy duties, however, on the same scale as those levied on the long-stages. Originally proprietors paid only a modest licence fee on each of their coaches, but in the later eighteenth century this was supplemented by a mileage duty raised at first at the same rate on all coaches and then (after 1804) on a scale which varied with the number of inside seats, *whether or not those seats were occupied.*[16] After 1815 coaches with not more than four inside seats paid 2½d. per mile and those with not more than six, 3d.[17]

The high cost of horse power and the very severe rate of taxation made it virtually impossible to make any significant cuts in fares to and from the outskirts of London. Given these handicaps, a major advance was possible only if operators could tap some of the short-distance passenger traffic within the streets of London itself and use the proceeds to reduce fares on longer journeys. The denser the population served, the greater was the likelihood of filling a higher proportion of seats and thus spreading costs. The coach proprietors were forbidden by law, however, from taking advantage of the lucrative short-distance traffic of central London. Once they reached the paved streets within the limits of the seventeenth-century Bills of Mortality— 'the stones' as they were called—the short-stages were not allowed to set down or take up passengers until they reached their City or West End termini. Similarly, on the outward journey, they were not permitted to stop for passengers until they reached the edge of the stones.[18]

The Hackney Coach Monopoly

This prohibition was enforced to preserve the monopoly enjoyed by the hackney coaches. It had originated in the seventeenth century when the number of vehicles plying for hire had increased so rapidly that the authorities had intervened in an effort to prevent any further jamming in the narrow City streets. As time passed and the metropolis grew, the permitted quota of hackney coaches was increased. In 1814 a lighter type, the chariot, was introduced taking only two passengers inside and a third on the box seat.[19] It was followed, in 1823, by a vehicle which was already fashionable in Paris, the one-horse cabriolet, a fleet two-wheeler which carried two passengers at a lower fare than a hackney coach; but, being open at the front, it was patronized only in good weather.[20] By the end of the 1820s licences were granted for 1,100 coaches and chariots and 165 cabriolets.[21] All these hackney vehicles were much more lightly taxed than stage coaches—they paid only 10s. per week plus a modest annual licence fee—but were subject to numerous regulations as to fares and conditions of hiring.[22]

The hackney coach monopoly came under increasing attack. It was an obvious target for the growing numbers who believed, on principle, that competition bred efficiency and, on a less doctrinaire plane, for the applicants who had been refused licences. A correspondent of *The Times* claimed that licences could be obtained only if the applicant knew the hackney coach commissioners;[23] the Receiver and Registrar at the Hackney Coach Office revealed that 65 cabriolet licences had been granted at the express instructions of the Treasury;[24] and Joseph Hume claimed in the House of Commons that twelve licences had gone to 'a banker and a barrister, whose rank in society should have placed them above such employment'.[25] The best criterion was the condition of the hackney coaches themselves, and it was generally agreed that this was deplorable. The practice was for the proprietors to buy gentlemen's carriages

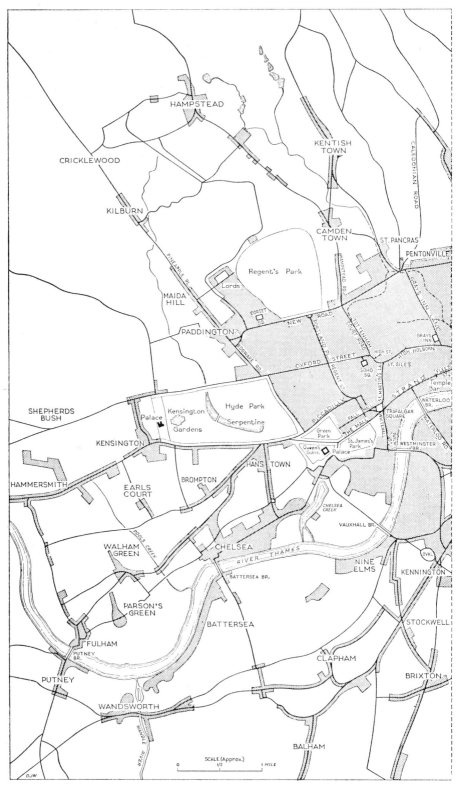

London in the 1820s based on John Luffman's map (1820);

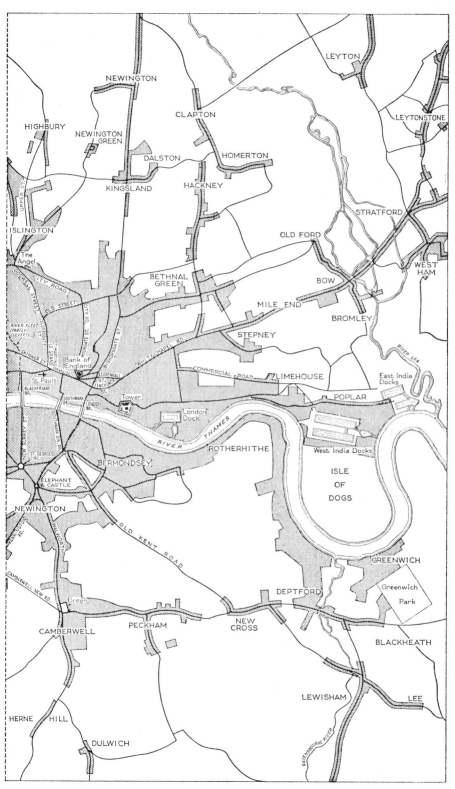

street improvements mentioned in the text have been added

9

after they had been discarded. They were decrepit and dirty—particularly those used at night—and always breaking down.[26] The owners complained that competition from the new cabs had made their business unprofitable and they could no longer afford to spend much money on their vehicles.[27] The cab proprietors retorted, more plausibly, that the fall in hackney coach profits was due to better policing and lighting of the streets at night 'which enable persons going to or returning from parties and places of public amusement to walk with safety'. More people, too, were taking short-stages to travel into town from the edge of the stones, and there had been a loss of traffic because of arrangements which the proprietors of long-distance coaches had made to carry London passengers between their homes and the long-stage termini by a system of branch coaches.[28]

Street Improvement

Because of its east–west growth, London was better served by roads running in this direction than by those running from north to south. There were, in fact, three main routes westwards from the City: along Fleet Street and the Strand; along High Holborn and Oxford Street; and by the New Road, which had been created as a kind of North Circular Road chiefly for the passage of animals on the hoof bound for market and had grown into a major thoroughfare for wheeled vehicles, serving inhabitants in its immediate vicinity as well as travellers from farther afield. Before the nineteenth century, however, a number of bottlenecks interrupted the easy flow of traffic along the High Holborn and Fleet Street routes. Along the former there was a deviation along the narrow St. Giles High Street and Broad Street (there was no New Oxford Street) and difficult descents into the valley of the river Fleet (no Holborn Viaduct). Along the latter, narrow streets at the west end of the Strand and another bottleneck at the top of Fleet Street, near

Temple Bar, slowed up the traffic. And, once St. Paul's was reached, there was the worst bottleneck of all, for these two routes then ran together along Cheapside and Poultry (no Cannon Street and, of course, no Embankment or Queen Victoria Street). To get from north to south, however, was even more tortuous, for, at the beginning of the nineteenth century, there was no good communication in this direction: no Regent Street; no Charing Cross Road (nor Shaftesbury Avenue); no traffic permitted through the Bedford estate, then being developed northwards from Russell Square (and no Kingsway); no Farringdon Road and no wide thoroughfare south from Finsbury Square.

Many of these new roads were not opened until the second half of the nineteenth century—and Kingsway was not built until the beginning of the twentieth. But an important start was made during, and after, the Napoleonic wars and these improvements strengthened the case for the removal of the hackney coach monopoly. The original exponents of the monopoly had based their arguments on the narrowness of the streets; the advocates of its removal were, in the later 1820s, able to point to the sweeping changes which had taken place, many of them within a comparatively recent period. The most important of these was Regent Street, begun in 1817 and all but completed by 1823.[29] It provided a good north–south thoroughfare from Portland Place (which itself connected with the New Road) to Oxford Street, from where it was cut through cheap property on the western fringes of Soho to Piccadilly and then down to Waterloo Place. A square was laid out at the top of Whitehall (named, in 1830, Trafalgar Square), linked by Pall Mall East to the lower part of Regent Street and, by the West Strand improvements, with the main road to St. Paul's through the Strand, Fleet Street (widened a little at the top near Temple Bar) and Ludgate Hill. To the north, the High Holborn route was also improved by the construction of a new street—Skinner Street—to ease the gradient on the east side of the Fleet valley.[30] And other minor improvements at the western end of Cheapside and at St. Martin's-le-Grand benefited both routes. In the heart of the City itself Moorgate Street was built, in the later 1820s, to link Finsbury Square and the Bank.[31]

Traffic from south of the river had the advantage of fine, wide highroads. Most of them had been laid out in the eighteenth century, first to secure better access to London Bridge and then to handle traffic to and from the first Westminster and Blackfriars Bridges (opened in 1750 and 1769 respectively).[32] Three new bridges were opened after the Napoleonic wars: Vauxhall (1816), Waterloo (1817) and Southwark (1819). But their usefulness was greatly restricted because of the tolls their owners levied on both vehicles and pedestrians. (Tolls had never been levied on Westminster Bridge, and Blackfriars Bridge had become toll-free in 1811.) The construction of the three new bridges did, however, lead to a further spate of road building on the south bank, where the marshy nature of the land still discouraged housing development. This made it easier for road builders to lay out Harleyford Road, Harleyford Street and Camberwell New Road as a direct route to Vauxhall Bridge,[33] and Waterloo Road as a link between St. George's Circus, where the existing roads already converged, and Waterloo Bridge.[34] Southwark Bridge Road, however, had to be cut through private property and was neither so wide nor so straight as the others.[35] Farther up the river a new suspension bridge was opened at Hammersmith in 1827. It, too, was a toll bridge, as were the older, wooden structures at Battersea and Putney. Most important of all, however, was the building, between 1824 and 1831, of the new London Bridge. This, too, had wide approaches. Many of the roads south of the river had carriageways 72 feet wide, while that of the new London Bridge was 52 feet, and even the narrower parts of Southwark Bridge Road were over 45 feet wide.

Another encouragement to traffic was the removal of turnpike gates. These not only barred the way out of London by all the main roads; they also stopped vehicles making short journeys along Oxford Street, Gray's Inn Lane and the New Road. In 1826, however, metropolitan turnpike trusts north of the river were consolidated into one Commission[36] and under its Surveyor-General, (Sir) James McAdam, $9\frac{1}{2}$ miles of roads were surfaced with stone for the first time, and other stretches under its control—and elsewhere in London—were re-surfaced on the macadam principle. (Whitehall, Parliament Street, Regent Street, Pall Mall, Oxford Street and part of Piccadilly were soon all macadamized.[37]) In March 1829 the Commission promoted a Bill to permit the removal of tolls within the built-up area, responsibility for the upkeep of the roads concerned being transferred to the parish authorities. An important aim of the measure was 'to remove all the gates from the Edgware Road to the City, so as to open a free communication between the east and the west of the metropolis'.[38] The Act freed from toll from 1 January 1830 Oxford Street and Edgware Road as far as Maida Hill, the New Road throughout its length, and the whole of Old Street and Gray's Inn Lane.[39] The Commission thereafter continued to raise tolls upon the main roads on the outskirts. It spent this income on macadamizing existing roads and laying out new ones, notably that from Camden Town to 'a clump of trees called the Seven Sisters near Tottenham'. The Caledonian Road, built in the later 1820s, was among the new roads which came under its jurisdiction but, rather remarkably, not the other fine north London highway of the same period, the road from Marylebone to North Finchley (the present-day Finchley Road, Regent's Park Road and Ballard's Lane).[40]

Between 1815 and 1830, then, the main thoroughfares of the metropolis had been greatly improved and many of them freed from tolls. As the demand for improved transport arrangements became more insistent, it became increasingly difficult to justify the hackney coach monopoly. In October 1828 a letter reached the Hackney Coach Commissioners to say that the Government had decided on the abolition of their office and was proposing to introduce a Bill in the following session to transfer their function to the Board of Stamps which was already responsible for the taxing of stage coaches.[41] The next session, however, saw no such measure and it was not until the following year, 1830, that a Select Committee was appointed to look into the whole position. It recommended the abolition of the Hackney Coach Office, the licensing of all comers by the Board of Stamps and the permitting of stage coaches to ply for hire within central London.[42] The fall of the Government in November 1830 again delayed action, and it was not until September 1831 that the existing hackney coach legislation was at last repealed. A new Act enforced the committee's recommendations about stage coaches by failing to renew the monopoly. It was to cease from 5 January 1832, and from January 1833 the limit to the number of hackney coaches was also to be removed. During 1833, 800 new licences were issued to more than 600 proprietors.[43] The old and rickety coaches were soon driven off the streets and replaced by cabs. These, in their turn, were within a short time replaced by a new type of cab, the hansom, and a new type of four-wheeler, the brougham.[44] In 1844, instead of 1,100 disreputable hackney coaches, whose owners claimed to be on the verge of bankruptcy, 2,450 cabs and 200 carriages of greatly improved design and upkeep were able to ply for hire profitably.[45] And this was in competition with short-stages. For short-stage work a new type of vehicle was also used: the omnibus.

The Omnibus

The omnibus did not involve any major development in coach design. In principle it was nothing more than a box

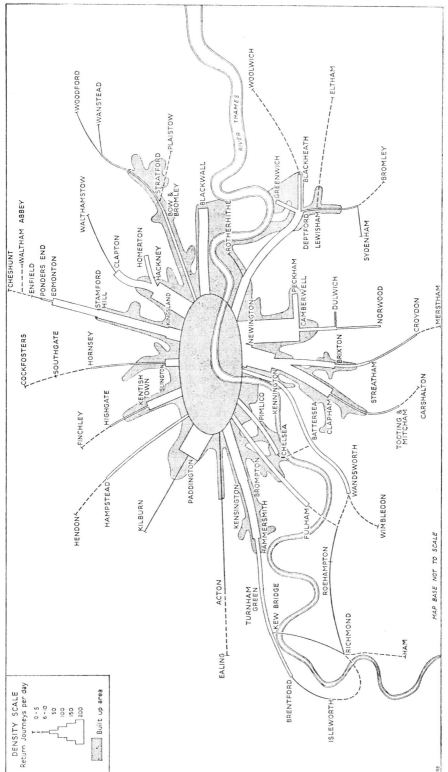

Short-Stage Coach Traffic in 1825 (Source: Appendix 1)

DENSITY SCALE
Return journeys per day

0 - 5
6 - 10
50
100
150
200

Built up area

MAP BASE NOT TO SCALE

RIVER THAMES

WOODFORD
WANSTEAD
WOOLWICH
ELTHAM
BROMLEY
STRATFORD
PLAISTOW
BLACKWALL
BLACKHEATH
GREENWICH
BOW & BROMLEY
DEPTFORD
LEWISHAM
SYDENHAM
ROTHERHITHE
CHESHUNT
WALTHAM ABBEY
ENFIELD
PONDERS END
EDMONTON
WALTHAMSTOW
CLAPTON
HOMERTON
HACKNEY
STAMFORD HILL
KINGSLAND
NEWINGTON
CAMBERWELL
PECKHAM
DULWICH
NORWOOD
CROYDON
MERSTHAM
COCKFOSTERS
SOUTHGATE
HORNSEY
ISLINGTON
KENTISH TOWN
BRIXTON
STREATHAM
CARSHALTON
FINCHLEY
HIGHGATE
PIMLICO
KENNINGTON
CLAPHAM
BATTERSEA
TOOTING & MITCHAM
HAMPSTEAD
KILBURN
PADDINGTON
KENSINGTON
BROMPTON
CHELSEA
FULHAM
WANDSWORTH
WIMBLEDON
HENDON
HAMMERSMITH
ACTON
EALING
TURNHAM GREEN
KEW BRIDGE
ROEHAMPTON
RICHMOND
HAM
BRENTFORD
ISLEWORTH

I5

on wheels with two forms placed lengthways inside, windows through which passengers could peer to discover where they were, and a door at the back providing easy entry and egress. There was nothing unique, or even new, about such a vehicle at the end of the 1820s. It was then said to be 'only a revival of the long stage-coach which was common in England about twenty or thirty years ago'.[46] This is confirmed by a painting of Blackfriars Bridge in 1798, a drawing ascribed to Rowlandson and dated 1799[47] and an entry in a diary in 1810 in which the writer records being carried from London to Kew Bridge in a coach which 'resembled a ship on four wheels; a sort of half cylinder, round below, flat above, very long and divided into three distinct apartments'. He 'was introduced into the cabin by an after-port and locked in with another passenger'.[48] The short-stages to Greenwich were also of this build; a drawing has survived of what a character in a farce of 1820 described as 'the great green Greenwich coach'.[49] This type of vehicle, however, was discriminated against so long as the mileage duty was raised on the number of inside seats. And it had no real advantage over the stage coach so long as a high proportion of passengers stayed on it for most or all of the journey. It was not much of a hardship, when most people travelled a distance into London from the outskirts, for them to clamber on to the roof or, as a print dated about 1830 shows, up a short ladder into an enlarged dickey.[50] Nor did riding in the open discourage them, since the lower fare paid by outside passengers was ample recompense for any discomfort. It was only when short-distance traffic became possible within London itself and people had to hop on and off at frequent intervals that clambering became both highly inconvenient and time-wasting. The ascendancy of the box on wheels and the eclipse of the short-stage coach was a direct result of the Hackney Coach Act of 1831; but—like the cabriolet—it came into its own only after its usefulness had been demonstrated in Paris.

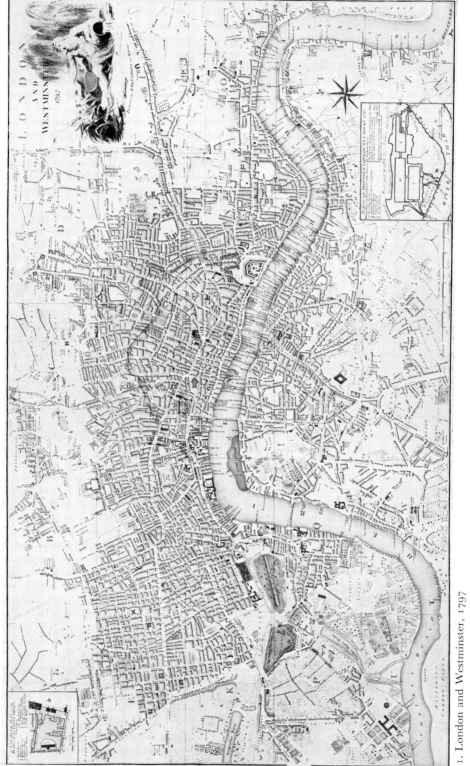

1. London and Westminster, 1797

2. Omnibus on Blackfriars Bridge, 1798

3. Shillibeer's Omnibus, 1829

4. The turnpike at St. George's Circus, 1813

5. The turnpike at Tyburn

6. Regent Street, 1822

7. The new London Bridge, about 1832

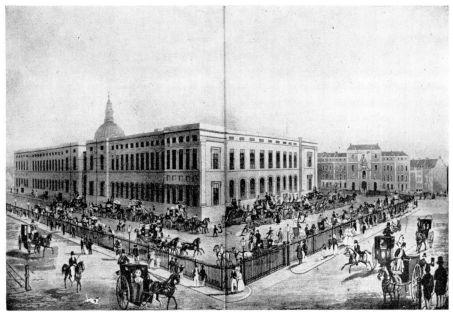

8. Coaches and cabs in the 1830s: the General Post Office, with an early Hansom Cab and Clarence 4-wheeler (left foreground)

9. Hammersmith Broadway with Omnibuses, 1840

10. George Shillibeer

MISERIES OF LONDON.

In going out to dinner (already too late) your carriage delayed by a jam of coaches — which choak up the whole street, and allow you at least an hour or more than you require to chafen your will for talkt'loth. "Breast against breast with ruinous assault And dissevering shock they come"

11. London Street Traffic, 1807

12. A suggested Pedestrian Crossing at Ludgate Circus, mid-19th Century

13. Inside a London Omnibus, 1859

Parisians were housed in taller buildings than were Londoners; they occupied premises which were usually five storeys high and often seven. Paris therefore lent itself more readily to the type of vehicle which could carry passengers satisfactorily for short distances. In January 1828 the Prefecture of Police gave permission to Stanislas Baudry, who already had had experience of operating a box on wheels in Nantes, and two collaborators to run a hundred of these coaches on ten fixed routes through Paris. They called them *omnibus* because (so it is said) the town terminus at Nantes had been the shop of a certain M. Omnes who had adopted the slogan *Omnes Omnibus*; the easy transition to naming the vehicle *omnibus* was irresistible. Omnibus, 'bus and bus it has since remained in Britain; William Morris's attempt to call it a 'folk-wain' found no favour. The word omnibus is used throughout this volume as it was the approved word for almost the whole of the nineteenth century.

According to the *ordonnance* granted by the Paris police, each omnibus was to be drawn by more than one horse and to carry between 12 and 20 passengers, all inside. In fact, the vehicles which *L'Entreprise des Omnibus* built carried 14 passengers and were divided into three classes, with a flat rate per journey for each class, the cheapest fare being 25 centimes. The venture was an immediate success; during the summer of 1828 each vehicle carried an average of 310 passengers per day. *L'Entreprise* had only taken up half of its permitted quota, and other concerns soon came on the scene to take the remaining licences and share the traffic.[51] On 6 September 1828 *The Times* was able to report the appearance in Paris of a new omnibus line called *Les Dames Blanches* 'painted white with a motto in gold upon a red ground; and at the back of each coach are sketches of Scotch scenery and costume from [Boieldieu's recent] opera *La Dame Blanche*. The horses and their harness are white and the drivers wear white hats and embroidered white coats . . . a kind of trumpet under the seat of the coachman,

D

and which is played by pressure, executes the principal airs of the opera . . .'

This early success of the omnibus in Paris was witnessed by George Shillibeer, who was then, at the age of 30, in business with John Cavill in Bury Street, Bloomsbury, as a coach builder and livery stable keeper—that is, the firm fed and watered horses at a charge or let out its own horses with or without carriages for hire. The directories mention this firm from 1826–27 but not earlier. In 1830 Shillibeer himself stated that he had 'an establishment' in Paris 'for the sale of carriages'[52] and claimed that he had been employed to make carriages for Jacques Laffitte, the Paris businessman and banker and in many ways the key figure in the French financial world of the 1820s.[53] H. C. Moore, in his article on Shillibeer in the *Dictionary of National Biography*, suggested that, though London-born and trained, Shillibeer had started business in Paris, transferred to London later and actually built omnibuses for Laffitte before beginning on his own account in London. While it seems probable that Shillibeer had had Paris connections for some time before 1830, it is not clear by what date these had ripened into 'an establishment', though it is certain that he did not give up his activities in Paris when, in the mid-1820s, he started to build vehicles in London. It is possible, indeed, that the Paris establishment may have grown out of Shillibeer and Cavill's business in London, as an outlet for their London-built carriages. Shillibeer had been trying to secure cabriolet licences in London since 1825,[54] which suggests that London was then already the main scene of his operations. This was certainly the case by 1828, as is made quite clear by the wording of a memorial he sent to the Treasury at the beginning of July of that year, seeking permission to operate in the London streets omnibuses of his own construction 'under the more English name of Economist':

Your Memorialist has no doubt but that your Lordships have heard of the new public vehicle, called *Omnibus* recently established at *Paris* and authorised by an ordonnance from the Prefecture of Police to convey passengers without luggage to and from the barriers of Paris at the moderate charge of 5 sous or 2½d. for a course of about one mile and a half English.

Your Memorialist having been to Paris for the purpose of viewing these carriages which commenced running about two months since, and being impressed by ocular demonstration of their extreme utility in London, contemplating establishing them in London under the more English name of Economist, their convenience being so greatly acknowledged at Paris notwithstanding there are 1,700 hackney coaches and 900 cabriolets in that city. It is with the strongest impression of their utility here, where the expense of conveyance is so high that the industrious part of the community are obliged to walk, that your Memorialist most humbly begs to solicit your Lordships' sanction to work these carriages upon the most frequented routes of the Metropolis according to the plan which your Memorialist has now the honour to submit, each vehicle being built to contain 18 persons, *all inside* without any luggage, to be drawn by 3 horses abreast, having a decent coachman on the box and a well conducted man inside as receiver, the price of each course being at the rate of less than 3d. per mile and subject to any regulations your Lordships may deem necessary to adopt, the object of your Memorialist being to give the public a safe and comfortable conveyance over the London stones at one fourth the price of the present hackney carriages.[55]

This application was refused because of the existing hackney coach monopoly. But Shillibeer was not for long deterred. He no doubt knew that the monopoly was under increasing pressure and felt that its overthrow was probable at no distant date. In the meantime there was one route on which he could demonstrate the merits of the new service he was proposing without breaking the law. This was along the New Road from Paddington to the Bank. It not only carried the heaviest traffic from the rapidly growing northwestern suburbs but also ran round the northern fringes of the metropolis just beyond the limits of the stones. It therefore lay outside the hackney coach monopoly, and vehicles could stop at will to pick up or set down their passengers. There would not be so much short-distance traffic as in the central streets but there was enough to make a start. And hardly any people at the Paddington and Marylebone end of the route had their own private transport; coach houses and stables were almost completely absent there.[56]

In a memorial dated 3 April 1829 to the Board of Stamps, Shillibeer announced that he was building two omnibuses and was going to operate these on the Paddington road under the Stage Coach Acts.[57] By then he had dropped the idea of calling his vehicles Economists, for he perceived that to anglicize them was a tactical error. The more French he could make them sound, the more fashionable they were likely to become. His first omnibus began to run on 4 July 1829, and his advertisement was at pains to stress that it was the latest from Paris:

OMNIBUS—G. Shillibeer, induced by the universal admiration the above vehicle called forth at Paris, has commenced running one upon the Parisian mode from PADDINGTON to the BANK.
The superiority of this carriage over the ordinary stage coaches for comfort and safety must be obvious, all the passengers being inside and the fare charged from Paddington to the Bank being one shilling, and from Islington to the Bank or Paddington sixpence.
The proprietor begs to add that a person of great respectability attends his vehicle as conductor; and every possible attention will be paid to the accommodation of ladies and children.
Hours of starting:— From Paddington Green to the Bank at 9, 12, 3, 6 and 8 o'clock; from the Bank to Paddington at 10, 1, 4, 7 and 9 o'clock.[58]

Shillibeer's original omnibuses were larger than those in Paris and were drawn by three horses instead of two; they could seat 20 passengers inside. The short-stages on the Paddington route were drawn by two horses and were,

therefore, allowed by law to carry seven outside passengers
as well as four or six inside. The single fare appears to have
been 1s. 6d. inside and 1s. out. The earning capacity of the
short-stage if every seat were taken by one person on the
journey was, therefore, 13s. or 16s. That of the omnibus on
the same basis (at one shilling all the way) was 20s. But as
it was drawn by an additional horse, that would add considerably to Shillibeer's running costs. He had also to pay
more duty than his competitors did, but here he was able
to take advantage of a clause in a stage coach act of 1822
which allowed vehicles carrying 'one description of passengers only, not distinguishing between inside and outside
passengers' to be taxed not according to the number of
inside seats but according to the number of horses drawing
the vehicle.[59] The rate was 1½d. per mile for one horse, 3d.
for two and 4½d. for three or more. As the short-stages paid
only 2½d. a mile if they were licensed to carry 11 passengers
and 3d. a mile for 13, Shillibeer, paying 4½d. a mile for 20,
had no tax advantage unless he was able to squeeze more
people into his vehicle from time to time. Nor was the ratio
of horse-power to passengers carried any lower on the
omnibus than on the short-stage. Shillibeer's costs rose in
proportion to the carrying capacity of his vehicle, and, in
the event, smaller omnibuses, capable of carrying 12 to 15
passengers—about the same number as the short-stages—
found general favour. The success of the omnibus clearly
depended not upon its size but upon its loading. The
operator had to fill a higher proportion of seats than was
usual on the short-stages, partly by attracting a succession
of short-distance passengers. Shillibeer no doubt hoped that
the novelty of his omnibus, with ease of access and protection against the weather, and its lower fares would achieve
this. And he placed great emphasis both on civility—two of
the conductors were said to be sons of naval officers[60]—and
on speed and punctuality. 'The other coaches,' Shillibeer
noted, 'hang about at the public houses a quarter of an

hour or ten minutes, but I go right away whether I have passengers or not.'[61] The omnibus picked up and set down on the road itself rather than at a number of public houses. Although one hour was allowed, it was possible to do the journey of five miles in 40 minutes.

The omnibus was from the first well supported by the public; 'fourteen or fifteen ladies and gentlemen were frequently to be seen running after it when it was completely full'.[62] It naturally aroused fierce opposition from the short-stage drivers, who on 11 July 1829, only a week after his service began, caused Shillibeer to be haled before the Lord Mayor's Court on a charge of permitting it to wait longer at Bartholomew Lane in the City than the Paddington stages were allowed to do. The Lord Mayor, however, gave him a very sympathetic hearing and, dismissing the case, expressed the opinion that the omnibus had 'advantages of a very high order'.[63]

Omnibus Competition and Association

Other operators were not slow to copy Shillibeer. George Cloud, for instance, who ran short-stages from Hammersmith, picking up as far as the limit of the hackney coach monopoly at Hyde Park Corner and then running direct to the terminus at St. Paul's, had replaced some of his coaches by four omnibuses by May 1830. These were smaller than Shillibeer's and more suited to the narrower streets near the City terminus of his route. Like the Paris omnibuses, they each carried 14 inside and were drawn by two horses, more powerful animals than those used by the coaches on account of the greater weight of the omnibus.[64] By then Shillibeer had six vehicles on the Paddington route and other operators there and elsewhere in London were running no fewer than 39.[65] As competition on the Paddington road became keener, Shillibeer was unable to keep up with his rivals. He was a man of ideas, conviction and courage, and was well able to make a case for himself whatever the circumstances;

but one suspects that he lacked the capacity for disciplined, hard work. There were soon clear signs of trouble. At the beginning of 1831 he and a number of other proprietors asked for relief of stage coach duty, and six days later he himself sent up an ominous petition begging for three months' grace in the payment of mileage duty.[66] His request was refused and on 4 March a Commission of Bankruptcy was issued against him.[67]

By the end of June the surviving operators on the Paddington road were referring to the Bill for ending the hackney coach monopoly as 'the New Stamp Act, the only means of saving them from ruin'.[68] On 19 July, when it was in the committee stage, Lord Althorp confirmed that its passing would allow stages to ply for fares within the streets of London.[69] In August, Shillibeer, describing himself as the 'inventor of the original Omnibus and late proprietor of several running from Paddington to the Bank', sent a personal petition in favour of the measure, urging 'the extreme convenience of the establishment of Omnibii on the same footing as in Paris . . . *especially to the middling class of trades-people whose finances cannot admit of the accommodation of a hackney coach* and are therefore necessitated to lose that time in walking which might be beneficially devoted to business at home . . .'[70]

While the Bill was in its final stages in Parliament, the competition on the Paddington road reached the point at which the operators decided to save themselves by collaboration. On 10 September 1831 they met together at the Wheatsheaf, Edgware Road, and elected Shillibeer as their chairman. (His affairs were then in the hands of assignees but, presumably, he was still managing his business on their behalf.) He roundly condemned the 'shameful scenes which were daily exhibited on the Paddington road between drivers and cads of the rival coaches and omnibuses' and proposed that, in order to reduce the competition, 33 vehicles should be stopped and the remaining 57 should together operate a three-minute service throughout the day from 8 a.m. to 10 p.m. Inspectors were to be stationed at the Wheatsheaf, Edgware Road; the Globe, Baker Street; King's Cross; the Angel, Islington; and Bartholomew Lane in the City, to see that the schedules were kept. A committee of 12 proprietors was formed to give effect to these decisions.[71]

So, while Parliament was passing a measure which aimed at improving London's transport arrangements by encouraging competition—invoking what the hostile hackney coach and cabriolet proprietors called 'abstract principles of Free Trade . . . quite inapplicable to the occasion'[72]—a group of the very operators who had been so loud in their advocacy of such competition were already curbing it among themselves on London's busiest route. When the streets of central London were thrown open after 5 January 1832, similar associations were soon to be formed on the new routes thereby created. The scope for competition in this field of activity was evidently strictly limited.

CHAPTER TWO

THE ASCENDANCY OF THE
OMNIBUS AND THE FIRST LONDON RAILWAYS

The omnibus, drawn by two horses, licensed to carry 12 or 15 passengers and charging sixpenny fares, displaced the short-stage coach within a very few years, and though Shillibeer himself was unable to make his business pay, other proprietors were successful. From 1842 the mileage duty was levied upon the vehicle itself irrespective of its seating capacity. Soon after this, most of London's omnibuses came to seat passengers on the roof as well as inside; but the vehicles themselves remained as cumbersome as ever. Keen competition gave rise to regulation, both by the authorities and by associations of the proprietors themselves. Meanwhile, the Thames steamboat services were being greatly extended, and the first suburban railways began to operate, mainly into London Bridge and Fenchurch Street. Pleasure traffic grew among all sections of society; but the 'commuter' traffic of people going to and from their work was still almost entirely confined to the middle classes. The Great Exhibition of 1851 produced an omnibus boom; more vehicles were provided; and when it was over, bitter competition ensued; but the second era of important street improvements was about to begin, and there was talk of an underground railway. The stage was set for significant developments.

THE ECLIPSE OF THE SHORT-STAGE COACH—
AND OF GEORGE SHILLIBEER

OMNIBUSES came into their own in London after 5 January 1832 when short-stages were allowed to stop for passengers in the central streets anywhere along the route for which they had been licensed.[1] As was to be expected, their appearance provoked much ribald comment from the various hackney coach stands,[2] and the hackney coach interests even

went so far as to seize upon a weakness in the wording of the
1831 Act in a last-ditch attempt to drive out their new competitors. But it was all to no avail;[3] more and more omnibuses came trundling through the streets. By the beginning
of 1834, no fewer than 376 of them were licensed;[4] but there
were then still 423 short-stages operating in the London
area, making a total of some 800 vehicles in all. This
probably represented an increase of about only one-third on
the total for the mid-1820s, before the omnibus came on the
scene and fares were reduced. Omnibuses were largely re-
placing short-stages rather than adding to the total vehicle
capacity; this is also indicated by the traffic to and from the
City.

SHORT DISTANCE TRAFFIC FROM THE CITY IN
DECEMBER 1825 AND JANUARY 1834

December 1825		January 1834		
Short-stages	Daily journeys	Short-stages	Omnibuses	Daily journeys
418	1,190	293		790
			232	770
				1,560

Source: A Statement of the Number of Short-Stage Coaches, Omnibuses and Flys
standing in and passing through the City of London, 1834 [45] LI.

Omnibuses alone, 109 of them, worked the two busy routes
to Paddington along the New Road and along High Holborn
and Oxford Street. They were in general use on roads north
of the river which passed through the main built-up area,
while the short-stages continued to preponderate on routes
in south London and on those to the north which served the
outlying villages. In 1837 Gracechurch Street and its con-
tinuation, Bishopsgate, were still the termini for these short-
stages.[5] But they were constantly being replaced by the
boxes on wheels, and by 1845 they were said to have been
almost entirely superseded.[6]

Shillibeer's larger omnibuses, pulled by three horses,
were not suitable for negotiating the narrow city streets,
particularly the bottleneck in Cheapside and Poultry
through which all east–west traffic had to pass whether it
took the High Holborn route or that along the Strand. The

smaller, two-horse vehicles of the kind used in Paris and by other operators in London[7] found general favour. Twelve or 15 came to be the number of passengers they were licensed to carry following the introduction of new rates of mileage duty in October 1832. The old distinction between inside and outside passengers was then abolished, and short-stages and omnibuses were taxed on exactly the same basis: vehicles licensed for not more than 12 passengers paid $2\frac{1}{2}$d. per mile and those for not more than 15, 3d.[8] This represented a very slight easing of the tax burden, both types of vehicle being allowed to carry one extra passenger for $2\frac{1}{2}$d. per mile and two extra for 3d. It also allowed two or three of the licensed quota to be carried on top beside the driver without fear of prosecution.[9]

It is not clear whether Shillibeer used his larger omnibuses when in January 1832 he was among the first operators to run from Paddington to the Bank along Oxford Street. He was certainly claiming an abatement of duty on three-horse vehicles in February and March 1832,[10] but, according to a return dating from the end of 1832 or beginning of 1833, his concern was operating seven two-horse omnibuses and only one larger one.[11] Although his affairs remained firmly in the hands of assignees,[12] he continued to be very actively engaged in the omnibus business, with head-quarters at St. Albans Place, Edgware Road, and other premises in Earl Street West. He also owned cabriolet licences and ran this branch of the firm from Bury Street, the scene of his original livery stable and coach-building activities. In the autumn of 1832, however, he was nego-tiating for the sale of his cabs, perhaps in anticipation of a flood of newcomers in the following January when the limit to their numbers was to be removed.[13] In addition to the two omnibus routes between Paddington and the Bank, he also ran a 'New Patent Improved Diligence' once a day from his St. Albans Place office to Brighton. This vehicle, again drawn by three horses, did the journey in six hours and carried passengers by coupé or chariot class for a guinea, by omnibus class for 16s. and 'exterior' for 10s.[14]

Shillibeer, however, was no better able to meet competition on the Oxford Street route than on the New Road. In January 1834 a partnership between him and William Morton was dissolved.[15] Perhaps Morton, said to have been a Southwell innkeeper, became his partner when he began to work the Oxford Street route; if so, this would explain why, in January 1832, some of his vehicles were licensed in his name only and others (newly licensed for the Oxford Street route) were entered in the name of Shillibeer and Company. Morton is said to have taken the New Road omnibuses as his share when the partnership was dissolved. There are, however, indications that Shillibeer did not withdraw entirely from the scene of his earlier and much-publicized exploits. In September 1835 he was buying horses for use between Paddington and the Bank and in the following March he still owned property in Paddington.[16] He may also have persevered on the Oxford Street route for a little time after the partnership was dissolved; but by May 1834 he had given up the struggle there and moved south of the river. In that month he started to operate a service from London to Greenwich and Woolwich while at the same time continuing to run to Brighton.[17] He then owned 16 vehicles and 120 horses and had his headquarters in the Old Kent Road at premises leased in October 1833 from Thomas Saunders Cave who had also promised to advance him £1,500. He no doubt hoped to succeed on a route where there was as yet hardly any omnibus competition. But routes south of the river did not then lend themselves particularly to the omnibus: there was comparatively little short-distance traffic. To add to his difficulties, at Easter 1835 a new and cheap steamboat service began operating between Greenwich and London (causing him to cut his fares by nearly one-half and his Woolwich–London fare to 1s.), and in February 1836 part of the London & Greenwich

Railway was opened to traffic. (These developments will be discussed later in this chapter.) Although his omnibuses were licensed to carry 15—obviously two-horse—in fact they carried on average only five. He fell into arrears with his payment of mileage duty and, towards the end of March 1836, all his property, which he valued at £4,000, was seized. It was later auctioned. He fled to Boulogne to escape his creditors and, on his return, was brought to the insolvent debtors' court by Cave, who testified that he had not paid any rent at all on the Old Kent Road property and had, in fact, borrowed not £1,500 but between £8,000 and £10,000. He was committed to the Fleet prison and spent several months there. On his release he got a job with the London & Southampton Railway but, after 130 gallons of uncustomed brandy (smuggled from Boulogne) were discovered on premises which he owned at Camden Town in 1839, he was again writing long letters of explanation and protest from inside the Fleet prison. In the following year, after his release, he sent indignant memorials to the Treasury claiming recognition for his services in introducing the omnibus to London and asserting that the seizure of his property in 1836 had been unlawful. He thought that a post as Inspector of Omnibus Duties should come his way as compensation and, when the Treasury demurred, had the effrontery to suggest that he be allowed to operate twenty omnibuses, tax free, for the following seven years. The deaf ears of those in authority at last discouraged even this persistent apologist. He looked round for another line of business in which Paris could teach London a lesson and found it in the organizing of funerals. He patented a new type of funeral carriage and, taking the Paris *Pompes Funèbres* as his model, set up as an undertaker in the City Road. Amid these sombre surroundings he at long last succeeded. It was a happier issue from his troubles than the Parisian pioneer, Stanislas Baudry, had found; he, too, became bankrupt in the midst of the success of his idea but committed suicide in the Canal Saint-Martin, opposite the omnibus stables, in February 1830.[18]

Shillibeer's later life was relatively tranquil and untroubled by clashes with those in authority. After 1840 his name appeared only rarely in the papers, but when it did it was to reveal him in a characteristic frame of mind. In 1850, for instance, he joined a committee of City Road inhabitants to protest against an 'illegal' paving rate, and in 1856 he allowed his name to appear on the prospectus of a small company which had been formed to fight the newly established and powerful London General Omnibus Company. He died in 1866 at the age of 69 and lies buried in the churchyard at Chigwell.[19] In 1929 the busmen of London erected a tablet in the church in memory of the 'inventor of the London Omnibus'—a slight exaggeration, perhaps, yet a fitting tribute to one who, chancing to be a vehicle manufacturer and to have links with Paris just at the right time, made the most of his opportunity. But he did not succeed in reaping the reward for his resourcefulness and for the persistence he showed in the face of hostility from the existing coaching interests and discouragement from officialdom. As so often happens, the pioneer lacked the business acumen to press home his initial advantage.

Omnibuses in the 1830s and 1840s

While Shillibeer was losing money on his omnibuses, others were managing to make theirs pay. Unfortunately no business records have come to light to provide explanations of their success. Nor have the annual mileage returns to the Board of Stamps and Taxes, but one of these happened to be printed in *Robson's London Directory* for 1839 and this provides details of the main routes and their operators (see Appendix 2). From this and other sources it is possible to piece together a picture, inevitably a rather impressionistic one, of the industry's early development.

The routes through the London streets were first

developed at sixpenny fares, longer journeys to the outskirts costing a shilling. Despite a further reduction in mileage duty in 1839—a cut of $\frac{1}{2}$d. per mile and an increase of one seat allowed in each tax category (i.e. 2d. per mile for 13 seats instead of 2$\frac{1}{2}$d. for 12; 2$\frac{1}{2}$d. for 16 instead of 3d. for 15)[20]—there do not appear to have been any important cuts in fares, and sixpence remained the standard rate until the middle of the 1840s. The 1838–39 mileage duty list (drawn up before the additional seat was permitted) shows that almost all omnibuses were then licensed to carry 12 inside and most of them also to take three other passengers on the roof, sitting by the driver. The conductor (very often known at this period as 'cad') stood outside at the back of the vehicle on a step. His job, in addition to collecting fares as passengers alighted, was to keep the omnibus as full as possible, and one advantage of the box on wheels over the short-stage was that it could easily be filled beyond the legal limit with less danger of detection. He achieved his objective by cajoling and enticing the hesitant into his brightly painted vehicle, occasionally, if Dickens is to be believed, even seizing them by main force and pushing them through the door at the back which was then slammed smartly behind them. One of these more determined cads, who makes his appearance in the pages of *Sketches by Boz*, dating from the middle of the 1830s, boasts 'that he can chuck an old gen'lm'n into the buss, shut him in, and rattle off, afore he knows where it's a-going to'.[21] Inside, the seats consisted of forms along each side, below windows which could be opened. The floor was covered with straw. There seems to be plenty of evidence that these early omnibuses were, in fact, 'lumbering, clumsy conveyances in which the public were packed like coal sacks and jolted through the streets . . .'[22]

Until the middle of the 1840s there were no significant innovations in omnibus design. The only experiment worthy of mention concerned means of attracting the driver's or conductor's attention when a passenger wished to get out. The original method had been to bang on the roof or prod the conductor with a walking stick or umbrella. In 1839, however, the London firm of Holtzapffel & Co. produced a bell which could be rung by pulling a cord inside the vehicle. They then had high hopes that it would be generally adopted. Two years later, however, a different device was being used. This consisted of two straps running along the roof, connected with two wooden rings, one on each of the driver's arms. A passenger pulled either the right or the left-hand strap according to the side of the street on which he wanted to be set down.[23] The 'rule of the road' did not prevent vehicles from crossing to the far side to make a stop; and there were, of course, no fixed stopping places along the route.

Efforts to initiate new routes and then to build up traffic upon them gave rise to very keen competition. Operators' attempts to fill their omnibuses at the expense of their rivals led not only to objections about conductors' sharp practices but also to complaints of crawling and obstruction in streets.

The driver and he who hangs behind—who opens the door and receives the money—are not satisfied with having their long box packed full of passengers at the first starting. The original occupants may nearly all leave the vehicle on its route, their business calling them out at different points. But driver and conductor are seldom disposed to move rapidly on with a half-empty omnibus. The one holds up his whip significantly, the other scans the pavement on either side to see if he can detect among the passengers any willing to fill the vacant places in his machine. The person who entered at the Bank to go to Piccadilly or Oxford Street may thus be considerably delayed.[24]

Some passengers who boarded an omnibus at Ludgate Hill on the driver's promise that he would take them to Charing Cross without delay, subsequently reported him and had him brought to court when he waited six minutes before

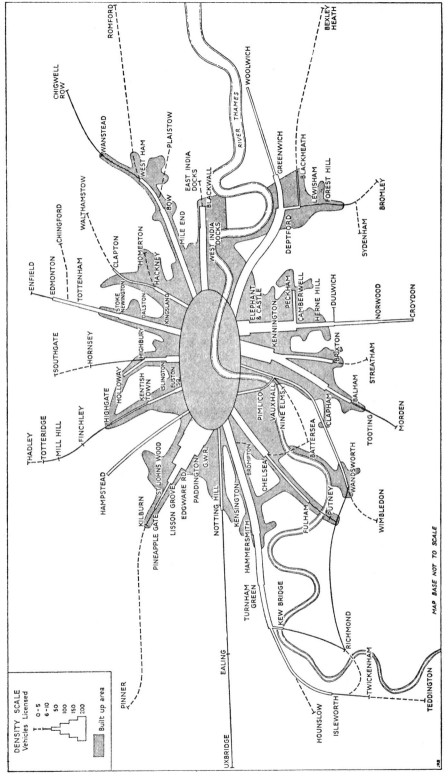

Omnibuses and Short Stages operating in 1838–9 (Source: Appendix 2)

starting and then took a further nine to travel 150 yards. (He was fined 40s.)[25] A few months after this, the firm of Chancellor of Kensington, who claimed to have run to Kensington from the King's Head, Ludgate Hill, for many years, appeared on a similar charge. Although they had replaced their short-stages by omnibuses, they continued to book passengers in addition to picking them up on the road, and it was the stop at their booking office which was partly responsible for the charge of obstruction. The drivers were again fined, the magistrate giving it as his opinion that 'omnibuses had a right to ply while they were moving on only; and if they stopped, it should be merely for the purpose of setting down or taking up passengers. To remain stationary even a minute longer than was actually occupied in taking up or setting down was a breach of the Act which he would rigidly punish.'[26] Having dawdled in order to fill as many seats as possible, drivers then went as fast as they could in order to get ahead of their rivals and so make sure of any passengers waiting ahead on the road. So general had racing become in Islington that the parish offered a reward for information leading to a conviction, and an indignant correspondent of *The Times* complained that unless drivers were checked it would soon be 'impossible for persons to cross the leading streets in the metropolis, particularly Holborn where they make a point of racing to such excess that the wide pavement is scarcely sufficient protection to pedestrians'.[27]

In order to discourage crawling and racing and the abusive behaviour of certain conductors, regulation was again needed. To this end Sir Matthew Wood, one of the M.P.s for the City, introduced legislation in successive sessions of Parliament,[28] but without avail until 1838 when an Act was passed obliging all conductors and drivers of Metropolitan Stage Carriages to take out licences, in applying for which each was to give his name, address and age. They were each given a metal 'ticket', on which was inscribed their licence number, and this they had to wear. This is the origin of the present-day licensing of drivers and conductors. If found guilty of obstruction or other road offence, they were originally liable to a fine of up to 20s.[29]

The omnibus proprietors were also forced to impose regulations on themselves in much the same way as the operators on the New Road had done in 1831. That pioneer association continued to yield most satisfactory results. In the later 1830s the timekeepers were still keeping the omnibuses moving punctually and the route continued to be worked by not more than 56 omnibuses, about the same number as in 1831 and 1834.[30] The second route to consider such action appears to have been that along the Commercial Road. When, in January 1834, residents of Poplar and Limehouse met at Poplar Town Hall to complain about the service to and from Blackwall, they were told that the operators concerned were to hold a meeting a few days later to regulate the traffic.[31] It is not known whether any effective action was then taken; the Metropolitan Omnibus Association, composed of proprietors working the Commercial Road, is said to have been formed only in July 1836.[32] An association is also believed to have been started in that year to regulate the Paddington–Bank route via Oxford Street.[33] Two years later, in August 1838, some 140 stage coach and omnibus proprietors met to form what was somewhat naively described by the press as a benevolent society. The account of its proceedings makes it quite clear that it was, in fact, intended as a pressure group to ensure that the proprietors' point of view was more strongly represented in Parliament than it had recently been.[34] The Act for the licensing of conductors and drivers had brought together the various owners in an attempt to protect themselves from what they considered to be further encroachments upon their freedom.

At sixpence the fare was still too high to be afforded— except on rare occasions—by any but the middle classes, and the omnibuses' morning starting times, from about 8 o'clock, were dictated by the needs of this section of the community.

'In the mornings from the hours of eight to ten', wrote an observer in 1837, 'the various short-stages and omnibuses are pouring in, bearing with them the merchant to his business, the clerk to his bank or counting-house, the subordinate official functionaries to the Post Office, Somerset House, the Excise, or the Mint, the Custom House or Whitehall. An immense number of individuals, whose incomes vary from £150 to £400 or £600 and whose business does not require their presence till nine or ten in the mornings, and who can leave it at five or six in the evenings; persons with limited independent means of living, such as legacies or life-rents, or small amounts of property; literary individuals; merchants and traders small and great; all, in fact, who can endeavour to live some little distance from London . . .'[35]

In the rush hour, journeys were often unpleasant so long as all but two or three of the passengers had to travel inside. The forms were hard and the straw on the floor often far from clean. A traveller on the New Road route during the evening rush hour one day in 1833 found himself in an omnibus filled with 'decent clerks, fagged and harmless and going home to their tea'. 'Here we are,' he commented, 'in all six and twenty [sic] sweating citizens, jammed, crammed and squeezed into each other like so many peas in a pod . . .'[36] The Times was moved to print a set of instructions which, if followed, would render omnibus travelling more bearable:[37]

OMNIBUS LAW

1. Keep your feet off the seats.
2. Do not get into a snug corner yourself and then open the windows to admit a North-wester upon the neck of your neighbour.
3. Have your money ready when you desire to alight. If your time is not valuable, that of others may be.
4. Do not impose on the conductor the necessity of finding you change: he is not a banker.

5. Sit with your limbs straight, and do not with your legs describe an angle of 45, thereby occupying the room of two persons.
6. Do not spit on the straw. You are not in a hogsty but in an omnibus travelling in a country which boasts of its refinement.
7. Behave respectfully to females and put not an unprotected lass to the blush, because she cannot escape from your brutality.
8. If you bring a dog, let him be small and be confined by a string.
9. Do not introduce large parcels—an omnibus is not a van.
10. Reserve bickerings and disputes for the open field. The sound of your own voice may be music to your own ears—not so, perhaps, to those of your companions.
11. If you will broach politics or religion, speak with moderation: all have an equal right to their opinions, and all have an equal right not to have them wantonly shocked.
12. Refrain from affectation and conceited airs. Remember that you are riding a distance for sixpence which, if made in a hackney coach, would cost you as many shillings; and that should your pride elevate you above plebeian accommodations, your purse should enable you to command aristocratic indulgences.

The Stamp Office return of 1838–39 (Appendix 2) gives a detailed account of the multitude of routes which were then being worked and the even more numerous army of men who were concerned in working them. The general picture is of a great mass of independent services being developed by a vast number of small-scale operators, the total of vehicles involved—about 825 (some 620 of them omnibuses and the rest short-stages)—being little more than that of four years before. But from this host of routes and hundreds of small operators, important exceptions stand out.

The two great routes from Paddington to the City still overshadowed all the others—the New Road with 55 vehicles licensed and Oxford Street with 65 (plus a further 13 on an extension of the route to Maida Hill). Other important routes had been built up which ran from one side of London to the other: Lisson Grove to the Elephant and Castle (29 vehicles); Chelsea to Mile End (27); Kennington Gate to Islington (15); Blackwall to Sloane Street (10); and Notting Hill to Mile End Gate (8). Among the operators, Richard Blore and Co. dominated the Oxford Street route with 31 vehicles to Edgware Road and a further nine on the Maida Hill extension. They also ran five between Lisson Grove and the Elephant and Castle, two between St. John's Wood and the Bank and one between Notting Hill and Mile End Gate. With 48 vehicles, Blore and Co. was by far the largest firm. It was either synonymous with, or else it dominated, the London Conveyance Co., which, in its turn, ruled the Oxford Street route. The London Conveyance Co. is said to have been formed in 1836 on the initiative of a man named Warburton.[38] The company was mentioned as a participant in the proprietors' meeting of 1838,[39] but does not appear in any of the directories until 1844 when Blore is described as its manager.[40] Among the other more important proprietors were J. Wheatley who had licences to run 16 vehicles from Greenwich and eight from Woolwich; T. Fardell (16 from Blackwall); A. Hamilton (15 from Hampstead); R. Lambert (17 from Blackwall and the East and West India Docks); George Cloud (four from Kew Bridge and eight from Turnham Green to the Bank); E. and J. Wilson (11 from Holloway to the City and two others from the same vicinity as E. Wilson and Co.); and George Chancellor (nine from Chelsea to Mile End).

Important questions remain which cannot be answered with the information at present available. To what extent, for instance, did omnibus operators concentrate upon omnibus operation and to what extent was this merely one of a number of their activities? Shillibeer, as we have seen, was a coach-builder and livery stable keeper and also ran cabriolets for a time. Wilsons were also job masters who hired out horses and carriages: the yard in Holloway where their omnibuses were kept was prominently labelled 'Wilson's Livery Stables'.[41] Thomas Tilling, who was to lay the foundations of his business at Peckham in the later 1840s, put advertisements on the sides of his omnibuses which bore the words: 'T. Tilling, Job Master, Wedding Carriages.'[42] The directories do not list omnibus proprietors separately; one for 1844, for instance, merely instructs the reader to 'see Job Masters'. Were all omnibus proprietors similarly engaged in these other activities? It is logical that they should have been, for the most costly item in the omnibus business was the horses, and it was in horses that job masters specialized. By the later 1850s, each two-horse omnibus needed a stud of 11 or 12 horses to keep it on the road for 14 hours or so each day. It is possible that some omnibuses may not have been so intensively worked in the 1830s and 1840s; and a large concern which sold out in 1852 had rather fewer than eight horses per vehicle. Nevertheless, at about £20 each, if the stud consisted of only six animals, their capital cost was greater than that of the omnibus itself which could usually be bought for about £100, and the working life of the omnibus was likely to be many times longer than the four years of a horse. Most important of all, omnibus horses had to be well fed; their feed at 15s. per week each probably totalled between £4 10s. and £9 per vehicle —between £234 and £468 a year. We should like to know to what extent economies of scale, involving all kinds of business connected with the stabling and hire of horses, allowed particular firms to buy their feeding stuff in bulk and so to operate more successfully than others.

There is, too, another set of questions which relate to the coming of railways. When the railways drove the long-stages off routes running parallel to their lines, did some of those who had interests in the long-stages which were displaced —particularly those out of London—move into the growing omnibus business? We know that two of them did this indirectly. William Chaplin and Benjamin Worthy Horne,

two London innkeepers very extensively concerned with
stage coaches, joined forces to become carriers for the
London & Birmingham Railway, and in addition to dealing
with freight from Camden Town they also ran omnibuses
from Euston Station.[43] They also operated omnibuses from
Paddington and Nine Elms. Similarly, Edward Sherman
became carrier for the Great Western.[44] Nelson's, whose
Bull Inn, Aldgate, was an important coaching house, also
became concerned with omnibuses.[45] How many others
switched resources from long-stages to omnibuses? This
would have been a very logical move, for the railways,
which drove the long-stages out of business, brought more
passengers into London than the stage coaches had ever
done, and thereby helped to stimulate the already growing
demand for omnibuses. The impact of steam on the passenger transport of London clearly merits our attention next.

Steamboats on the Thames

Steam came into quite widespread use on the Thames before
the advent of railways. Steamboats began to ply regularly
from London to other places on the river in 1815.[46] Although some of the earliest trips were up-river to Richmond
and Twickenham, traffic downstream, where larger vessels
could operate, soon became much more important. Between
1820 and 1830, there was a considerable growth in the
steamboat activity to Gravesend, Margate and Ramsgate,[47]
and in 1831 a Member of Parliament went so far as to
describe these places as 'recently built to accommodate the
citizens [of London], a great majority of whom took
advantage of steam communication'.[48] Margate was
reached in six hours, and the fare was 8s. or 9s. according
to the cabin.[49] These steam packets would call at various
places on the way, and small boats were sometimes used to
connect with them in mid-stream.[50] Among the places of
call on the Gravesend route were Greenwich and Woolwich.
In 1834 Woolwich, and in 1835 Greenwich, secured a

service of its own provided by smaller boats of from 70 to 100 tons (to be compared with those from 170 to 225 tons running down to Gravesend).[51]

The steamboats had considerable advantages over the coaches. They could carry hundreds of passengers at a time and were not burdened by any mileage duty. On the other hand, wharfage dues were often quite heavy—3d. per passenger at London and at Gravesend[52]—and some would-be travellers were, no doubt, discouraged by the frequency of accidents on the river: between May 1835 and November 1838, for instance, 12 steamboats were seriously damaged in collisions, 43 people were drowned and five injured by steamers upsetting other craft, and a further 72 were thrown into the river but rescued.[53] In the early days, too, the process of boarding and landing from these vessels was rather hazardous. In 1830, for example, the inhabitants of Tower Ward complained to the Corporation about the 'incessant tumults' caused by watermen seeking fares at the various stairs which served the steamboats. They proposed that a barge be moored off the eastern part of Custom House Terrace with a platform over it 'from which passengers may at once embark without the necessity of trusting themselves to any wherry or scrambling on board in the ordinary style . . .' In the next few years, however, such improvisation gave way to proper landing places: six new wharves were built to accommodate steamboat passengers.[54] The chief deterrent to steamboat travel, how-ever—the weather—still remained. The river became singularly unattractive, if not positively repulsive, when the winds blew and the rains poured. Nevertheless, the various proprietors contrived to run services in winter as well as in summer at frequencies, speeds and fares which compared very favourably with those of land transport. To Green-wich, for instance, boats ran every half hour in winter and every quarter of an hour in summer.[55] To Gravesend the fare was 1s. 6d. or 2s. and to Woolwich 9d. or 1s. (for cabin or saloon), the latter journey taking an hour and a quarter with the tide and an hour and a half against it.[56] These services, which still ran after dark in winter,[57] were very frequently used by the middle classes of those places. In 1837 the secretary of the Woolwich Steam Packet Company claimed: 'Nearly the whole of the Government Departments and I should say nineteen persons out of twenty in the town who want to come to London for business, use this mode, for the simple reason that it saves them at least 100 per cent. in money and they go quite as quickly, if not more quickly, by steam boats.' In the early 1840s, a yearly season ticket from Gravesend cost only six guineas.[58]

There was certainly very heavy traffic at holiday times when a much larger cross-section of the community poured on to the boats. The fair at Greenwich at Easter and Whit-suntide, in particular, was a most popular attraction. On occasions such as this the more hair-raising examples of overloading were to be found—1,100 brought up from Gravesend on a Margate packet on Whit Monday in 1835, for instance, and, on another holiday, 500 in a 77-ton vessel from Woolwich.[59] In an effort to check these excesses, the Lord Mayor's Court in September 1835 approved by-laws ordering steamboats not to carry more than three passengers per registered ton.[60] Some idea of the extent to which these vessels were being used may be seen from the fact that 500,000 people used Gravesend Pier for embarking and disembarking between the middle of 1834 and the middle of 1835.[61] Between June 1836 and June 1837 the Woolwich Steam Packet Company alone carried 250,000 passengers.[62] The steamboat wharves in London—and notably the one on the north bank to the east of London Bridge, together with Nicholson's in Thames Street and Hungerford Market Pier—were becoming important passenger termini.

The steamboats were challenging the interests of the watermen on the river in much the same way as the short-stages and omnibuses had attacked the hackney coach monopoly on land. The final blow fell in April 1837 when small steamboats, capable of carrying 120 passengers at a time, began to run between London and Westminster Bridges (and occasionally on to Putney), calling at Southwark Bridge on the way, the whole journey taking 15 to 30 minutes and costing 4d. These boats were soon running every quarter of an hour from 8 a.m. to 9 p.m. and in the first few months they carried 500 to 600 passengers per day. The next year the Iron Steam Boat Company started a half-hourly service from London Bridge to the newly opened London & Southampton railway station at Nine Elms, Vauxhall, calling at the north side of Waterloo and Westminster Bridges. The journey all the way cost 4d.[63] By 1843, eight iron steamboats were providing a 15-minute service between London Bridge and Chelsea and carrying more than 2,000,000 passengers a year.[64] In 1846 the Citizen Steamboat Company was formed to share some of this lucrative business.[65] Sharp competition ensued, and by the end of the year the fare from London Bridge to Chelsea had been cut to 2d.[66] Meanwhile, in the same year the Dyers' Hall Company started to operate a fleet of small boats, sporting such names as *Ant*, *Bee*, *Cricket* and *Fly*, between their wharf near London Bridge and the Adelphi at ½d. fares.[67] Cheap fares and frequent services brought a large traffic to the river. The piers and arches of the bridges attracted the attention of enterprising bill-stickers.[68]

Steam on the roads

It was much more difficult to employ the steam engine to power transport on land in London than to use it to propel river craft. The heavy steam engine of those days was not suited for driving omnibuses, and the building of railways presented particular problems in such a heavily built-up area as London.

Between 1821 and 1840 a number of steam carriages seating eight or more people were built, and many more were designed and publicized. Indeed, it is difficult to discover how many actually ran on the roads. But there were some interesting developments, which were frustrated by the inadequacy of engineering techniques then available, the unsatisfactory state of road surfaces, hostility from the authorities and horse interests, and—most importantly— the success of steam locomotion on rails. Goldsworthy Gurney, Sir Charles Dance, Col. Francis Macerone and Walter Hancock were the principal persons concerned. Hancock was the most significant, for he had, in 1827, patented a lighter and more efficient boiler. His first omnibus was run as a showpiece from his factory at Stratford into London 'as a means of dissipating any remaining prejudices and establishing a favourable judgment in the public mind as to the practicability of steam travelling on common roads'.[69] The public, however, was not greatly impressed and it was not until 1833 that financial support was forthcoming to encourage further efforts. The London & Paddington Steam Carriage Company was then formed to run three of Hancock's vehicles along the New Road, but, after one 14-seater omnibus had been operating for just over a fortnight, Hancock and the company quarrelled over the company's obvious reluctance to order the other two. Hancock took over the service himself and ran it during that and the subsequent summer. He was otherwise occupied in 1835, but in the following year he ran three vehicles on the New Road, one of which was a 22-seater. This bid was an utter failure; even in the height of the summer he carried only about 90 passengers per day. The novelty of steam could not then compete with horse power, even on this extremely busy route.

The first railways in London

The very year that Hancock was involuntarily demonstrating that the steam omnibus as then built had no commercial future, the opening of London's earliest railway—

the first part of the London & Greenwich, opened from Deptford to Spa Road, Bermondsey, on 8 February 1836 and to London Bridge on the following 14 December—showed that steam locomotives could, in fact, be used successfully for short-distance passenger work in London. Here, however, the main problem was that of keeping down costs in an area where site values were often notoriously high. In this the London & Greenwich was fortunate, for most of the line ran through market gardens and at the London Bridge end the property which had to be demolished was of low value. The engineer, Col. George Landmann, a retired officer of the Royal Engineers, built it throughout on arches which raised it above the adjacent property. Some of these arches proved a source of income when leased as warehouses, workshops, private dwellings or—in one case—a public house. Raising the track above ground level in this way was a device to be widely copied later by builders of London's railways, for they had usually to pass through congested districts for a much greater distance. A novel feature of the Greenwich line was a 24-foot walk, planted with trees, which ran at ground level on each side of the viaduct. This was intended for pedestrians who were charged a penny toll. It was for a time moderately well patronized: in 1839, for instance, 120,000 people used it.[70]

The railway to Deptford was much more direct than the road, and the journey much shorter for those who lived near the station. In the first 15 months of its existence the railway carried more than 650,000 passengers. In November 1837 it was advertising a 15-minute service between 8 a.m. and 10 p.m. on weekdays (until 11 p.m. on Sundays) at fares of 1s. single for 'imperial carriages' and 6d. single for 'open cars'. When the line was opened across the Ravensbourne into Greenwich on 24 December 1838, it was announced that omnibuses from Blackheath, Lewisham and Woolwich would meet every train. As with the steamboats, the railway did its briskest business at holiday time. On Whit Monday 1839, for instance, a six-minute service was run and 35,000 passengers carried. On Easter Monday 1841, 7,000 were carried in two hours alone and the railway stayed open until 2 o'clock the next morning to get everyone home. Confronted with stronger steamboat and omnibus competition, the fares were cut in 1843 to 1s., and 10d. return for 1st and 2nd class passengers and 4d. single for 3rd; and seasons were introduced, costing 12 or 10 gns. a year. In 1844 the line carried more than 2,000,000 passengers.

Although London Bridge station was at first much criticized for its meagreness—in its early days it consisted of little more than uncovered platforms and a handsome pair of iron gates[71]—it was well situated, being within easy walking distance of the heart of the City, and the railway owned adjacent land so that the station could be extended when required. Other lines connected with the London & Greenwich in order to run into this well-sited terminus: the London & Croydon, a railway intended to build up a local traffic through New Cross, Forest Hill, Sydenham, Penge and Norwood, in 1839—extended to Carshalton and Epsom in 1847; the London & Brighton in 1841; the South Eastern, opened from the Brighton line at Reigate Junction (later Redhill) to Ashford in 1842, Folkestone in 1843 and Dover in 1844.[72] As a result, traffic into London Bridge grew quickly. The London & Greenwich doubled the number of tracks into it in 1842, and additional station accommodation was brought into use two years later. The South Eastern and Croydon companies, however, as a protest against what they considered to be excessive tolls charged by the London & Greenwich for the use of its lines, promoted a new terminus at Bricklayer's Arms, at the top of the Old Kent Road. This was opened in May 1844. Its situation was, however, greatly inferior to that of London Bridge for passengers, if not for goods. Yet it served its immediate purpose, for the Croydon company soon

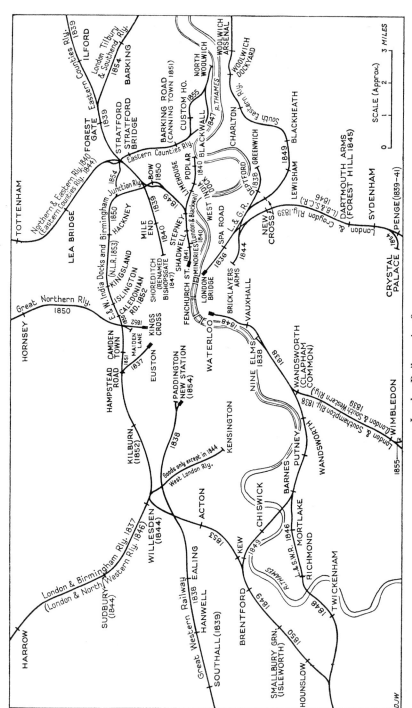

London Railways in 1855

47

succeeded in negotiating more favourable rates with the London & Greenwich and gave up using Bricklayer's Arms, and the South Eastern was helped to obtain a 999-year lease of the London & Greenwich as from 1 January 1845. It thereafter ran most of its regular passenger trains into London Bridge, although after the opening of its North Kent line in 1849—to Gravesend in the first instance—some of this new traffic was fed into Bricklayer's Arms for a couple of years or so.

Meanwhile, in 1846, the London & Brighton had amalgamated with the Croydon to become the London, Brighton & South Coast. It brought its own quite separate terminal accommodation at London Bridge into use in 1850, and extended it in 1853 in anticipation of heavy excursion traffic to Sydenham when the Crystal Palace was reopened there. The South Eastern's terminus had also been enlarged, and in 1850 two further tracks had been laid, making six in all. So, by the middle of the 1850s, London Bridge had separate platforms for the Greenwich, North Kent and South Eastern main-line traffic (forming the South Eastern's station on the north side) and for the Brighton main line, the Croydon line and the Crystal Palace (in the London & Brighton's station on the south side).

The London & Greenwich Railway soon had its counterpart on the north side of the river. This was the London & Blackwall which, like the Greenwich, started as a self-contained unit but became increasingly reliant on passengers from other lines, for it, too, had a well-situated terminus. The City Corporation had, in 1836, opposed the entry of the Blackwall, and indeed all railways, within its limits, on the ground that street congestion would be worsened and improvements already planned would be frustrated; but its opposition was withdrawn.[73] The railway was opened to a temporary station at the Minories on 8 July 1840 and extended to Fenchurch Street on 2 August 1841. It was originally promoted to tap some of the lucrative river

14. Omnibuses and Rifle Volunteers at the Mansion House, about 1860

15. Exhibition Omnibus with Knifeboard Seat in difficulties

MISERIES of LONDON.

Entering upon any of the bridges of London, or any of the passages leading to the Thames, being assailed by a groupe of watermen, holding up their hands and bawling out Oars Sculls. Sculls. Oars Oars.

16. London Watermen, 1812

17. Margate Steam Yachts at the Custom House, 1820

18. A Thames Steamer at Gravesend, 1828

19. Building the London & Greenwich Railway, near the Surrey Canal, 1835

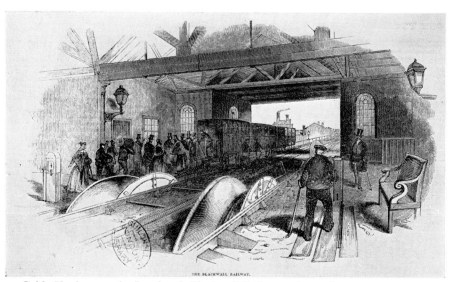

20. Cable Haulage on the London & Blackwall Railway, about 1840

traffic, the distance to Brunswick Pier, Blackwall, being seven miles by water round the Isle of Dogs and just under four by railway; the trains took 15 minutes and the steamers over an hour. The success of the venture, however, depended upon the willingness of the steamboat companies, and particularly those sailing to Gravesend, to run to Blackwall instead of all the way to London; but they, not surprisingly, were not very eager to carry their passengers for only part of the journey. Nor did haulage by stationary engines and ropes help to attract steamboat traffic to the railway. The system was rather involved* and the ropes were often breaking; the wire cables which replaced them in 1841 also gave much trouble for at least two years longer. Although in 1841 the railway carried about 2,000,000 passengers at a fare of 6d. or 4d. single, according to class, fewer than half of them went to or from Blackwall, and by no means all of the Blackwall passengers connected with steam vessels. In an effort to secure more of the Gravesend traffic, the railway arranged for three boats to operate in conjunction with the trains. Eventually, at the end of 1842, agreement with the steamboat companies was reached. A single ticket Gravesend–London was fixed at 2s. and 1s. 6d., and Gravesend–Blackwall 6d. less in each case. But, despite this equalizing of the fare by boat and rail, steamboat passengers do not seem to have shown any greater inclination to desert the river. Most of the railway tickets were still bought by those living or working at Blackwall or in those

*The train left Fenchurch Street hauled by a rope attached to one of the stationary engines at Poplar, and dropped carriages at the various stations on the way. On the return journey, at a signal by electric telegraph—a very early use of this new form of communication—the carriages at each station were re-gripped to another rope which had been trailed by the Blackwall section of the outward train, and hauled back along the line by one of the stationary engines at the Minories. The same method was employed on the other track which also had its own stationary engine at each end, but in that case the completed train started its journey from Blackwall. A 15-minute service was maintained, but passengers could not travel between intermediate stations. 'The section between Poplar and Blackwall was traversed by momentum up the slight rise to Blackwall, and by gravity from Blackwall, and the cable attached at Poplar . . . The extension from Minories to Fenchurch Street . . . was worked similarly by gravity, the trains "being started by a slight push from the porters in attendance".' (Charles E. Lee, 'The London and Blackwall Cable Railway', *Railway Magazine*, 87 (1941), 425.)

F

parts of east London served by the stations at Cannon Street Road, Shadwell, Stepney, Limehouse, West India Docks and Poplar. In the first half of 1848, for instance, receipts from local traffic totalled £16,857 while those from Gravesend passengers amounted to only £4,670 and from Woolwich £1,441.[74]

Fenchurch Street station, like London Bridge, became important when other lines began to use it as a means of getting a terminus close to the centre of the City. Its value was considerably enhanced when the Royal Commission on Metropolitan Termini, which was set up at the time of the Railway Mania in the mid-1840s to consider a number of proposals for building new lines into the very heart of London, reported against all these schemes. It supported the Government's view that no future railway north of the river should penetrate nearer to the City than a line drawn along the New Road, City Road, Finsbury Square and Bishopsgate Street.[75] The London & Blackwall soon seized its new opportunity and set about improving its line. The continuous cable system was scrapped and replaced by locomotives; the gauge was changed from 5 ft. to the standard 4 ft. 8½ in. and the approach to Fenchurch Street improved. A new branch was built and opened in 1849 to a station at Bow, operated jointly with the Eastern Counties Railway, in an attempt to deflect to Fenchurch Street traffic bound for the Eastern Counties' terminus at Shoreditch.

The Eastern Counties Railway, which had been opened from a temporary station at Mile End (Devonshire Street) to Romford in 1839, was a constant butt of criticism and source of amusement: it had taken a further seven years and the launching of another company to reach Ipswich. Long before then, however, traffic was being fed on to it at Stratford from another line running up the Lea valley. This had been opened as far as Broxbourne in 1840 by the Northern & Eastern Railway and was leased by the

Eastern Counties four years later; a branch was opened from Edmonton to Enfield in 1849. Farther to the south another branch was built, in 1847, from the Eastern Counties' main line at Barking Road to connect with steamboats at North Woolwich. Despite the growing traffic which was generated by these feeders, however, very few passengers chose to change trains at Bow when the joint station was opened there in 1849.[76] It was left to the North London to bring prosperity at last to the struggling, but never downcast, London & Blackwall.

The London & North Western Railway which ran into Euston (this line, built by the London & Birmingham, had been opened as far as Boxmoor in 1837 and Birmingham in 1838) soon found itself in need of a branch to take its goods traffic to the docks. In 1846 a company known as the East & West India Docks & Birmingham Junction Railway secured parliamentary authority to build a line from the London & North Western at Camden Town to Blackwall via Canonbury, Kingsland, Homerton and Bow. Although intended initially for goods traffic, its possibilities as a suburban passenger line were soon realized, and powers were obtained in 1850 to link it with the Eastern Counties and the London & Blackwall. Through passenger trains started running from Islington into Fenchurch Street via Bow on 26 September 1850, from Camden Town by the end of the year, and from Hampstead Road (Chalk Farm, where it joined with the London & North Western) in the middle of 1851.[77] Although this was a very roundabout way for people to get into the City, the line did serve a large residential area and was both quick and cheap. In the first six months of 1851, when a 15-minute service was operated from 8.30 a.m. to 10 p.m. at a fare of 6d. single, first class, and 4d. second (there was no third), more than 1,750,000 were carried, half of them using the new railway as a means of getting to the City via Fenchurch Street.[78] This doubled the traffic on the London & Blackwall which at once

started to improve its terminus. The new line was performing a similar function north of the river to that of the railways running into London Bridge from the south. In 1853
the trains of the North London Railway (as it was then
re-named) started to run also right round the western
suburbs to Kew over the newly opened North & South
Western Junction Railway, first using the London &
North Western lines to West London Junction, near Kensal
Green (there was no Willesden Junction at that time), and
then (after 1860) the Hampstead Junction through Kentish
Town (Gospel Oak), Hampstead Heath, Finchley Road
and Edgware Road (Kilburn). At Kew the North & South
Western Junction joined the South Western's Windsor loop.
This allowed North London trains to run on by a rather
roundabout route via Barnes to Richmond, Twickenham
and (later) Kingston.[79]

During the fifties also the traffic which was ultimately to
take over Fenchurch Street completely began to flow into
the station in a very modest trickle—that derived from the
London, Tilbury & Southend Railway. This line, authorized
in 1852, originally ran from a junction on the Eastern
Counties' main line at Forest Gate through Barking, Pur-
fleet and Tilbury to Leigh-on-Sea and Southend. Trains
began working at the London end on 13 April 1854; and
on 31 March 1858 a new direct line from Gas Factory
Junction, Bow, through Plaistow and East Ham to Barking
was brought into use, giving a railway service to more
rapidly growing suburbs.[80]

London Bridge and Fenchurch Street were the only
London stations to handle much short-distance traffic in
the 1840s. The London & South Western's Nine Elms
station, Vauxhall (opened in 1838 by the London &
Southampton), also catered for some, though its distance
from the City made it relatively unattractive; the omnibus
journey to Gracechurch Street took 45 minutes and the
steamboats, though cheaper and in some ways more

convenient, were little used in bad weather or at night.[81] In an effort to overcome this disadvantage and to encourage short-distance traffic, which, according to its general manager, was already starting to grow rapidly, the London & South Western brought its terminus forward to Waterloo Road in 1848.[82] By then a line had been opened to Richmond (1846) striking due west from Clapham Junction through Wandsworth and Putney, and this was extended to Windsor three years later. A branch to Chertsey was opened in 1848 and to Hampton Court (worked for some years by horse traction) in 1849. A loop from Barnes to Isleworth was also opened in 1849 and continued to Hounslow in the following year. In order to handle this growing volume of shorter-distance traffic, four tracks were laid into Waterloo at the outset.[83]

Concessionary fares, schemes for workmen's trains and the growth of excursion traffic

The other main line termini—Euston (1837) and Shoreditch (1840), which have already been mentioned, and Paddington (1838) and King's Cross (1852, a temporary terminus at Maiden Lane having been used from 1850)— were concerned almost entirely with long-distance traffic. The average journey travelled from Euston, for instance, was over 60 miles.[84] Such efforts as these lines might make to attract short-distance passengers by offering concessionary fares achieved poor—indeed, surprisingly poor— results. From Harrow, for instance, the London & North Western offered a six-months' season ticket for £7 10s. 0d., or about a shilling a day. The company also offered a free pass for 11 years to anyone taking a house there at a rental of not less than £50 a year (for Tring and Leighton [Buzzard] the concession was extended to 21 years); but in 1857 only 60 passes had been issued. The Eastern Counties also offered concessionary fares or free passes on several lines, but fewer than a hundred of these were taken up.[85] It is

quite clear that the overwhelming majority of people continued to live sufficiently near to their place of work to be
able to get to it by road. In 1850 *The Railway Times* put this
total at 250,000 and asked why 100,000 or more could not be
persuaded to live further out and be brought in by train.

If house rent, twenty miles from the City, and travelling by rail,
could be made to be not more than equivalent to house rent in
crowded streets, is it not clear that the same motives which promp-
ted the citizen to fix his habitation within an hour's walk of his
place of business, would at once induce him to exchange the dirty
suburb for the pure and invigorating atmosphere of the country?
Who, for instance, would prefer living at Paddington, Islington,
Kingsland or Walworth, if he could for the same cost reside at
Kingston, Banstead Downs, Stanmore Common, Bushey Heath,
Northfleet, Slough, Epsom, Hainault Forest, Barnet or Reigate?
These pleasant salubrious sites are all accessible by railway and
are within half an hour's ride of the metropolis.[86]

Charles Pearson, Solicitor to the City of London, shortly to
feature prominently in the beginnings of the underground,
had already developed this idea and extended it. In 1846 he
argued that, if a central station were to be built at Farringdon Street (as some people were then urging), a concerted
effort should be made to build 10,000 cottages for artisans
and clerks in a planned estate radiating outwards from
another station some seven miles away up the line. There
it would be possible to buy land for £60 or £70 an acre
and lay out the estate in such a way that nobody would
have to walk more than 600 yards to get to the trains.
Arguing that railways could carry freight profitably for
1d. per ton mile and calculating 14 men to the ton, he
concluded that the railway could transport those who lived
in his new town to their work and back for 1d. per day. The
saving in site value would not be offset by such a low fare
even if it were 2d. per day, and the standard of housing—
each cottage having four rooms plus kitchen and back yard
—would be infinitely better than anything which could be

had at a comparable rent in London itself. And, moreover, each cottage was to have 400 square yards of garden attached to it if it was near the perimeter of the estate, or on the outskirts if it was near to the station.[87] Five years later, Pearson was still campaigning for a central station[88] and, when a Select Committee investigated metropolitan communications in 1855, he was extolling the merits of a new town at Hornsey or Tottenham, on the recently opened line to King's Cross, where land cost £100 to £200 per acre (as compared with upwards of £15,000 in the built-up area itself). He went on to make an interesting observation:[89]

The desire to get out of town is not a mere desire, it is not a passion, it is a disease. . . . The passion for country residence is increasing to an extent that it would be impossible for persons who do not mix much with the poor to know. You cannot find a place where they do not get a broken teapot in which to stuff, as soon as spring comes, some flower or something to give them an idea of green fields and the country.

Although at least one railway company, the London & Croydon, considered seriously the possibility of introducing reduced fares to encourage the higher-paid workmen to move farther out and use its line,[90] some years were to pass before workmen's fares were introduced and even more before those who used these tickets could enjoy well-laid out housing estates. But the railway was already helping an increasing number of people to take day excursions into the country or to the seaside.

Londoners had long been in the habit of going out into the surrounding country either on foot or by cart, particularly at Easter—described by a writer in the *Illustrated London News* as 'peculiarly the holiday of the poor'[91]—and at Whitsuntide. Greenwich Fair was a special attraction, as was Fairlop Fair in a remnant of Hainault Forest, held at the beginning of July 'for the people of London and particularly the East-Enders'.[92] Hampton Court was another popular spot frequented during the summer on Mondays when those engaged in outwork in their own homes often took the day off. They travelled on open carts, each carrying about 20 people; sometimes as many as 800 went on one day.[93]

It was this kind of traffic which the railways sought to attract and extend. For the Greenwich, the task was easy. The Croydon, too, was quick to issue day tickets at 2s., 1s. 6d., and 1s. return 'to afford the public an opportunity of viewing the beautiful scenery' on their line. They put up marquees in the woods close to Anerley station and encouraged anglers to fish in the nearby canal. (At Croydon itself a porter used to come out into the road and ring a big dinner bell five minutes before the train started.)[94] Excursion trains soon began to run farther afield. The first one to Brighton, on Easter Monday 1844, consisted of 57 carriages and had to be drawn by six engines.[95] The Southampton line, which took thousands of passengers for part of the way to Epsom races even before its official opening, later made a speciality of running trips by boat round the Isle of Wight.[96] By 1855 some 1,800 excursion passengers travelled from Waterloo every Sunday during the summer—they could go as far as Winchester for 3s. 6d. return;[97] the excursion fare to Brighton and back was also 3s. 6d. and the recently-opened branch from Sydenham to the place where the Crystal Palace had been re-erected was doing Derby Day traffic—10,000 passengers there and back every day;[98] 'whole shoals' of people went on Sunday trips from Shoreditch down the Eastern Counties' line[99] and even uninviting Blackwall became quite popular: the visitors were said to 'swarm into the docks and parade up and down the pier'.[100]

The omnibus retains its ascendancy

By the 1850s the railway's main function, so far as short-distance passenger traffic was concerned, was to provide for the occasional pleasure trip rather than the regular journey to work. Even the North London, which quickly established itself as a commuters' line, did more business on Sundays than on weekdays.[101] It is true that the foundations had been laid on which the commuters' traffic was later to be built up, and the number of commuters coming into London Bridge, Fenchurch Street and Waterloo was probably growing quite fast during the 1850s. But those Londoners who rode to work still for the most part went by omnibus. It is most significant that the main drive in London's suburban development continued to be to the north-west, to the district then known as Tyburnia (which was largely built between the later 1830s and the 1850s) and beyond,[102] and it was from this direction that the omnibus still derived its main support. While effective railway competition was held off by the difficulty of getting railways into central London, omnibuses continued to gain traffic. Indeed, the increase in railway travelling, by bringing more passengers into the metropolis (particularly at the time of the Great Exhibition) and providing Londoners themselves with greater opportunities for excursions, so causing more traffic movement within London, was feeding many more passengers on to omnibuses than it was taking from them. But on certain routes, such as those in the direction of Greenwich and Lewisham, the railways were said to have captured the omnibus traffic.[103]

The period we are at present considering lies well before the days of traffic censuses and it is, therefore, impossible to obtain any reliable estimate of the numbers who came to work every day either on foot or by the three modes of public transport, the omnibus, the steamboat and the train. An inquiry in 1854, however, provides us with a very rough outline of the picture.[104] It was then believed that 200,000 people came into the City daily on foot and 15,000 by steamboat. The numbers passing through the various termini (on either the outward or return journey) bound

for either the City or the West End during the previous
year were also given:

NUMBERS PASSING THROUGH THE LONDON TERMINI IN 1854

London Bridge group	10,845,000
Blackwall Company	
(all passengers using the line and not merely those	
using Fenchurch Street)	8,144,000
Waterloo	3,308,000
Shoreditch	2,143,000
Paddington	1,400,000
Euston	970,000
King's Cross	711,000

Source: Report from the Select Committee on Metropolitan Communications,
1854–55 [415] X.

On these returns, it can be roughly calculated (see below*)
that there were about 6,000 commuters a day by railway;
even if there were 10,000, this would have been fewer than
the 15,000 estimated as using the steamboats and considerably fewer than those coming in every morning by
omnibus, for the latter could then handle about 26,000
people. Omnibuses started running about eight o'clock in
the morning and it seems unlikely that each one could make
more than a single journey with commuters as the journey
to the centre from the outskirts usually took about an hour.
On this basis, and assuming a 75 per cent. loading of commuters on this first journey of the day, the omnibuses might
have brought in nearly 20,000 people. And, throughout the
day and evening, they carried a great volume of traffic from
one part of London to another, a service only supplemented
by the more expensive cabs and (for certain places) by the
steamboats. Clearly, until a means could be contrived of
getting the railways into the central built-up area, the

*It is safe to assume that hardly any commuters came into Paddington, Euston or
King's Cross and very few into Shoreditch. The Blackwall Railway carried about
22,000 passengers per day in all i.e. a maximum of 11,000 return passengers. We know
that in the early days of the North London 4,000 people bought tickets per day to go
on that line either to or from Fenchurch Street, a maximum of 2,000 return passengers.
If a half of these were commuters in 1851, then 2,000 seems a reasonable figure for the
number of commuters using Fenchurch Street from the North London and Blackwall
railways together in 1855. If, say, 3,000 came into the London Bridge termini (the
Greenwich service, like the North London, ran every 15 minutes but started at
7.30 instead of 8 and there were, in addition, six trains arriving from the Croydon line
between 7.45 and just after 10) and about 1,000 came into Waterloo (where the
morning service was much less frequent)[105] that would make some 6,000 commuters
in all.

omnibus was likely to dominate London's transport both for regular commuters and for more casual journeys.

Cheaper omnibus fares

Omnibus traffic grew rapidly while railway competition was held off. Early in 1839, as we have seen, some 620 omnibuses were licensed, most of them to carry 15 passengers (and there were still about 200 short-stages running). By 1850 there were nearly 1,300 omnibuses licensed, and the capacity of many of them had been increased to 22.[106] This represented perhaps a doubling of seating capacity within 11 years. Such rapid growth was made possible by a big reduction in mileage duty and, particularly, by a change in the way it was levied. In 1842, the duty of $2\frac{1}{2}$d. per mile for a vehicle by then licensed for 16 passengers and 2d. for 13 was repealed, and a flat rate of $1\frac{1}{2}$d. per mile per *vehicle* imposed in its place, whatever the capacity of the vehicle might be. This was not only a considerable reduction in duty on existing omnibuses; it was also an encouragement to experiment with ways of increasing their carrying capacity and so spreading costs. The safety regulations, which also formed part of the 1842 Act, showed the way in which this was to be done. A ratio of roof to inside seats— each to average 16 inches in width—was laid down for vehicles above a certain height.[107]

It is not clear exactly when the knifeboard seat running lengthwise along the roof first appeared on a London omnibus. On 1 May 1847 the *Illustrated London News* described an improved design of vehicle which Adams and Company of Bow had recently patented and were making at their works. The roof was shaped so as to provide a long seat for passengers, but it is by no means clear that this was the first such omnibus. Long before that date, passengers had been riding on the roof. In the later 1830s, as we have noticed, many omnibuses were licensed to carry three passengers on top, sitting by the driver; and after 1842 when the permitted number was raised, more passengers sat beside the driver on his seat, and immediately behind him on the front edge of the roof. Seven men, for instance, are shown on top of one of Wilsons' 'Favorites' in a painting dated 17 March 1845.[108] To provide a roof seat and access to it was the logical outcome of this; by 1850 it was usual for omnibuses to carry 22 passengers, nine of them on the roof.[109] The means of getting on to the roof were very primitive, however, and a correspondent was moved to write to *The Times* in 1851 to complain of having 'to displace the conductor and scramble up at considerable personal risk by the aid of an iron step, generally placed on the edge of the window, to the inconvenience of the inside passengers'. He claimed that they ordered things better in Belgium; there a spiral staircase was provided and the seats were sometimes placed across the roof instead of length-wise.[110] In Paris, however, passengers were still not allowed to travel on the roof and it was only in 1853, following visits to London, that this innovation was adopted there, being named the *impériale*.[111]

The cut in mileage duty and the greater earning capacity of each London omnibus enabled fares to be reduced; but these reductions do not seem to have come until towards the end of 1846. A new line of omnibuses which started to run from Paddington to Hungerford Market, Charing Cross, on 21 October of that year provided 2d. fares for short distances; and on 18 November a number of omnibuses running from the Bank to Oxford Street [*sic*] started to charge 3d. and others, from the Bank to Brompton, 2d.[112] Three weeks later it was reported that

The omnibuses at 2d. and 3d. each passenger, now running to and from Paddington and Hungerford Market, the Bank and Charing Cross, the Bank and Tottenham Court Road etc. have been found so productive that it has been determined to extend the cheap travelling system; and accordingly omnibuses have begun to run between Paddington and the Bank via New Road, City Road etc.

at the rate of 4d. each passenger for the whole distance, and 2d. to and from Tottenham Court Road.[113]

In 1847 some even cheaper fares were introduced, culminating in the middle of July in a 1d. fare between Hungerford Market and Camden Town. It is not clear who initiated this new round of competition; but the omnibus owners on the Hungerford Market–Paddington and Hungerford Market–Camden Town routes seem to have been among the first. And it may also be relevant to recall that this was the period when competition among steamboats was bringing down fares on the river. None of the lowest fares, however, came to stay. *The London Omnibus and Thames Steamboat Guide*, published in February 1851, shows that by then steamboats were charging 3d. from London Bridge to Chelsea and omnibuses had reverted to 6d. fares across London and 3d. fares for part of the way—from the Bank to Knightsbridge, for example; or from Tottenham Court Road to either the Bank or Paddington; or from the Angel to either Portland Place or the Bank. The halfpenny steamboats continued to operate but penny and twopenny ones were also well supported. The most lasting result of competition in the later 1840s appears to have been the spread of 3d. fares for half the total distance instead of a fixed rate of 6d. for all or half of the way.[114]

The International Exhibition of 1851 caused a great increase in traffic as many thousands of people poured into London from the provinces and abroad. Fares were put up and additional vehicles brought into service. The income from licence duty in 1851 was 30 per cent. higher than it had been in the previous year and from mileage duty 20 per cent. higher.[115] When the Exhibition was over the omnibus proprietors were left with an excess of capacity. Bitter competition resulted and led to a second phase of fare-cutting. By October 1851 it was said that between 200 and 300 omnibuses were laid up. At a meeting of proprietors, one of their number, Crawford, who had started the Hungerford and Camden Town line, proposed that an association be formed to run cheap omnibuses on the most lucrative stretches of the main routes. These would be exploited one by one, any of their number being allowed to put vehicles on the road until a total of twenty was reached. Then they would turn their attention to part of another route. The new association began running from Bayswater to Tottenham Court Road for 2d. and from there to the Bank for 2d.[116] The older-established associations, running right through to the Bank, also had to cut their fares, and those on the Piccadilly and Strand lines followed suit.[117] By the beginning of December it was possible to ride all the way from Notting Hill to Charing Cross for 3d. During the winter of 1851–52, competition was extended by further subdivision of the main routes and the offer of even cheaper fares on these shorter sections. Penny fares were introduced, for example, from Paddington to Portland Place, Portland Place to King's Cross, Edgware Road to Tottenham Court Road, Tottenham Court Road to Holborn Hill and Holborn Hill to the Bank.[118] Although there are no reports of 1d. fares having resulted in omnibuses being 'literally besieged by the working classes' as had happened in Liverpool,[119] the omnibuses with cheaper fares do appear to have been quite well supported. A journalist who went in one from Holborn Hill to Tottenham Court Road noted that, although 12 inside passengers started the journey and only four completed it, the conductor took 22 fares altogether. 'Passengers, paying their money before they alight, are seen to step out while the vehicle goes on at an easy pace, and others clamber in or on to the roof in the same manner.'[120]

The older-established firms which operated along the whole length of a route were particularly vulnerable to competition from the newcomers who charged 1d. or 2d. fares along its busiest stretches. Both the London Conveyance Company, which dominated the Oxford Street line, and the Paddington Association, which worked along the New Road, tried to hold their own by starting a large number of vehicles at the same fares and for the same distances as their competitors.[121] But the former, though still probably the largest single firm in the business, was not equal to the struggle. Its 65 omnibuses and 508 horses were put up for auction in October 1852.[122] Its downfall appears to have spurred on the survivors to greater efforts; the mileage duty paid in 1852 was slightly greater than that of the Exhibition year itself, though the amount collected in licence duty makes it clear that the number of vehicles was only a little greater than it had been in 1850.[123] Each omnibus was being run more intensively than before and profit margins were cut to a minimum. But while operators were willing to make little or no profit for a limited period in an attempt to consolidate or improve their position in relation to their rivals, such a fierce contest could obviously not continue indefinitely. And in 1853 there were two developments which promised to raise costs and so make business even less remunerative. The outbreak of war between Turkey and Russia in October, soon to become the Crimean War, threatened the price of horse feed, and a new Act, which came into force in the same month requiring all vehicles to be inspected by the Metropolitan Police,[124] made many fear that more money would have to be spent on the omnibuses themselves.

There are signs that, by the autumn of 1853, the operators were again growing tired of fighting. A well-attended meeting of proprietors, held on 26 September to petition for a further reduction in mileage duty,[125] was a straw in the wind; and the setting up of a committee of 21 of their number to further that cause was an even stronger indication. By 1854 the total mileage was a little less than it had been in 1850 and the number of omnibuses had fallen to 1,160. In 1855 the omnibus total was said to be fewer than 1,000 and continuing to fall; in 1856, with mileage still about the 1854 figure, it reached 810.[126] If the 1830s had been notable for the spread of omnibuses and the 1840s for the advent of additional seats on the roof, the mid-1850s clearly saw each vehicle travelling a greater mileage. But this more intensive use of vehicles seems to have been possible only as a result of closer collaboration among proprietors, as we shall see. Such a course was also favoured by others, not proprietors, as a means of dealing with London's growing traffic problems.

Traffic congestion in London's streets and proposed remedies

The traffic jam is not the product of the motor car age. When the main thoroughfares were narrower and fewer, and when vehicles were more ponderous and speeds slower, it did not take much traffic to cause serious congestion. And, in the 1830s and 1840s, the volume of traffic was rising quickly. Between 1830 and 1850 the population living in the City and Metropolitan Police areas grew from 1,900,000 to 2,700,000.[127] The number of stage carriages increased from 800 to 1,200 and of hackney carriages from just under 1,500 to just over 3,000. The advent of railways introduced more goods as well as passenger traffic, and all this merchandise had to be carried in slow, lumbering carts from the railway yards on the outskirts to markets and warehouses in the centre. Sometimes raw materials came in to be sold, were sent out again to be manufactured, and then returned as finished products. In the case of the leather trade, two double journeys were necessary. The skins were brought to Camden Town and loaded on carts to be taken to Leadenhall market for sale. The hides were then returned to the railway to be sent for tanning. The tanned hides returned to be stored in London warehouses and then made their fourth slow journey across the capital, bound for the boot and shoe manufacturers of Northampton.[128]

Yet, despite this great increase in the volume of both passenger and goods traffic, and despite the protracted deliberations of first a Select Committee and then a Royal Commission on Metropolitan Improvement,[129] the chief thoroughfares in 1850 were in much the same state as they had been in 1830. There were still only the three major routes into the City from the west. The Oxford Street route had been improved during the 1840s by the cutting of New Oxford Street between Tottenham Court Road and Holborn,[130] but there was still no Holborn Viaduct and the Fleet valley remained a considerable obstacle. The Fleet Street route was only 23 feet wide at Temple Bar and 25 feet up Ludgate Hill; and the crossing with Farringdon Street was a particularly bad bottleneck on account of turning carts.[131] The two trunk routes still ran together down Cheapside and Poultry. New Cannon Street was made in the early 1850s in an effort to divert some of this traffic. It may have attracted some of the goods vehicles; but the omnibuses and, to some extent, the cabs clung to the busier routes where the fares were to be found.[132] Traffic from the south was similarly impeded, but in this case the bridges caused the main delays. Again, there had been little or no progress since the early 1830s when the new London Bridge had been opened. This was a free bridge, like Blackfriars and Westminster—and Blackfriars had been repaired and improved during the 1830s; but tolls still discouraged the use of Southwark and Waterloo Bridges and forced most of the traffic on to the other three.[133] The only new bridge on this stretch of the river was the Hungerford suspension bridge, opened in 1845. But this was built for pedestrians only, and they had to pay a toll of $\frac{1}{2}$d. Nevertheless it was soon used by 3,000,000 people per year.[134]

As the traffic built up, so the murmurs of complaint became louder. Those who had to get from the London Bridge stations to Charing Cross had the worst of both worlds—the jam on London Bridge and the jam down Ludgate Hill and up Fleet Street—and were particularly

G

outspoken. Already, by 1846, a regular traveller from Brighton had reached the conclusion that it was quicker to walk from the railway terminus to his office in Trafalgar Square than to go by omnibus or cab,[135] and eight years later even the chairman of the London, Brighton & South Coast Railway himself confirmed that this was true; he never took a cab if he was anywhere east of Temple Bar because he could not calculate to a quarter of an hour the time it would take to cross London Bridge.[136] By then it took less time to travel from Brighton up to Town than to get from London Bridge to Paddington.[137] So bad was the congestion at Ludgate Hill that, because of parking and traffic problems, its popularity as a shopping centre was on the wane and at least one shopkeeper had been driven to move elsewhere.[138]

A Select Committee was set up to investigate these growing traffic problems in 1855 and heard evidence from a wide range of witnesses. The success of the Crystal Palace had fired people's ideas, and iron and glass featured in several imaginative, yet utopian, solutions. One witness proposed to knock down 400 houses in order to build what he called a Crystal Way from Oxford Circus to Cheapside, with a branch leading from near Seven Dials to Piccadilly. This Crystal Way was to consist of a 30-foot walk poised in the air 25 feet above street level and flanked on each side by shops. Pedestrians were to be charged a penny for the privilege of climbing up and using it. Twelve feet below street level was to run a railway to be worked by the (discredited) system of atmospheric pressure.[139] Sir Joseph Paxton himself had an even grander scheme which he called his Great Victorian Way. This was to encircle the whole of the central area with a vast new thoroughfare, linking Paddington with Euston and King's Cross, and then sweeping southwards in a wide arc, smartly bisecting Cheapside and crossing the river a little to the west of Southwark Bridge. It was then to continue south of Waterloo station, crossing the Thames again just up-river from Westminster Bridge, brushing past the Houses of Parliament and returning, via Sloane Square and Kensington Gardens, to Paddington. Nor was this all: from Waterloo a branch was to cross the river and cut through to Piccadilly. This remarkable thoroughfare was to be 72 feet wide and entirely covered by a glass arcade and lined with Staffordshire tiles. Within the arcade, and at each side, were to run four railway tracks at a height above street level. (The trains were also to be powered by atmospheric pressure.) Nearer to the centre of the arcade were to be rows of shops in busy districts and private houses elsewhere, the advantage of having the latter under glass being that 'it would prevent many infirm persons being obliged to go into foreign countries in the winter'. In the centre of the arcade there was to be a road which would be open to carts by night and passenger vehicles by day.[140]

The committee also heard more realistic suggestions, and these they commended in their report. They advocated the removal of bridge tolls and the linking of stations by underground railway. They also urged that railway building be undertaken in conjunction with street improvement when the Bill to establish the Metropolitan Board of Works, then passing through Parliament, became law, and London obtained, for the first time, a rate-aided improvement authority with powers over the entire metropolis.

The establishment of the Metropolitan Board of Works —the forerunner of the L.C.C.—in 1855 ushered in a new era in road improvement. It was to be followed, within months, by the merging of most of the omnibus undertakings to form the London General Omnibus Company, which in its turn led to greater order and discipline on the most congested routes. But it was already evident that, even with further street improvement and a better-run omnibus service, the horse omnibus could not handle all central London's passenger traffic in a reasonably satisfactory way.

In particular, the omnibus was an inadequate adjunct to the railway, as an increasing number of travellers through London Bridge had already found to their cost. There was an overwhelming case for bringing the railways from the south across the river to termini on the north bank. No matter how much the streets might be widened or new ones built, no matter how much omnibus services might be streamlined, horse omnibuses from London Bridge to Trafalgar Square could never compete with an extension of the railway tracks across the river to Charing Cross. And, so far as the railways into Paddington, Euston and King's Cross were concerned, no road link with the City using horse traction could be so satisfactory as an underground railway. The years between 1855 and 1870, which saw the Metropolitan Board of Works in its early vigour, the beginnings of the omnibus combine, and, above all, the railway's further penetration into central London to supplement its first foothold at Fenchurch Street, clearly mark a new phase in our story.

CHAPTER THREE

THE EARLY YEARS OF THE
LONDON GENERAL OMNIBUS COMPANY

In 1855 the road transport services of Paris were formed into a monopoly with the blessing and support of the Commission Municipale. *Taking advantage of the wish for closer association which was already evident among several of the London omnibus proprietors, two Frenchmen attempted a similar take-over in London; but in this they were only partly successful. The* Compagnie Générale des Omnibus de Londres, *the original French company financed mainly with French capital, acquired most of London's omnibuses but never a complete monopoly. An improved design of vehicle was introduced and street tramways were envisaged; but so well had the French promoters lined their pockets that the company was soon in financial difficulties. Competition became sharp in 1858 and at the beginning of 1859 the languishing concern was transferred to a British company. After several very lean years its fortunes picked up during 1862 when another international exhibition again brought hundreds of thousands of visitors to London.*

PARIS AGAIN SETS THE EXAMPLE

In the autumn of 1853, the London omnibus owners began to draw closer together, as we have seen. The harvest that year was poor, and the price of horse feed—the main item in operating costs—rose.[1] The proprietors formed a committee to campaign for further reductions of mileage duty; it was claimed that the duty amounted to as much as 20 per cent. of total expenditure on two routes and on others to about 15 per cent. The committee, which was widely representative, included Arthur McNamara of Finsbury, James Willing of Walworth Gate (its treasurer) and John Wilson of Holloway (the largest individual owner), three men who were soon to be deeply concerned in the launching of the London General Omnibus Company; and its secretary, John Edwin Bradfield, a particularly able pamphleteer and special pleader, was to be the L.G.O.C.'s parliamentary agent.[2] The committee's efforts bore no success in 1853, but in November of the following year, Gladstone, the Chancellor of the Exchequer (for whom, personally, omnibuses had a certain fascination[3]), received a delegation of 17 proprietors, representing the owners of 437 vehicles—less than half of the total—and heard from Bradfield a sad tale of woe. According to the proprietors, business had been unprofitable ever since November 1851 and 'on the average' some of the tax had to be paid out of savings. Several of them testified to the truth of this assertion[4] and subsequent evidence, compiled when the L.G.O.C. started publishing its accounts, proved beyond dispute that the duty still imposed a burden on the omnibus business which was very difficult to bear when times were hard. The Chancellor of the Exchequer was impressed by the information laid before him, and from 1 July 1855 the mileage duty was reduced by a third, from $1\frac{1}{2}$d. to 1d.[5]

The Crimean War, which was declared in March 1854, and consequent grain shortages, despite a good harvest that year, drove up operating costs sharply. The basic fare was advanced from 3d. to 4d., and an attempt was even made, during the winter of 1854–55, to put it up to 6d., but this had no success.[6] In June 1855 there were further gloomy reports of omnibuses having been taken off the streets.[7] Clearly, even if the trade had not become so unprofitable as the owners made out for purposes of gaining tax concessions, at the time they met Gladstone it was obviously not so flourishing as formerly. Some proprietors, taking their cue from the greater profits which, from 1831 onwards, had resulted from the formation of associations on the various routes, saw a way out of their troubles in an even more complete pooling of their interests.

Events in Paris again pointed the way to the future and, as in 1828, the first move came from the Prefect of Police there. In May 1854 he recommended to the *Commission Municipale*, Napoleon III's nominees, that the existing omnibus firms in the French capital, already reduced in number to 11, should be formed into a single undertaking and given a monopoly. Who was behind this move is not known, though it is evident that the *Crédit Mobilier*, the recently formed and highly successful banking concern in which some of the leading figures of the Second Empire were represented,[8] soon became deeply involved and may have been prominent in the scheme's initiation. The *Commission Municipale* granted monopoly rights for thirty years but laid down strict conditions of working. The fares were to be fixed at 30 centimes (3d.) for inside passengers and 15 centimes for those who travelled on top, and there was to be no reduction in the frequency of service in off-peak periods. The merger proved difficult to arrange, and negotiations between the existing omnibus owners dragged on for several months. At the end of November 1854 Isaac Pereire of the *Crédit Mobilier* was called in to bring the talks to a speedy conclusion.[9] They were finally completed in February 1855 and the *Compagnie Générale des Omnibus* started to operate on 1 March, just in time for the opening of an International Exhibition which for several months greatly increased the traffic in the French capital.

One of the visitors to the Exhibition was Edwin Chadwick, the leading advocate in Britain of administrative reform and centralization, whose activities in connection with the Poor Law and public health had gained him wide respect from many supporters as the outstanding civil servant of his day —and the constant criticism of a powerful group of opponents to whom he appeared merely as an archbureaucrat. In the previous year, 1854, the opposition had succeeded in having him retired from government service when the General Board of Health, of which he was a

member, was ended. At the age of 54 he found himself freed
from the ties of regular employment and, with a pension of
£1,000 per year, able to undertake many voluntary duties.
Among them was that of serving on a small sub-committee
of the Society of Arts, set up on Prince Albert's initiative
towards the end of 1854 to study documents about Hauss-
mann's rebuilding of Paris.[10] When he visited the Paris
Exhibition in the first half of September 1855, therefore, he
already had an interest in the changes that were then
taking place in the French capital.

Chadwick was well aware of the shortcomings of competition when applied to public services. He had already
experienced, for instance, the harm done by rival water
companies competing for custom within the same streets. In
cases such as this, the consumers' free choice was (in his
opinion)

a free choice as between several rotten oranges—and as a general
rule it cannot be otherwise for it is a competition of services made
inferior as well as kept dear in the long run because unavoidably
extra weighted with disproportionately heavy establishment
charges, which restrict the profits and the means of improvement
—and these charges and the consequent restrictions as to the
quality of the service must be augmented by the very number of
competitors permitted within the field of supply.[11]

Omnibuses came into the same category as water pipes, and
Chadwick was immensely impressed by the superiority of
the services provided by the recently merged Paris undertaking when compared with those of the independent
operators in London, despite the associations on the various
routes. He was introduced to Léopold Foucaud, a Paris
businessman, 'as having done much and as being most
versed in the principles of improvement and of the practical
means of applying them . . .' and was surprised to learn that
Foucaud was already actively engaged in bringing about a
merger of the London omnibuses, not by authoritative

means as in Paris, but by 'voluntary agreements'.[12] In this venture Foucaud was associated with Joseph Orsi, who had thrown in his lot with Louis Napoleon some years after the family banking business in Italy had failed, and had been a member of the ill-fated expedition to Boulogne in 1840. From 1849, if not earlier, Orsi was in partnership with Anthony N. Armani at an office at 6 Guildhall Chambers, Basinghall Street, trading, according to the directories, as 'pat[ent] metallic lava [sic] mfrers'. With Louis Napoleon's rise to power, he moved to more lucrative enterprises. He was connected with one of the Paris omnibus concerns and had been closely involved in the creation of the omnibus monopoly there, being one of the three promoters named at the time of the *Compagnie Générale*'s formation.[13] Having seen how profitable that venture had been, he was not slow to appreciate the possibilities of a similar merger in London where, as he well knew, the traffic was even greater. Foucaud told Chadwick that the 'chief omnibus proprietors' in London had already agreed to sell their stock and goodwills to a French company. This assertion was, to say the least, highly misleading. Two or three of the leading London proprietors may have come to terms by September 1855 when Chadwick was in Paris, but the others knew nothing about the scheme nor had any French company then been formed. Foucaud and Orsi were adopting a confident pose in order to secure Chadwick's support. It appears, however, to have been a pose with substantial financial backing. The *Illustrated London News*, reporting the promoters' first approach to the omnibus trade in London in mid-October, stated that these overtures were made by the *Crédit Mobilier*; and the *Economist* later asserted that the *Crédit Mobilier* had 'a pretty considerable interest in the omnibuses of London'. Although no confirmation of this is to be found in Aycard's *Histoire du Crédit Mobilier* and no list of shareholders survives from this early date to allow us to document the *Crédit Mobilier*'s interest, there are certain hints in the L.G.O.C.

records which suggest that it was, in fact, involved.*[14]

The report of Orsi and Foucaud's first approach to the London omnibus proprietors tried to give the impression that by then (mid-October) negotiations for the take-over were well advanced:

The discussion [at a meeting held at the Hungerford Hall] was very protracted, turning chiefly on the precise terms which ought to be accepted. Ultimately it appeared to be the general feeling that the *Société* should be required to pay £500 for each omnibus with its horses, that sum to include the goodwill as well as the stock . . .

This was followed, on 3 November 1855, by a report in *The Times* which gave the name of the proposed company, based on its Paris counterpart's, in its English version, and suggested that the omnibus proprietors were rapidly coming to terms:

THE LONDON GENERAL OMNIBUS COMPANY. The arrangements for the formation of this company are progressing favourably and it is expected that by the commencement of next year it will have completed the purchase of 500 omnibuses for the purpose of introducing the new service. They comprise the omnibuses running on almost all the leading lines of thoroughfares between the eastern and western suburbs of the metropolis and several of the chief north and south communications . . .

These were obviously both inspired reports, aimed at potential shareholders. The second of them grossly exaggerated the promoters' success and aroused strong opposition, particularly from the committee which had campaigned for the reduction in mileage duty, prominent among whom were Gray, its chairman, and Bradfield, its secretary. The opposition went so far as to make provisional

*The shares which the company issued in England were handled by Theodore Uzielli of Threadneedle Street (B.T.C. Records, LGOC 1/1, Minutes of *Gérants*, 2 January 1856) and Theodore and Mathieu Uzielli were the only two Londoners who held shares in the *Crédit Mobilier* (Aycard, *op. cit.*, 10). Later, when a new French representative was required on the board, Félix Cahaquet who 'held a high position in the service of the *Crédit Mobilier*' was elected (B.T.C. Records, LGOC 1/42, General Meeting 15 March 1864).

registration, on 3 November, of the London Omnibus Company Ltd.—one of the first companies to be registered under the new limited liability Act—as a counterblast, Bradfield being named as its promoter. They were slow to move, however, and do not seem to have got out their prospectus before the French company had issued theirs.[15]

Meanwhile, events occurred in mid-November which left nobody in doubt either of the opposition's strength or of the scant success which Orsi and Foucaud had had up to that time. It was then revealed that McNamara, Willing and Wilson had thrown in their lot with the Frenchmen and a meeting was advertised to be held on the evening of 15 November to hear their proposals. The opposition swiftly organized a protest meeting for that afternoon with Henry Gray, who described himself as chairman of the Metropolitan Stage Carriage Proprietors, in the chair. When this counter-demonstration was over, those who had been present and claimed to represent 'nine-tenths in number and seven-tenths in value' of the trade, publicly denied that anyone had been authorized to sell their property. They then turned up in force at the evening meeting. McNamara acted as chief spokesman for the proposed merger. He reported having been to Paris with Willing and Wilson and asserted that a company had already been formed there to buy out the London proprietors. It was proposed that £500 should be paid for each vehicle and its horses. It did not take the opposition long, however, to bring out the true state of affairs. Some of the exchanges are worthy of quotation:

Proprietor: With whom are the London proprietors treating?
McNamara: The Company, to be sure.
Proprietor: Are the shares of the new company in the market?
McNamara: They are at 35 prem.
Gray: 35 what?
McNamara: 35 francs. (Laughter.)

Gray: Has any of the capital been paid up? What are the names of the principal persons forming the company?

McNamara: None of the capital has yet been subscribed. I have heard the names of the leaders in the company but cannot pronounce French names. (Loud laughter.) . . . When I went to Paris, I found the company had an office and everything looked very respectable; but I do not believe that any money has been paid up. I think they are to pay up in full by 8 December. (Ironical cheers.)

In the end, the meeting—described, no doubt justly, as 'somewhat unruly'—decided to adjourn until the purchase money had been deposited. The French had obtained no acceptance of their terms but there was a hint that a section of the trade might not be averse to selling, at a reasonable price. 'Many proprietors', claimed one of their number, 'would have no objection to sell, and if half a million of money were hanging over them, they might seriously consider whether they would retire from the business or not in the face of so great a threatened opposition.'[16] As matters stood, however, only McNamara, Willing and Wilson had openly declared their intention of selling. Wilson, owner of the Favorites which operated routes from Highbury, possessed 48 vehicles, more than any other proprietor; McNamara of Finsbury had 27 and Willing of Walworth only nine. Together their 84 vehicles represented about one-tenth of the total. Willing and Wilson admitted that they were to become joint managers of the company, each at a salary of £800 per year plus a percentage of the profits, and McNamara also revealed that he was to take office under the company, but what that office was to be, or its remuneration, he did not divulge.[17] There was something to be said for Gray's view that the take-over was 'a job on the part of five or six members of their own trade to help themselves at the expense of the smaller proprietors whom eventually they would throw overboard'.[18]

The formation of the French company

Having tried, unsuccessfully, to persuade the omnibus owners in London that adequate compensation was forth-coming, the promoters next attempted, this time with success, to persuade investors (chiefly in France) that the omnibuses had, in fact, been bought. The *Compagnie Générale des Omnibus de Londres* was formed in Paris under Acts of 4 and 17 December with a capital of 25,000,000 francs (£1,000,000) divided into 250,000 shares, each of 100 francs (£4) of which 200,000 were to be issued at the outset.[19] According to the *Statuts*,[20] Orsi and Foucaud had already succeeded in purchasing 600 omnibuses (quite untrue) for which they were to be paid 100,000 shares as the vehicles were delivered between then and the following 5 February. A further 26,312 shares were to be paid for an additional 210 omnibuses, which would bring the figure to 810, the total then at work in London.

The *Compagnie Générale des Omnibus de Londres* was a *société en commandite*, that is to say it offered limited liability and was run by *gérants* (or managing directors) subject to the advice and supervision of a *Conseil de Surveillance*, the watch-dogs of the shareholders. There were to be three *gérants*, Nicolas-Felix Carteret in Paris and McNamara and Willing in London. (For some inexplicable reason, Wilson did not become one of the managing directors, as had been forecast at the meeting on 15 November, but one of the district managers. The prospectus also named three other district managers, all of them existing proprietors: John Barber, Richard Hartley and John Trevett.) The *Conseil de Surveil-lance* was divided into two parts, the Paris section consisting of the Comte de Lantivy; Vacossin, a director of the *Com-pagnie d'Assurance Urbaine*; Frédéric Toché, banker; Augustin Dubois, director of ironworks at Montataire; and Marziou, *gérant* of the *Union Maritime*. In London were Chadwick, Robert Keating, M.P., director of the London & County Bank, and Thomas Harrison. The Paris office was at 14 Rue

Vivienne; the London office, originally at 21 Old Broad Street, was removed in January 1856 to 454 West Strand.

The London *gérants* held their first meeting on 21 December with Orsi and Foucaud present.[21] The four men met again on the 24th and on that occasion were joined by a fifth member, whose name had not previously been mentioned in any of the published reports. This was Sir Cusack P. Roney. It seems probable that he was the Paris financiers' agent in London whose existence, but not his name, had been mentioned at the meeting on 15 November.[22] The first London office, 21 Old Broad Street, was Roney's address,[23] and he attended most of the *gérants'* meetings during the first month of the company's existence and was afterwards for a time a member of the *Conseil de Surveillance* in London.[24] How he came to be connected with the company is not clear, though, following his resignation from the post of secretary of the Eastern Counties Railway in 1851,[25] he had been actively concerned with railway promotion and finance. He had become, in 1853, secretary of the London board of the Grand Trunk Railway, the largest single investment project undertaken in Canada up to that time.[26]

Like Roney, the *gérants'* first staff were also former employees of the Eastern Counties Railway, though unlike him they had all left that company under a cloud; all three had tendered their resignations on the same day in January 1855 following an official inquiry.[27] Augustus George Church, who had been coaching superintendent in charge of passenger stock, became secretary of the omnibus company at a salary of £500 per year; Sandys Britton, stores accountant, became the book-keeper at £250; and Alfred Feeny, a clerk, came to serve in the same capacity at £120.

Roney visited Paris at the end of December and returned with £3,267. A further £20,000 arrived at the beginning of January and was followed quickly by further instalments, Orsi himself being present again on 4 January and handing over £67,000. We do not know how many of the original issue of 200,000 shares were disposed of at the outset, but in October 1857 150,000 were said to be in circulation, the remaining 50,000 being still in the company's hands.[28] Two-thirds of the 150,000 shares were held by French investors.[29] One hundred thousand of them were given, as agreed, to Orsi and Foucaud in payment for the 600 omnibuses which they claimed to have bought. These shares were not all transferred at once, however, for the *gérants*, who were better informed than the shareholders, needed some security that the vehicles would, in fact, be acquired. They therefore transferred them as the omnibuses were received. They later explained this course of action to the investors (who had been led to believe that the omnibuses had already been bought) on the grounds that 100,000 shares were too many to place on the market all at once and would have caused a sharp fall in their value.[30]

The buying-out of the existing proprietors did not start before the beginning of January 1856, after the arrival of money from Paris. The take-over aroused considerable feeling at first. The *Illustrated London News* reported on 5 January:

The project for the formation of a new omnibus company has met with a sturdy resistance on the part of a great number of the regular 'Bus-men' and placards of a very exciting nature have for some days been posted in the City to counteract what is considered to be a 'foreign innovation' [*sic*]. As every available point is posted with these bills, the congregation of idlers and the jeering of the 'Bus-men' have created such a perfect nuisance that the police were diligently employed on Wednesday [January 2] in preventing more bills being posted and in pulling down and defacing any already put up.

But the company's purchase price, now raised to £510 per omnibus with payment in hard cash at the time of delivery (the minutes of the *gérants*, which give details of purchases during January, make no mention of payment in shares) soon proved irresistible to most of the proprietors, particularly when backed by the threat of crushing competition if such a generous offer were to be refused. McNamara was able to report on 3 January that the owners of 22 omnibuses on the Kingsland and Newington roads—he himself was the proprietor of six of them—had agreed to sell. They were paid for at the rate of £510 each and passed into the Company's hands on 7 January, together with five Hackney omnibuses, also paid for at the same price. On that day, too, Wilson's fleet of vehicles was worked for the first time by the new company.[31] On 13 January he received £24,000 for his 48 omnibuses (£500 each) plus £7,000 for the lease of his premises, £5,000 for the machinery and equipment there, and a strange and unexplained £8,000 'on behalf of Orsi and Foucaud'—£44,000 altogether. These successes in north and north-east London were soon followed by others at the opposite side of the capital. Willing's stock was transferred on 7 January, although he was not paid for it until later.[32] Hartley, another district manager, brought in the 12 vehicles he ran from Putney, Brompton and Wimbledon and with them came 35 others operating from those places and from Chelsea, to be followed, in the ensuing weeks, by yet others. (Details will be found in Appendix 3.)

The take-over pattern was becoming clear: those who had agreed to serve the company either as *gérants* or as district managers had between them interests in all the main routes and were able to carry with them most of their associates on these routes. And most of those who were reluctant to sell at first did so later when they realized how powerful the company was becoming. Even J. E. Bradfield threw in his hand and became the company's parliamentary agent.[33] Altogether more than 250 omnibuses, nearly a third of the total, had been paid for by the end of January, and by the end of March the figure had risen to more than 400, almost half the total. The company was by then in a strong position, for it ran on so many routes that it could meet

21. Wilson's 'Favorite' Omnibus, 1845

22. The Upper Clapton Omnibus, 1852

23. The London Bridge Railway Terminus, 1845

24. The South Western Railway's Nine Elms Terminus

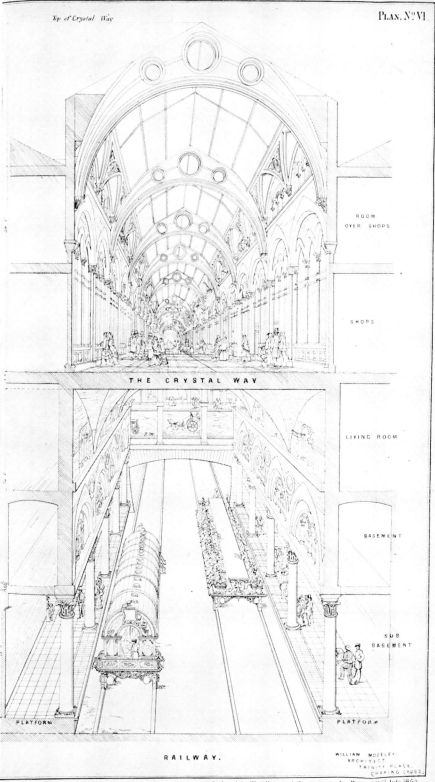

Top of Crystal Way

PLAN. Nº VI.

ROOM OVER SHOPS

SHOPS

THE CRYSTAL WAY

LIVING ROOM

BASEMENT

SUB BASEMENT

PLATFORM

PLATFORM

RAILWAY.

WILLIAM MOSELEY,
ARCHITECT.
TRINITY PLACE,
CHARING CROSS.

Nº 415.   Ordered by The House of Commons, to be Printed 25ᵗʰ July 1865.

25. 'The Crystal Way', a suggestion of 1855

PROSPECTUS

OF THE

Compagnie Générale des Omnibus de Londres

(THE LONDON GENERAL OMNIBUS COMPANY).

Established in Paris, under Acts of the 4th and 17th December, 1855, as a *"Société en commandite*, by which the liability of each Shareholder is limited to the amount subscribed.

CAPITAL:

TWENTY-FIVE MILLIONS OF FRANCS—ONE MILLION STERLING,

In 250,000 Shares of 100 Francs, or £4 each.

In Two Series.—The First, 200,000 Shares (£800,000.)
The Second, 50,000 Shares (£200,000.)

The First Series only will be issued at present.

Gerants of the Company.

MACNAMARA, CARTERET, WILLING & Co.

Managers in London.

Messrs. JOHN WILSON,
,, JOHN BARBER
,, RICHARD HARTLEY.
,, JOHN TREVETT.

Members of the Council of Surveillance.

ROBERT KEATING, Esq., M.P., Director of the London & County Bank....LONDON.
LE COMTE DE LANTIVY...PARIS.
VACOSSIN, Administrateur de la Compagnie d'Assurance l'Urbaine.........PARIS.
FRÉDÉRIC TOCHÉ, Banquier ....PARIS.
EDWIN CHADWICK, Esq., C.B. ....LONDON.
AUGUSTIN DUBOIS, Administrateur des Forges de Montataire.............PARIS.
MARZIOU, Directeur-Gérant de l'Union Maritime ....PARIS.
TH. HARRISSON, Esq..LONDON.

Bankers.

In **Paris**....MESSRS. GREENE & Co.

In **London**.. { THE LONDON AND COUNTY BANK.
{ MESSRS. ROBARTS, CURTIS & Co.

Solicitors.

In **Paris**....MR. PETIT BERGONZ, Avoué au Tribunal de Première Instance.
In **London**....MESSRS. WILKINSON, GURNEY & Co.

THE undoubted advantages produced by the amalgamation of the Omnibuses of Paris, have originated the plan of concentrating, in one Great Enterprise, the several Associations now working the Omnibuses of London.

26. The L.G.O.C's original Prospectus in the English Version

27. L.G.O.C. Knifeboard Omnibus, late 1850s

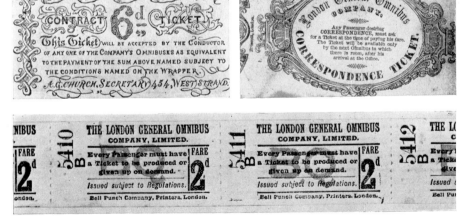

28. L.G.O.C. Correspondence and Contract Tickets, 1856–58 (above); Bell Punch Tickets, 1893 (below)

29. Smithfield Market, about 1830

30. The New Cattle Market in Copenhagen Fields, about 1853

31. The North London Railway Viaduct over the Great Northern at Maiden Lane, 1851

32. The first Station at Willesden, London & North Western Railway, about 1845

33. King's Cross Terminus, Great Northern Railway, 1852

34. King's Cross Station, Metropolitan Railway, under construction, 1862

opposition on any of them by cutting fares, while continuing to operate profitably on the others. Under these circumstances the purchase of further vehicles took place remarkably slowly: 44 in April; 48 in May, June and July; 54 in August and September; and 50 in October, November and December. By then just over 600 vehicles had been acquired, the number which Orsi and Foucaud claimed to have bought a year earlier. For reasons which will be discussed later in this chapter, no attempt was made to purchase the remaining 210 as agreed in the *Statuts*, and the amount Orsi and Foucaud were to be allowed in compensation for not being permitted to make their profit on these remaining vehicles was settled by arbitration, the arbitrator being John Johnson, corn factor, director of the Bank of London and 'one of the largest shareholders of the company resident in England'. He ruled that the cancelled contract was worth £24,000, or just under £1 for each of the 26,312 shares which they had been promised for these remaining vehicles.[34] In addition, if we assume that the 100,000 shares received for the 600 omnibuses were sold at par—not an unreasonable assumption, for the company reported good trading results at the outset—they would have fetched £400,000. At £510 each, the omnibuses cost Orsi and Foucaud altogether £306,000. They (and the financial interests supporting them) seem to have made considerably more than £100,000 on the deal, or over one-sixth of the paid-up capital.*

Their chief London collaborators also did well out of the operation, though it would be wrong to underestimate the scale of either McNamara's or Willing's business activities before the merger. Both men already bore the unmistakable

---

*Léopold Foucaud died some time between January 1857 and November 1858 (University College, London, Chadwick Papers, letter from Foucaud written from 37 Rue Joubert, Paris, 5 January 1857, and draft letter from Chadwick, 27 November 1858, referring to 'the late M. Foucaud' among his letters and notes to unknown persons). Joseph Orsi apparently lived his last years in penury, for in 1888 he wrote to the L.G.O.C. begging for £6 10s. to settle a pressing debt occasioned by the death of his wife. This was refused. (B.T.C. Records, LGOC 1/20, *Minutes*, 26 April 1888.)

H

stamp of success. McNamara, who appeared in the London directories of the later 1840s merely as a railway carrier with an address in Bishopsgate Without, was described in 1851 as both carrier and contractor with premises at the Coal Exchange and in Castle Street, Finsbury. In that year he came to share with its existing holder the contract for carrying the Royal Mails throughout the London area. He already owned omnibuses, and some of them were used to transport the mails from St. Martin's-le-Grand to and from post offices on the outskirts of London. His Royal Day Mail, for instance, according to a contemporary, 'light, elegantly built and splendidly horsed', ran to Barnet. We do not know the value of this Post Office work but it is on record that for a single month in 1857, by which time McNamara's firm appears to have held the contract alone, he received £930 for carrying the London District letter bags.[35] Out of this sum he had to defray his own expenses for vehicles and horses; but, even so, these payments from the Post Office clearly represented a considerable, regular source of income.

Willing, too, had other interests besides the running of omnibuses. From 1849 the directories list him as a tobacconist of Bolingbroke Row, Walworth Road. We know that he also collected turnpike tolls and at the time he became one of the *gérants* of the L.G.O.C. a newspaper gibed at him as being a 'fortunate toll collector at the Walworth Gate, expert in the monetary errors of conductors'. A few years later he also had an interest in the important gates at Notting Hill and Kensington. When he eventually left the board of the company in 1862, it was because it was decided on legal advice that he was disqualified from being a director 'by reason of his being a lessee of tolls and turnpikes through which the omnibuses of the company passed'. He had already started the advertising agency which still flourishes and had held the contract for advertising on the omnibuses from the formation of the L.G.O.C. until 1859. In 1864 he was also referring to himself as a contractor for coals throughout England and Wales but it is not clear how long he had been engaged in this branch of business.[36] He was obviously an entrepreneur of some resourcefulness.

Both men maintained their other business interests after they had become *gérants* of the new omnibus concern. Nevertheless McNamara found time to be personally responsible for the management of one of the districts and Willing acted as traffic manager. We do not know how much they received for these services, though £800 per year, the figure stated at the meeting of 15 November, may not have been far wide of the mark in view of the secretary's known salary of £500. They also, together with the third *gérant* in Paris, shared $1\frac{1}{2}$ per cent. of the company's profits.

The district managers were also well rewarded. They, too, received liberal compensation for their omnibuses. And then they found themselves in charge of all the vehicles operating from the areas which they had formerly served. They were paid £400 per year, Hartley's and Trevett's salaries being raised after a time to £500. In addition they continued to run their own private businesses as job masters, though this practice was stopped at the end of 1859.[37]

The handful of proprietors who now found themselves in charge of what was, by the close of 1856, the largest omnibus undertaking in the world, had to evolve a means of controlling such a vast concern. Already, by the end of January 1856, the book-keeper was explaining methods by which records should be kept in the districts, depots, and stables. He produced ten different forms on which regular returns were to be made. By the end of February the district managers were attending the *gérants'* weekly meetings as a matter of course, and they soon turned their attention to cutting operating costs. When the shareholders met in Paris 14 months later, in April 1857,[38] they were told that 33 omnibuses had been taken out of service and 63 routes were then being worked by 567 vehicles. New stables had been built and most of the old ones repaired, thus contributing to the horses' health and prolonging their working life. Veterinary surgeons had also been appointed with the same end in view. Above all, the managers had made efforts to cut the costs of horse feed, which amounted to about half the company's total expenditure. Steam-driven machinery had been installed at the Bell Lane depot in Spitalfields to clean and prepare the grain, cut the straw and bruise the oats. By April 1857 a third of the 6,000 horses were being supplied with their feed from this centre. It had also been possible to reduce the diet a little—the daily ration of 18 lb. of oats being cut to 16 lb. of bruised oats, plus a mixture of 10 lb. of hay and straw in place of 10 lb. of hay alone. In the following year, 1857–58, large-scale processing of feed was started at three other centres, Paddington, Chelsea and Highbury[39] which, with Bell Lane, were then able to supply all the company's horses.[40] In 1858 this activity was further extended at Irongate Wharf, Paddington, and Bell Lane, the processing formerly carried out at Chelsea and Highbury being concentrated at those two depots. Highbury then became the main vehicle and repair centre, and omnibuses were also built there. This enabled the company to dispense with the services of some of their outside contractors.[41]

Operating economies, an improved design of omnibus and a trial of the correspondence system

The *gérants* also tried to give the public a better service, but their efforts in this sphere do not appear to have been so determined or sustained as their efforts to cut costs. They had, in fact, to be constantly prodded by the French section of the *Conseil de Surveillance*, who wanted them to build more new omnibuses and to press on more vigorously with a correspondence system (as in Paris) whereby passengers could transfer from one route to a second without paying any additional fare. The *gérants* did, however, start off in fine fashion by offering a prize of £100 for an improved design of omnibus. The various entries were inspected in mid-February 1856 and the occasion was used by Chadwick to outline some of the benefits which the public would soon reap from the new merger. He looked forward to the day when 'a passenger from any part of London, by placing himself in the first omnibus passing, would be conveyed to whatever part of the metropolis or suburbs he might wish to reach . . . at one fare'.[42] But although the competition gave Chadwick the opportunity to engage in some useful public relations activities, it did not produce any entirely satisfactory entries. As the *gérants* later reported, they had come to the conclusion that if a vehicle had a track much wider than 6 to 6½ feet, it was unsuitable for the narrow London streets, and if it weighed more than 21 cwt. it was really too heavy to be hauled by a pair of horses. The problem, therefore, was that of building an omnibus which would give greater space inside without materially increasing the size outside.[43] The judges—Charles Manby, secretary of the Institution of Civil Engineers, George Godwin, editor of the *Builder* and Joseph Wright of Birmingham, the maker of railway carriages—came to the conclusion that none of the 75 entries was of 'supereminent merit', but that one, that of R. F. Miller of Hammersmith, had possibilities if it could be further developed.[44] The advantages of the Miller omnibus in its eventual form were those of greater height inside (6 feet instead of 4½ or 5 feet) and greater width (5 feet instead of 4½ feet), fixed side windows but better ventilation in the roof, brass rods to mark each person's share of the form on which he sat, and improved handles and rails to enable outside passengers more easily to scramble up the projections from the back of the vehicle, which served as steps, on to the roof.[45] Mats were substituted for straw on the floor but these were found objectionable in wet weather, so it was decided to try instead 'the French system of fixing strips of wood longitudinally'. Coconut matting was, however, still in general use two years later.[46] The company also experimented with Palmer's Patent Carriage Telegraph as a means of making it easier for passengers to warn the driver when they wished to get out, but it gave so much trouble that the experiments were stopped and the conductors issued with whistles instead.[47]

Omnibuses of improved design were put into service comparatively slowly. Miller delivered his first experimental model towards the end of April 1856,[48] but discussions about the design were still going on in the following November.[49] Fourteen omnibuses were then being built; 46 were in service by April 1857, 124 by the end of that year and 236 by the end of the next.[50] Meanwhile, to fill the gap, McNamara had been to Manchester and Glasgow to look at the larger three-horse omnibuses which ran in those cities.[51] Although they could not be used on the central routes, they were well suited to some of the broader roads out of London, and in May 1856 some vehicles of this kind, built by Menzies of Glasgow and capable of carrying 19 passengers inside and 20 out, started to run on the Kingsland Gate–Bank route.[52] At the same time, some of the better omnibuses among the existing stock were improved; their roofs were raised to give a six-foot standing height inside, the ventilation was increased, and rails were added to enable outside passengers to clamber up to the roof seats.[53] Seventy-nine vehicles had been improved in this way by April 1857, 177 by the end of the year and 221 by the end of 1858.[54] However, the fleet still left much to be desired. In August 1858, for instance, Willing reported that 'very many' of the omnibuses were in 'a very indifferent condition such as he feared would preclude them from passing the examination of the Police'.[55]

The correspondence system, on which Chadwick had set such store and which had featured very largely in the propaganda at the time of the company's formation, was also embarked upon by the *gérants* with great restraint. Here there was something to be said for their lack of enthusiasm, for a system which worked well within the more limited confines of Paris did not really lend itself to the much more extensive routes of London, radiating as they did in all directions from the main central thoroughfares. The company did, however, introduce a modified version of the Paris system which allowed passengers from the suburbs to change on to other routes in order to reach parts of the City or West End not served by their local line. In April 1856 passengers from Barnet bound for the G.P.O. at St. Martin's-le-Grand (who paid 1s. 6d. inside and 1s. out) were allowed to change at either Highbury or the Angel, Islington, without extra charge.[56] During the following year correspondence points were opened at Regent Circus in Oxford Street (now Oxford Circus), 56 High Street, Whitechapel, 109 Bishopsgate Street and the Gunter Arms, Brompton; and on 1 May 1857 two more points were added to serve north and north-west London, at Notting Hill Gate and Edgware Road.[57] At all these places offices were opened at which passengers had to have their correspondence tickets stamped before transferring to the second route. They were not allowed to break their journey but had to go on without any delay.[58] The system proved for a time quite popular with housewives. For 6d. they could travel from their homes in the immediate suburbs to shops in various parts of London.[59] It was an off-peak traffic, however, and was not much used by those going to and from their work. And correspondence never became so cheap or general in London as in Paris, where a 30 centimes (3d.) ticket allowed the holder to ride on any two omnibuses and to get from any point in the French capital to any other. In London Chadwick's hopes were never realized, and support for the system in its modified form was never great. The number of people taking advantage of it fell quite sharply during 1858, and at the end of that year it was abandoned. To compensate for what amounted to a rise

in fares, the basic rate on the two trunk routes (Oxford
Street and the Strand) was reduced from 4d. to 3d. It was
then possible to ride for that price from Tottenham Court
Road or Charing Cross to London Bridge and from Marble
Arch to Farringdon Street. From Orchard Street or Praed
Street to London Bridge cost 4d.[60]

*The French press for more omnibuses, river steamers and the
building of tramways*

Soon after the company was formed, differences of opinion
between the shareholders in Paris and the management in
London began to reveal themselves. The Frenchmen had
assumed that what could be done in Paris could be reproduced in London: not the last time in transport history that
this error has been made. And they expected profits on the
Paris scale. But the conditions were totally different since
the London company possessed no municipal monopoly.
The Paris members of the *Conseil de Surveillance* were, however, very slow to grasp the full implications of this fact and
were constantly urging the *gérants* to hurry on with the purchase of all London's omnibuses, not realizing, apparently,
that this was no guarantee against future competition.[61]
The *gérants*, however, refused to buy more than 600 vehicles
because, they claimed, the remaining 210 were working the
less profitable routes.[62] This however, was by no means the
whole of the story. It is quite clear that the *gérants'* policy
was to buy their way into the associations which already
existed. They soon came to dominate, but not necessarily to
monopolize, them. Some of the remaining 210 omnibuses,
therefore, belonged to operators who ran amicably within
these associations at fares and times decided by the company. They included the vehicles belonging to Mrs. Birch,
later Birch Brothers, which then ran from Westminster to
the Bank. There had been two of them in 1851; by 1858
the total had grown to seven, and in that year it was agreed
that Mrs. Birch should run five on that route and the

company eight.[63] Others among the operators of the remaining 210 omnibuses worked roads on which the company did not run. Notable among them were those south
of the river. The *gérants* claimed that these services were
only marginally profitable; another explanation may be
that Thomas Tilling, who was strongly established in the
south-eastern suburbs, and Balls Brothers, his counterpart
in south London, refused to come to terms. Be that as it
may, at the end of 1856, when the 600 omnibuses had been
acquired, the company faced no competition; there were
no independent operators outside the associations on the
routes it operated.[64] After much discussion—and often
heated argument—the *gérants* were able to persuade the
Conseil that the purchase of more vehicles over and above
the ones they already possessed, which would involve the
issuing of the remaining shares, would lead to a smaller
return on the existing capital.

The *Conseil's* hankering after the control of as much
passenger transport as possible was also evident in its concern that the company should have an interest in the Thames
steamboats and should also build its own tramways. While
Orsi was concerned with the purchase of omnibuses, his
partner in other business enterprises, Armani, attempted to
launch another French company to take over the steamboats on the river. The *gérants*, in September 1856, declared
that they wished to have no hand in this matter,[65] but the
Conseil insisted. By January 1857 the company had subscribed £10,000 to the venture, and a prospectus was then
published. The concern was to be financed by the issue of
2,225 shares of £20 each and the capital used to purchase
and operate 27 boats belonging to the London & Westminster and Citizen lines. The boats were then to be brought
into correspondence with the omnibuses.[66] This take-over
did not succeed, however, and the L.G.O.C. later decided
on 'amicable arbitration' with Armani as the best means of
deciding what was to become of its £10,000.[67] Armani had

meanwhile joined the London section of the *Conseil* and was soon to become a prominent figure in the company.

The attempt to launch London's first tramway came in 1857. This method of urban transport had started in New York and New Orleans in the 1830s and had spread to other American cities in the 1850s. In North America the railways themselves often ran through streets of towns, and on these urban stretches locomotives had to be replaced by horses. As a leading British authority, W. Bridges Adams, explained to the Society of Arts in February 1857: 'Once familiarized with railway carriages drawn by horses, the observant American mind was not slow to perceive that the arrangement was very superior to omnibuses for town transit.'[68] Loubat, who is said to have been concerned with tramways in New York, introduced them to Paris in 1853, when a line was opened from the Place de la Concorde to Passy, with a 'new Parisian omnibus' carrying 16 passengers inside and 24 out. The Loubat tramway—the *Chemin de Fer Américain* as it was called—was extended to Sèvres in 1854 and in the next year it became part of the Paris transport monopoly.[69] The *Conseil* of the *Compagnie Générale* was soon urging that tramways should be built in London. On 6 October 1857 they were told that 'the *gérants* had fully and seriously considered the scheme of tramway conveyance on the American plan' and had reached the conclusion that it would be possible to introduce such a system. The prospectus of the London Omnibus Tramway Co. Ltd., an English company, was issued from the omnibus company's offices before the year was out.[70] It was proposed to lay a track from Notting Hill Gate through Bayswater and along the New Road, City Road and Moorgate to the Bank, with a branch from King's Cross via Farringdon Street to Fleet Street. The amount of capital needed, £50,000, was based on information gleaned from working tramways in Paris.[71] According to James Samuel, the engineer, 'the tramway omnibuses' were to weigh two tons and to carry 60 passengers, three times the capacity of the existing omnibus. Yet they were to be hauled by two horses, apart from the ascent to the Angel, where a third would be needed. The double-line track was, according to the company's prospectus, to be laid in the centre of the roadway 'perfectly flush with the surface' so as not to interfere in any way with the passage along it and across it of ordinary road vehicles. The project, however, met strong resistance from municipal interests and from Sir Benjamin Hall, M.P. for Marylebone and Chief Commissioner of Public Works, whose carriage had been overturned on at least two occasions by plateways in his native South Wales; he was determined not to allow anything similar to endanger wheeled vehicles in London. The Bill to authorize the laying of the track was defeated at its second reading.[72]

The *Conseil* also tried to impose other Parisian practices upon the reluctant *gérants*. They demanded, for instance, the speedy introduction of indicators, a means of counting the number of passengers and so keeping a check on conductors' takings. The *gérants* ordered a trial but were quick to declare this an utter failure.[73] They fell back upon the existing method of employing a road inspector to keep an eye upon any conductors whose earnings were lower than usual, though they did introduce, at the beginning of 1857, a new scheme whereby vouchers could be purchased in advance and used in payment of fares. There was a 10 per cent. reduction if a sovereign's worth was bought at once. At the time of this innovation some of the larger shops declared their intention of offering these 'tickets' to their lady customers instead of small change.[74]

The movement against the 'French monopoly'
The fundamental cause of dissension between London and Paris, however, lay deeper than these initial misunderstandings and the *Conseil's* wish to impose Parisian practice upon a management determined to act instead upon London

experience. National feeling was also involved; France was then the traditional enemy. Although the two countries found themselves fighting for a short time on the same side during the Crimean War, this was just a short-lived episode, soon to give way to the customary animosity which within a few years was to focus itself in the Volunteer Movement. This anti-French feeling gave a considerable advantage to rival omnibuses when they appeared in 1857. Passengers were urged to give their support for patriotic reasons, and the omnibuses of one of these competing firms even went so far as to parade the French flag as an object of derision.[75] Much later on, a rival was to take the Union Jack as its distinguishing mark.

The first opposition, ironically enough, arose out of the omnibus competition which the *Compagnie Générale* had held at the beginning of 1856. One of the disappointed entrants threatened to start a rival concern if the company refused to buy his design. The *gérants* offered him £800, but refused to go any higher; whereupon the disgruntled competitor enlisted the support of Sir R. W. Carden, a former Lord Mayor, Sir John Kay, Chamberlain of the City of London, and others in a crusade against the 'French monopoly'. They registered the Metropolitan Saloon Omnibus Company Ltd. as a joint-stock company on 26 September 1856 and issued a prospectus at the beginning of November.[76] The capital, a modest £20,000, was to be raised in £1 shares, an unusually low denomination at that time, the aim being to attract investment from patriotic Londoners who would use the new company's omnibuses. A specimen vehicle, heavier and larger than those of the *Compagnie Générale* and, as events proved, too burdensome for the horses and too unwieldy for the narrower London streets, made its appearance in mid-November.[77] Little progress appears to have been made that winter, however, and in February 1857 the secretary had to deny a rumour that the company had ceased to exist.[78] In April they had six omnibuses on the streets and 12 by August, but they never appear to have worked more than 15.[79] At first they ran on various routes to the north as well as to the south-west, but later in 1857 they concentrated on the Brompton and Putney roads; perhaps it was in that quarter that most of their shareholders were to be found. Meanwhile, other independent operators appeared, notably on the Kingsland Road. In order to meet this competition, the *gérants* had to reduce their fares drastically—that from Kingsland Gate to Elephant and Castle, for instance, was cut to 2d.[80]—and put on additional vehicles to 'nurse' those of their rivals. These measures, however, failed to banish competition, although the Saloon Company was in a very weak state by the end of 1858 and was driven, as a last desperate step, to take legal action against its powerful rival, accusing the members of the *Conseil* and the *gérants* individually with conspiring to libel and injure its trade. The Saloon Company eventually lost its case in the courts, but only in 1862 and after a very protracted series of hearings.[81]

The reduction in fares and increase in expenditure required to meet this opposition narrowed the company's profit margin and revealed its fundamental weakness. The take-over had, in fact, been excessively costly. Not only had Orsi and Foucaud lined their pockets with, perhaps, upwards of £100,000, but £32,500 had also been spent on initial publicity and brokerage.[82] Possibly £150,000 or more had been taken out of the company right at the start. And it was generally agreed that compensation had been paid to the existing proprietors on a very generous scale. The comment of one newspaper that 'enormous sums [had been] paid for rattling, old, greasy vehicles'[83] reflected the general opinion and was, perhaps, allowing for a little journalistic licence, not too exaggerated. In other words, so much capital had had to be raised that unusually high profits were needed in order to pay a rate of dividend which would command the respect of financial circles and so establish the company's credit-worthiness.

Returns of revenue and expenditure on the first $2\frac{1}{2}$ years' working show how the company, having made less money in 1857 than in 1856, ran into serious trouble in 1858.

REVENUE AND EXPENDITURE OF THE L.G.O.C.
IN 1856, 1857 AND THE FIRST HALF OF 1858

	Revenue	Expenditure	Profit
1856	£474,262	£399,862	£74,400
1857	£603,770	£550,331	£53,439
Jan.–June 1858	£291,605	£282,523	£9,082

All the first year's profit was paid out to shareholders in a $12\frac{1}{2}$ per cent. dividend ($12\frac{1}{2}$ francs or 10s. per share) totalling £75,000. In 1857, despite the beginnings of competition, receipts per vehicle fell only slightly, but since there were more vehicles, an average of 571, operating throughout the year, total receipts were much greater. It was higher costs which caused the quite considerable fall in profit. Despite this warning sign, an 8 per cent dividend was declared on the year's working and £48,000 distributed to the shareholders. The crisis arrived in 1858 when competition was intensified. Despite a fall in the cost of horse feed, total costs continued to rise and, at the same time, income fell quite dramatically. For the first six months of the year receipts were nearly £17,000 down. This depressing news at last caused the shareholders in Paris and the *gérants* in London to resolve their differences.

The L.G.O.C. is naturalized

The *gérants*' view—in which they were supported by the London members of the *Conseil*—was that the company should be turned into an English one and all the meetings be held in London. The London members were urging this course so early as January 1857,[84] and Chadwick wrote to Foucaud at that time to express his conclusion that

the undertaking cannot be safely or agreeably conducted by any set of persons on the present footing; . . . safe opinions can only be formed on the spot and . . . with the best intentions misunderstandings will be sure continually to arise and . . . the present constitution, were it attempted to be maintained, could not last or give satisfaction. We are unanimously of the opinion that it is in the interest of the French shareholders that the management must be undivided and concentrated at the seat of administration.[85]

The Paris *Conseil* would not listen to these suggestions at that time and continued to advocate the introduction of Paris methods as the only sure way to Paris dividends. This was the constant theme contained in the minutes of their meetings which were sent to London and pressed by their representatives on frequent visits. The sharp fall of profits early in 1858, however, caused the French shareholders to think again. By June the Paris *Conseil* was already considering the possibility of making the company English, and this was decided upon by the end of the summer. In persuading the French to adopt this course, the *gérants* made much of the way in which their rivals were able to invoke anti-French feeling against them:

'We are at length forced to the conclusion', they asserted, 'that the weapon constantly used against us really possesses a much greater influence with the English public than we were at first willing to believe—we refer to the cry so continually raised against us that we are a FOREIGN MONOPOLY . . . We have heard this charge of foreign monopoly made against us in pleadings in the Superior Law Courts for the purpose of biasing the administration of justice when otherwise the cause has been favourable to your interests, and the Company spoken of as foreigners, and almost the agency of an enemy . . . Political circumstances have also turned against us. The respective positions of the two countries were changed for a time, at least in appearances . . .'[86]

The British London General Omnibus Company Ltd. took over from the French company on 1 January 1859 by an exchange of shares, those of 100 francs being changed for new ones of £4. (Shares worth over £5,000 'disappeared' in the Paris office during the exchange, and it was decided that since the French company was then extinct, nothing could be done to recover the loss.) The nominal capital of the L.G.O.C. was £800,000, the same as that of its predecessor, and just over 25,000 shares still remained unissued. While the French kept for a time their major financial interest, they no longer exercised any real control, for only four of the twelve newly-created directors were French and the shareholders' meetings were moved to London.[87] The Paris office was closed and a branch opened in more modest premises at which a register of French shareholders was kept. In 1862 the French shareholders started to gather a few days before the general meeting in London to decide what points of view their representatives should take on the various issues to be discussed.[88] Although the French still held most of the shares in 1864, by 1867, 94,000 were held in England and only 54,000 in France.[89] When, in the next year, the number of directors was reduced from 12 to 9, the French representation was cut to two.[90] The reports and balance sheets, however, continued to be printed in French as well as English and this practice was continued until 1911.[91]

Difficult years for the new English company

The original board of the L.G.O.C. consisted of the four leading members of the Paris *Conseil*, Vacossin (who had been first its secretary and then its president), Lantivy, Toché and Carteret (the *gérant* in Paris); the two English *gérants*, McNamara and Willing; two members of the London *Conseil*, Armani and William Halliday-Cosway (a London property owner who had joined the *Conseil* in November 1857 when Roney and Harrison had resigned); together with Farmery John Law, Joseph Dugdale, a barrister, Richard Thornton, a former East India Company judge, and William Sheldon, a former coach proprietor. Chadwick was also named in the preliminary list but did not actually join the board; whether this was at his own wish or that of the directors, is not clear. He handed in his ivory pass entitling him to free travel at the end of December 1858, but it was presented to him by the board 'as a trifling acknowledgement of his past valuable services in connection with the company'.[92] McNamara remained in fact, if not in name, the managing director and the *gérants*' committee (McNamara and Willing, attended by the district managers) became the managers' committee. Halliday-Cosway was chairman of the company until 1860, when he was succeeded by Law.

The new board inherited a sorry legacy. The company was burdened with debts to the tune of over £100,000.[93] Their origins are obscure, though it is evident that such improvement as had been carried out must have been undertaken, for the greater part, by borrowing from the bank rather than by reinvestment. There was a profit of £23,888 on the operations during the whole of 1858, but since this was made during the lifetime of the French company, it was left to the Paris shareholders to decide whether to divide or reinvest it. Not surprisingly, they took the former course and declared a dividend of 3 per cent., thus disposing of £18,000 among themselves. In order to meet a most difficult situation, the directors made an effort to improve the management by forming three of their number —McNamara, Law and Sheldon—into an executive committee which met daily.[94] The salaries of district managers were cut and, towards the end of the year, Wilson and Barber resigned.[95] Despite every effort to reduce expenditure, the profit for 1859 at £24,046 was little more than it had been in 1858, but on this occasion no dividend was paid. At the beginning of the next year an attempt was made to issue £30,000 worth of debentures, but there were only two applications for them. So McNamara took £3,000 worth himself and the board resolved 'that each member . . . do undertake to make enquiry of Solicitors and other parties of their acquaintance likely to have trust funds in hand for investment'.[96]

I

Meanwhile competition continued unabated; 78 rival omnibuses were operating in December 1859 and 85 in the following April.[97] And 1860 proved a year of unprecedented difficulty, for not only did competition continue to reduce revenue, but also—and more important—bad weather caused a very sharp rise in the price of horse feed. The company made no profit at all that year; there was even a slight loss.[98] Hardly any money was made in the first half of 1861 either, but better business in the second half of the year produced a final profit of £13,225 and a dividend of 1s. 6d. was declared on each share. The company's debt, however, still remained at about £100,000.

Despite its disappointing trading results, the L.G.O.C. was carrying more passengers year by year without having to put more than 580 vehicles on the road.

NUMBER OF PASSENGERS CARRIED
BY THE L.G.O.C., 1859–62

1859	38,899,247
1860	40,123,366
1861	41,360,893
1862	42,768,248

1862 was an exhibition year, and, as in 1851 in London and 1855 in Paris, the additional traffic brought great prosperity to public transport undertakings. The L.G.O.C.'s profits rose to £72,503; but only 3s. per share were distributed in dividend, the rest being used to pay off part of the debt which was reduced to £64,000 by the end of that year.[99] The worst was past, although the company still had to contend with competition from some 100 rival omnibuses. And in 1863 it was also confronted for the first time with competition from an underground railway.

CHAPTER FOUR

THE FIRST CLIMAX

(I) THE COMING OF THE UNDERGROUND RAILWAY

By the later 1850s, improved communications were called for to prevent the congestion in London's busiest streets from growing worse as the volume of traffic continued to increase. One solution was to bring railways closer to the heart of London, to within walking distance of each passenger's destination, so providing him with an alternative to the omnibus on those central routes where traffic congestion was worst. North of the Thames, this was achieved by an underground railway which served three of the main-line companies. Built by the Metropolitan Railway, opened from Paddington to Farringdon Street on 10 January 1863 and extended to Moorgate Street on 23 December 1865, it was the first underground railway in the world. The Great Western gave it financial support, and the Great Northern and Midland also used it as a means of securing entry into the City. The Metropolitan, however, asserted its independence of the main-line companies from the outset, and concentrated on its own large 'omnibus' traffic, shortly to be supplemented by that from feeder lines to Hammersmith, Kensington and Swiss Cottage. In order to handle an increasing number of trains, two additional tracks were laid from St. Pancras and King's Cross to Moorgate Street for the accommodation of Midland and Great Northern traffic. Meanwhile the North London, representing the North Western's interests, opened its own city terminus at Broad Street in 1865, but the Great Eastern—as poor and struggling as its predecessor, the Eastern Counties—having planned a new terminus at Liverpool Street and suburban lines to Edmonton and Chingford in the middle of the 1860s, was prevented by financial difficulties from maturing them until the early 1870s.

THE FLEET VALLEY IMPROVEMENT SCHEME

THE VERY HIGH COST of property in central London caused would-be railway promoters to explore the possibility of constructing lines underground long before the 1850s. As the law obliged anyone who burrowed under buildings to buy them outright, even though he might undermine only a part of the foundations, it followed that the only routes likely to pay their way were those which ran under roads and open spaces and passed underneath as few buildings as possible. When Robert Stephenson, for instance, in the mid-1830s, considered extending the future London & Birmingham Railway to the Thames, he proposed to do this by means of a line running under Gower Street and down to the north end of Waterloo Bridge.[1] But while engineers were tolerably well versed in building tunnels and cuttings in open country or where only a few buildings were involved, the hazards of constructing a railway just below the surface in the midst of expensive property, where the slightest subsidence would lead inevitably to a succession of extravagant claims for compensation, were too great. The risks deterred even Stephenson.

At about the same time as Stephenson was pondering the possibility of a line under Gower Street, another underground scheme was also under consideration. This was to run from King's Cross, down the valley of the river Fleet as far as the main Holborn–Cheapside road at Snow Hill. But this, too, came to nothing.[2] It did, however, arouse the interest of Charles Pearson* who, as we noticed in chapter two, was a keen advocate of cheap railway travel as a means

*Charles Pearson was born on 4 October 1793 at Clement's Lane, Lombard Street, where his father, Thomas, carried on business as an upholsterer and feather merchant. He was educated at Eastbourne and articled to Andrew Burt, a solicitor in John Street, Minories. Having completed his articles, he was admitted on the roll of attorneys in Hilary term 1816, and, taking chambers in John Street, Adelphi, soon acquired a large and lucrative practice. He married in 1817 Mary Martha Dutton of Brixton, the daughter of a member of the Corporation. A member of the Haberdashers' Company, he became Common Councilman for the ward of Bishopsgate from 1817 to 1820 and again from 1830 to 1836. He achieved early fame by bringing to light the system of packing juries for the trial of political offences, which was suppressed as the result of his exertions. His progressive opinions led to an association with Radical politicians for a time, but this adversely affected his business and was not persisted in. In the City he campaigned successfully against the bar on the admission of Jews to the freedom and as sworn brokers, and also for the removal of the lines in the inscription on the Monument attributing the Great Fire to Roman Catholics. From 1831 to 1833 he was chairman of the City Board of Health which dealt with the severe outbreak of cholera,

of enabling the poor to live in healthy surroundings outside London, and John Hargrave Stevens, an architect and civil engineer.[3] Both men were shortly to become influential City officials, Pearson as City Solicitor and Stevens as Surveyor for the City's Western Division. They realized that an underground railway could profitably form part of the City's plans for the improvement of the Fleet valley and the building of a new road north from Farringdon Street.

Although the first part of Farringdon Street, between the bottom of Fleet Street and Holborn Hill, had been opened to traffic in 1830,[4] land to the northward was still covered with a maze of narrow streets and insanitary property. Down the valley flowed that notorious sewer, the river Fleet, open to the air in a number of places. To the east Smithfield still remained a market for live animals, surrounded by cattle sheds, slaughterhouses, and dark dens devoted to what were then called the 'noxious trades'. In 1838 the City was empowered to begin the improvement of this area by building a new street northwards from Farringdon Street towards Clerkenwell Green. Two years later the Clerkenwell Improvement Commission was formed to add to this road-building programme a more general plan for clearing dilapidated and tumbledown property.[5] Progress was slow, however, and money short. When, therefore, during the Railway Mania of the mid-1840s, there was a proposal to terminate a new trunk line from the north in

and in 1834 and 1835 he served as under sheriff. On his retirement from the Common Council in 1836, a special court was summoned to present him with a valedictory address and a candelabrum was presented to him in recognition of his services.

In 1839 he became City Solicitor and Solicitor to the Irish Society, both of which posts he held until his death. He was also Solicitor to the Commissioners of Sewers from July 1859 until his death, and a Member of Parliament for Lambeth from July 1847 to July 1850. As City Solicitor, in addition to his interest in the underground railway, he also supported schemes for the embankment of the Thames, the establishment of a new meat market and the promotion of the Great Central Gas Consumers' Company. He was also interested in prison reform and the problem of juvenile crime, and served for a year as governor of Whitecross Street Prison. He wrote many pamphlets on these and other subjects.

He died on 14 September 1862 at Oxford Lodge, West Hill, Wandsworth, having suffered from dropsy for the last twelve months of his life, though this did not prevent his attention to business until a week before his death. He was buried at Norwood. (*The Times*, 16 September 1862; *The City Press*, 20, 27 September 1862; Boase's *Modern English Biography*.)

the Fleet valley, many people in the City welcomed it, for they realized that it would bring capital to their languishing improvement schemes as well as more business to City firms. Prominent among the railway's champions was Pearson, who had no qualms about speaking out, despite his official position. He wrote a pamphlet on the subject, advocating the merits of a covered way—not a tunnel—down the Fleet valley which would be 'as lofty, light and dry, as airy and cheerful as the West End arcades' and through which trains would be drawn by atmospheric power. He also made much not only of the economic benefits which would accrue to the City but also of the social advantages.[6] The Corporation, which stood to gain financially, supported the railway scheme and hoped it might be worked into its other plans for cutting a new road from Carey Street to Cheapside; but the railway promoters were unable to proceed with their line from the north, and the whole idea had to be dropped. Meanwhile the Clerkenwell Improvement Commission fell further and further into debt, and in 1851 the City Corporation was obliged to come to its rescue.[7]

The City's further financial involvement was the signal for Pearson and Stevens to press their railway scheme once again. The Great Northern Railway had been opened to a temporary terminus at Maiden Lane in the summer of 1850 and was in process of building its permanent station at King's Cross. It was hoped that this new arrival, together with the London & North Western and Great Western, might be persuaded to support a railway down the Fleet valley as a means of gaining direct access to the City. Again, the Common Council lent a sympathetic ear, and in November 1851 it formed a large and influential committee to study Pearson's Railway Terminus and City Improvement Plan.

The plan consisted of a 100-ft. road connecting the then northern limit of Farringdon Street at Holborn Hill with King's Cross. Under it was to run an arched tunnel wide enough to accommodate no fewer than six narrow-gauge and two broad-gauge railway tracks. There was to be a link with the Great Northern Railway a quarter of a mile north of King's Cross, and the provision of broad-gauge rails makes it clear that Pearson already had in mind the railway's extension to the Great Western. South of the tunnel a viaduct was to be built to carry the main Holborn–Cheapside road across the Fleet valley, and under this Holborn viaduct the railway was to pass, to end, beyond the viaduct, in stations covering over six acres of ground on both the east and west sides of Farringdon Street. These stations were to accommodate the main-line traffic. To the north of them was to be yet another one for short-distance passengers with platforms 200 to 300 yards in length, partly under the new street; and, further north still, a thirteen-acre site for goods traffic and engine sheds.[8]

Pearson attended the meetings of the Corporation's committee when it met to consider this plan and was also engaged in a considerable amount of lobbying behind the scenes. At the end of November 1851, for instance, he gave a *soirée* to members of the Institution of Civil Engineers.[9] Three weeks later he proposed tackling the project in two stages, stopping the line at the Holborn–Cheapside road in the first instance and leaving the Holborn viaduct and the stations to the south of it until later. 'I intend to employ my Christmas vacation', he told the committee, 'in company with the Engineers and Surveyors engaged in the preparation of plans, surveys and estimates, and I shall endeavour to prevail upon wealthy parties to provide the capital to carry a Bill through [during] the ensuing session for a line stopping at Holborn Valley.'[10] The technical experts reported favourably on the plan, and the committee reported on 15 January 1852 that it would be

most desirable to secure if possible to the public and Corporation of London the great Benefits which will arise from such a terminus and street improvements which will be the necessary consequence of the construction of the line, which may be secured without any risk being incurred by the Corporation.

The Common Council endorsed this recommendation on 11 March, and on the 16th the committee resolved that Mr. Pearson be authorized to give any information he may be in possession of to the respective Railway Companies if desired by them on the understanding that such information be given by him as the projector of the plans and not as an officer of the Corporation.

The main-line companies were, however, no more anxious to bear the risks of such an adventurous speculation than the City Corporation was, and it was left to Pearson and the few supporters who joined him in the City Terminus Company to press on with the scheme. They got so far as preparing a Parliamentary Bill.

The origins of the Metropolitan Railway

The efforts of the City Terminus Company were soon being supplemented by those of another venture, known at first as the Bayswater, Paddington & Holborn Bridge Railway, which aimed at building an underground line from Paddington to King's Cross and there joining the one proposed by the City Terminus Company. The men behind this second line seem to have been quick to realize its financial possibilities without any prodding or encouragement. Unlike the City Terminus, they did not have to build a road and knock down houses: a fine, wide thoroughfare already existed—the New Road—which could be cut and recovered without the purchase of much property. The capital needed was estimated at £300,000, less than half that required by the City Terminus even in its abbreviated form. Upon this the considerable local traffic on one of the busiest routes in London could be expected to earn a good return. The promoters were impressed by the large passenger traffic which the East & West India Docks & Birmingham Junction (soon to be re-named the North

London) Railway had already gained, despite its round-about route into the City.[11] Their underground railway ran out to a much more prosperous area, the district known as Tyburnia from which the omnibuses derived their great source of income. The Bayswater line obviously had strong financial attractions of its own once the possibilities of underground travel were realized and the more difficult and costly stretch to Farringdon Street was being actively promoted. It was the real origin of the Metropolitan Railway as it was finally carried out.

Stevens became the surveyor of the projected line, and among its original sponsors was William Burchell, also connected with the City Terminus Company. He was a solicitor, and it was at 47 Parliament Street, where he had had his office ever since the Railway Mania of the mid-40s, that the board held its first meeting. He was then in partnership with John Parson, who, since 1850, had been waging a vigorous—and unscrupulous—contest with the Great Western Railway as legal adviser and virtual dictator of the Oxford, Worcester & Wolverhampton Railway.[12] He was an associate of the well-known railway contracting firm of Peto and Betts who had come to the rescue of the floundering O.W. & W. ('The Old Worse and Worse') in 1850 and eventually completed the line. This firm, too, was involved in the Bayswater, Paddington & Holborn Bridge Railway, each partner promising to subscribe £20,000.[13] And (Sir) John Fowler,* engineer of the Oxford, Worcester & Wolverhampton from March 1852, was appointed engineer of the

*John Fowler was born on 15 July 1817, the eldest son of John Fowler of Wadsley Hall, Sheffield. Having served his apprenticeship to a hydraulic engineer, he entered the as yet young but rapidly-growing railway industry. He was engaged under J. U. Rastrick on the design and superintendence of the London & Brighton Railway and then for a time resident engineer and then locomotive superintendent of the Stockton & Hartlepool. He became an independent consultant at the age of 26, in good time to make the most of the Railway Mania of the mid-1840s. Among his later activities he is particularly remembered (together with Benjamin Baker) for his engineering work in Egypt, including the Aswan Dam, and for the building of the Forth Bridge. On the completion of the latter he was created a baronet. He became a member of the Institution of Civil Engineers in 1844 and was its president in 1865–66 and 1866–67. He died on 20 November 1898. (*Proceedings of the Institution of Civil Engineers, 135* (1899), 328–37; *D.N.B.*)

underground project.[14] These were men well versed in the various stages of railway promotion: the legal processes in Parliament, the raising of capital, and the actual building of the line.

The prime mover in the scheme, however, and the company's first chairman, was William Malins, a practical man 'very conversant with mining' (his own description of himself) who had been recommended by Robert Stephenson for the post of chairman of the City Commission of Sewers a year or two before.[15] In 1853 he lived at a fashionable address in Savile Row and had contracted to take shares in the company to the value of £15,000. In some respects his transport career resembles Shillibeer's. He always claimed that the original idea of a railway under the New Road was his, and when the line was open and making money he sought compensation from the company.[16] But, like Shillibeer's, his claim was not so clear-cut as he liked to believe. Obviously Pearson deserved consideration, and Burchell also made a case for himself.[17] In these circumstances Malins was no more successful in gaining recognition in terms of hard cash than Shillibeer had been. The New Road was an unprofitable scene of activity for transport pioneers, either above or below ground.

William Malins looked upon the projected line right from the outset as the beginning of an underground railway network which would spread throughout London. Growing congestion on the roads, he believed, had made this inevitable.

'It must be obvious', he claimed, 'that the constantly accumulating number of omnibuses, wagons and conveyances of all sorts would, if it continued two or three years longer, render London almost insupportable for purposes of business, recreation and all ordinary transit from place to place . . . doubling the thoroughfares by means of *sub via* railways was the only mode of accommodating the increased traffic of London.'[18]

Malins and his expert associates showed great ability and

adroitness in the way they went about promoting their scheme. They persuaded the banking firm of Heywood, Kennards & Co. to advance the deposit required to meet Parliamentary Standing Orders, in return for the appointment of that firm as the company's bankers.[19] They withdrew the proposed terminus of the line from the Westbourne Terrace end of Sussex Gardens to the Edgware Road in order to avoid opposition from the Paddington Vestry,[20] and they gained the support of the local authorities in St. Marylebone by emphasizing how much the ratepayers would save in road repairs. As a result, the Bill was not opposed in Parliament and got through its committee stage in a single day. The line was then renamed the North Metropolitan.[21]

Pearson's scheme, however, did not even reach a second reading. No money was forthcoming from the main-line railway companies, and the City Corporation therefore refused its support of the Bill. It instructed the Improvement Committee to confer with the Government 'on the whole projected improvements in Holborn Valley and Farringdon Street in order to ascertain if [the] Government will co-operate with the Corporation in accomplishing the whole of the plan proposed'; but decided that, 'in the meantime, the progress of the Bill now before Parliament be suspended'.[22] A deputation visited the Home Office at the beginning of May 1853, but the Home Secretary was unwilling to offer any help.[23] 'Thus,' commented the *Railway Times* with relish, 'expires Mr. Charles Pearson's notable project.'[24]

The directors of the North Metropolitan, however, could not afford to let Pearson's plan die; and they saw how it could be profitably improved. They were chiefly interested in the short-distance traffic and only incidentally concerned with providing a route into the City for the main lines. They therefore dropped the notion of a large City terminus. This not only saved money but also spiked the guns of those who had opposed Pearson's scheme on the grounds that it had run counter to the recommendations of the Royal Commission on Metropolitan Termini in 1846 that the main-line companies north of the river should not be allowed to penetrate farther into the built-up area than they had already done. As soon as it had obtained its Act in the middle of 1853, therefore, the North Metropolitan began to take over the City Terminus scheme and amend it. Acton Smee Ayrton, a lawyer who had recently returned home after a profitable spell in India and had become a leading member of the City Terminus, joined the board of the North Metropolitan at the end of August 1853 and became its deputy chairman in the following November.[25] At the end of October arrangements were made whereby City Terminus scripholders could, on advantageous terms, take options on the additional North Metropolitan shares which were to be issued to finance the extension to the City. This was now no longer to run to the main Holborn–Cheapside road but to veer south-east at Cowcross Street and go from there to the General Post Office at St. Martin's-le-Grand and enter the basement there so that mails could be loaded on trains without being moved from the building. At the Paddington end of the line there was to be an extension along Praed Street to a station in the road directly in front of the Great Western's main-line terminus with a branch under South Wharf Road to join the main line itself. In return for this extension and the laying of broad as well as narrow gauge track throughout the line, the Great Western promised to subscribe for shares totalling £185,000.[26] It was proposed to issue shares to the value of £700,000 altogether for these extensions, making, with the £300,000 already authorized, £1,000,000 in all. At the end of the year John Jay, who had been responsible for excavation on the Great Northern line immediately to the north of Maiden Lane,[27] was appointed contractor for the extension from King's Cross to the Post Office, and Tredwell

Brothers, who had been associated with Peto & Betts on the Oxford, Worcester & Wolverhampton, became contractors for the western part of the line. Jay agreed to take the largest individual block of shares (£100,000), and Thomas and Solomon Tredwell between them held shares worth £50,000.[28]

This time the Bill was contested in Parliament; Malins and his supporters had to fight hard to secure its passage. They made light of the technical problems and much of the benefits to humanity and the Post Office. (On the latter point Rowland Hill himself gave supporting evidence.) Fowler was closely questioned about the method of traction which was to be used. His argument was deceptively simple. It was well known, he claimed, that locomotives continued to run for some time after the fire had been removed from them.

'What we propose to do', he went on, 'is to have no fire . . . To start with our boiler charged with steam and water of such capacity and of such pressure as will take its journey from end to end and then, by arrangement at each end, raise it up again to its original pressure . . . Without any actual experiment I think neither Mr. Brunel nor myself nor any engineer would consider this as a question of doubt. It is a mere practical mode of working.'[29]

I. K. Brunel, the celebrated engineer of the Great Western Railway, agreed, adding (just to emphasize the utter simplicity of the whole thing): 'If you are going a very short journey, you need not take your dinner with you or your corn for your horse.' Brunel also took the view that the ventilation of tunnels would be an equally simple matter:

Generally speaking, the passage of a train through a tunnel creates such a commotion and change of air that I do not know of any difficulty in any tunnel I am acquainted with . . .[30]

Although the opposition produced engineers who dissented from these optimistic opinions, the Parliamentary committee was convinced that Fowler could build and operate the underground railway. And Malins showed himself a past master in the art of pleading a case. Indeed, when he was nearing the end of his evidence, counsel for the opposition paid him a fitting tribute. There had been some discussion whether the previous year's Bill had been disputed, Malins wishing to give the (quite erroneous) impression that it had been subjected to the opposition's careful scrutiny:

Counsel:	Counsel often appear against a Bill. It was not really opposed as we understand the word here.
Malins:	I am not bound to know how you understand the word.
Counsel:	You are almost as old a hand at this sort of thing as I am.
Malins:	I am much your senior.
Counsel:	Senior in this kind of thing, too.

Thanks very largely to a careful and skilful presentation of its case, the North Metropolitan secured its Act.[31] All that now remained was to raise the million pounds needed to build the railway.

It was, however, a very bad moment for raising capital. War with Russia had just broken out, and the Government itself was borrowing money. The Metropolitan, as the company was now re-named, had to bide its time and content itself with making minor amendments to its plans.[32] In February 1856, however, just after the Crimean War had ended, the shareholders grew restive and refused to accept the directors' half-yearly report.[33] Malins resigned, though he continued to take an interest in the company's affairs as a shareholder.[34] A few months later, J. L. Ricardo was elected in his stead.[35] Ricardo had previous railway experience as chairman of the North Staffordshire, but the choice in this case appears to have been connected with a previous decision to give the Electric Telegraph Company, of which he was founder and chairman, exclusive rights to use the Metropolitan's tunnels in return for financial support.[36] His appointment, in July 1856, was followed by an attempt to make calls on the 40,000 £10 shares which had already been issued; but money was still scarce—bank rate was high during the autumn and winter of 1856–57— and the date of the calls had to be postponed. In February 1857 Ricardo resigned.[37]

The Crisis

It was at this juncture that Pearson reappeared on the scene. The City Corporation had opened its new cattle market at Copenhagen Fields (north of King's Cross) in the middle of 1855 to replace Smithfield, and in the following year the new road had at last been built to Clerkenwell Green, Jay being the contractor.[38] The Corporation was now pressing on with further improvements in the Fleet valley. If the Metropolitan acted quickly, it could obtain at a reasonable price land which had been cleared; but if it delayed for long, the land would be redeveloped and so made prohibitively costly. Pearson, who was in a better position to know the true state of affairs than most other people, urged the Metropolitan to 'tell the Corporation that if they do not come forward to help, you will wind up the affair and that will be the end of it'.[39] This advice was taken, and at the next half-yearly meeting, in August 1857, the directors announced their intention of seeking powers to wind up the company during the next Parliamentary session.[40] A Bill was accordingly prepared and presented to Parliament at the beginning of 1858. Meanwhile a financial crisis late in 1857, during which bank rate was up at 10 per cent. for some time, made it seem all the more likely that all hope would, in fact, have to be abandoned. There was, however, 'never a more serious crisis nor a more rapid recovery',[41] and money was soon more plentiful than it had ever been since the company's formation. Thoughts of winding-up gave place to yet another attempt to raise capital. At the half-yearly meeting in February 1858 it was resolved that:

as a considerable number of shares were taken when money was in great demand for commercial purposes and as the intrinsic merits of the project have since rather increased than diminished, it is reasonable to expect, as money is now abundant, that if the undertaking were once more placed before the public, they would take further shares . . .[42]

It was, therefore, decided that £1,000 should be spent on publicity in an effort to find takers for the remaining 60,000 shares on the understanding that no allotment would be made unless at least 50,000 were taken. At the end of March and beginning of April the directors addressed public meetings at Hammersmith and Notting Hill, and as far afield in Great Western country as Bristol, Gloucester, and Windsor, in an effort to enlist the necessary support.[43] But it was all to no avail: the 50,000 shares were not taken.[44]

This, it might be supposed, would really have been the end: the winding-up Bill would pass into law and the whole venture abandoned. That this did not happen seems to have been due to the activities of William Arthur Wilkinson, a member of the Stock Exchange and chairman of the London & Croydon Railway from 1839 until its amalgamation with the London & Brighton, who had been brought on to the Board in August 1857 because of his 'position, energy and experience'.[45] He became chairman of the company on 26 April 1858, and on that day it was decided that the winding-up Bill should be dropped. Soon afterwards, John Parson himself, who had been a subscriber to the list submitted for the 1854 Bill, joined the board and from then onwards played a prominent part in the company's affairs. His rule over the Oxford, Worcester & Wolverhampton had ended in the middle of 1856, some time after he had been openly accused of jobbing in shares and bringing a vast amount of lucrative business to the firm of Burchell & Parson.[46]

On 3 August 1858 Charles Pearson attended a meeting of the board and promised his support in a final effort to

35. Charles Pearson

36. Sir John Fowler

37. Sir Benjamin Baker

38. Sir Myles Fenton

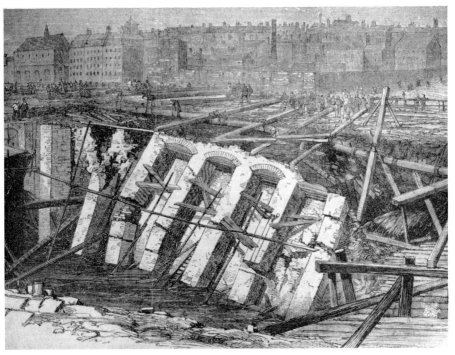

39. The Collapse of the Metropolitan Railway works at the Fleet River, 1862

40. Constructing the Metropolitan at Coppice Row, Clerkenwell, 1862

41. The Metropolitan Cutting and Tunnel at Wharton Street, King's Cross, 1862

42. The new Farringdon Street and the Metropolitan station, showing clearance of property

43. 'Fowler's Ghost' in Reality: near Edgware Road

44. Trial Trip at Edgware Road, 24 May 1862: Mr. and Mrs. Gladstone, John Fowler and invited Party in Smith & Knight's open Wagons

45. Praed Street Junction

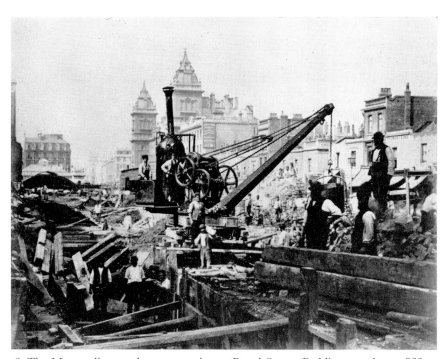

46. The Metropolitan under construction at Praed Street, Paddington, about 1866

47. Metropolitan Train at Hammersmith with 'A' Class Locomotive, built 1864

48. Metropolitan Railway Workmen's Train, about 1864

49. The Skew Bridge at Ray Street, Clerkenwell, 1868

50. The Midland Railway Terminus and Tunnel to the Metropolitan, St. Pancras, 1868

51. The London, Brighton & South Coast Station at Victoria, 1861

52. Workmen's Train arriving at the London, Chatham & Dover Railway Station at Victoria, 1865

push the scheme through. From then, throughout the next few critical months, he attended board meetings regularly. In October he made further representations to the Corporation, and his petition, as in 1851, was considered by its Improvement Committee.[47] All this activity culminated in a large public meeting held in the City on 1 December 1858 at which the Lord Mayor took the chair.[48] Pearson explained yet again the merits of the project, and among others who spoke in its support was Lord John Russell. After lengthy negotiations, the Corporation at last came to terms with the Metropolitan and agreed to subscribe for shares worth £200,000—which it later sold at a premium.[49] The Metropolitan, on its side, was to pay £179,157 to the Corporation (one-third in cash and the rest in rent charges) for land in the Fleet valley, and to reduce the total cost of its scheme to £950,000 by abandoning the line between Cowcross Street and the Post Office.[50] (In the event it also abandoned the line along Praed Street, only building the link with Paddington station itself in the first instance.)[51] The company also agreed to make a siding from the Great Northern to the new cattle market at Copenhagen Fields, the intention being to use the underground for bringing the slaughtered cattle from there to the dead meat market which the Corporation was to build at Smithfield. At King's Cross, no fewer than three underground curve lines were to be built to the Great Northern, two being single-track connections eastwards and one (the Maiden Lane curve or western branch) to the west, towards Paddington. This last, though built, was probably never used.[52]

The first part of the underground is built
With the Corporation's support, the Great Western's £185,000, and bank rate down to 2½ per cent. throughout the last half of 1859, sufficient capital was at last forthcoming to enable a start to be made on the line. In October 1859 Parson was put in charge of building operations, and in

K

December Jay was awarded the contract for the stretch between King's Cross and the City. The rest of the line was to have been constructed by R. Brotherhood, but he withdrew, and the contract was subsequently given to Smith & Knight.[53]

Benjamin Baker, then a young engineer in London,* later recalled 'anxious discussions and criticism' of the engineering problems. This is hardly surprising, for the peculiar difficulties to be overcome had no precedents for their solution. What stress could brick arches bear when weighted on one side only? How much room should be allowed for the expansion of iron girders? How could sewers and pipes be best diverted?[54] These and many other questions had to be answered before work could proceed. Smith & Knight's section consisted of a covered cutting which ran through gravel and was crossed by only one main sewer, the Tybourne, at Baker Street. Jay's was an open cutting, but it ran through clay, had to be tunnelled for 728 yards, and crossed the notorious Fleet sewer three times. The whole undertaking proved more costly than was at first expected. More capital was needed, and a further £300,000 had to be raised by the offer of additional shares. In order to find takers, these had to be issued as 5 per cent. preference stock.[55]

The original contracts specified that the line should be completed within 21 months and so be open in good time to catch the exhibition traffic in 1862.[56] The contractors fell

*Benjamin Baker was born on 31 March 1840 at Keyford, Frome, Somerset, and was educated at Cheltenham G.S. Having served his apprenticeship at the Neath Abbey Ironworks, he came to London and was engaged for two years on work connected with the building of Victoria Station and Grosvenor Road railway bridge. In 1862 he joined Fowler's staff, in 1869 became Fowler's chief assistant on the extension of the District Railway from Westminster to Mansion House, and was thereafter closely associated with Fowler in many engineering ventures, particularly the Egyptian work and the building of the Forth Bridge (on the completion of which he was created a Knight Commander of St. Michael and St. George). Both men were consultants to the City & South London Railway, and Baker was also connected with the building of a number of other London tubes. He became an associate of the Institution of Civil Engineers in 1867, a member in 1877 and president in 1895–96. He became an F.R.S. in 1890. He died on 19 May 1907. (*Proceedings of the Institution of Civil Engineers,* *170* (1907), 377–83; *D.N.B.*)

behind schedule, however, and it was not until May 1862 that the company got so far as the appointment of an operating superintendent. In Myles Fenton they secured a youngish man of proved ability with 15 years of railway experience behind him, much of it in Lancashire. He was soon appointed as general manager and stayed with the Metropolitan until 1880 when he became general manager of the South Eastern. He was knighted in 1889.[57]

Fenton was given longer than he had expected to work out timetables and fares. The Fleet sewer burst into the workings east of King's Cross in the middle of June 1862 and further delayed the railway's completion.[58] It was sufficiently advanced by August for two parties of shareholders and their friends to go from Farringdon Street to Paddington and back. Some of them travelled in carriages and others in contractors' wagons. Presumably it was on one of these occasions that the well-known photograph was taken (too often misdescribed as a view of the opening ceremony) in which Gladstone and his wife are shown sitting in one of these open wagons along with Fowler, the engineer, and an impressive array of dignitaries.*[59] Signalling difficulties, however, further delayed the start of a regular passenger service. It was not until the middle of December that all was ready for the Board of Trade inspecting officer's final check, and then a few more modifications were called for. The final inspection took place on 3 January 1863; from then until the 8th empty carriages were worked to train the staff and test the signalling; on the 9th the official party travelled the length of the line and banqueted, with speeches, at Farringdon Street; and on the 10th the long-awaited opening at last took place.[60]

Charles Pearson had the satisfaction of seeing the line well on the way to its completion, but he did not live to

*The photograph was taken at Edgware Road station where there was a stop for refreshments. Presumably these ladies and gentlemen travelled in one of the carriages but were persuaded by the photographer to pose in an open wagon so that there would be sufficient light for his photograph.

take part in the opening celebrations; he died on 14 September 1862. In his last years, however, he was able to return to his main interest: the provision of workmen's trains. He told a parliamentary committee in April 1860 that the Great Western had agreed to carry up to 1,000 'mechanics' to Farringdon Street in time for their work every morning and back home again at night for a fare of 1s. per week. The service, it was proposed, would operate from a place between $7\frac{1}{2}$ and 10 miles out, where a specially-planned estate would be built. (He thought he could raise enough capital for this.)[61] The London, Chatham & Dover Railway (a new concern which will be discussed in the next chapter) was also approached by Pearson[62] and included a clause in its Act of 1860 to provide workmen's trains.[63] Although nothing came of the specially-designed estate in West London, the Metropolitan was in fact the first company actually to operate workmen's trains in the London area. Two of them, one starting at 5.30 in the morning and the second ten minutes later, began to run in May 1864 at a fare of 3d. return.[64] Charles Pearson clearly deserves some share of the credit for the introduction of workmen's trains into London as well as for being such a persistent supporter of the underground. At the time of his death, the Metropolitan's directors recorded their appreciation of 'the very valuable services so long and cheerfully rendered by him to this Company without fee or reward'[65] and they later granted his widow a small annuity.[66]

If Pearson had been the devoted and ultimately successful propagandist for the idea of an underground railway, the engineer, Fowler, was no less entitled to credit for having carried the work through in the face of great physical difficulties and frequent discouragement among the promoters; for he alone had maintained the board's confidence in the scheme from the engineering point of view throughout the later 1850s. Much of the responsibility for the detailed execution of the railway is to be attributed to Thomas Marr

Johnson,* for he was engaged exclusively on this work under Fowler's direction.

The public opening of the first 3¾ miles of underground railway brought large numbers of people flocking to see it. On the opening day—a Saturday—thousands of eager sightseers queued up at Farringdon Street to get on the trains and the company took nearly £850 in fares.[67] In the first six months the railway carried an average of 26,500 passengers per day.[68] One of these early passengers, (Sir) William Hardman, has left a brief account of a journey he made on 25 January, in the third week of the line's operation:

... Mary Anne and I made our first trip down the 'Drain'. We walked to the Edgware Road and took first class tickets for King's Cross (6d. each). We experienced no disagreeable odour, beyond the smell common to tunnels. The carriages (broad gauge) hold ten persons, with divided seats, and are lighted by gas (two lights); they are also so lofty that a six footer may stand erect with his hat on ...

A little later, Hardman recorded of another journey that it went very smoothly and not rapidly; it felt very safe and quiet. It was, however, difficult to recognize the stations because they all looked alike, and many people were carried past the one they wanted to get out at.[69]

To overcome so completely the public's initial anxieties about underground travel was no mean achievement. Only just over a year before the opening, *The Times* had noted that many people regarded the whole scheme as one which

*Thomas Marr Johnson was born on 29 June 1826 at Appleby, Lincolnshire. He entered Fowler's office six years after leaving school and remained there until 1870. He was in charge (under Fowler) of a number of railway schemes including the Mid-Kent line and the Farnborough extension of the West End & Crystal Palace. From 1860 to 1869, apart from a few months spent in the United States, he was 'exclusively occupied', under Fowler's supervision, in the building of the Metropolitan Railway. In February 1870 he left to become a partner in the firm of G. Smith & Co., builders and contractors, which built the new Manchester Town Hall and Eaton Hall, Chester. He was jointly responsible, with William Mills, for the design and building of the Holborn Viaduct station. He became an associate of the Institution of Civil Engineers in 1852 and a member in 1863. He died on 20 July 1874 aged 48. (*Proceedings of the Institution of Civil Engineers, 39* (1875), 268-9.)

even if it could be accomplished, would certainly never pay. A subterranean railway under London was awfully suggestive of dark, noisome tunnels, buried many fathoms deep beyond the reach of light or life; passages inhabited by rats, soaked with sewer drippings, and poisoned by the escape of gas mains. It seemed an insult to common sense to suppose that people who could travel as cheaply to the city on the outside of a Paddington 'bus would ever prefer, as a merely quicker medium, to be driven amid palpable darkness through the foul subsoil of London . . .[70]

That these fears were allayed and the public attracted underground in ever-increasing numbers, despite the smell and the darkness, was largely due to the extremely safe and efficient working of the railway. Had there been any bad accidents, as could well have happened in the early days of new and untried equipment, passengers would certainly have been scared away. In fact, during the whole period of steam operation, there was no fatal accident to any passenger in these cuttings and tunnels.

Signalling and rolling stock

The chief credit for this must be given to new methods of block signalling. The electric telegraph had been used for railway signalling since the early 1840s—the London & Blackwall used it, for instance—and the Great Western had introduced the block system in the Box Tunnel in 1847. It was the Great Western's Telegraph Superintendent, C. E. Spagnoletti, who devised a disc block telegraph instrument which was first used on the new underground.[71] This device, operated by the signalman at the next box by means of a red or white key, gave a visual indication of whether or not the line was clear. Spagnoletti's 'lock and block' system was introduced about 1880.*[72]

*Some method of automatic locking seems to have been tried out before the line was opened, but it was not used. *The Times* reported that signals 'are so arranged that while any signal-man can put them on to "danger", they cannot possibly be taken off but at the station to which the train is going. Thus, with a train starting at the Paddington terminus, the signal-man puts on the danger signal to prevent others following, and in the act of putting it on, the "points" which give entrance to the line are shut and locked so that it becomes mechanically impossible for another train to enter the

There was obviously a difficult problem to be overcome in regard to the kind of locomotive power to be used for this tunnel-railway. Fowler developed his hot-water (but fire-less) locomotive idea, expounded before the 1854 Parliamentary committee, to the point of having an experimental machine designed and constructed by Robert Stephenson and Co. in 1861. This contained a small firebox and 'a large mass of fire brick stowed away in a chamber in the barrel of the boiler; the idea being to work it as an ordinary locomotive with full blast in the open portions of the line, burning there an excess of fuel in order to convert the white-hot firebrick into a reservoir of heat for use in the tunnels'. This contraption was run down the Great Western main line for $7\frac{1}{2}$ miles in October 1861, but it had much difficulty in getting home again, and after a further trial in the tunnels was judged a failure. It had cost over £4,500. Robert Stephenson and Co. designed a successor to 'Fowler's Ghost', as it was derisively called, but this was never proceeded with. If it had been, it might have been the first locomotive with a true bogie to run on an English railway; but the Metropolitan had had enough of hot bricks.[73] The Great Western was to work the new line, and its famous locomotive engineer, (Sir) Daniel Gooch, designed a coke-burning locomotive intended to consume its own smoke and have a quick rate of acceleration. The result was a 2–4–0 tank engine with outside cylinders—the only ones on the broad gauge apart from Stephenson's experimental machine —weighing 38 tons, with 6-foot driving wheels; flap valves, worked by rods from the footplate, directed the exhaust steam either up the chimney when the engine was running in the open or into tanks under the boiler, between the

line till the one that has started has passed the station ahead, from which point only can the danger signal be removed. These signals are not used now the line is being worked by the Great Western Company by telegraph, but they must come into use as soon as the number of trains is increased . . .' (Quoted in *The Engineer*, 30 January 1863.) The *Illustrated London News* had reported in its issue of 27 December 1862 that there was 'a self-acting apparatus' which put the signal up when a train entered a section of line. When it was clear of the section, the signal was given back 'Line clear', and the arm lowered 'which has been put up by the passing action of the train'.

frames, when it was working in the tunnel. The fumes were thus left to be consumed by the passengers. The water tank had a capacity of 375 gallons and the condenser of 420 gallons. There were 22 of these engines, built between June 1862 and October 1864. The first six, from the Vulcan Foundry, were named, as A. R. Bennett observed, after busy but aggressive insects—*Bee, Mosquito, Gnat, Hornet, Locust,* and *Wasp*; the second six, from Kitson's of Leeds, after foreign despots—*Czar, Kaiser, Khan, Shah, Mogul,* and *Bey*; the last ten, from Swindon after the opening of the line, after flowers, not all correctly spelt.[74]

For carriages, the Great Western used long vehicles which could be formed into short trains capable of carrying many more passengers than the rolling stock then normally used. Some were specially built; others were existing stock suitably modified. Among the latter were some 'Long Charleys', taken off the Birmingham route, where they had been operating since 1852, and fitted, like the rest, with coal-gas lighting.[75]

The stations, though not architecturally striking—their style would probably be described now as 'debased Italianate' on the original Metropolitan and 'engineers' utilitarian' on the Metropolitan District which followed it —were well designed for their purpose, and many of them were spanned by imposing wrought-iron and glass roofs. (The disappearance of one of the last survivors of these roofs moved Mr. John Betjeman to write a poem about Aldersgate station.) They were well lit, and the gas lamps encased in large glass globes are a prominent feature of all the early illustrations of underground stations. They soon had book-stalls and poster advertising, too. James Willing, who, as we have seen, left the board of the L.G.O.C. in 1862, was soon doing well as an advertising contractor. In March 1863 he put in a successful tender for the sale of books and for the posting of advertisements at the Metropolitan's stations, for which privileges he was to pay the company £1,150 for the year.[76] Later, he started to advertise on its tickets, on the walls between certain stations and inside carriages. In 1866 he agreed to pay £34,000 for the whole advertising and bookstall contract over the following seven years.[77] The company also gained an income from allowing refreshments to be sold at its stations. It accepted a tender from Spiers and Pond, who, having previously made money in Australia by supplying refreshments to railway travellers between Melbourne and the gold-mining town of Ballarat in the booming 1850s—and organized the first All-England cricket tour of Australia in 1861–62—shifted their railway catering activities to London soon afterwards. In 1864 they agreed to pay 10 per cent. of their gross takings (and a minimum of £4,000 per year) for the refreshment rights at stations between King's Cross and the City for the following 14 years, and in 1865 opened a refreshment room at Edgware Road on a percentage basis.[78] The same company still continues catering at certain Metropolitan stations today.

The ventilation west of King's Cross was poor and the air often unpleasant to breathe.[79] A few days after the line's opening, the board resolved that

the trains should be composed of only as many carriages as the Engine is capable of drawing without emitting steam and smoke . . . and . . . special trains should be employed to convey any accumulation of passengers who cannot be conveyed by the ordinary trains.[80]

These special trains took the form of rush-hour expresses—seven in each direction—which set off from the termini ten minutes after the regular trains and did the journey in 14 minutes instead of 18. They did not last for long, however, being replaced, in April 1863, by a ten-minute service between 9 and 10.30 in the morning and 4 and 6.30 in the afternoon. At other times between 8 a.m. and 8 p.m. there was a 15-minute service, and between 6 and 8 in the morning and 8 and 12 midnight a 20-minute service. The single fares were 6d. (first), 4d. (second) and 3d. (third) with returns for 9d., 6d. and 5d. respectively and season tickets for £8 a year (first) and £5 10s. od. (second).[81]

The clash with the Great Western

The Metropolitan soon expressed dissatisfaction with the frequency of the service which the Great Western provided. In April there are references in the directors' minutes to 'misunderstandings' with the Great Western, and in May the Metropolitan decided to explore the possibility of working the line itself.[82] The Great Western's position was quite clear: it had put up £185,000 of the capital with the intention of getting direct access to the City. The Metropolitan, however, wanted to place all the emphasis on the local traffic and to run such a frequent service as to leave little or no room for through trains during the daytime. Nor was there as yet any provision at all for goods traffic. And, no doubt, the presence of its old enemy Parson, now deputy chairman of the Metropolitan, gave support to the Great Western's darkest suspicions. Matters came to a head in the middle of July, when a junction with the Great Northern was about to be opened. The Great Western raised difficulties about it in an attempt to defer further congestion of the line.[83] A few days later, in an effort to bring the Metropolitan to terms, it refused to work any trains after 30 September, a date subsequently brought forward to 11 August. It also refused to sell the locomotives and carriages to enable the Metropolitan to work the line itself.[84] The Great Northern came to the rescue with engines and rolling stock—on the narrow gauge, of course, with smaller carrying capacity; the London & North Western also supplied some coaches. Even so, the Metropolitan had to revert to a 15-minute service throughout the day. The middle rail, provided for narrow gauge working but not hitherto used, gave some trouble.[85] Traffic fell off: as may be seen from the table on p. 125, 200,000 fewer passengers were carried in the second half of the year than in the first, and receipts fell by £4,500.

The Great Northern equipment was, however, only intended to serve as a stop-gap. The Metropolitan placed orders for its own carriages and locomotives, the latter from Beyer, Peacock and Co. of Manchester.[86] The new carriages, made in a great hurry by the Ashbury Railway Carriage & Iron Company, also of Manchester, were first put into service at the beginning of October—'an unmistakable improvement on those that were used in the early days of the line,'[87] but lack of locomotives was still dictating a 15-minute service in the following spring,[88] and it was not until July 1864 that the Metropolitan began to dispense with plant hired from the Great Northern. It then ran a ten-minute service throughout the day and a more frequent service—sometimes a train every two minutes— at busy periods.[89]

The new locomotives, of the 4–4–0 tank type, solved the Metropolitan's traction problem for a generation and more; they were in fact so successful that Beyer, Peacock, as well as supplying 66 to the Metropolitan, sold nearly 90 more of the same type, with only slight modifications, to other railways for similar work; some were even bought by the L. & N.W.R. and the Midland, proud companies which few people thought would ever accept an 'outside' product. The design owed something in its origins to some inside-cylindered tanks running on the North London since 1855; more to an engine built in 1859 by J. C. Craven for the London, Brighton & South Coast, which was a 4–4–0 saddle tank with outside cylinders; and most to a Beyer, Peacock design of 1862, supervised by John Ramsbottom of the L. & N.W.R., for the Tudela & Bilbao Railway in northern Spain. The Metropolitan engines were powerful outside-cylindered machines, comparatively heavy, weighing $42\frac{1}{2}$ tons and carrying 1,000-gallon water tanks. Though they were credited to Fowler's design, it seems that he contributed little more than the steam-condensing arrangement, and that R. H. Burnett (later, on the strength of this, appointed locomotive superintendent of the Metropolitan) did most of the detailed work. The original engines still had a Bissell truck in front, not a bogie; that was adopted in the 1870s after it had proved its worth on the North London's outside-cylindered class of 1868. The engines did not for many years have cabs, only weather-board protection for the driver. All of these Metropolitan engines, either of the original A class (44 built 1864–70) or of the later and heavier B class (22 built 1878–85), were in service when the line was electrified in 1905, except the first, No. 1 *Jupiter*, scrapped after an accident in 1897. They were originally painted dark green with large brass numerals and classical names appropriate to the stygian gloom of the tunnels they inhabited—*Mars, Medusa, Cerberus,* and so on. Having selected 18 names, the Metropolitan gave up, and after that there were only numbers. From about 1885 the livery was changed to a colour described as chocolate, which might mean various things. After electrification of the line, a few of these remarkable engines went on working ballast trains and in remote parts of the Metropolitan's empire, so that it was possible for London Transport in 1948 to decide to preserve one; this, No. 23, has been restored to its steam-age condition and remains as a witness to the most memorable, next to the idea of the underground railway itself, of the Metropolitan's contributions to the art and science of the railway.[90]

For carriage stock, R. H. Burnett ordered both four-wheelers and eight-wheelers, the latter not having bogies but side-play in the axle-boxes. Trains of five of these long carriages were described as being 'so constructed as to carry more than 20 ordinary railway carriages and to occupy very much less station room'. The four-wheelers were close-coupled in pairs with a central buffer. Round-topped doors made their appearance in 1867, and this feature of design continued throughout the Metropolitan's existence; the idea was to avoid damage from striking the tunnel wall if the door was left open. Various refinements were made from time to time, such as the introduction of the Pintsch high-pressure oil gas system of lighting which needed re-charging only once a day, and new four-wheeled 'jubilee' stock was introduced after 1887. Some of the eight-wheeled variety survived on the Brill branch until the 1930s; the four-wheelers departed unregretted on electrification in 1905.[91]

The condition of the air in the tunnels continued to cause some concern. Ventilator shafts were built and glass removed from some of the stations in an attempt to increase the circulation of fresh air; but still there were complaints. In 1871–72 'blow-holes' were cut from the crown of the tunnel into the middle of the road above at intervals between King's Cross and Edgware Road (the iron gratings in the middle of the road are still to be seen). It was, however, said that so long as the engines dropped their condensing water regularly and refilled with fresh, the atmosphere was tolerable; but later, with the pressure of traffic, they simply 'topped-up' and the condensers became much less effective.[92]

Despite its early difficulties, the Metropolitan soon proved that an underground railway could be a paying proposition. It provided a service which was invariably quicker and often more convenient than that of the omnibuses, and it soon won an assured traffic. After the temporary setback in the second half of 1863, the number of passengers and receipts grew rapidly.

PASSENGERS CARRIED AND RECEIPTS EARNED BY
THE METROPOLITAN RAILWAY IN 1863 AND 1864

	Passengers	Receipts
10 January–30 June 1863	4,823,437	£53,058
1 July–31 December 1863	4,631,731	£48,649
1 January–30 June 1864	5,207,335	£54,740
1 July–31 December 1864	6,614,554	£61,749

On the first year's working, the company paid 5 per cent.; on the first half of the second, at the rate of 5½ per cent. per annum and on the second half at the rate of 7 per cent.

Extension into the City and feeders from Hammersmith, Kensington and Swiss Cottage

The Metropolitan Railway took the wise precaution of getting Parliamentary sanction for the extension of its line farther into the City while the Paddington–Farringdon Street stretch was still under construction. In 1861 powers were secured to take the railway as far as Moorgate Street and to build a terminus there, just to the north of Fore Street and within easy walking distance of the Bank.[93] Shares to finance this extension (£500,000 with the usual borrowing powers of one-third) were issued in February 1863 in the wake of the underground's successful opening.[94] The purchase of property was started without delay and, at the beginning of November 1863, the contract was awarded to John Kelk. Work was started in the following spring.[95] Narrow-gauge trains started to run to Moorgate Street—to a temporary station at first—on 23 December 1865 and broad-gauge trains on 1 July 1866.[96]

A feeder to Hammersmith was then already in service, having been opened on 13 June 1864. It was also engineered by Fowler, but built by the Hammersmith & City Railway, an independent company which had the backing of both the Great Western and the Metropolitan. It ran from the Great Western main line at Green Lane (now Great Western Road)—about a mile out of Paddington—through the fields south of Porto Bello and Notting Barn farms and round the north-western limits of suburbia to a terminus near the north side of Hammersmith Broadway. (Parson, one of the directors nominated by the Metropolitan and then chairman of the Hammersmith & City, again gained notoriety by being concerned in purchases of land through which the railway was to pass.)[97] There was a station at the northern end of Ladbroke Road (now the middle of Ladbroke Grove) and another near Shepherd's Bush Green. The railway was intended not only to win traffic from the growing residential areas of Notting Hill, Shepherd's Bush, and Hammersmith, but also to provide a connection between Paddington and the recently-opened outlet to the south via the West London Extension. This link between the railways north and south of the river will be dealt with in the next chapter. The northern section of it formed part of the West London Railway, and it was with this line that the junction from the Hammersmith & City was opened on 1 July 1864.[98] (A map will be found on pages 136–7.)

The West London Railway ran from the main lines of the Great Western and London & North Western in the Willesden area down to Kensington canal basin, close to the road bridge where Olympia now stands. The only section of the high-sounding Birmingham, Bristol & Thames Junction Railway to be built, it had been opened on 27 May 1844. But so spectacularly unsuccessful was it as a passenger line—the passenger service had to be withdrawn after a few months—that it became an even greater source of amusement than the Eastern Counties had been. It featured so often in the pages of *Punch* that it came to be known as *Punch*'s Railway. 'Omnibuses have been put on to meet the trains,' quipped *Punch*, 'but the meetings have been so strictly private, no one having been present but the driver of the 'bus and the guard of the train.'[99] The Great Western and London & North Western had taken a joint lease of the moribund line in 1845, and it had seen nothing but the occasional goods train until the beginning of the 1860s when the connection with the south at last breathed a little life into it. Now, advantage was taken of the junction with the Hammersmith & City to run passenger trains from Kensington on to the underground.

At the outset a half-hour service was run to Farringdon Street from both Kensington and Hammersmith, the carriages being joined together beyond the junction to form a single train.[100] Even with only a half-hour frequency, the use of the stretch of Great Western main line from Green Lane caused much delay at busy times of the day, and in 1865, when the Great Western and Metropolitan settled their outstanding differences, it was agreed that the Great Western should lay two additional tracks.[101] When this was done, at the end of May 1867, the two companies took a joint lease of the Hammersmith & City Railway.[102] The line was worked at the start by the Great Western. Metropolitan trains began to run through to Hammersmith on 1 April 1865, and a joint Metropolitan-Great Western management committee took charge from the following June.[103]

The underground's second local feeder was itself an underground railway, the Metropolitan & St. John's Wood, promoted by an independent company in 1864 to run from Baker Street to the Hampstead Junction Railway near its Finchley Road station.[104] This company, of which Fowler was also engineer-in-chief, started with high hopes and in 1865 secured powers to extend its line to Hampstead.[105] But it soon encountered financial difficulties, and it was only with the Metropolitan's help that it managed, on 13 April 1868, to open a single-track line as far as Swiss Cottage.[106] At Baker Street there was a junction with the Metropolitan, but when the St. John's Wood Company proposed, early in 1869, to double the frequency of its service and run trains on to the Metropolitan every ten minutes, it was agreed that the St. John's Wood trains should stop at Baker Street and passengers be made to walk along the 'communicating galleries' to the Metropolitan's platforms.[107] This line out of Baker Street, which was later to become of considerable importance, had very unpromising beginnings.

Some special locomotives were built to work the St. John's Wood line when it was opened, as the steepness of the gradient on the rise from Baker Street to the bridge over the Regent's Canal at St. John's Wood was thought to be beyond the steaming capacity of the existing engines. Five 0–6–0 tanks, exceptionally powerful for their day, were designed by R. H. Burnett and built by the Worcester Engine Company in 1868; but it was found that the standard engines could in fact do the job, and after 1872 the heavy tanks were laid aside and then sold, most of them to the Taff Vale Railway.[108]

The 'widened lines', the growth of the suburban traffic on the Great Northern, and the arrival of the Midland

The Great Northern began to run trains from Hatfield and Hitchin into Farringdon Street on 1 October 1863.[109] Its suburban traffic was then just starting to grow. The line from King's Cross then passed through rather sparsely populated territory once it had left its station near Holloway Road; but on 1 July 1861 a couple of wooden and uncovered platforms had been laid at Seven Sisters' Road—to develop in due course into Finsbury Park station.[110] And in 1867 the Great Northern was to acquire a company which had promoted a railway from near Seven Sisters' Road through Crouch End and Finchley, where it forked into two, one line striking north to Barnet and the other west to Edgware. The Edgware line was opened on 22 August 1867 and the fork to High Barnet on 1 April 1872.[111] A short branch, from Highgate to Muswell Hill, was built in time for the opening of the original Alexandra Palace in May 1873.[112] Meanwhile, another short branch had been built north-eastwards from the main line at Wood Green to Palmer's Green and Enfield. This was opened in April 1871.[113] These suburban extensions called for the enlargement of the Seven Sisters' Road station which was re-named, in 1869, after the newly-opened Finsbury Park nearby. In the early 1870s it was entirely reconstructed.[114]

The Metropolitan soon realized that it could not hope to

L

handle the Great Northern's growing suburban traffic on its own two tracks from King's Cross into the City. It was, therefore, decided to double the existing line from King's Cross to Farringdon Street and build four tracks to Moorgate Street, instead of the two as originally planned in 1861.[115] The 'widened lines' from King's Cross to Farringdon Street were authorized in 1864 (£450,000 in shares and £150,000 by borrowing), and Kelk, who was building the extension to Moorgate, also received this contract, which involved the building of a second Clerkenwell Tunnel.[116] The new tracks ran to the north of the original line from King's Cross but later went under it, under a remarkable skew bridge near Farringdon Street, known as the 'gridiron'. This enabled the 'widened lines' both to connect with the London, Chatham & Dover Railway, a new company which, as we shall see in the next chapter, had started to operate to Ludgate Hill, and to provide access for goods traffic to the Corporation's meat and poultry market at Smithfield which was then being built. Passenger trains started to use the 'widened lines' from 17 February 1868.[117] Smithfield Market, which had railway goods facilities beneath it, was opened in November 1868.[118]

The Midland Railway, whose lines to London first started to carry passenger traffic on 13 July 1868, had a connection with the underground from the outset.[119] Indeed, Midland passenger trains ended their journeys in the City for several weeks before they were able to run into St. Pancras, for their London terminus, perched high above Euston Road to avoid sharp gradients on the line and to provide storage space underneath for Burton beer, was not ready for use until 1 October.[120] The Midland was quick to begin suburban services from its stations at Camden Road, Kentish Town, Haverstock Hill, Finchley Road and Hendon. (West End, Child's Hill and Cricklewood, and Welsh Harp were opened soon afterwards.) From 1 July 1870 suburban passengers also started to reach the Midland line from the Tottenham & Hampstead Junction Railway which ran from the Great Eastern's Lea Valley line at Tottenham through Harringay and Crouch Hill to Highgate Road and had been opened two years before. Midland suburban trains ran to Crouch Hill at first and then (from 1 May 1871) to South Tottenham, a newly-opened station at the foot of Stamford Hill on the High Road.[121] In 1875 the Midland began to operate passenger trains on the line from Cricklewood to Acton, running them first through to Richmond, then to Earl's Court on the District, and finally to Gunnersbury only.[122]

Broad Street, Willesden Junction and Liverpool Street

The London & North Western Railway, in contrast to the Great Northern and the Midland, was not obliged to take an interest in local traffic and formed no junction with the Metropolitan under Euston Road. But the North London, which it dominated, had a flourishing suburban traffic which did not interfere with its own relatively heavy long-distance passenger and freight business into Euston and Camden Town. The North London's attractiveness as a suburban line was considerably increased by the opening, on 1 November 1865, of a branch striking south from Kingsland Road at Dalston to a new terminus at Broad Street, for this both saved the long, roundabout journey into the City through Hackney and provided the North London with a well-situated terminus of its own.[123] Nearly a year later, on 1 September 1866, another station was opened, this time down the line, which was to become one of the busiest on any railway out of London—Willesden Junction. It was built on two levels, the upper serving the North London's suburban service which bridged the North Western's main line at that point, and the lower the main line itself and a few local trains from Watford which then started to run on to the Hampstead Junction and so round to Broad Street. The original bridge carried the line to Kew and Richmond;

a year later a second was built at the opposite end of the main-line station to take trains via the West London Railway to Kensington and beyond. The Broad Street service ran alternately on these two routes—much to the annoyance of many passengers who, having climbed the steps to the higher level at one end of the station and just missed a City train, then had to come down again, walk the length of the station and climb another set of stairs.[124] These developments, however, did bring a 15-minute service as far as Willesden. Such a service had been customary on the North London's own rails to Chalk Farm (Hampstead Road) from the outset; now, in addition to this, the Willesden trains, starting ten minutes later than the locals—a technique already worked out in the earlier, Fenchurch Street days, though with many fewer trains[125]— ran with only one or two stops to Camden Town from where they became stopping trains, serving such stations as Gospel Oak, Hampstead Heath, Finchley Road and Edgware Road (Brondesbury).[126]

At the end of 1874 a junction was opened from Canonbury to the Great Northern just south of Finsbury Park station. By then the season ticket holders on the Great Northern had become very indignant about the delays caused by the tunnels between Finsbury Park and King's Cross. Following a protest meeting held early in January 1875, an agreement was reached between the Great Northern and the North London under which the North London was to run suburban passenger trains from Broad Street on to the Great Northern system in order to relieve the congestion. These through services began to Barnet (later New Barnet) and High Barnet on 18 January 1875 and to Enfield on the following 1 February.[127]

The Great Eastern, as the Eastern Counties had now become, although later than the other main line companies to develop its railways in the London area, soon succeeded in adding considerably to its existing local services and

building up a very bu
suburban traffic. Althoug
Parliament in 1864,[128] th
early 1870s. They had a tw
almost due north from the
through Stoke Newington a
existing Enfield line at Edmo
Hackney Downs to Walthamstov
connected by single line to the mai
Bridge in 1870) and Chingford; and
from the cramped station at Shoredit
spacious terminus at Liverpool Stre
branch was opened in stages during 1872
of Liverpool Street in February 1874, and
November 1875.[130] Five months later Liverpool Street
obtained its own direct link with the networks south of the
river when the East London Railway was extended to join
the Great Eastern's main line.[131] The East London had
been formed in 1865 to purchase Sir Marc Brunel's Thames
Tunnel between Rotherhithe and Wapping (which had
taken from 1825 to 1843 to build and, when completed,
could only be used by pedestrians and not by wheeled
traffic as had originally been planned[132]). The railway had
been opened through the tunnel from the Brighton and
South Eastern lines at New Cross on 6 December 1869. In
the subsequent extension northwards, the building of the
tunnel through the Thames gravel under the London Docks
presented (Sir) John Hawkshaw, the engineer,* with
unusual difficulties; but these were overcome and the line
was opened to Liverpool Street on 10 April 1876.[133]

*John Hawkshaw was born in 1811 in the West Riding of Yorkshire where his
father's family for some generations were farmers in the neighbourhood of Otley,
Leathley, and Bramhope. After leaving Leeds Grammar School he learned from first-
hand experience about road and harbour engineering, and then spent the years
1832–34 in Venezuela as engineer of the Bolivar Mining Association, a concern which
had copper smelting interests in Lancashire. On his return to England he became
involved in railway work, particularly in Lancashire and Yorkshire. He removed from
Manchester to London in 1850, and during the following 38 years he was 'constantly
employed in designing and superintending engineering works, and in reporting and
advising as to their practicality, not only in this country, but in many other parts of

tself

nained just a line from

t was a sound and profit-

pts rose quite impressively

attracted to its trains and as

ffic on to it. By 1868 Fowler

de that

was in many respects different from

nc was immense and he had to wait

ur trains before he could get into the train

CARRIED AND REVENUE EARNED BY
ETROPOLITAN RAILWAY 1865–68

	Passengers	Revenue	Net Traffic Receipts
January–June 1865	7,462,823	£69,072 ⎫	£86,008
July–December 1865	8,301,084	£72,441 ⎭	
January–June 1866	10,303,395	£102,947 ⎫	£125,683
July–December 1866	10,969,709	£107,295 ⎭	
January–June 1867	11,488,358	£114,442 ⎫	£143,109
July–December 1867	11,916,924	£118,738 ⎭	
January–June 1868	12,994,223	£128,474 ⎫	£150,278
July–December 1868	14,713,788	£155,769 ⎭	

When the railway was first opened, just under £1,400,000 had been invested in it. The extension to Moorgate, the 'widened lines' and various small additions roughly doubled this figure, £1,800,000 of the grand total being in ordinary shares.[135] Even so, the balance of earnings over expenses was sufficient to pay 5 per cent., and rising income promised higher dividends to come. But shareholders were not to reap the full reward of this important pioneer venture, for the board had already become involved in much

the world. His practice was not confined to any special branch of professional work.'
As consulting engineer of the South Eastern Railway from 1861 to 1881, he was in charge of the extensions to Charing Cross and Cannon Street. He was engineer of the East London Railway and (with (Sir) John Wolfe Barry) of the Inner Circle Completion Railway. He was also joint engineer of the Channel Tunnel Company from 1872 to 1888. Among many assignments overseas was that of advising the Khedive of Egypt to proceed with the building of the Suez Canal. He became a member of the Institution of Civil Engineers in 1838 and president in 1862–63. He was knighted in 1873. He died on 2 June 1891, 'leaving a reputation such as few have achieved for variety of good and honest work'. (*Proceedings of the Institution of Civil Engineers, 106* (1891), 321–35; *D.N.B.*)

less remunerative expenditure. The initial successes had played into the hands of those who had a vested interest in extending the line: the contractors who built the railway, the engineers who supplied the technical advice, and the solicitors who looked after the parliamentary proceedings and the subsequent conveyancing. The point had been reached where the interests of London's travelling public— and of the railway promoters—ceased to be identical with those of the investors.

To understand how this state of affairs came about, it is necessary to turn to railway developments south of the river, for they provided powerful arguments to those who were interested in the extension of the underground.

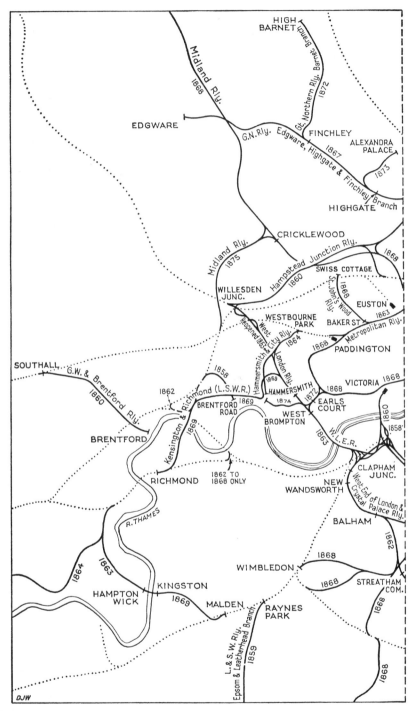

Railways opened between 1855 and 1875:

136

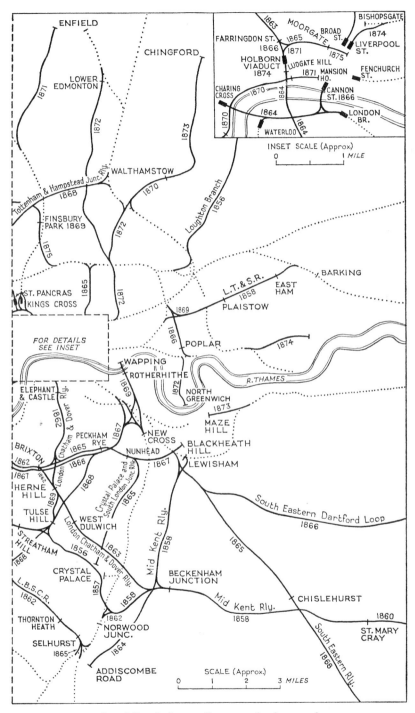

ENFIELD

CHINGFORD

LOWER
EDMONTON

1871

1872

1873

BISHOPSGATE

1874

BROAD
ST.

MOORGATE

FARRINGDON ST.
1866

1863

1865

1871

1874
LIVERPOOL
ST.

HOLBORN
VIADUCT
1874

LUDGATE HILL

1875

1871

MANSION
HO.

FENCHURCH
ST.

CHARING
CROSS

1870

1864

CANNON
ST. 1866

1870

1864

LONDON
BR.

1864

WATERLOO

INSET SCALE (Approx.)

0   1 MILE

Tottenham & Hampstead Junc. Rly.
1868

WALTHAMSTOW

1870

FINSBURY
PARK 1869

1872

1875

Loughton Branch
1856

BARKING

L.T.&S.R.
1858

EAST
HAM

1865

1872

ST. PANCRAS
KINGS CROSS

1869

PLAISTOW

1866

POPLAR

1874

FOR DETAILS
SEE INSET

WAPPING
ROTHERHITHE

R. THAMES

1869

ELEPHANT
& CASTLE

London Chatham & Dover Rly.

1862

NORTH
GREENWICH

1872

1873

MAZE
HILL

1867

PECKHAM
RYE

NEW
CROSS

BLACKHEATH
HILL

1865

BRIXTON

1862

NUNHEAD

1867

LEWISHAM

1866

1867

1862

1868

Crystal Palace and
South London Junc. Rly.

HERNE
HILL

1869

1869

TULSE
HILL

1865

South Eastern Dartford Loop
1866

WEST
DULWICH

London Chatham & Dover Rly.

Mid Kent Rly.

1858

STREATHAM
HILL

1868

1856

1863

1865

L.B.S.C.R.
1862

CRYSTAL
PALACE

1857

1858

BECKENHAM
JUNCTION

Mid Kent Rly.
1858

CHISLEHURST

THORNTON
HEATH

1862

NORWOOD
JUNC.

1860

ST. MARY
CRAY

SELHURST
1865

1864

South Eastern Rly.
1868

ADDISCOMBE
ROAD

SCALE (Approx.)

0   1   2   3 MILES

dotted lines indicate railways previously opened

137

CHAPTER FIVE

THE FIRST CLIMAX

(II) RAILWAYS OVER THE RIVER AND THE EXTENSION OF THE UNDERGROUND

Railways from the south could be brought nearer to the City and West End by bridging the river and building stations on its northern bank. These developments, and the construction of new suburban lines, were south London's counterpart to the extensive network of railways which was then being built in north London. Between 1860 and 1866 Victoria, Charing Cross and Cannon Street were opened to relieve the pressure on London Bridge, and Ludgate Hill (and later Holborn Viaduct) to provide a city terminus for a thrusting newcomer, the London, Chatham & Dover Railway, which also shared Victoria. Confronted with a host of competing schemes for building railways within central London itself which were submitted during the height of this railway boom in 1863 and 1864, Parliament recommended the extension of the underground to form an 'inner circuit' so as to link the new main-line termini. The District Railway was formed to build the southern part of this circuit, and the Metropolitan undertook to extend its line round to South Kensington to join the District in the west, and through extremely expensive city property to Tower Hill to meet it in the east. The District, however, ran into financial difficulties even before the first part of its line was opened at the end of 1868, and the dividends of the Metropolitan fell sharply in the following year. Out of this adversity ill-will developed between the two companies which had been intended originally to work together as one; and, by the middle of the 1870s, the 'inner circuit' was still no more than a horseshoe ending at Aldgate and the station inexactly described as Mansion House. All this new competition from surface and underground railways deprived the river steamboats of most of their regular passengers; but the omnibuses generally managed to hold their traffic, though with lower earnings.

THE GROWTH IN TRAFFIC FROM THE
SOUTHERN SUBURBS

PASSENGER TRAFFIC into both the South Eastern and the London, Brighton & South Coast stations at London Bridge grew rapidly during the 1850s. The number of passengers arriving and departing rose from $5\frac{1}{2}$ millions in 1850 to nearly 11 millions in 1854.[1] The rate of growth appears to have slowed down a little after that, but in 1858—by which time the recently-opened Mid-Kent Railway from Lewisham to Beckenham and the Caterham line had also started to feed in traffic[2]—more than $13\frac{1}{2}$ millions used the two stations.[3] The number of trains then running daily on the various routes emphasizes the importance which suburban traffic into London Bridge had by that time assumed:

NUMBER OF TRAINS PER DAY USING THE
LONDON BRIDGE STATIONS IN 1858

South Eastern	*Down*	*Up*
Main Line	13	13
Greenwich	49	49
North Kent	27	27
Mid-Kent	9	10
London, Brighton & South Coast		
Main Line	14	14
Croydon/Crystal Palace/Epsom	48	47

Source: Evidence of C. W. Eborall to the Commons' Committee on the London Bridge and Charing Cross Railway Bill, 22 March 1859 (House of Lords Record Office).

Of 320 trains regularly using the London Bridge stations, 266 were carrying what the South Eastern's general manager then considered to be a 'very large' suburban traffic.[4] Although London Bridge itself provided a fine, wide thoroughfare into the City, it was not wide enough to go on accommodating this growing traffic in addition to the increasing number of vehicles which converged upon it from roads south of the river. In 1850 13,000 vehicles per day had been crossing London Bridge; by 1857 this number had risen to 18,000, and by 1859 it was more than 20,000, nearly half of which were omnibuses.[5] Such were the traffic

jams which developed that omnibuses were known to be
held up for twenty minutes at a time, and it was 'sometimes
very uncomfortable even crossing the bridge on foot'.[6] The
City Police eased the position by organizing traffic lanes—
a new development—and keeping the slower-moving
vehicles on the left of the bridge at each side; but this did
not prevent the twice-daily tidal wave from and to the
railways from reaching an ever-higher crest. It was time
for other stations to be created to draw some of this traffic
away from the London Bridge termini and distribute it
more widely.

In the middle of the 1840s, when the Royal Commission
on Metropolitan Termini had reported on the multitude of
railway schemes that were then being promoted, it had
reached the conclusion that quite a good case could be
made for railway-building south of the river even within the
built-up area; and it does not seem to have been opposed
to the idea of railways being projected from there on to the
north bank.[7] The need for such extensions had not then
arisen; but by the later 1850s there were those, both in
Parliament and outside it, who were coming to realize that
one means of easing the worst of London's traffic jams was
to carry passengers arriving from the south by railway
across the river and nearer to their destinations.

This is the background to the quite remarkable spate of
railway building south of the river during the later 1850s
and 1860s which led, within six years, both to the opening
of termini at Victoria, Charing Cross, Ludgate Hill and
Cannon Street and to the bringing of railway communications to many parts of south London which had not
previously been served by the main lines. The railways out
of London Bridge and Waterloo had already staked their
claim to suburban traffic; now, with much better access to
the City and West End, they consolidated their position
and established an ascendancy which they have never
since lost.

The details of all this activity are tedious and tend to confuse rather than enlighten; but the main outlines are clear enough, and the map on pages 136–7 may be helpful in following these developments.

The origins of Victoria and Charing Cross

The need for another terminus to relieve London Bridge was anticipated by the West End of London & Crystal Palace Railway, a company promoted in 1853. It ran from a steamboat pier on the south side of the river just east of Battersea Park, through Wandsworth Common, Balham, Streatham Hill, West Norwood and Gipsy Hill to the Crystal Palace, from where there was a link to the Brighton's line. The stretch from the Crystal Palace to Wandsworth Common was opened on 1 December 1856 and to Battersea on 29 March 1858, to coincide with the opening of the Chelsea suspension bridge which adjoined the new terminus. The whole line was bought by the Brighton Company in the following year.[8]

It had never been intended that the railway should stop south of the river. In 1854 Samuel Beale, its chairman, and several of its original promoters had been instrumental in forming the Westminster Terminus Railway to cross the river and run via Millbank to a station which was to be built near the Victoria Street end of Horseferry Road.[9] Although it obtained Parliamentary sanction, it was in its turn succeeded by another scheme promoted by a different company, the Victoria Station & Pimlico, in which the Brighton had a majority interest. In 1858 this company secured powers to construct a railway along the Grosvenor canal which ran down to the river just opposite the Battersea terminus of the West End of London & Crystal Palace line, and to build a station on the site of the canal basin, close to the junction of Victoria Street and Vauxhall Bridge Road. As a West End terminus, this site had much to commend it. Passengers bound for Whitehall, Trafalgar

Square and that part of London could get away down Victoria Street, a fine, wide thoroughfare, which having been 'silently but unceasingly in progress' for nine years, had at last been opened in 1851;[10] and those who wanted to strike west to Chelsea, north-west to Brompton, or north to Park Lane and Mayfair were also well served by good, clear roads. With the energetic John Fowler, not yet actively at work on the Metropolitan, as the engineer, the Thames was quickly bridged and the new extension built. Passengers from the Brighton line started to reach Victoria on 1 October 1860.[11]

While this, the first of the West End termini, was under construction, a new and pushing intruder used it—with the aid of those familiar figures, the contractors Peto and Betts —as a means of gaining access to London. This concern, the East Kent, which had begun life as a client of the South Eastern, feeding traffic from the district east of Chatham on to the South Eastern at Strood, sought powers in 1857 to build a railway from Strood to St. Mary Cray from where it planned to run its trains over another company's tracks on to those of the West End of London & Crystal Palace.[12] Parliament refused to sanction this line, but only after the South Eastern, which served that part of Kent, had promised to build its own West End terminus.[13] By the following year, however, although the South Eastern's secretary, Samuel Smiles, soon to become the Victorians' favourite writer of non-fiction, had put his name to a pamphlet outlining a scheme for a West End terminus,[14] the company had not made any formal proposals to Parliament. Parliament thereupon approved the Strood– St. Mary Cray line when it was re-submitted. In recognition of its new status the East Kent changed its name to the London, Chatham & Dover. Its trains started to steam into Victoria on 3 December 1860.[15]

By this time the South Eastern had belatedly matured plans for its own West End terminus. As most of its suburban traffic came either from its Greenwich or North Kent lines,[16] a route round south London to Victoria would be too circuitous. What was needed was an extension almost due westwards from London Bridge through relatively inexpensive property to Waterloo Road (where there could be a junction with the South Western), then over the river to a terminus on the north side, where Hungerford Market provided the most attractive site. This was the origin of the Charing Cross scheme, presented to Parliament in the session of 1859. It entailed the purchase of Hungerford Market—rebuilt, less than thirty years before, by a firm in which Peto was a partner[17]—and compensation (£296,000) to St. Thomas's Hospital which had to move first to temporary quarters and then to its present site, much to the gain of Florence Nightingale's new training school for nurses.[18] It also meant the destruction of the Hungerford suspension bridge, although the piers were used for the railway bridge (on which footpath accommodation had to be provided) and the chains were sold to form part of the high-level suspension bridge over the Avon Gorge at Clifton. Outside the terminus a large hotel was put up—'one of the first buildings in London in which terra-cotta has been so largely used'[19]—with the facsimile Eleanor Cross in its forecourt. The Charing Cross extension was opened for local traffic on 11 January 1864.[20] The junction with the London & South Western was used between 1865 and 1867 by a London & North Western Railway Kensington–London Bridge (later Cannon Street) service.

Ludgate Hill, Cannon Street and the South London loop

Meanwhile the London, Chatham & Dover had grown more ambitious. Not content with running powers over the West End of London & Crystal Palace, it had in 1860 secured Parliamentary sanction to build a new line from near Beckenham Junction through Penge, Sydenham Hill, West Dulwich, Herne Hill, Brixton and Clapham to

Battersea, where it was to join the existing railway into Victoria. At the same time, and with even greater boldness, it applied for and obtained powers to build a branch northwards from Herne Hill via the Elephant & Castle and Blackfriars and across the river to Ludgate Hill. From there there was to be a link with the underground and so with the main lines entering London from the north and west, thus making possible branch train services between south and north London. Building was started without delay: the clay won from the burrowing of Penge tunnel was soon being turned into bricks for the building of the miles of viaduct to the north.[21] These extensions were opened between the middle of 1862 and the beginning of 1866, to a temporary station on the south side of Blackfriars Bridge on 1 June 1864, another temporary station at Ludgate Hill on 21 December, and a permanent, though unfinished, one there on 1 June 1865. Most of the London, Chatham & Dover's local services ran through to Farringdon Street on the Metropolitan from 1 January 1866; Holborn Viaduct station came into use on 2 March 1874, the Viaduct, built by the City, having been opened in November 1869.[22]

The London, Chatham & Dover's new line to Victoria and the thrust into the City itself spurred on the other companies to greater efforts. The South Eastern's retort to the Ludgate Hill line was to cause a City branch to be promoted from its Charing Cross extension: yet another bridge was built over the river, this time to Cannon Street. The station was opened to traffic on 1 September 1866.[23] By contrast, the Brighton's reaction to the Chatham company's obvious bid for suburban traffic was to collaborate rather than fight. It promoted a railway from its main line at South Bermondsey through Peckham Rye and Denmark Hill to Brixton. From there the Chatham built two extra tracks to Battersea, alongside the existing ones, to accommodate this new traffic, and the Brighton also doubled its tracks between Brixton and Peckham Rye so that the

Chatham could secure access to a new protégé, the Crystal Palace & South London Junction, which ran through Nunhead, Honor Oak and Lordship Lane to a high-level terminus at the Crystal Palace. Trains started to run on this railway on 1 August 1865;[24] and the South London loop was opened from South Bermondsey to Brixton on 13 August 1866 and along the doubled track to Battersea on 1 May 1867.[25] The viaduct into London Bridge was widened and an additional track laid to help handle the frequent suburban trains to and from this line.[26]

Suburban extensions to the south-west and west

At the South London's other terminus, Victoria, the original facilities were no longer adequate. Built to handle only traffic arriving along the West End of London & Crystal Palace Railway's two tracks, the new terminus was soon receiving, in addition, trains first from the Chatham's West End line and now from the Brighton's South London loop. Nor was that all: a link was also made between Victoria and the two great systems of the London & North Western and the Great Western via the West London Railway, which, as we saw in the last chapter, was leased by those two companies. When, in 1858, the Victoria station scheme had been approved, making use of the Grosvenor canal, the lessees of the West London decided to follow suit. In an effort to bring business, particularly passenger business, to their moribund line, they proposed to turn most of the Kensington canal into a railway and to carry it on to join the other lines south of the river. In 1859, together with the South Western and the Brighton who subscribed one-sixth share each of the £300,000 capital, they promoted the West London Extension Railway to continue the original line through West Brompton and Chelsea and carry it over the river to Clapham Junction, where it connected with both the Crystal Palace and the South Western. The extension was opened at the beginning of March 1863, and the

M

Great Western began to run trains from Southall into Victoria (on the broad gauge) on the following 1 April.[27]

In order to handle this rapidly-growing traffic into Victoria, the station accommodation had to be increased and the two approach lines multiplied. A new terminus, for the use of the Chatham and Great Western, who leased it jointly, was built to the east of the existing one. It consisted merely of a series of unimpressive wooden buildings and a wooden palisade and was ready for use in the middle of 1862, in time to handle traffic from the Chatham's newly opened route via Herne Hill.[28] The Brighton's original terminus was improved and arrangements made to allow North Western trains to use it. The two stations were separate entities and there were no internal means of communication between them. A new bridge across the river, right up alongside the original one, was completed at the end of 1866 and enabled the number of lines to be increased from two to six but put an end to broad gauge traffic. Three separate high-level tracks were opened during 1867 to give a good approach to it from the south for South London, Chatham and Brighton main-line traffic.[29] (The Brighton main line, from 1 December 1862, only used the West End of London & Crystal Palace Railway as far as Balham; from there it went via a newly built cut-off through Streatham Common and Thornton Heath to Croydon.[30]) So, within less than a decade, not only had the original Victoria stations been built, but the maze of lines from them just south of the river—the so-called 'Battersea Tangle'—had also been created.

The London & South Western made its contributions to the 'Tangle' when it, too, joined in the scramble to secure an alternative metropolitan terminus. In return for a subscription to the London, Chatham & Dover's capital, it obtained running powers over the Chatham's rails from Battersea to Ludgate Hill, and in order to gain access to the Chatham's lines, put in a link between its own main line at Clapham Junction and the Chatham's at Battersea. South Western trains started to use this route into the City on 3 April 1866.[31] A second connection with the Chatham was made at the beginning of 1869. The South Western and the Brighton companies had joined forces to take over the building of a line from Wimbledon to Streatham where it joined one promoted by the Brighton company from Peckham Rye (on the South London loop) to Sutton. Both lines were opened on 1 October 1868.[32] The Chatham, in the meantime, was building a spur from the Brighton's line at Tulse Hill to their own at Herne Hill. From 1 January 1869, therefore, South Western trains were able to travel from Wimbledon via Streatham and Tulse Hill and so on to Ludgate Hill.

New Year's Day 1869 saw three other new developments which also helped to build up the South Western's suburban traffic: the opening of the South Eastern's Waterloo Junction station which enabled passengers arriving at Waterloo, having walked a distance under a covered way, to catch trains to Charing Cross, Cannon Street or elsewhere on the South Eastern's system;[33] the linking of Kingston (previously, since 1 July 1863, served only from the Windsor line via Twickenham) with Wimbledon which enabled people in the Kingston area to have an alternative route into London;[34] and, most important of all, the opening of a line from Kensington to Richmond which enabled the South Western to stake its claim to traffic north of the river. As we have seen, the South Western had an interest in the West London Extension Railway which joined it south of the river and ran to Kensington. From a little to the north of Kensington station it built a railway which curved westwards, passing close to Hammersmith Broadway and then proceeding via Chiswick (with connections to the North & South Western Junction) and over the river through Kew Gardens station to Richmond on its Windsor line.[35] At Hammersmith this new line connected with the

Hammersmith & City Railway, and the two companies' stations lying to the north of the Broadway were linked by a footbridge. The Metropolitan was later to run its trains on to Richmond by this route. The through service started on 1 October 1877.[36]

The 'inner circuit'

The boom in railway promotion in the London area reached its height in 1863, following the initial success of the underground. Plans were soon afoot for no fewer than 174 additional miles of railway at an estimated cost of some £44,000,000. This giant onslaught on the metropolis by the railway promoters was said to be 'creating alarm amongst the holders of a vast amount of property'. Residents in one neighbourhood agreed to pay five per cent. of the rental value of their houses towards a campaign fund to fight the proposed railways. One of the contributors to the fund noted in December 1863:

Next year we are to have a revival of the Railway Mania which will surpass in intensity the celebrated season of 1846. London is to be burrowed through and through like a rabbit-warren, and its main thoroughfares and rivers bridged over in every direction . . . Solicitors will make a good thing out of these projects, and shareholders will spend their money, but the rush of railways is so vast that public feeling has been very strongly aroused. If London is to be cut up in such style, London will have to move elsewhere.[37]

Parliament intervened, as it had done during the Mania of the mid-1840s. In 1863 a select committee of the House of Lords considered in general terms how London's communications could best be improved; and in the following year a joint committee of both Houses reported more specifically on the host of railway schemes with which Parliament was then confronted. The 1863 committee came out in favour of a railway connecting the main-line termini; it believed that this could best be achieved by 'an inner circuit' formed by extending the Metropolitan in both directions, from Moorgate Street and Paddington, 'and connecting the extremities of those lines by a line on the north side of the Thames'.[38]

This brought into the discussion the plans for making a wide embankment along the north side of the Thames from Westminster to Blackfriars. Advocated at intervals for at least thirty years by a succession of engineers, this project at last reached the realm of practical politics in 1860 and 1861,[39] largely because of the activities of the Metropolitan Board of Works which wanted the embankment as a route for an important trunk sewer as well as a means of diverting some of the traffic from the Strand and Fleet Street. The necessary legislation was obtained in 1862 and, in the following year, powers were also gained to build a new road, the future Queen Victoria Street, from Blackfriars to the Mansion House.[40] The ever-vigilant Fowler lost no time in pressing the merits of a railway from the Metropolitan at Farringdon Street via Blackfriars and along the proposed embankment to a terminus at Westminster[41] and by the time the Lords' select committee heard evidence in 1863 his ideas had grown. Now he advocated an extension of the Metropolitan from Paddington to Notting Hill Gate and back through Kensington Gardens to Westminster, where it was to join the branch he had already proposed.[42] Once the idea of an 'inner circuit' had won Parliamentary support, it became imperative, if other promoters were to be kept out of the field, that detailed proposals should be presented to Parliament without delay: the recent Parliamentary victory of the Chatham because the South Eastern was not ready with plans for a West End terminus was still fresh in people's memories.

In the session of 1864, therefore, measures were introduced to extend the existing underground at both ends so as to form an inner circuit. By then, however, the scheme had become even more extravagant, for the Lords' select committee of the previous year had advocated that the

Metropolitan's extension should run east from Moorgate Street and not south from Farringdon Street.[43] It was now proposed that the line should be cut through very expensive City property from Moorgate Street to Trinity Square (Tower Hill) and then back again to Cannon Street and Blackfriars. The Metropolitan, therefore, sought powers, in two separate Bills, to extend its line eastwards from Moorgate Street to Trinity Square and westwards from Paddington via Notting Hill Gate and High Street, Kensington, to Brompton (South Kensington). At the same time another company, the Metropolitan District, promoted a railway to join Brompton and Trinity Square via Westminster and the proposed embankment, thus serving the new termini at Victoria, Charing Cross and Cannon Street. It was also to extend its tracks westwards from South Kensington to Gloucester Road (running alongside those of the Metropolitan) and then on through the fields of Earl's Court to the West London Extension Railway at West Brompton. Another line was authorized from the West London south of Addison Road through Earl's Court and round to Kensington High Street. (In the event, arrangements to run the Brighton and the South Western companies' trains over the Metropolitan District fell through and the physical connection at West Brompton was never made.[44])

The Metropolitan District

As its full name suggests, the Metropolitan District was in the beginning a very close associate of the Metropolitan. At the end of December 1863, the Metropolitan nominated four directors to sit on the board of the new company;[45] Fowler was to be its engineer and Burchell to attend to its Parliamentary business. At the Metropolitan's half-yearly meeting early in 1864, Parson told the shareholders that they were

much indebted to Mr. Fowler for promoting the Metropolitan District scheme because, had he not done so, they must either have

abandoned their position in Parliament or have promoted some
such scheme themselves. What he had done was to relieve them,
by preventing Parliament from saying that no scheme had been
submitted in compliance with the recommendation of the Lords'
Committee last session.[46]

In fact, the Metropolitan District was the work of Fowler in
association with the Metropolitan, backed by a powerful
group of contractors, Peto, Betts, Kelk and Waring Brothers,
and headed by a member of the House of Lords, the Earl
of Devon, who had been a (non-attending) member of the
Lords' committee of 1863. This other company appears to
have been a stop-gap device for meeting a particular
emergency. The amount of capital required for the whole of
the inner circle was so large—even in terms of the original
underestimates—that the Metropolitan on its own could
not have embraced more of the undertaking than it did. As
it was, it had to raise £1,900,000 in shares and one-third
more by loans, and the Metropolitan District (the contractors for the time being) £3,600,000 plus one-third. But
it was intended at the start that the two companies should
merge their interests as soon as it was financially possible
for them to do so. This was the view expressed by Fowler
himself,[47] and, at the first formal meeting of the Metropolitan District's board on 11 July 1864, attended by Peto
and Waring, terms were drafted for such an amalgamation.[48]
But the Metropolitan's shareholders, who were then receiving a good dividend—$5\frac{1}{2}$ per cent., soon to be raised to 7
per cent.—were not anxious to subsidize what promised to
be a less profitable undertaking. The reasons for allowing
a second company to promote this extension to the underground may have seemed sound at the time; but to allow
it to maintain its separate existence was a fatal decision and
the Metropolitan must often have regretted it bitterly.

The Metropolitan avoided, for the time being, some of
its heaviest expenditure by postponing the building of its
city section east of Moorgate Street. Even so, the western

extension was costly enough. It involved the driving of a tunnel through Campden Hill and much compensation to property owners, particularly in residential Bayswater. In Leinster Gardens, where the line crossed the road at right angles, false-fronted houses had to be built to conceal the railway's existence.[49] This length was opened to Gloucester Road on 1 October 1868 and to Brompton (South Kensington) on the following 24 December.[50] Fowler was the engineer in charge of all this work and for the building of the District Railway.

Although the District Railway also halted its line before it reached the City's more costly acres, it was nevertheless involved in very heavy expenditure. From South Kensington through Sloane Square and Victoria to Westminster it passed through land that was built up all the way. In Westminster its construction was accompanied by slum clearance and the widening of Tothill Street.[51] A remarkable series of contemporary photographs gives a vivid impression of the heavy labour involved.[52] In the middle of 1866, 2,000 men were said to be hard at work, assisted by 200 horses and 58 engines. Two immense kilns at Earl's Court were busily baking the 140,000,000 bricks needed for the cuttings and tunnels.[53] With great effort the stretch from South Kensington to Westminster was completed in just over three years and was opened to traffic on 24 December 1868. It was worked at first by Metropolitan trains.[54] A further section, from Gloucester Road to West Brompton, was opened on 12 April 1869, and a shuttle service was run upon it until 1 August 1870 when the link with South Kensington, finished months before, at last came into use. The Kensington High Street–West London stretch, in fact two curves connecting with the central portion of the existing line to West Brompton, was completed by 7 September 1869, but the junction with the West London Railway was not used for regular services until 1872; however, the Cromwell Curve, put in on the night of 5 July 1870 (without statutory authority) provided a through route between Kensington High Street and Gloucester Road by District, as well as Metropolitan, rails.[55]

The District Railway had spent some £3,000,000 by the end of 1868, the whole of the capital so far taken up (£2,225,000 in ordinary shares and £750,000 in debentures).[56] Had the company been able to dispose of all of its authorized share capital (£3,600,000 in ordinary shares) soon after its incorporation, its later history would almost certainly have been very much less troubled. As it was, railways in the London area had become much less attractive to investors. As the new lines were opened, it became clear that the returns were very much less than had been estimated. Moreover, the financial crisis following the collapse of Overend, Gurney and Co. in May 1866—an event 'without parallel in the recollection of the oldest men of business in the City of London'[57]—was particularly damaging to railway promotion and above all to the Metropolitan District, for the contracting firm of Peto and Betts, its leading backers, went down for £4,000,000.[58] Their failure also put the London, Chatham & Dover Railway in grave difficulty. But its line was built: that of the District was still under construction.

The delays caused by the financial crisis led to arguments between the railway company and the Metropolitan Board of Works.[59] Because of the shortage of capital the railway was anxious to avoid building along the embankment until the line was open and making money between South Kensington and Westminster. The Metropolitan Board of Works, however, was keen to press on with its embankment, for the trunk sewer was urgently needed. Building was started between Westminster Bridge and Temple Gardens in 1865 and this stretch was opened to pedestrians in July 1868.[60] It was impossible to complete the work as far as Blackfriars, however, because considerable compensation had to be paid to the owners of a continuous line of wharves and quays along the river and round Whitefriars Dock.[61] The original idea had been to preserve these wharves by building this part of the embankment as a viaduct,[62] but the railway, promoted after the embankment had been authorized by Parliament, obviously made this impossible and the wharf owners had to be compensated for their loss. There were long negotiations between the District and the Metropolitan Board of Works about how compensation should be apportioned between them; agreement on this point was not reached until May 1868.[63] The Metropolitan Board of Works then went ahead quickly with the rest of the embankment, but a year later was still complaining that railway building was 'fitful and uncertain, the number of men employed varying considerably'.[64]

The trouble was that the Metropolitan District, having built its line to Westminster, was having great difficulty in raising capital to continue it to the City, but in 1869 Parliament sanctioned the issue of an extension capital of £1,500,000 of 5 per cent. preference stock in place of the unissued ordinary shares.[65] Work then proceeded quite briskly under the supervision of (Sir) Benjamin Baker, Fowler's chief assistant on this stretch. The line was finished to Blackfriars on 30 May 1870, and the road along the embankment (which had to await the railway's completion) was opened to traffic on the following 13 July.[66] The District tried to take its line under the whole of the new Queen Victoria Street as far as the Mansion House itself, but its Bill was defeated in the Lords.[67] Instead, it had to be content with a station at the corner of Cannon Street, which for several years became its City terminus. Trains began to run into this 'Mansion House' station on 3 July 1871.[68]

Until this time the District had been worked by the Metropolitan under an agreement whereby the Metropolitan was paid 55 per cent. of the gross receipts from both local and through traffic.[69] In fact, however, the District ultimately received only about 38 per cent. because it was soon demanding more trains than were stipulated in the agreement and for these it had to pay extra.[70] The arrangement was most unsatisfactory and the District, therefore, decided to run its own trains, and embarked upon the building of repair shops and sheds at West Brompton (now called Lillie Bridge depot). At the beginning of 1870 it gave the necessary 18 months' notice to the Metropolitan for the ending of the agreement between them. With the opening of its new city terminus, it began to work its own part of the underground, and by the end of July 1871 was providing half of the trains from Mansion House right round via the Metropolitan to Moorgate Street as well. This provided a ten-minute service to Moorgate Street and a five-minute frequency between Mansion House and Gloucester Road. South Kensington, Gloucester Road and Kensington High Street were worked as joint stations and the lines between them as joint lines. Receipts from traffic over this section were divided between the Metropolitan and the District in the ratio of 66:34 until 1874, 60:40 from then until 1878, and 50:50 thereafter.[71]

The District decided that it could not do better than copy the Metropolitan's example and order more 4–4–0 tank locomotives of the well-tried design supplied by Beyer, Peacock to its neighbour since 1864. The Manchester firm ultimately supplied 54; 24 came in the first batch (originally lettered, not numbered) in 1871, followed by further batches of six, all numbered consecutively, in 1876, 1880, 1883, 1884 and 1886. They were painted dull green and latterly had the words 'District Railway' on the tank sides. All survived until electrification in 1905, no. 33 until 1925 and no. 34 until 1932. In steam days, all the coaching stock was four-wheeled, made up first of eight and then of nine carriages—two first, three second, four third. All the compartments seated five a side but first class coaches contained only four compartments while the other two classes had five. Each train, therefore, had a seating capacity of 380 at the outset and of 430 when the additional second class coach was added. The firsts were roomy and well upholstered; third class upholstery was confined to a strip of carpet on the seat and a padded back strip at shoulder height. The carriages were gas-lit, braked first by chain, then by Westinghouse non-automatic. Both Metropolitan and District railways originally secured exemption from the requirement of the Railway Regulation Act, 1868, to provide smoking compartments, but they had to comply with public pressure and provided them from 1874. The District copied the Metropolitan in its use of Spagnoletti's disc block telegraph and, like the Metropolitan, introduced 'lock and block' about 1880, although using Sykes's, not Spagnoletti's, instruments.[72]

The underground rivals

From 3 July 1871, the two underground companies, originally intended to be amalgamated, came to own not only separate track but also separate trains. To some extent the traffic itself then dictated an individual existence for each company. Each provided a service from the City to the western suburbs along a major trunk route. The Metropolitan followed the busy New Road to Paddington and from there had extended its services to Hammersmith and Kensington (Addison Road) on the one hand, and to Bayswater, Notting Hill Gate and South Kensington on the other. The District ran parallel to the even busier Fleet Street–Strand route and served Westminster, Pimlico and the Brompton side of Kensington. The Metropolitan linked the main-line termini in north London and the District those of the main lines crossing the river from the south. The Metropolitan actually carried trains from the Great Northern, the Midland, the Great Western and the Chatham railways. The District was at a disadvantage here, for it had no direct junctions with the main lines, but it did connect with the West London, and so early as 1866 it was already negotiating for passenger traffic from the London & North Western.[73] The latter, as we have seen, started to run two trains an hour from Broad Street via Willesden Junction and the West London to Kensington (Addison Road) and, from 1 January 1869, one of these trains was sent on via the West London Extension to Victoria main-line station.[74]

Clearly the District Railway, which ran more directly to Victoria and then went on into the City, offered a much more satisfactory route. Accordingly, the London & North Western agreed in 1871 to contribute £100,000 towards the cost of the Mansion House station and to pay to the District a proportion of the through fares in return for powers to operate over its line up to six trains per hour in each direction.[75] From 1 February 1872 the service over the West London Extension to Victoria ceased and the two trains per hour were both sent on to Mansion House.[76] On the following 1 August, two Great Western trains per hour also started to use the District's line, although in this case they did not add to the total but merely replaced two District trains. Having reached the West London, they then took the Hammersmith & City line on to the Metropolitan and so to Moorgate Street.[77] These horseshoe-shaped routes came to be known as the Outer and Middle Circle respectively; rather battered horseshoes, as Hamilton Ellis has observed.[78]

By the early 1870s the Metropolitan was carrying about 40,000,000 passengers per year and earning about £400,000. The District, however, was only carrying half as many and earning half as much. Yet the share capital of the Metropolitan was only about one-fifth greater than that of the District (£5,330,000 compared with £4,620,000). The District was a relatively unattractive business proposition, heavily burdened with debenture and preference stock. It could irritate the Metropolitan by lowering its fares in an effort to compete for traffic in the zone which was common

to the two companies—a zone which was enlarged after 9
September 1874 when the District Railway was extended
to Hammersmith Broadway.[79] But these irritations were
not sufficient to cause the Metropolitan to make any offers
of amalgamation which seemed sufficiently attractive to the
District's various ranges of shareholder.[80] And, in the years
to come, as the two companies extended their systems, the
District to the south-west and the Metropolitan to the
north-west, their separateness was emphasized, though
enough points of common interest remained to provide
opportunity for increasing friction.

To bring life and vigour to these fundamental differences
and difficulties came two of the most powerful figures in the
railway world of their day—men who, having been at
daggers drawn because of their previous railway experiences,
now chanced, each for a different reason, to become chairmen of the two underground companies and, what is more,
to remain chairmen for most of the last quarter of the
nineteenth century.

The District at first lacked an able manager of the calibre
of Myles Fenton. It decided, therefore, to take the rather
unusual course of securing the part-time services of James
Staats Forbes, the very competent general manager of the
London, Chatham & Dover Railway, who had already
been assisting it in an advisory capacity. In the summer of
1870, when independent operation was only a year away,
he was appointed managing director at an annual salary of
£2,500 and, at the end of November 1872, he became
chairman of the company, a position he was to hold until
September 1901. (In 1873 he also became chairman of the
Chatham; he retained that position until 1904.)[81] This
appointment would not have aggravated the differences
between the District and the Metropolitan had not Parson,
who had succeeded Wilkinson after the latter's death in
1865, been evicted from the chairmanship of the Metropolitan and Sir Edward Watkin, since 1866 chairman of

the Chatham's bitter rival, the South Eastern, been called
in to put an end to a period of considerable irregularity in
the Metropolitan's affairs. Having arrived in 1872 to deal
with a crisis, he stayed until 1894.[82]

Upheaval in the Metropolitan

There were already signs by the end of the 1860s that the
Metropolitan's board was taking rather more than usual
liberties with the company's capital. From the second half
of 1864 until 1868, the company had paid 7 per cent. on its
ordinary shares even though, as we saw at the end of the
previous chapter, the balance of earnings over expenditure
was sufficient to pay only 5 per cent. in the latter year.
Clearly, some of the dividend was being paid out of the
new capital raised for the extensions of the line. Several
legal cases in 1868 and 1869 resulted in the company's
being prevented from doing this, and when it sought to
continue the practice in another way—by paying the shareholders the estimated capital gain on its surplus lands—
this, too, was forbidden.[83] As the new capital on the less
remunerative extension to South Kensington came liable
for dividend, the honeymoon period came to an end. For
1869 the dividend on ordinary shares fell to 4 per cent. and
for 1870 to $3\frac{1}{4}$ per cent. On the first half of 1871, a return
at an annual rate of $3\frac{3}{4}$ per cent. was declared; but when this
was reduced to $2\frac{3}{4}$ per cent. for the second half of that year,
the shareholders rose in revolt and caused two of their
number, Henry Davis Pochin and Benjamin Whitworth, to
be placed on the board.[84] A preliminary investigation
showed that the books had been kept very unsatisfactorily
and that there was a considerable amount of slackness and
waste in the stores and engineering departments. (The
storekeeper absconded, and the engineering superintendent
was given three months' notice.[85]) It was these circumstances which caused the chief shareholders to meet the
board on 31 July 1872 and to bring with them Sir Edward

Watkin. What transpired at that meeting is not recorded in the minutes, but on 7 August the board received a letter from Watkin agreeing to become the company's chairman. A ballot was taken to decide which director should retire to make way for him, and the lot fell on Parson. Two days later Watkin presided over the board for the first time.[86]

Watkin's arrival on the scene was, therefore, somewhat fortuitous. It seems to have owed much to Manchester interests among the shareholders. Pochin was a chemical manufacturer in Manchester and Whitworth was in cotton. Both were strong Liberals and had represented the Liberal interest in Parliament. (Pochin had had the distinction of taking the chair at the first public meeting ever held in Britain in favour of votes for women. It took place at the Manchester Free Trade Hall.[87]) Both had also been engaged, along with other Manchester men, in purchasing coal and iron businesses and turning them into public companies. These included John Brown and Company, Palmer's Shipbuilding Company, and Bolckow Vaughan, the Middlesbrough iron concern.[88] It was not surprising, therefore, that in a difficult situation, they called to their aid one of their Manchester friends. Watkin was a Manchester man born and bred and a keen Free Trader; even before he was twenty he was organizing an Operative Anti-Corn Law Association in Manchester as a counterblast to Chartism.[89] He still lived near Manchester; although he was chairman of the South Eastern Railway, he was also chairman of the Manchester, Sheffield & Lincolnshire. And it is significant that when the existing directors were swept out of office at a shareholders' meeting in October 1872— not without a warm word from Watkin for one of them, James Nasmyth, the inventor of the steam hammer, who was particularly associated with the famous works at Patricroft near Manchester[90]—there were elected in their place, in addition to Pochin (who became vice-chairman) and Whitworth, Andrew Cassels, a member of Peel, Cassels

53. Charing Cross Station, South Eastern Railway, in its early days

54. Cannon Street Station, South Eastern Railway, at the time of its Opening, 1866

55. West Street Junction, Smithfield: Metropolitan Train on left, Chatham Lines to right, 1866

56. The Crystal Palace and the High Level Station, L.C. & D. R., 1865

63. The Thames Tunnel as a Footway

64. The Thames Tunnel converted to a Railway: Wapping Station, 1870

61. Building the Metropolitan District along the Victoria Embankment in front of Somerset House, about 1869

62. The Metropolitan District near Blackfriars, about 1869

59. Kensington (High Street) Station under construction, about 1867

60. Building the Metropolitan District at Victoria, about 1867

57. Building the Metropolitan under Leinster Gardens, Bayswater, about 1866

58. The Dummy Houses, 23 and 24 Leinster Gardens, above the Railway today

65. Liverpool Street Station, Great Eastern Railway, 1875

66. House-building in Progress at Walthamstow, late 1870s: Great Eastern Railway near Hoe Street Station (at left)

67. The Fleet of the City Steamboats passing in Review Order off Chelsea, about 1855

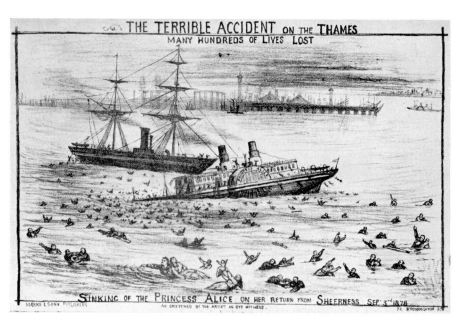

68. The *Princess Alice* Disaster, 3 September 1878

and Company of Manchester, Joseph Shuttleworth, partner
in an agricultural machinery firm with a branch at Manchester, and John R. Lingard, the Stockport man who, in
1862, had become solicitor to the Manchester, Sheffield &
Lincolnshire Railway.[91] The railway promoting clique had
been ousted by a railway investing clique centred largely on
a group of Manchester business men.

As was to be expected, this new régime was not slow to
expose its predecessors' shortcomings. It was calculated
that, since the railway's opening, about a quarter of the
dividends had been paid out of capital.[92] Half of the total
expenditure had been on land purchases and compensation.
All this had passed through Burchell's hands but none had
ever been examined or agreed to, and the books were in a
state of great confusion. In 1865, notices had been served
on tenants and lessees of property east of Moorgate Street
at an estimated cost of about £150,000, but no railway
had yet been built there.[93] The engineer, Fowler, had also
done very well for himself. He had received £152,000 in all
(and a further £157,000 from the District). 'No engineer
in the world,' exclaimed the indignant Watkin in a very
straight letter to him,

was so highly paid. Taking it any way you like—time, speciality,
risk, quantity, value or all combined, you have set an example of
charges which seems to me to have largely aided in the demoraliza-
tion of professional men of all sorts who have lived upon the
suffering shareholders for the past ten years.[94]

He went on to demand a detailed breakdown of contractors'
charges on the extension lines, but this was not forthcoming.
The new chairman went as near to the truth as the law of
slander would allow when he declared at an emergency
meeting of shareholders, held in October 1872:

What is it we see in the world around us? At the opera, if we look
at the lady occupants of the best boxes, who are glittering with the
best diamonds, and ask who they are, we are told that they are
the wife and daughters of Clodd, the great railway contractor. In

N

the park whose carriages, horses and equipages are the most fashionable? Why, those belonging to Plausible, the great railway engineer. And if we hear of some poor nobleman's estate being in the market who buys it? Why, Vampire, the great railway lawyer.[95]

The fact remained, however, that while Clodd, Plausible and Vampire lined their pockets, they did succeed, by skilful manœuvrings and lavish promises—such as those contained in a sixpenny pamphlet entitled *The Metropolitan Railway: A Fifteen Per Cent. Paying Line* which claimed to have gone through ten editions by 1868—in raising the capital needed to build the railway. The public owed a considerable debt to them, even if the shareholders, having enjoyed an unreal 7 per cent. for a few years, had subsequently to put up with a more modest return on their investment. Their discomfiture, however, did not prevent Watkin himself from being voted £2,000 per year for his services. The motion was proposed by Edmund Potter, M.P., the great calico printer and a former president of the Manchester Chamber of Commerce.[96]

The new board raised a further £250,000 and pressed on with the building of the railway to the east of Moorgate Street through the property for which notice of purchase had been given in 1865. The new terminus at Liverpool Street was under construction and the Metropolitan thus seized the opportunity to extend its line to join the Great Eastern's system. This junction was opened on 1 February 1875 and the Metropolitan then started to run its Hammersmith trains into Liverpool Street main-line station for a short time until its own station, then called Bishopsgate, was completed.[97] The underground was further extended to Aldgate in 1876, a shuttle service from there to Bishopsgate starting to run on 18 November and through trains on 4 December.[98] This was to remain the limit of its penetration of the City until the completion of the Inner Circle was made possible a few years later.

London railways in the mid-seventies

By the middle of the 1870s the railway map of central London presents a remarkably modern appearance. Only the line into Marylebone and the tubes remain to be added to it. There has, of course, been considerable widening and improvement of these routes, and much enlarging and rebuilding of the termini. But, fundamentally, the surface and underground railways (as distinct from the tubes) that are used in central London today were the creation of early and, particularly, of mid-Victorian times. The underground, as we have seen, cost more than £10,000,000; the Chatham spent nearly £6,000,000 on its metropolitan lines[99] and the Brighton over £4,300,000 on theirs between 1855 and 1866 alone.[100] The Broad Street extension cost over £1,000,000,[101] the building of Charing Cross and Cannon Street more than £2,500,000[102] and that of Liverpool Street not much less.[103] It seems probable that, when the London section of the Midland Railway (built with four tracks between Hendon and St. Pancras, except in the Belsize Tunnel, in order to accommodate the suburban traffic) and the various smaller ventures are added to the sum, the total invested in these mid-Victorian years was at least £40,000,000. (For comparison, the total invested in all the railways of Britain by 1860 was, perhaps, a little under £350,000,000.[104])

Some idea of the wide range of City and suburban services made possible by these new lines may be gained from a list of some of the more important routes which were being operated by the early or mid-1870s—the list is by no means complete:

Victoria–Brixton–London Bridge
Victoria–Brixton–Ludgate Hill–Hendon
Victoria–Brixton–Ludgate Hill–[New] Barnet
Victoria or Moorgate Street–suburban stations on the Chatham main line

Victoria–suburban stations on the Brighton main line and via
  Crystal Palace (Low Level)
Victoria–Brixton–Crystal Palace (High Level)
Victoria–Addison Road–Southall
Paddington–suburban stations on Great Western main line
Charing Cross–Cannon Street–Greenwich or North Kent lines.
  (The trains usually ran to Charing Cross via Cannon Street,
  thereby providing a frequent West End–City service.)
Waterloo or Ludgate Hill to stations on the South Western main
  line and Windsor, Brentford and Kingston branches
Ludgate Hill/Holborn Viaduct–Swanley, Bickley or Beckenham
Moorgate Street or Broad Street–Finsbury Park–Finchley–[High]
  Barnet
Broad Street–Finsbury Park–[New] Barnet or Enfield
Moorgate Street–Kentish Town–Tottenham
Moorgate Street–Windsor (via Great Western)
Fenchurch Street–Blackwall
Fenchurch Street–Loughton
Fenchurch Street–North Woolwich
Fenchurch Street–Barking
Liverpool Street–Enfield or Chingford
Liverpool Street–Peckham Rye (via Thames Tunnel, East London
  line)
Liverpool Street–Brentwood
Liverpool Street–Hertford
City–Hammersmith (Metropolitan Railway)
Aldgate–Paddington–Kensington–Mansion House (Inner Circle)
Moorgate–Addison Road–Mansion House (Middle Circle)
Broad Street–Willesden Junction–Addison Road–Mansion House
  (Outer Circle)
Broad Street–Willesden Junction–Richmond[105]

By 1875 the Metropolitan was carrying more than
48,000,000 passengers a year and the District still no more
than half that total.[106] Numbers for the other lines are not
easy to come by, but in the first half of 1863, some years
before the opening of the South London loop and the
direct line to Sutton, the Brighton already carried more
than 4,000,000 passengers on its suburban trains[107] and in

1866 the Chatham accommodated nearly 9,000,000 on its metropolitan extensions. By the later 1860s about 20,000,000 passengers travelled on the North London every year.[108] According to a calculation made some years later by the L.C.C.'s Statistical Officer, in 1875 106,000,000 journeys were made on the Metropolitan, District, North London and East London railways alone.[109] This would suggest that, when the traffic of the main-line companies is added, perhaps somewhere between 150,000,000 and 170,000,000 train journeys were then being made every year by people wishing to get from one part of the London area to another.

Steamboat and omnibus traffic

Did this large increase in railway travel represent quite new traffic—people who had rarely ridden before or, if they had, were persuaded to ride more often? Or did it represent a gain from the two other types of public transport, the steamboats and the omnibuses? Or was it a combination of both?

The steamboats on the river were, clearly, at a heavy disadvantage when they had to compete directly with steam trains running along its banks. The extension of the railway down-river to Gravesend and up-river to Richmond had put an end to the regular steamboat services to those places in the 1850s:[110] now the building of the new main-line termini, particularly Charing Cross, and the cutting of the underground, particularly along the Embankment, greatly reduced the steamboat traffic through London itself. In 1876 the existing firms—the Iron, Citizen, London & Westminster, Waterman's and Woolwich Steam Packet Companies—merged to form the London Steamboat Company Limited, in an attempt to keep a half-hourly service running all the year round between Chelsea and Greenwich and Woolwich. At the time of the merger it was claimed that the steamboats had carried 200,000,000 passengers during the previous ten years; but, although the river still provided the cheapest route between the City and Westminster, the traffic had already become very seasonal. Summer excursions became the steamboats' mainstay; but the appalling disaster which befell the *Princess Alice* in September 1878 when returning from one of these trips—more than 700 people were drowned—hastened the company's decline. Its boats and plant were eventually sold in 1884, and when its successor also came to grief two years later, there were no bidders for the 57 paddle wheelers which it then owned.[111]

The omnibuses, in contrast, managed to maintain their traffic quite well in the face of the new railway competition, but their traffic revenue fell with significant regularity for several years. The returns of the London General Omnibus Company indicate what was happening.

THE L.G.O.C.'S TRAFFIC AND RECEIPTS
FROM ITS OMNIBUSES, 1863–75[112]

Year	Total number of passengers carried	Receipts from omnibuses
1863	40,199,838	£601,324
1864	42,648,936	£613,145
1865	44,006,581	£624,086
1866	44,352,288	£615,094
1867	41,424,428	£572,442
1868	40,968,187	£568,854
1869	41,047,521	£542,687
1870	42,935,471	£537,852
1871	42,556,545	£519,303
1872	44,523,357	£518,488
1873	46,066,247	£516,091
1874	48,538,896	£533,546
1875	49,720,038	£537,905

These figures show that in the underground's earliest years, when it ran only from Paddington to Farringdon Street and while some of the surface railways were still being built, the L.G.O.C. managed to increase its traffic and revenue; but it did so only by cutting its fares on those routes where it encountered competition. Myles Fenton claimed, soon after the opening of the underground, that some omnibus fares had been reduced by so much as 50 per cent.[113] When the Metropolitan was extended to Moorgate Street and other suburban lines opened, omnibus traffic still continued to grow but at the expense of an even more drastic cut in fares, resulting in a fall in revenue. Meanwhile the management took advantage of the greater manœuvrability of the omnibus and developed new routes. In September 1866, for instance, it was claimed that alternative traffic had been found which more than compensated for the losses caused by the recent opening of the new railway termini at Broad Street and Moorgate Street.[114] In the following two years, however, more new traffic was not forthcoming to compensate for further gains by the railways. The L.G.O.C. lost more than 3,000,000 passengers and it was not until 1872 that they were regained. At the same time receipts fell year by year until 1874, when they started to move upwards again. And then this upward turn was to be explained, in part at any rate, not by more money being collected in fares but by more money being paid in; several of the conductors were convicted of pilfering and, according to the half-yearly report, this had had 'a very salutary effect' on all the others.[115]

The omnibus holds its own for shorter journeys but the train attracts the longer-distance traffic

Under the direction of A. G. Church, who became general manager as well as secretary on the death of McNamara in January 1867,[116] the role of the omnibus was adapted to meet the changed circumstances. It had ceased to be the main means of passenger transport for Londoners. In the 1860s, while the number of omnibus journeys remained relatively stationary, the number of journeys by train rose rapidly. If to the total of passengers carried by the L.G.O.C. in the mid-1870s is added an estimate for the traffic of its 200 or so associates and (perhaps) 20 rivals, the number of journeys by train was probably by then between two or three times as great as that by omnibus. Yet the omnibus still had advantages over the train in that it picked up and set down in the street itself; it involved no clambering up or down flights of stairs as at railway stations which, in the London area, were usually perched upon viaducts or buried in tunnels, and it could often carry passengers from very near their point of departure direct to their destination. 'Where railways come in direct competition with omnibuses', commented the L.G.O.C. early in 1870, 'the through traffic often goes to the railway; where the distance travelled is short and the destination of the passenger is more conveniently reached by omnibus, the omnibus service gains preference.'[117]

The omnibus interests enjoyed a great measure of freedom from control by local authorities; indeed, it was only after 1867 that omnibuses were obliged to set down passengers on the left side of the road, and then only within a four-mile radius of Charing Cross.[118] Although the City had powers to prescribe routes within its jurisdiction from 1863,[119] it does not seem to have used them. A mass of omnibus routes picked their way unobstructed through many parts of the metropolis which the railways still did not serve. In particular, the omnibus plied unchallenged in many of London's central streets; no railways ran near Oxford Street, Piccadilly or Knightsbridge, for instance. Added importance was given to areas of London such as these by developments in retail trade. There were more shops, and several of the department stores date from before 1875. Many of their customers arrived by omnibus and found the omnibuses all the more necessary as they staggered home again, tired out after shopping and laden with parcels. But further consideration of the growth of this important off-peak traffic may be deferred until a later chapter.

The railway companies themselves stimulated omnibus travelling, although most of the journeys to and from railway stations were short ones. Both the underground companies encouraged the L.G.O.C. to operate such feeder services. In 1879, for instance, Forbes the chairman of the

District recalled that when the underground was first opened

there was no public conveyance whatever between Regent Street . . . on the one hand, and Church Lane, Kensington, [Kensington Church Street] on the other hand. There was nothing up Park Lane. There was nothing up Palace Road. There were not any public conveyances of any kind upon those roads.

This being an area where most of the inhabitants owned their own carriages and did not require public transport, the District Railway had to subsidize the first omnibuses from Victoria to Paddington via Park Lane. 'For years they could not live without the subsidy,' Forbes added, 'but now [1879] they live very well.'[120] The Metropolitan, too, was concerned with omnibus feeder services. When the line was first opened, it had asked the L.G.O.C. to run services to and from certain stations, and in August 1866 the railway company itself started to run omnibuses from Regent Circus, Oxford Street (Oxford Circus) to Portland Road (Great Portland Street) station; in 1874 the service was extended to Piccadilly. From 1872 to 1874 another feeder line was operated by the Metropolitan between Camden Town and its station at Gower Street (Euston Square).[121] Short journeys such as these may have kept the omnibus traffic from declining, but they also help to explain the fall in revenue. In so far as this was the case, the buoyancy of the journey totals may be misleading; people may have been riding almost as often as previously but they did not travel as far.

The train was so much faster than the horse-drawn omnibus, however, that for journeys from the outer suburbs the railway had an overwhelming advantage. By the 1860s London had spread so far in some directions that the journey time and fare by omnibus had reached a limit beyond which regular travellers were reluctant to go. The north-western thrust, for instance, had by then reached Kilburn, four miles west and nearly two miles north of

St. Paul's; this must have meant something like an hour's journey by omnibus. There was still much room for house building less than this distance out, but the pressure for new houses on the outskirts, where land values and rents were lower, remained insistent. The population continued to grow rapidly—that of Greater London rose from nearly 2,700,000 in 1851 to nearly 3,225,000 in 1861 and nearly 3,900,000 in 1871[122]—and, as the professions grew in size and as business, large and small, prospered, so an increasing number of middle-class people sought dwellings farther out of London, on its more agreeable fringes. The railways now enabled them to continue to do this. Indeed, trains allowed those who worked in London to live well beyond the bounds of the built-up area. It was now not just a matter of pushing forward the housing frontier but rather of siting communities around, or on roads radiating from, railway stations often far beyond that frontier. Frequently this entailed the rapid development of existing villages. Finchley, for instance, was a small village outside London before the railway reached it. Only three omnibuses ran from Church End, Finchley, to Tottenham Court Road and Charing Cross, and two or three others passed through what we would now call East Finchley on their way from Barnet to the Bank. From Whetstone in the north of the parish the journey took about 1¾ hours and the fare was 1s. single. By 1870 the railway provided 20 trains each way from Church End (six of them between 7.30 and 9.30 a.m. and five back between 4.30 and 6.30 p.m.), the journey took about half an hour, and a yearly season (second class) cost £10 10s. to Moorgate, which worked out at about 8d. return per working day. After the railway was opened, the population of Finchley began to grow rapidly and it has been estimated that, by 1874, two and a half times as many commuters were travelling from Finchley and other suburban stations on the Great Northern as had travelled in 1867, only seven years before.[123] The same story was repeated many times at a number of other places similarly situated beyond the housing frontier—at South Croydon, for instance, by 1866, and between Gloucester Road and Hammersmith by 1875.[124] To this extent the railways were creating new longer-distance suburban traffic. But this was a process which, despite rapid initial growth, took time to reach substantial proportions; chairmen of railway companies were constantly urging their shareholders to wait patiently for the traffic to grow. The really big developments were to come in the last quarter of the nineteenth century rather than in the years immediately after the railways' construction.

Fares and workmen's trains

Once inside the housing frontier, horse power was not at such a complete disadvantage, and it could often hold its own in direct competition with the locomotive. The Chatham's trains from Brixton, for instance, were often quite empty while the competing omnibuses were full; and the Brighton company had the same experience in that area.[125] The North London directors, too, were made aware of omnibus competition.[126] In the older suburbs there was not a great difference in the total journey times, for the trains' greater speed was offset by the omnibuses' greater accessibility. Nor could the railways undercut the omnibuses' fares on these shorter distances. They were, however, able to provide several fares over the same distance and in the same trains, whereas the omnibuses, while they were sometimes known to charge less for roof passengers, were essentially one-class vehicles. First class on the railway was more expensive than the omnibus fare, and the journey much more comfortable. Third class, on the other hand, was often cheaper. (Most London underground and suburban trains provided for third class passengers in the 1860s, the North London being a notable exception; but in the North London's case, the first and second class fares were extremely reasonable.[127]) As we have seen, the Metropolitan at the outset charged 6d. first, 4d. second, and 3d. third for any distance between Paddington and Farringdon Street. These were the same fares as those charged in 1866 by the Chatham from Camberwell to the City and almost the same as those of the South Eastern between Cannon Street and Charing Cross (its third class was 2d.).[128] Longer distances cost a little more. For instance, the Chatham and the Brighton charged 8d., 6d. and 4d. from Peckham Rye to their respective City termini, and the fares from Hammersmith to Moorgate Street were 9d., 7d. and 5d.[129] The railways also offered returns at less than twice the single fare and season tickets which cut the price still further. The Metropolitan's original returns cost 9d., 6d. and 5d. and its seasons £8 and £5 10s. When trains started to run from Hammersmith to Moorgate Street, the return journey cost 1s. 3d., 11d. and 8d. and seasons £12 and £8 10s. These figures suggest that the key to the railways' fare structure was the second class single, which seems to have been fixed at about the same rate as that charged by competing omnibuses. In the early days of the new competition, at all events, omnibus fares dictated those on the railway. In 1864, for instance, Forbes admitted that the Chatham's charges from Brixton were 'very much regulated by those of the omnibuses . . .'[130] Above the omnibus rate was the more expensive (and exclusive) first class and below it were the third, the return and, for regular travellers who paid in advance, the season. Fowler probably summed up the situation accurately when he observed:

the character of the omnibus traffic is lower than it was and on the railway we have a higher and a lower class than originally travelled by omnibus. We carry many who would not ordinarily travel by omnibus and we carry, in the third class, many persons who are rarely seen on omnibuses.[131]

This remark was made about traffic on the underground soon after its opening and before many of the cuts in fares had taken place. The Metropolitan subsequently introduced lower fares (4d., 3d. and 2d.) between adjoining stations, and in August 1865 it reduced these to 3d., 2d. and 1d. The 1d. fare trebled the number of passengers who used the underground for such short distances.[132] By 1874, 28,000,000 journeys on the Metropolitan, 64 per cent. of the total, were made by third class passengers.[133]

The railways, and particularly the underground, were securing much new traffic within the built-up area as well as outside it: by greater speed and comfort they were attracting to public transport some first class passengers who disliked travelling in congested omnibuses and, by lower fares, many third class passengers who would otherwise have walked. And the spread of workmen's trains added to this second category many who would certainly have had to walk. Some of the men employed in building Victoria station, for instance, could not find lodgings nearby at rents they could afford and had to walk to their work from as far away as Paddington.[134] The Metropolitan, as we have seen, introduced these trains to London in 1864 and by the end of 1865 between 1,800 and 2,000 workmen were using them every weekday.[135] In February 1865, the Chatham had also started to run workmen's trains on its recently-opened lines between Ludgate Hill and Victoria.[136] One of these set off from each terminus at 4.55 a.m. and, having stopped at every station, covered the whole journey in just under an hour. Trains to carry these passengers home again left at 6.15 p.m. on Mondays to Fridays and at 2.30 p.m. on Saturdays. *Bona fide* 'artisans, mechanics and daily labourers, both male and female'—they had to give names and addresses both of themselves and their employers when taking their weekly tickets—could travel from any station on the route for 2d. per day return. These trains, which soon increased in number,[137] were run under a clause of the Chatham's Act of 1860 which, as we have seen, was inserted on Pearson's initiative. After 1864 it became usual for all railways which promoted new stretches of line in the built-up area of London to be required by Parliament to provide workmen's trains. And, at the same time, other companies started to run them, as the Metropolitan had done originally, without any such statutory obligation. The North London came into the former category because of its extension to Broad Street in 1865, and (most notably) the Great Eastern because of its suburban lines to Edmonton and Chingford in 1872 and 1873; while the South Eastern's workmen's trains along its Woolwich branch, started in 1865, and those provided by the Brighton Company, started in 1870, came into the latter class. Watkin took up Pearson's cry and hoped that these trains might lead to new housing schemes outside London. Addressing the South Eastern's shareholders shortly after its workmen's trains had started to run, he said:

Let us find the wealth of London ready to grapple with this great evil of the crowding out of the working man. Let us see the capital raised at 5 per cent. to build working men's houses for 100,000 in any healthy place down our line and we shall be ready to recommend you to contract to carry the people at times to suit [them] and at prices not greater than the difference in rent and taxes between unhealthy London and the healthy open fields beyond.[138]

But the housing schemes were not forthcoming—at that time.

The railways with rapidly-growing traffic pay poor dividends; the L.G.O.C. with no such increase in traffic pays well

From the traffic figures, it might be supposed that London's rapidly-growing railways would give a better return on capital than the hard-pressed L.G.O.C. With the notable exception of the North London, however, which continued to pay 5 or 6 per cent. on its ordinary shares in the early 1870s, this was not the case. So much capital had been invested in London's railways that even the quite impressive passenger traffic which was built up within the later 1860s and early 1870s was unable to provide more than a very modest return on it. The Metropolitan was reduced to a dividend of 2 or 3 per cent. once it had embarked upon less profitable extensions and could no longer pay its interest out of newly-raised capital, and the District was hard put to it to pay anything on its preference shares, let alone its ordinaries. The Chatham's metropolitan extensions had brought it to the Court of Chancery by the middle of the 1860s, and the Brighton's heavy investment in suburban lines had also landed it in difficulties at about the same time.[139] The capital of the L.G.O.C., however, which, at £600,000, had seemed excessive in the dark days immediately after the merger in the middle of the 1850s, came to look almost insignificant when set against the millions so readily expended by the eager railway contractors. On £600,000 it was not necessary to earn a big profit to pay a quite respectable dividend. In fact, apart from the critical year 1867, from which it was still recovering in 1868, the L.G.O.C.'s profits did not fall appreciably during these years.

THE L.G.O.C.'S PROFITS, 1863–75

1863—£49,457	1869—£47,978
1864—£66,936	1870—£64,443
1865—£55,317	1871—£48,900
1866—£37,479	1872—£76,230
1867— -£2,833	1873—£62,527
1868—£21,174	1874—£40,287
1875—£52,004	

The loan debt of the company was paid off completely by the beginning of 1865, and a proportion of the profit thereafter was devoted to building up a reserve fund. From 1862 to 1866 the company paid its shareholders between 5 and $7\frac{1}{2}$ per cent. In 1867 and 1868 it could pay only $3\frac{3}{4}$ per cent. (for the former year by dipping into the reserves). The dividend rose to $6\frac{7}{8}$ per cent. in 1869 and $8\frac{3}{4}$ per cent. in 1870, fell back to $7\frac{1}{2}$ per cent. in 1871 but from 1872–74 was 8 per cent. and in 1875, 9 per cent.

Horse feed continued to be by far the largest item of expenditure and its price could vary by so much as £36,000 between a year of good harvest and one of bad—

enough to wipe out most of the profit.[140] If the railways' dividends were determined mainly by the large number of shares on which they had to be paid, those of the L.G.O.C. were decided chiefly by the weather, for the weather determined the yield of the harvest (and also, to some extent, the number of passengers). In 1866, however, Church began to defeat the English weather to some degree by buying imported maize instead of home-grown oats;[141] the opening up of a world economy, which was to have such a dramatic effect upon grain prices from the later 1870s, was already beginning to exert an influence.

There were also substantial savings in tolls and taxes. It is impossible to discover how much the omnibuses paid altogether in tolls to the various turnpike trusts. It was put at £26,000 for the year 1854 and this figure may be of the correct order of magnitude, for the L.G.O.C. paid £9,500 in turnpike tolls for the first half of 1859.[142] Most omnibus concerns managed to avoid payment by ending their routes at the turnpike gates, and some proprietors, such as those operating to Camden Town, succeeded in winning nominal tolls by threatening to run their services down side streets if these were not granted.[143] On most routes, therefore, the turnpikes limited the length of journey rather than added to operating costs. Many of these restrictions were removed after 1 July 1864 when a number of the remaining turnpike gates in and about London were swept away, including those at Notting Hill, Kensington, Islington and City Road, 25 gates and 56 side bars in all. Southwark Bridge was also freed of tolls in 1864, and other turnpike gates were removed during the following few years.[144]

Of greater importance than the removal of tolls was the abolition of mileage duty. Once the L.G.O.C. began to publish full accounts, the Commissioners of Inland Revenue, who had formerly found it 'very difficult to ascertain the proportion which the duty . . . bore to the earnings and profits of the proprietors', were no longer left in any doubt on the matter. In 1864, for instance, the L.G.O.C. paid over £53,000 in duty in a year when receipts totalled £613,000 and profits were £67,000, a result which even Her Majesty's Commissioners found 'very startling'.[145] In 1866 the rate of duty was cut from 1d. to ¼d. a mile and this, together with a reduction of 16 in the total number of omnibuses, saved the L.G.O.C. nearly £19,500 in the first half of 1867.[146] From 1 January 1870 the mileage duty was abolished altogether.[147]

All these economies, and particularly those in horse feed, led to a big reduction in costs during the difficult period after 1865 when receipts were falling year by year. In 1869 costs were £50,000 lower than they had been in 1868 and £80,000 lower than in 1867; in 1870 they were £20,000 lower still. By then, however, the company had found another source of income which, together with the £5,000 a year or so which it gained from the sale of manure and advertising rights, added nearly £40,000 to its omnibus receipts in 1871, £90,000 in 1872, £100,000 in 1873 and nearly £120,000 in 1874 and again in 1875. Clearly, without this windfall, the balance sheets for these years would have looked very sorry indeed. Paradoxically, the new revenue came from a competing source. At the beginning of the 1870s the L.G.O.C. obtained contracts for horsing a number of tramcars which, operated by rival companies, then began to trundle through some of the streets of London and its suburbs.

O

CHAPTER SIX

HORSE TRAMWAYS

The horse-drawn tram, after a false start in 1861–62, was successfully introduced to London in 1870. It could carry many more passengers than the omnibus and cost little more to operate. The tramway companies could therefore offer low fares and, by adding to existing transport users a section of the community hitherto little catered for by public transport, quickly built up as large a traffic as that of the L.G.O.C. Most of their passengers travelled from the inner suburbs to the fringe of central London within which tramcars were not allowed to penetrate; the authorities believed that tramways in the central streets would make traffic congestion much worse, and many interested parties feared that they would reduce the amenity value of property in fashionable residential areas.

SCHEMES AND EXPERIMENTS

THE GREAT ADVANTAGE of the tramcar, running on a smooth railed track, was that it made more efficient use of horse power, the operators' main expense. The rolling resistance of iron wheels on rails was much lower than that of omnibus wheels on ordinary road surfaces; so, with the aid of a tramway (or street railway, as it was often then called, using the American name), two horses could pull a vehicle weighing a couple of tons or so and accommodating up to 50 passengers—about twice the weight and capacity of an omnibus. A successful design of tramcar had been developed in America, its country of origin, where there had been a considerable spread of tramway building during the 1850s. Its small wheels were tucked away underneath its body, thus giving extra width and spaciousness inside the car, and, as the floor level was low, passengers could easily climb on and off. The ride, too, was smoother and, so its advocates claimed, safer, for the tramcar was fitted with a brake; stopping did not have to depend on pulling up the horses, the old stage coach practice which had been passed down to the omnibus. On the other hand, tramway companies had to build and maintain their track and the part of the road which it occupied. Yet it was relatively inexpensive to lay lines on the public highway, and although a little more fixed capital was needed to run a tramway than to work an omnibus route, the interest which had to be paid on this larger outlay could be more than offset by the greater earning power of the vehicle. Tramway companies could operate profitably at considerably lower fares than those charged by omnibuses, and by doing so they could generate a new and greatly increased volume of traffic. The railways had provided a faster and cheaper service than the omnibuses over longer distances; now the tramways threatened to undercut them for shorter journeys along the main roads.

Tramway promoters, however, had first to obtain permission to lay their rails through the streets, and this was no easy task, for the road authorities were quick to realize that such a concession automatically carried with it a certain monetary value.[1] In fashionable neighbourhoods, however, the authorities made a stand, not for bargaining purposes, but because they did not want a tramway at any price. Authorities in these areas were sensitive to pressure both from residents, who felt that tramways in the vicinity would reduce the value of their property, and from the owners of high-class shops, whose customers often came by carriage and who considered that tramways would interfere with this well-to-do traffic. These were interested parties on whose sensibilities the most interested party of all—the L.G.O.C.—could play with effect.

As we noticed in chapter three, the L.G.O.C.'s own attempt to promote a tramway in 1857–58 had foundered largely because of such local hostility. An American, George Francis Train, and an Englishman, William Joseph

Curtis, had similar experiences when they each tried to introduce tramways into London a few years later. In 1860 Marylebone refused permission—but only after prolonged debate and under considerable pressure from the L.G.O.C.[2] —for Train to lay a trial line from Finchley Road down Baker Street and Wigmore Street, through Cavendish Square to Regent Street, and back along Oxford Street, Portman Square and Gloucester Place. He did, however, succeed in persuading the Turnpike Commission to allow him to attempt a more modest demonstration along the south side of Bayswater Road between Marble Arch and Porchester Terrace (opened on 23 March 1861). This was followed by another single line beginning outside Westminster Abbey and extending some way down Victoria Street (opened on 15 April 1861), and a third—perhaps more than a demonstration line—from the Surrey side of Westminster Bridge to Kennington Gate (opened on 15 August 1861). All these lines aroused fierce criticism, and after a few months they had to be removed—but not before Train had managed to convince a good many people of the merits of his single-deck cars.[3]

Train had, in fact, made two mistakes. First, he failed to see that tramways were likely to gain support in middle class and, particularly, in working class neighbourhoods whose inhabitants were likely to use them, rather than in fashionable Portman Square, Gloucester Place and Bayswater Road, many of whose residents had their own carriages or could afford to take a cab. To propose at the outset a line down wealthy Wigmore Street, for instance, where not even the omnibuses had chosen to penetrate,[4] was an error of the first order. The Kennington line, the last to be opened, might have succeeded had it not been for Train's second and greater mistake, the type of rail he used. Rails which could be laid quite flush with the road were well known—they were used on some American tramways and James Samuel, one of Train's technical advisers, had recommended a rail of this sort in 1857–58 when he was engineer for the L.G.O.C.'s scheme. Yet Train favoured another variety, the so-called step rail the outside of which, if not very carefully laid, protruded above the macadam road surface and became a hindrance to traffic crossing it. These rails had been recently laid for Philadelphia's new tramways, and the choice seems to have been dictated by Train's connection with that town.[5] They provided a wide, flat surface a little below road level which could be used by ordinary cart and carriage wheels, as well as the stepped up part of the rail, which was supposed to be flush with the road, to accommodate the tramcars' flanged wheels. But the advantage of providing an iron road for the general use of carts and carriages, though apparently welcomed in Philadelphia where wheel gauges of private vehicles were even altered to fit the flat part of the new rails,[6] was considerably diminished in London's thoroughfares where the macadam surface was tolerably well maintained, by the standards of the day. And it was more than offset by the disadvantage that the raised part of the rail when badly laid was an obstacle to traffic because it protruded above road level. The unsuitability of this edge rail, allied to Train's own bombastic manner, prejudiced tramway promotion in London for several years to come, and it may have been to some extent responsible for keeping the tramcar permanently out of most of the West End. As a civil engineer later observed, Train's 'highly objectionable and futile' attempts had 'contributed more than any other cause to bringing public misconception, disfavour and discredit, upon the Tramway question as applied to London Streets'.[7]

In some ways, however, Train was the victim of misfortune as well as of miscalculation. As we noticed in the last chapter, 1861–62 were years of feverish railway-building activity in the London area. It was railways which then caught the imagination of the investing public and even of local authorities; the Marylebone Vestry, which turned down Train's application, was at that time actively supporting the building of the Metropolitan Railway under one of its main roads. Only when the railway boom was over did tramways come into their own. After the downfall of Peto and Betts and the recognition that railways built at a cost of hundreds of thousands of pounds per mile were yielding little or nothing, it became possible to kindle a little interest in undertakings which, if American and European experience was valid, were also capable of winning a large urban traffic at a cost of only a few thousand pounds per mile. In 1865 John Noble and Company, a firm of financial agents, put out a pamphlet called *Tramways as a Means of Facilitating Street Traffic of the Metropolis* and began to act on behalf of the Metropolitan Tramways Company Ltd., an undertaking which was incorporated in December of that year. It proposed to use rails which would not in any way interfere with other traffic passing over them;[8] and it also realized from the outset that tramways on a public road required not merely the permission of the local road authority but also the sanction of Parliament.

Train had also understood the need for such sanction if he was to get beyond the building of small demonstration lines. But when, in 1861, he promoted a private Bill to give wide powers to his Street Rail Company, a £300,000 concern which had been incorporated on 7 February of that year, the measure was strongly attacked in the Commons on the grounds that it would give the company a monopoly of part of the public highway and should have been promoted as a public, and not as a private, Bill. It was thrown out on the second reading, and another Bill, introduced in the following session by Acton Smee Ayrton (whom we have already encountered as an early supporter of the underground) was also rejected. John Bright, however, spoke up on the tramways' behalf, and his advocacy at this juncture deserves notice in view of subsequent events.[9] In 1866 and 1867 the Bill sanctioning the activities of the Metropolitan Tramways Company Ltd.—with which, as we have just seen, John Noble's firm was concerned—got no farther than its predecessors had done. Indeed, it did not even receive a hearing, being objected to on Standing Orders.[10] Standing Orders were, however, amended in 1867,[11] but in 1868 when the measure was proposed yet a third time, it was rejected on the second reading. Nevertheless, in that session, Parliament did pass a Bill authorizing extensive tramway building in Liverpool's streets, and this at last opened the way to a more sympathetic hearing of the case for tramways in London.

London's first successful tramways

There is no doubt that public—and investing—opinion was now veering round in favour of tramways, and in December 1868 John Bright, their warm supporter, became President of the Board of Trade, the Government department directly concerned. In 1869 Bills were presented by three companies. Two of them, the Metropolitan Street Tramways and the Pimlico, Peckham & Greenwich Street Tramways, sought to build lines south of the river; the third, the North Metropolitan Tramways, applied for powers in east London. The Commons decided to treat these three applications together and sent them all to the same committee.[12] There the promoters were able to point to the success of tramways not only in the United States but also in other towns in Europe and elsewhere. William Sheldon, for instance, a former director of the L.G.O.C., who had horsed Train's tramway on the Kennington Road, gave evidence about tramways he had subsequently worked in Geneva and Copenhagen and a line soon to be opened in Brussels. Henry Gore, a civil engineer, told of a tramway he had built in Valparaiso and others he had inspected in New York, Philadelphia, New Orleans, Havana, Vera Cruz, and

Mexico City. George Hopkins, engineer of both the Metropolitan Street and North Metropolitan companies (and also of the Liverpool venture), and Thomas Bouch, engineer of the Pimlico, Peckham & Greenwich, set the committee's mind at rest as to the type of rail to be used. There was, however, some mystery about the backers of these schemes and, in particular, the extent of American interest in them. John Morris, a partner in the legal business of Ashurst and Morris which specialized in company promotion and was acting for the two companies which proposed to operate south of the river, would go no farther than to speak generally of 'some gentlemen in Copenhagen, some gentlemen in this country and some gentlemen connected with the American Tramways'. In 1870, of the Pimlico, Peckham & Greenwich Tramways' shares then issued (three-quarters of the total authorized), more than half were held by John Morris's brother, William, the contractor, and nearly one-sixth by Thomas Bouch, the engineer. The only other large shareholder was Morton O. Fisher, a former New York resident, who held an eighth. The rest was in the hands of various Danes. Unfortunately, no similar list survives for either of the two other companies, but American influences seem to have been strong in the North Metropolitan line. Its contractors were the American firm of Fisher and Parrish (who were also responsible for the first Liverpool tramways), and the North Metropolitan's first tramcars were built by Stephenson of New York. The Metropolitan Street also ordered its first cars from New York.[13] In the end Parliament authorized all three tramways, though not before it had halved the amount of capital to be raised by the North Metropolitan and Metropolitan Street companies.[14]

The L.G.O.C. reacted with considerable adroitness to the menacing developments of these years. After its own unsuccessful venture (which had been largely foisted on the London *gérants* from Paris), it never actively promoted

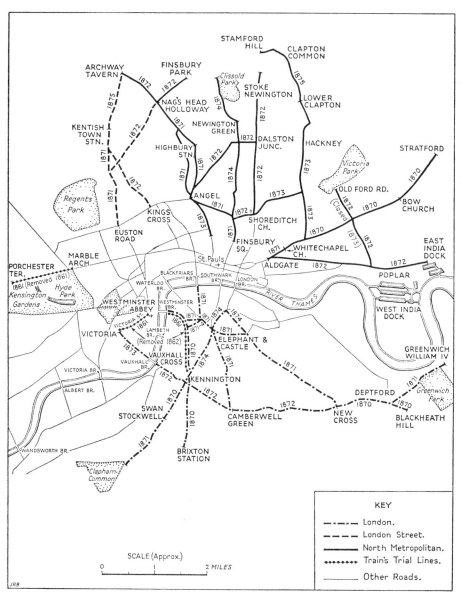

London's Tramways in 1875
(The Shepherd's Bush and Acton Line is shown on map on page 258)

tramways itself, though it did revive the London Omnibus Tramway Company Ltd. in 1860 as a means of opposing Train's activities.[15] At the same time, however, it was willing to negotiate with other tramway promoters. In 1860, for instance, when a Boston man named Ridley, who had been backing Train financially, decided to act on his own because of the way in which Train was alienating 'the existing interests',[16] the L.G.O.C. supported his Metropolitan Improved Transit Company.[17] This, however, came to nothing; nor did the even more optimistic scheme of another American, Dr. Holland, who proposed to float a £2,000,000 company to build tramways and take over the L.G.O.C. *in toto*.[18] The resumption of tramway promotion in the later 1860s, however, again found the L.G.O.C. in opposition. The faithful Bradfield was kept busy writing both anti-tramway pamphlets and Parliamentary petitions and enlisting the aid of the omnibus proprietors' committee.[19] At the end of May 1869, however, when the L.G.O.C. received word that 'the Government were determined to grant the three experimental lines',[20] it promptly changed its tactics. An agreement was signed with the North Metropolitan Company on 11 June,[21] and the omnibus proprietors' committee decided to call off its opposition to the Bills in return for the promoters paying £1,500 to cover its costs. In May 1870 an agreement was made with the North Metropolitan to horse its trams, and the income from this, as we have seen, added considerably to the L.G.O.C.'s profits. The North Metropolitan also gained from the agreement, for there was then an acute shortage of suitable horses; although the L.G.O.C. did not possess its own private source of supply, its agents knew the market well and could buy on the most advantageous terms. Another benefit to the tramway company was that the L.G.O.C. was not averse to reducing the omnibus service along tramway routes which it horsed.[22]

None of the 'experimental' tramways authorized in 1869

was allowed to penetrate into the heart of London. They were, in fact, confined to four main approach roads, and they provided additional transport facilities only to and from the fringes of central London. The Metropolitan Street Tramways were to run from the north end of Kennington Road (where it joined Westminster Bridge Road) to Kennington Park Road and then to divide into two, one route going down Brixton Road to a point just north of Brixton station and the other down Clapham Road as far as the junction with South Lambeth Road. A further line along Stockwell Road was to join the southern ends of the two routes.[23] Trams built to carry 22 passengers inside and 24 out (with space on the platform for others, standing) started to rumble down Brixton Road from Brixton to Kennington Church on 2 May 1870. They were described at the time as 'very commodious', and attention was drawn to their sun blinds—an obviously American touch—and to the velvet cushions.[24] The route was completed to its northern terminus at Westminster Bridge Road on 5 October 1870, and cars started to serve Clapham Road on 7 December.[25] It was not until later that month that the other company south of the Thames, the Pimlico, Peckham & Greenwich, opened the first part of its route. It had been authorized to build a tramway (much of it single line) from the junction of Kennington Lane and Harleyford Road via Kennington Oval, Camberwell New Road, Peckham High Street and Queen's Road to New Cross, and from there via Deptford Bridge to a terminus at the junction of Lewisham Road and Blackheath Hill.[26] The first section, from Blackheath Hill to New Cross, was opened on 13 December. On the other side of the river, the first $2\frac{1}{2}$ miles of the North Metropolitan's line, from Whitechapel Church along the Mile End Road to Bow Church, was opened on 9 May 1870.[27] All three companies had agreed to charge not more than 1d. per mile, subject to a minimum fare of 3d. which could, after three years, be reduced to 2d. if the

Board of Trade thought that the circumstances warranted this. In fact, on the two original routes the fare was 2d. The companies were also obliged to provide workmen's fares at not more than ½d. a mile with a 1d. minimum. Workmen's trams were run by the North Metropolitan from the outset; they started at 4.45 in the morning. South of the river workmen's trams operated between 5 and 7 a.m. The returning workmen could take any tram leaving after 6 p.m.; but they had to travel on the top deck.[28] Normal fares on a number of journeys, however, soon fell to the level of workmen's and made workmen's tickets unnecessary for such distances.

Extension and amalgamation

Even before the first trams started to run, the three companies came to Parliament with development plans. The North Metropolitan, which had been allowed to raise up to £112,500 for its Mile End Road scheme, now sought to raise a further £300,000 to extend its activities to north London. It proposed to build a tramway from the foot of Highgate Hill (by the present Archway underground station) down Holloway Road, Upper Street and High Street, Islington, to the Angel, and from there along City Road to Finsbury Square and Moorgate. It also proposed to bring its other terminus forward from Whitechapel to High Street, Aldgate, and to extend its original lines in the east along the Romford and Leytonstone Roads. The Pimlico, Peckham & Greenwich had equally grandiose schemes south of the river. In 1869 it had been allowed to raise £56,250: now it applied to raise a further £200,000 to extend its lines over both Lambeth and Vauxhall Bridges into Victoria Street and in almost all directions from the Elephant & Castle: to the south side of the Blackfriars, Westminster and Lambeth Bridges, down Walworth and Camberwell Roads, and along the New and Old Kent Roads. Compared with these proposals, those of the third company, the Metropolitan Street Tramways, were quite modest. Having been authorized to raise £150,000 in 1869, it now sought only a further £37,000 to take its northern terminus nearer to Westminster Bridge and its southern termini to Clapham and Acre Lane, Brixton. There was already a move afoot, however, for the two companies south of the river to join forces. The Pimlico's Bill of 1870 contained a clause giving it powers to make traffic arrangements with the Metropolitan Street, and at the end of the year the two of them merged to form a new concern, the London Tramways Company Ltd.[29] Moreover, this company developed interests north of the river. Four of its leading members had, in fact, already been named as promoters of a new undertaking, the London Street Tramways, which sought to open up an area to the west of the North Metropolitan's proposed new line through Holloway.[30] It applied to Parliament to raise £125,000 to build tramways from the south end of Hampstead Road (by Euston Road) to Holloway Road via Camden Town and Camden Road; and from King's Cross along (Royal) College Street to the Midland Railway station in Kentish Town.

Parliament passed the Bills of all four companies.[31] (The L.G.O.C. noted that 'the influence of the Board of Trade' would make impossible any serious opposition to them.[32]) Although not all the tramways then authorized were built, by the end of the session of 1870 rights had been allotted for all the most valuable thoroughfares in the immediate vicinity of London—in those districts, that is, where the street authorities were agreeable to tramways being laid. But no lines had yet penetrated the central area itself, During the second half of 1870 it was clear from the tramways already open that the new cars were attracting a great volume of traffic. The North Metropolitan, for instance, carried more than 1,000,000 passengers on its Bow–Whitechapel route during its first six months and its chairman

confidently forecast a dividend of 12 per cent.[33] The traffic
would become even greater if passengers could be carried
into central London instead of being set down at its
boundaries. History was now repeating itself. Just as in
1831 the omnibus proprietors had made a great and successful effort to be allowed to share in the traffic of London's
central streets in order to exploit their new vehicle to the
full, so the tramways now made a similar attempt to exploit
theirs. The time was clearly ripe to close in on at least the
Thames bridges and the great east–west route through Oxford
Street and High Holborn. But history rarely manages to
repeat itself exactly. A similar situation had recurred but
the underlying circumstances were quite different. The
opposition was much stronger in 1870 than it had been in
1831. When the tramway companies tried to penetrate the
central area, they received from the authorities not a
sympathetic hearing (as in 1831) but the same unrelenting
hostility which had defeated Train nine years before. This
hostility was to prove too strong for them, too.

Failure to penetrate into central London

The three tramway schemes which had been authorized in
1869 had all been situated in friendly territory. Nobody
ever imagined that these tramways would obstruct other
traffic, for they ran for most of their length down wide,
welcoming roads. The local residents in these suburbs
looked on them with favour, for they promised additional
transport facilities and lower fares. The street authorities
were also well disposed towards them, for they promised to
help with the upkeep of the roads. The companies' responsibility for maintaining those parts of the road through
which their track ran was, a tramways spokesman claimed,
worth up to £500 per mile per year.[34] Moreover, there was
also the possibility of further gains in the future, for the
Acts of 1869 gave the street authorities the right of com-
pulsory purchase after 21 years. The new form of transport

had much to commend it to inhabitants in suburban areas both as residents and as ratepayers.

The tramway schemes authorized in 1870 were also supported by the street authorities concerned; but such support could obviously not be expected when the tramways sought to penetrate central London itself. In 1870, however, the Board of Trade, in its efforts to encourage tramway promotion, had introduced a Bill which, if it had been passed in its original form, would have greatly weakened the street authorities' position. The view was taken that tramways had already proved themselves of value to the community. If only the relationship between the companies and the local authorities and such details as the maximum fares and the minimum street widths could be generally agreed, then it should be possible to authorize tramways merely by Board of Trade certificate, without the need for a number of separate private Bills. In formulating these basic conditions the Board of Trade drew upon experience gained during the two previous Parliamentary sessions. Tramways were made more attractive to local authorities by a modification in the 21-year purchase arrangements. According to the three private Acts of 1869, the purchase price was to include a payment for the goodwill of the undertaking: now the local authorities were to pay only for the property and materials.[35] On the other hand, the powers of a local authority to veto a tramway proposal were to be much reduced. If, after a public inquiry, it was decided by the Board of Trade that a tramway should be built, even though the local authority objected, the local authority would have very little means of redress. It is true that the Board of Trade's certificates had to be laid on the table of both Houses of Parliament, but this would be something of a formality.[36] Parliament did not have to approve them; they assumed the force of law if not objected to within a given length of time. If the Bill had been passed in this form, there can be little doubt that tramways would have been laid in central London. It was an astute move on the part of the tramway supporters; but how much was the work of a favourably disposed Board of Trade and how much of tramway pressure groups, it is impossible to say. The surviving Board of Trade papers are silent about this episode.[37]

The whole scheme, however, miscarried. The Bill was badly mauled in the Commons' committee, and the Board of Trade had to beat a retreat—a withdrawal no doubt made all the swifter by the absence of its President: John Bright fell seriously ill in February 1870 and for a long time was unable to read or even to sign his own name.[38] Indeed the Board of Trade was virtually without a minister until the following December when Bright resigned. The Bill suffered in consequence. Board of Trade certificates requiring no formal Parliamentary sanction were rejected in favour of Provisional Orders, which needed such approval. Not only had the sanction of street authorities still to be obtained but a new category of opponents, known as frontagers (owners and occupiers of property along roads where tramways were proposed), had the right of appearing both at Board of Trade inquiries and before Parliamentary committees. They, too, were to have a power of veto on the issuing of a Provisional Order in cases where a tramway ran within nine feet six inches of the kerb for a length of 30 feet and a third of their number objected.[39] By the time the Tramways Bill reached the statute book, therefore, the local property-owning interest had successfully reasserted itself. The only concession which the tramway promoters were given was the right to overcome local authority vetoes in cases where their track ran through several areas and had local authority support along two-thirds of its total length.[40] This clause, however, did not help the companies in their efforts to enter central London, for two of the key vestries, St. Marylebone and St. George, Hanover Square, were adamantly opposed to them.

69. George Francis Train

70. Train's Victoria Street Tram, 1861

71. Metropolitan Street Tramways Car at Kennington Church, 1870

72. An early North Metropolitan Tram at the Aldgate terminus

73. The Crystal Palace at Sydenham in 1854 (before erection of the end towers)

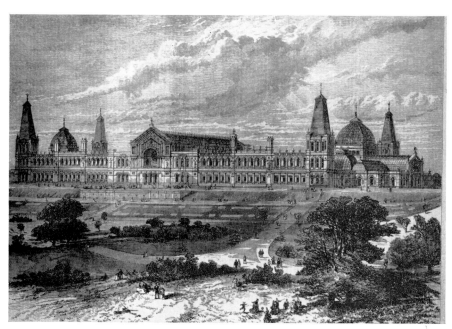

74. The Alexandra Palace, Muswell Hill, as rebuilt in 1875

75. The Fair at Fairlop Oak

76. The (second) Canterbury Music Hall, Lambeth, opened 1854

77. The Design for Watkin's Tower at Wembley

78. All that was built of Watkin's Tower

79. Sir Edward Watkin
80. James Staats Forbes

81. Sir John Wolfe Barry
82. Sir John Hawkshaw

83. The Metropolitan in the Outer Suburbs: train passing Kingsbury (now Neasden), about 1896

84. The Metropolitan arrives at Chesham, 1889

85. District Railway Train at West Brompton, May 1876

86. The District Station at Hounslow Town, opened in 1883 (photographed in 1905)

The way seemed to be blocked as surely as it had ever been. But all was not yet lost. The debate on the Tramways Bill did bring upon the scene another local authority and, for a time, it seemed as if its friendly intervention might offset the vestries' hostility. In most towns the local authority and the street authority were one and the same; but in London since 1855 the Metropolitan Board of Works, elected not by direct vote but by the vestries and district boards, had been responsible for major improvements (such as the building of the Victoria Embankment, which we have noticed), while the vestries and district boards themselves continued to look after more strictly local affairs, including the upkeep of the streets. While the Tramways Bill was passing through its committee stage, the Metropolitan Board of Works demanded to be recognized as the authority responsible for sanctioning tramways in the London area (apart from the City), and on 11 April the Parliamentary committee agreed to this by the Chairman's casting vote.[41] These new powers did not allow the Metropolitan Board of Works to overrule the vetoes of the street authorities when promoters sought their franchise by Provisional Order under the 1870 Act. But the tramway companies were still, of course, at liberty to proceed by the traditional method of a private Bill, and in this case the tramway authority's support, if forthcoming, was likely to go far to cancel out the street authority's opposition.

The Metropolitan Board of Works did, in fact, take a favourable view of tramways in central London, for, representing as it did all smaller authorities, it was not so vulnerable to pressure from any particular locality. It had the interests of the metropolis as a whole at heart and was concerned to form a co-ordinated tramway system for the whole of London. In the session of 1871 it was asked to comment on a vast number of new schemes, including some which were promoted by companies other than those already in operation. There were in all 105 miles of tramway

P

proposed (to be compared with $10\frac{3}{4}$ miles then open, $1\frac{1}{4}$ miles about to be opened, and 31 miles already authorized and under construction).[42] It decided not to build any tramways itself (as it was permitted to do under the Tramways Act) but laid down a number of general principles which it would follow when deciding on the merits of the various applications from private concerns. Every main line from the centre to the suburbs, for instance, was to be in the hands of a single company for the whole of its length. Applications were to be refused in cases where it was proposed to use roads through which there was not already a well-supported omnibus route and, therefore, no large potential traffic. Acting on these principles, the Board raised no objection to the existing companies building certain lines in central London. It approved, for instance, a line along Bayswater Road, Oxford Street and High Holborn; another along Knightsbridge and Piccadilly; and a third down Haymarket, Cockspur Street and Whitehall Place to the Embankment and then across Westminster Bridge.[43] In every case, the Parliamentary committees on the private Bills supported the Metropolitan Board of Works' recommendations even when the street authorities were in opposition.[44]

With the prospect of tramways down Oxford street and across the Thames bridges, including Westminster Bridge, the opposition, led by Alexander Beresford-Hope, M.P., who had been one of Train's leading opponents, really roused itself. Sclater-Booth, chairman of the 1869 committee and a member of the committee on the Tramways Bill, later confessed that that Bill was 'passed like all Acts of last session, at 2 or 3 o'clock in the morning in solemn silence. The Board of Trade alone was responsible.' Another member claimed that 'the Board of Trade had acted in the most secret manner' and urged that the sooner it was reformed, the better.[45] As a result of this mounting opposition, all the proposals for building tramways in central

London were, on their third reading, postponed until the following session, and a joint select committee of both Houses was then formed to consider them. This committee recommended that the procedure on private Bills should be brought into line with that on Provisional Orders.[46] Consent of street authorities thus became a prerequisite of all tramways schemes whether promoted by Provisional Orders or private Bills, and frontagers had rights of veto in narrow streets. So, in the session of 1872, Parliament declared central London a zone prohibited to tramcars, and, by doing so, it postponed for many years the building of anything approaching a tramway system in the London area. Even the route from the northern end of Vauxhall Bridge Road to Blackheath—the only one to cross the river—was, in fact, interrupted at Vauxhall Bridge, considered to be too steep for safe operation; passengers had to be carried between the northern and southern section by omnibus.[47]

The three tramway companies win a large traffic

The existing companies, excluded from central London, settled down to developing traffic in their own suburbs. The London Tramways secured as managing director Thomas Kenworthy Rowbotham, who had been previously for 15 years general manager of the North British Railway; and A. J. Mundella, M.P., the Nottingham manufacturer and a future President of the Board of Trade, was a director in the early years and sometimes presided at shareholders' meetings. Both served the company until 1875. The London Street Tramways appointed as their secretary J. Barber Glenn, who was to make a considerable reputation for himself as a tramway administrator. It was the North Metropolitan, however, under the chairmanship of George Richardson, which was able to show the greatest progress in the early 1870s. It gained extensive new powers in 1871 to enlarge its system in north and east London, and these lines were completed by 1874.[48] In June of that year $1\frac{1}{2}$ miles of tramway were also opened in west London, from Shepherd's Bush along the Uxbridge Road, the original promoters being a new company known as the Southall, Ealing & Shepherd's Bush Tram-Railway.[49]

The tramways' failure to penetrate the streets of central London gave the omnibuses another lease of life. The omnibuses alone could tap the densest traffic of the central area, and since few of those who travelled in from the suburbs wanted to be set down on the fringes of London, they still retained much of the traffic along the tram routes too, but only at the cost of cutting—sometimes halving—their fares.[50] Nevertheless, despite these reductions, the omnibuses could not compete with tramway fares. From Westminster Bridge to Greenwich, for example, a journey of $6\frac{1}{4}$ miles, cost 4d. by tramcar. By 1872, 69 per cent. of the London Tramways' fares were 2d. ones.[51] The tramways were not only carrying the middle classes; they were more particularly catering for sections of the working classes who previously had not been able to afford to ride. This probably explains the very large rate of growth of tramway traffic at a time when the omnibuses' own traffic was also on the increase. After just over six years' operation the tramways could boast almost as many passengers as the L.G.O.C. In 1875, 48,900,000 travelled by tramcar and 49,720,000 by L.G.O.C. omnibus.[52] More than half of the tramways' total—27,750,000—was carried by the North Metropolitan in over 160 cars on its busy system in north and east London. The London Tramways in that year carried nearly 15,800,000 in 140 cars over its 20 miles of track; and the London Street, a very much smaller undertaking—it had only $5\frac{1}{2}$ miles in operation—5,350,000 in 48 cars. The three tramway companies' returns show that two of them, at least, had already developed into sizeable business ventures. Their traffic receipts and working expenses were:

TRAFFIC RECEIPTS AND WORKING EXPENSES OF THE
THREE LONDON TRAMWAY COMPANIES IN 1875

	Traffic receipts	*Working expenses*
North Metropolitan (capital expended £684,566)	£234,266	£175,942
London Tramways (capital expended £418,665)	£138,050	£123,811
London Street Tramways (capital expended £94,900)	£43,947	£34,860

Source: Robinson Souttar, 'Street Tramways', *Minutes of Proceedings of the Institution of Civil Engineers, 50* (1876-77), 25-26.

On these figures the tramways were clearly not so profitable as had originally been promised by their capital-hungry promoters. The 12 per cent. dividend on the ordinary shares promised—and paid—by the North Metropolitan in its first year was soon reduced, but even so the company continued to give a very respectable return. In 1875 it was 8¼ per cent. The London Street paid 7¼ per cent. that year. The London Tramways were also accustomed to paying dividends of this order, but they had run into difficulties; having recently opened an unremunerative stretch of line and being also involved in heavy compensation claims, they were unable to pay anything in 1875. Tramways, like other forms of passenger transport in London, were a considerable gain to the community but by no means always so valuable an asset to those who had invested in them.

CHAPTER SEVEN

LATE VICTORIAN LONDON

(I) THE RAILWAYS

During the later nineteenth century, as the outward movement to homes in the suburbs gathered pace, the resident population of the inner areas declined. From 1873 to 1896 prices fell, real earnings rose, and more people could afford public transport. As the number of 'commuters' increased, so did the 'off-peak' traffic: the spread of department and multiple stores brought housewives to the West End and the suburban shopping streets; and the reduction in working hours allowed more time for leisure activities of all kinds. The railway companies, both main-line and underground, extended their suburban systems as London spread outwards, but within central London the only new development was the completion of the Inner Circle. This was achieved only at immense cost and with wretched commercial results—which exacerbated the already poor relations between the Metropolitan and District companies.

THE INCREASE OF PURCHASING POWER

THE SPREAD of transport facilities described in the previous two chapters was a response to greater needs as London's population grew. The tax returns show that middle-class incomes were then growing very rapidly,[1] and London, the financial and commercial centre of the country—and, in terms of numbers employed, its leading manufacturing area[2] —was the great stronghold of the middle classes. These were the people who were seeking houses farther and farther away from their places of work, and as their numbers grew, so their craving for suburbia brought into existence more and better transport facilities. Improved transport services, in their turn, made suburban living more attractive, and so the outward movement gained pace, demand creating new facilities and new facilities generating more traffic. In the 1880s the four places with the most rapid rate of population growth in the whole of England and Wales were all suburbs of London, and in the following decade eight London suburbs were among those at the head of the list.[3]

These forces of attraction from the fringes continued to be associated with others, no less powerful, of repulsion from the centre. Economic growth which made possible the rapid rise of the middle classes also created a demand for more and more central sites for business purposes of one sort or another, including railway building and road improvement. This was an old trend but, from the middle of the nineteenth century, it became much more pronounced. The extent to which private dwellings were removed to make room for shops, offices and warehouses may be seen in the census returns for the City. Its residential population, more or less stationary in the first half of the century, fell sharply after 1850: between 1851 and 1871 it dropped from 128,000 to 75,000.[4] Westminster, Holborn, Finsbury and St. Marylebone also started to lose residents after 1860, but during the 1860s the rate of loss was low. The real decline in population in these districts dates from the early 1870s. A change in the economic climate then began which gave fresh impetus to London's outward growth.

Prices, having generally moved upwards in the third quarter of the nineteenth century, began to fall after 1873. This was caused partly by the opening up of primary producing areas abroad—resulting in a cheapening of food and raw materials—and partly by the introduction of new cost-reducing techniques in industry. Competition was greatly intensified in all sectors of the economy and profit margins shrank. This in turn led business men to seek further ways of cutting their costs in an effort to maintain, or increase, their profits. In this laudable task many were successful. The income tax returns show that the middle classes continued to grow in numbers, although perhaps not so quickly as during the 1860s.[5] And all sections of the community benefited from the prolonged fall in the cost of living. Real incomes per head probably rose at the remarkably high rate of about 25 per cent. per decade in the 1880s and early 1890s.[6] Now, while the middle classes continued to multiply and flourish, the working classes also had more to spend; and some of their extra income was used to ride when they would otherwise have walked—or not made the journey at all.

Under these circumstances the number of commuters increased even more rapidly than before, and the traffic as a whole came to be much less predominantly middle class. Workmen's fares which, as we have noticed, were introduced to London in 1864, were greatly extended; and, as we shall see later in this chapter, a widespread cut in fares generally enabled many others to ride to work from areas where, or at times when, workmen's fares were not available. Central London's resident population went on falling as its working population grew.

RESIDENT POPULATION OF THE CITY, WESTMINSTER
AND HOLBORN 1871–1901

	1871	1881	1891	1901
City	74,897	50,652	37,702	26,923
Westminster	248,363	229,784	201,969	183,011
Holborn	93,423	78,634	66,781	59,405

By contrast, the day population of the City grew very fast. It increased from 170,000 in 1866 to 261,000 in 1881, 301,000 in 1891, and 360,000 at the beginning of the twentieth century.[7]

In addition to making possible a greater number of journeys to and from work, rising earnings and lower fares also led to a big increase in travelling about for other purposes—short trips from one part of London to another, for instance. It is also likely that the spread of new methods of retail trade and the growing popularity of various forms of entertainment had some considerable influence on traffic receipts.

Travel for shopping

These years saw the real growth, if not the beginnings, of the department store. Shoolbred's of Tottenham Court Road could already claim in the middle of the nineteenth century 'a larger stock and greater choice of every description of drapery and furnishing goods than at any other warehouse in the kingdom'.[8] Well-known firms of today such as Peter Robinson, Marshall & Snelgrove and Swan & Edgar also have a history which dates back to the earlier part of the nineteenth century, although they did not begin to take on their modern appearance until later Victorian times. The earliest development of a department store on the modern pattern is traditionally attributed to Aristide and Marguérite Boucicaut, who, in 1852, took over the direction of a small Paris drapery shop, the *Bon Marché*, and in 1863 began to branch out into other lines.[9] Prominent among the first English department stores were the Civil Service Supply Association (1865) and the Civil Service Co-operative Society Ltd.(1866), soon to be followed by the Army & Navy, which was launched in 1872 as the Army and Navy Co-operative Society Ltd. By the end of the 1870s the annual sales of the C.S.S.A. and the A. & N. had each reached the impressive total of £1,500,000.[10] Harrods, in developing from a small one-shop family business into a department store, appears to have owed something to the example of these middle-class consumer retail societies. By 1880 the firm was employing nearly 100 people and, by 1889, when it became a limited company, its turnover had reached £250,000 per year. Subsequently, under Richard Burbidge's management, the business made even more rapid progress, and the now familiar terracotta frontage in Brompton Road, put up in the early years of the present century, was the visible evidence of this.[11]

Burbidge had received part of his training at Whiteley's. The Universal Provider's rise in the world was the most impressive of all among London's department stores.

Whiteley's first shop had been opened in Westbourne Grove in 1863. By 1867 he was leasing others nearby and going into new lines of business. By 1872 he occupied ten shops and employed more than 600 assistants, and when the business was turned into a company in 1899, its assets were valued at over £1,600,000.[12] While stores such as these had their local *clientèle*—Sala, for instance, particularly noted the residents of 'the aristocratic and refined Tyburnia' shopping at Whiteley's[13]—they also attracted customers from other parts of London. By 1885 more than 700 omnibuses per day brought customers to Whiteley's, and when the L.G.O.C. refused to put on a special service to bring in well-to-do shoppers from fashionable Regent's Park and prosperous Maida Vale, the Universal Provider for a time ran one of his own.[14] The underground, too, began to run to Paddington only a few weeks before he opened his first shop and came much nearer, to Queen's Road, Bayswater, in 1868. It brought many customers, as it was already doing, by way of its Gower Street station, to Shoolbred's.[15] By 1892 the District Railway even found it worth while to start a parcels service, chiefly to relieve shoppers on their homeward journey.[16] All in all, the spread of department stores must have generated a considerable traffic for the various transport undertakings, and, conversely, good transport services were a prerequisite of the department stores' success. A few wealthy shoppers still continued to travel in their own carriages and some others took cabs. But the majority came by train or omnibus, and this was a particularly valuable source of income to the operators. Coming outside the peak hours, it caused seats to be filled which would otherwise have been quite unremunerative.

The other important development in retailing—the spread of multiple shops—also occurred during this period. Again, the beginnings are to be found before the 1870s, in ventures such as W. H. Smith's railway bookstalls or the shops of the Singer Sewing Machine Co.; but the real growth occurred after 1870, particularly in the grocery and footwear trades.[17] The International Tea Co., the Home and Colonial, Eastmans, Freeman, Hardy & Willis, Stead & Simpson, and George Oliver all became familiar names. Notable, too, in the London area were the ventures of the Sainsburys, who opened their first shop in Drury Lane in 1869,[18] and of the Scot, Thomas Lipton, who, having previously concentrated his activities outside London, came to the capital at the end of the 1880s and opened 70 branches within three years.[19] In so far as these multiples replaced the small shopkeepers, they would not cause more travelling about. But if they provided certain busy shopping centres with bargains which could not be had elsewhere, perhaps they did cause a greater use of London's transport facilities. As fares became much cheaper, it may have paid the careful housewife to venture farther afield to visit shops where perhaps a copper or two could be saved on each purchase. Nowadays every main shopping area has its multiples; but in the later nineteenth century, while they were spreading—and before the days of resale price maintenance—presumably certain areas were better served than others.

Travel for pleasure

While the housewife was being offered more bargains, her husband was enjoying a slightly shorter working week. The Saturday half-holiday became general, and this greatly stimulated the spread of outdoor activities of one sort and another. The sports club came into its own, and the better teams started to win a following, particularly when cups and trophies were introduced into the games. The Football Association, for instance, held its first cup competition in 1872. The Cup Final, held first at the Kennington Oval and then (after 1895) in the grounds of the Crystal Palace, aroused a growing interest. By the end of the century it had become a major attraction, 'one of the sights of the London year, when over 100,000 screaming people are standing upon the slope at Sydenham'.[20] Besides the Saturday afternoons, extra general holidays had been added to the two existing ones, Christmas Day and Good Friday. By the Bank Holiday Act of 1871 Boxing Day, Easter Monday, Whit Monday and August Monday also became 'days off'.[21] Excursion traffic, which, as we have seen, was developing in the middle of the nineteenth century at fares of up to three or four shillings return, grew more extensive. The Great Western, for instance, did good business up the Thames Valley to Windsor for 2s. 6d. return or to Henley for 3s. 6d.[22] Excursion fares to Margate or to the south coast appear to have varied at different times between 3s. 6d. (the excursion rate to Brighton in the middle of the century and the rate to Margate, Hastings and Dover at the end of the 1860s) and 5s.[23] Despite the sabbatarians' protests, cheap tickets continued to be issued on Sundays, too, and these enabled large numbers of Londoners to get away into the country or to the seaside for the day. So early as 1868 the total for a fine summer Sunday was estimated at 250,000.[24]

Exhibitions, too, continued to enjoy great popularity, and from the 1870s there were many more of them. At first they were held on land in Kensington to the south of the Albert Hall. The Fisheries Exhibition (1883), the Health Exhibition (1884), the Inventions Exhibition (1885), and the Colonial & Indian Exhibition (1886) drew large crowds. Every year more people flocked to Kensington, 2,750,000 visiting the first of these exhibitions and 5,500,000 the last.[25] The railway companies contributed considerably to this success by issuing from stations in the London area special return tickets which included the price of admission. At first passengers had to walk up the road from South Kensington station, but in 1885 a subway was opened which led to the exhibition site, 1d. toll being charged.[26] By 1886, if not before, artisans' tickets were on sale which enabled the holder to travel to South Kensington, visit the exhibition and return home again, all for a shilling.[27] After 1886, when the site was needed for the building of the Imperial Institute, the series of exhibitions was continued on land at Earl's Court which belonged to the District Railway. In 1894 London Exhibitions Ltd. took a lease of the Earl's Court site to develop it as an exhibition and pleasure ground, and among the attractions was a Great Wheel, based on a very popular and profitable feature of the 1893 World Fair in Chicago.[28] A little to the north, just over the main road to Hammersmith, the vast Olympia building, opened in 1886, was also used for exhibitions and shows of all kinds. In the winter of 1889–90, for instance, Barnum's Show drew huge crowds there, and during 1890 it was a centre for the then current roller-skating craze. Olympia was well served by public transport. By the later 1880s, 331 trains stopped at the nearby Addison Road station every day and 226 omnibuses passed the entrance doors.[29] In another part of London there was another exhibition hall which attracted a different *clientèle*. This was the Agricultural Hall in Upper Street, Islington, a much older building, which dated from the early 1860s. By the later nineteenth century it had become the home of many trade shows, and these attracted business men from all over the country.[30] And, of course, that even older creation, the Crystal Palace, still remained the popular resort in south London. Its north London imitation at Alexandra Palace (rebuilt in 1875, after the fire which had gutted the original building a few days after its opening) also had its attractions, including one of the largest organs in the world.[31]

The irrepressible Sir Edward Watkin was among those who became interested in the exhibition business. He was attracted to it by the huge success of the 985-foot Eiffel Tower, the receipts from which in its first year alone (1889) were said to have repaid more than two-thirds of the initial cost. In August 1889, Watkin and several of his associates in the Metropolitan Railway decided to go one better and put up a tower over 1,000 feet high. They acquired 280 acres of land at Wembley Park to which, as we shall see later in this chapter, the Metropolitan Railway had by then been extended.[32] This site, Watkin confidently hoped, would become the greatest of London's pleasure and exhibition grounds, the huge mass of ironwork, visible for miles around, serving as a constant reminder of its existence and attracting large crowds down the railway from Baker Street. But Watkin's tower, unlike the similar and more modest structure which was then put up at Blackpool, never rose to such heights. The Metropolitan Tower Construction Company, which had been formed to build it and to develop the site, was able to raise only £27,000, and although the Metropolitan Railway came to the rescue with a further £60,000, the tower could only be built to the first stage, a mere 200 feet up. This rather grotesque and completely useless product of misplaced determination was eventually opened to the public in May 1896; but during its first six months—when, one would have supposed, curiosity alone might have produced a substantial number of visitors —only 18,500 people paid to ascend. By then, however, a cycle track and sports ground had been laid out, and during the same six months more than 100,000 people in all entered the park.[33] The Tower Construction Company went into liquidation a year or two later and surrendered its lease to the company owning the land,[34] which in 1907 was renamed the Wembley Park Estate Company Ltd. In the same year Watkin's tower was taken down, being finally removed with explosives.

Despite Watkin's great miscalculation, there could be no doubting the growing taste for all kinds of enlightenment and entertainment. This was also to be seen in the spread of theatres and musical performances of various kinds at, for instance, the Albert Hall (opened in 1871) or the Queen's Hall (1893). The Gilbert and Sullivan operas were a product of these years, and promenade concerts came into vogue at the end of them. Of far greater interest to most Londoners, however, were the music halls which then reached their heyday. They developed from singing rooms at public houses, the first of them, Canterbury Hall off the Westminster Bridge Road, having opened in 1849. By the early 1860s there were 23 music halls in London, and one of them, the recently-opened Oxford Music Hall at the corner of Tottenham Court Road and Oxford Street, counted 428,000 customers within the course of a single year.[35] In the later nineteenth century some of the earlier music halls were pulled (or burnt) down, and new and larger ones were put up. By the early 1890s there were 35 major music halls in London entertaining altogether an average of 45,000 people per night, or 14,000,000 per year. The largest of them, the Alhambra, the Empire, the Pavilion, the Canterbury, the Paragon and the Victoria Palace, each had nightly audiences of about 2,000 people.[36] 'The multitudes of all classes of the people who attend the theatres and music halls of London', declared a parliamentary committee in 1892, 'find no parallel in any other part of the country.'[37]

It is quite impossible to assess the significance, from a transport point of view, of all this increase in leisure-time activity; but the numbers visiting exhibitions and entertainments of all kinds were so considerable that it must have been an appreciable item in increasing traffic receipts. Certainly the exhibitions were of importance to the District Railway.[38] People were moving about much more extensively, and while some—probably the majority—usually walked, these activities must have brought many more fares to the trains, omnibuses, trams and cabs. And the more London emerged as the centre of not only government and business but also of entertainment, the more it attracted visitors from other parts of the country and from abroad. The great increase in the number of hotels is a clear indication of this. Not only were Londoners riding about much more, but an increasing number of visitors to the capital was helping to swell the total.

The population of Greater London (the City and Metropolitan Police areas) grew from just over 4,200,000 in 1875 to about 6,000,000 in 1895. From information collected for the Royal Commission on London Traffic at the beginning of the present century and from other sources,[39] it would seem that the number of journeys made by train, tram and omnibus perhaps increased from some 275,000,000 per year to about 1,000,000,000 per year during the same period. So, while London's population grew by rather less than 50 per cent. in these 20 years—in itself a remarkable rate of growth—the number of journeys in the London area appears to have risen by nearly 300 per cent. and the number of journeys per head of London's resident population from about 65 to over 165.

Clearly, these were years full of opportunity for London's transport undertakings. Which of them was able to make the most of the growing traffic?

The Metropolitan and District Railways extend their lines into the suburbs and beyond

As has been seen in the three preceding chapters, the various forms of public transport were each developing specialized functions before the 1870s. The railway was best suited to carrying people medium or longer distances across London and, in particular, to and from the suburbs. The omnibus flourished on the short-distance traffic, especially that in the busiest streets. The tram could also attract short-distance passengers but was restricted to main roads in certain of the suburbs. And, finally, the cab carried the more expensive fares, chiefly in the central area.

Since the railways' brightest prospects lay in the suburbs, it is not surprising that such railway building as there was in the last quarter of the nineteenth century was almost entirely confined to extensions into the suburbs and beyond, and to the improvement of the facilities for handling suburban traffic in and out of the central termini. The District Railway, for instance, fanned out from the outer limits of its original line to serve many areas to the west and south-west. A short link at Hammersmith to the London & South Western Railway allowed District trains to run over South Western tracks to Richmond from 1 June 1877. Two years later, on 1 July 1879, a three-mile branch was opened from Turnham Green to Ealing (Broadway) and on 1 March 1880 another from West Brompton through Walham Green to the north side of Putney Bridge.[40] These extensions were accompanied by considerable house-building activity in the areas concerned; together with similar growth in other suburbs where new, or better, railway services had become available, this may explain the prolonging of the building cycle in London at that time.[41] On 1 May 1883 an independent company opened a railway from the District's Ealing branch at Mill Hill Park (now Acton Town) to Hounslow and this was worked by the District's trains.[42] Finally, on 3 June 1889, the London & South Western opened a four-mile stretch of railway from its route centre at Wimbledon through Wimbledon Park, Southfields and East Putney—stations described at the time as 'of that style of architecture known as Early English'[43]— and across the river to make an end-on link with the District on the north side of Putney Bridge. This was the result of years of scheming to take the District to Barnes or Kingston, which the South Western successfully held off.[44]

Although the Metropolitan was only a few months behind its rival in running trains over the South Western's rails to Richmond—the Metropolitan's through service started on 1 October 1877—its own railway-building activities were directed to the north-west. By 1890 it had penetrated much farther in this direction than the District had advanced to the west and south-west; but whereas the District, in association with the London & South Western, contrived to seek

Q

traffic along a number of branches covering quite a wide
arc of territory—Ealing, Hounslow, Richmond and Putney/
Wimbledon—the Metropolitan concentrated, with one
minor aberration, upon gradually extending one line, its
St. John's Wood feeder, and thrusting right out into the
country. The exception was the Latimer Road & Acton
Railway, promoted by a nominally independent company
to run from the Hammersmith & City to Acton, on the
Great Western main line. An Act was passed in 1882 and
some construction was begun; but finance was never
secured and an abandoning Act was obtained in 1900.[45]

The Metropolitan Extension, as the line out from Baker
Street came to be called, was opened from Swiss Cottage
to West End Lane, Hampstead, on 30 June 1879; to
Willesden on the following 24 November; and to Harrow
on 2 August 1880.[46] One of the advantages of this extension
was that the locomotive and carriage repair shops could be
removed from overcrowded quarters at Edgware Road to
more suitable premises at Neasden. In 1883 the Metropolitan & St. John's Wood lost even its appearance of
independence by becoming part of the Metropolitan. Its
single track had by then been doubled.[47] The line was further
extended to Pinner (25 May 1885), Rickmansworth (1
September 1887), Chesham (15 May 1889) and Aylesbury
(1 September 1892); and so at last brought to an end the
working of the mail-coach which left the Old Bell Inn,
Holborn, for Wendover at 3 p.m.[48] By 1897, 231 trains were
running to stations as far out as Rickmansworth every day
(both ways) and a further 18 to and from Aylesbury. New
locomotives and rolling stock were needed to work this
extra mileage. The Metropolitan departed from its well-
tried policy of using one standard type of locomotive
throughout its system when in 1891 it bought from Neilson
of Glasgow four 0-4-4 tank engines, numbered 67 to 70,
which were generally similar to James Stirling's Q class on
the South Eastern Railway. On the carriage side, two sets

of nine close-coupled, four-wheeled vehicles, built by Craven Brothers and Company of Sheffield in 1887, became the prototype of what came to be known as the Jubilee Stock. This was used on the Inner Circle as well as the Extension.[49]

The building of this long line into the country—at least, beyond Harrow—may be explained in terms of Watkin's determination to bring the Manchester, Sheffield & Lincolnshire Railway, of which he was also chairman, to London—and, indeed, to send trains on via the East London and South Eastern (which he also dominated) to the coast and, perhaps, even through the Channel Tunnel, in which far-sighted idea he also became very interested from the early 1880s. In 1887 he had told the Metropolitan's shareholders that one of the aims 'always discussed by proprietors and quite approved by them' was 'to break through the circle of railways to the north of their district which prevented them from getting out into the country and shaking hands with any new or old neighbours who wanted to get their traffic through London . . .'[50] This undoubtedly is one explanation of the Metropolitan's yearning for the open fields, miles away from London. Its long line did in fact become the route whereby the Manchester, Sheffield & Lincolnshire (by then renamed the Great Central) found its way to a terminus at Marylebone at the end of the 1890s.[51] But even so, the Metropolitan was never used as a means of getting the Great Central's traffic through London. Indeed, Baker Street remained an interchange station, not a junction. Passengers still had to change there as had always been the case ever since 1869, soon after the opening of the St. John's Wood Railway. By the later 1890s, when the Great Central's London Extension was opened, the Metropolitan's main line from Baker Street to the City, already carrying 528 passenger trains and 14 goods every day,[52] was in no position to handle any more traffic on its two tracks.

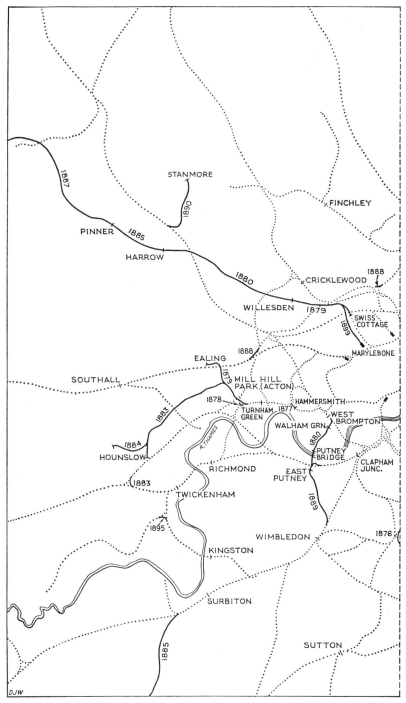

Railways opened between 1875 and 1900:

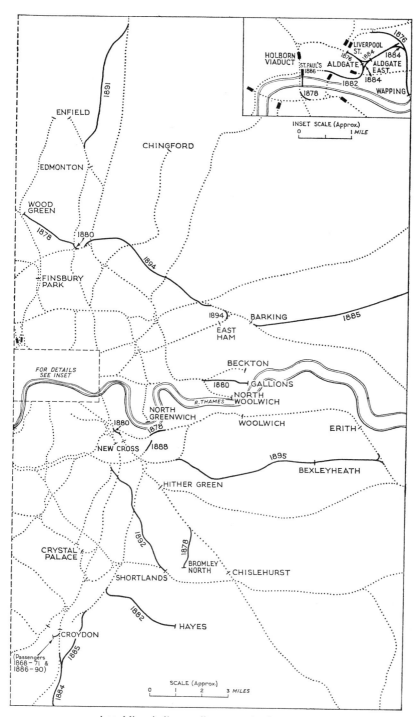

INSET SCALE (Approx.)
0   1 *MILE*

SCALE (Approx.)
0   1   2   3 *MILES*

dotted lines indicate railways previously opened

213

Another—and more plausible—explanation of the north-western thrust is to be found in the 'circle of railways to the north', to which Watkin referred. Each of these power-ful trunk lines had its own sphere of influence and would have reacted violently had the Metropolitan tried to fan out in the same way as the District had done. In any case, the Great Northern and the Midland, which between them had staked their claim to the traffic from all the suburbs from Tottenham round to Edgware, already fed many passengers on to the Metropolitan via the 'widened lines' from King's Cross to Moorgate Street.[53] The Great Western had an even longer tradition of association with the Metro-politan and also supplied it with traffic. There remained the London & North Western (which supplied the Metro-politan's rival, the District, with passengers round the Outer Circle), and it was into the London & North Western's territory that the Metropolitan in fact built its line. Watkin would, no doubt, have welcomed the possi-bility of a broad suburban network as a means of increasing the company's revenue. He was constantly stressing the importance of the growing yield from suburban traffic, as against the more static earnings of the underground in London itself. But, unlike the District, the Metropolitan had been largely forestalled in its efforts to develop its own suburban traffic on a wide front and, with the exception of its one long line into the country, had to be content with the revenue from passengers fed on to it by the Great Western, the Chatham, the Midland and, particularly, the Great Northern.

The Great Northern, the Great Eastern and the North London
Suburban traffic on the Great Northern grew so rapidly that it soon became an embarrassment to that company, for it started to interfere with the main-line goods traffic, the Great Northern's most profitable source of income. By the early 1880s, the company's chairman was commenting

upon the 'towns . . . springing up within two or three miles
of King's Cross' as fast as they could be built[54] and another
observer remarked upon the 'immense suburbs of working
class residences' which were covering sites by the railway
line towards Hornsey, 'occupied by people . . . connected
in their work with London'.[55] The return fare from Hornsey to the City was then (1884) 1s. 1d. first class, 9d. second
and 8d. third; and there were cheaper tickets on two
workmen's trains which ran at about 5 o'clock in the
morning.[56] Meanwhile similar growth in traffic was occur-
ring along the Edgware, High Barnet and Enfield branches.
Finchley, for instance, was served by 36 trains each way in
1876. In 1884 it had 45 and in 1887, 51.[57] Cheap and rapid
railway travel was creating new areas of population more
rapidly than ever. Finchley's population doubled between
1881 and 1901, and its rate of growth was in no way
exceptional. More and more trains were needed at the peak
hours. By 1890 they were passing Finsbury Park, the focus
of the Great Northern's suburban system and point of
interchange between the various lines, at the rate of one
every three minutes at the busiest times.[58] All this extra
traffic involved the Great Northern in heavy expenditure,
for the track had to be doubled, and then trebled, to
accommodate it, and on that route out of London this
entailed tunnelling as well as widening.[59] By the 1890s,
despite the greater capacity of the lines and of the carriages
(which were altered to seat ten in each compartment),[60]
rush-hour travelling was a constant cause of complaint.
There were not the serious accidents that there had been,[61]
but the service was as unsatisfactory as ever. And by the
early 1890s there were signs that the Great Northern's
suburban traffic had grown so large that the North London
and Metropolitan were starting to have difficulty in handling it.[62] By 1895 the annual total had reached about
25,000,000 single journeys and was growing at the rate of
about 1,000,000 per year.[63] That is to say, about 40,000

people were using the Great Northern's suburban services every day. Perhaps about a fifth of them travelled on early morning trains at reduced fares. Seven workmen's trains ran up to London before six o'clock, return tickets costing, for instance, 2d. from Finsbury Park, 3d. from Wood Green, 4d. from New Southgate or Finchley, and 5d. from High Barnet. They were followed by others on which reduced, but not drastically reduced, return fares were available— 3d. from Finsbury Park, 4d. from Hornsey, 5d. from Wood Green, 6d. from New Southgate, 7d. from Finchley and 9d. from High Barnet.(For comparison, the ordinary 3rd class returns were, respectively, 5d., 8d., 10d., 1s., 1s. 2d., and 1s. 6d.)[64]

The development of the Great Northern's 'suburban incubus' merits further investigation than is possible here. By encouraging this huge peak-hour traffic, the Great Northern was interfering with its profitable long-distance goods trains and involving itself in large outlays of capital. Was it driven to do this solely by the commuters themselves —more trains at cheap fares producing more traffic and, therefore, needing even more trains? Or do the land and property speculators enter the picture? Were they able to bring pressure to bear on the Great Northern directors? Indeed, were any of the directors or leading shareholders themselves involved in developing the areas which the new lines served?

The Great Eastern also developed a huge suburban traffic. Like the Great Northern, it had opened suburban lines in the years before 1875—and it added a branch to Wood Green (Palace Gates) in 1878[65]—but unlike its western neighbour it did not possess a heavy main-line goods traffic. It was obliged by its Act of 1864, which authorized the metropolitan extensions to Edmonton and Chingford, to run a workmen's train on each of those lines at the remarkably low return fare of 2d.[66] In fact, it provided early morning trains for this fare from so far north as

Enfield Town, 10¾ miles away, as well as others along its main line to the east. This led to a considerable migration to the places served by these trains where, presumably, for the same rent—or for a shilling a week less, to compensate for the rail fare—much better accommodation could be had than was available in central London. The workmen's traffic grew quickly. In 1884, the Great Eastern's general manager remarked, rather ungratefully perhaps, on the change which had come over Stamford Hill, Tottenham and Edmonton:

That used to be a very nice district indeed, occupied by good families, with houses of from £150 to £250 a year, with coach houses and stables, a garden and a few acres of land. But very soon after this obligation was put upon the Great Eastern to run workmen's trains . . . speculative builders went down into the neighbourhood and, as a consequence, each good house was one after another pulled down, and the district is given up entirely, I may say, now to the working man. I lived down there myself and I waited until most of my neighbours had gone; and then, at last, I was obliged to go.[67]

By 1884 more than 8,000 people were going to work every weekday on those trains from various stations, such as Ilford and Forest Gate, on the main line, and from the Edmonton and Walthamstow branches, the largest workmen's traffic on any of London's railways and, indeed, more than a quarter of the total of such traffic for the whole of the London area.[68] The trains ran at, or just after, five o'clock in the morning in time to get their passengers to work by six. For a time, special workmen's trains were run back at night but, remarked the disapproving general manager,

the men all came on to the station at whatever hour they might have left their work and accumulated in such large numbers and were such a constant source of annoyance by expectorating all over the station and smoking very much with short black pipes that we felt we had far better let them go home.[69]

Workmen's trains were later made available up to 7 a.m. Considerable extensions to Liverpool Street station were opened on 1 April 1894, enabling increased services to be provided to Forest Gate and Ilford, and by the beginning of the present century 19,000 people were using workmen's trains coming into the station.[70] After these trains came others loaded with clerks, 9 o'clock being 'a very common hour for the clerks to begin their work'.[71] In the 1880s this traffic was heavier than the workmen's,[72] and at the beginning of the present century (when 3d. returns were available for journeys starting 7 to 7.30 and 4d. returns for those starting between 7.30 and 8) this appears still to have been the case.[73] These cheap trains brought in 35,000 clerks every day, Walthamstow being then noted as 'largely the home of the half-fare traveller'.[74] In order to accommodate this vast host, second as well as third class carriages could be occupied. Firsts, the seats covered with oilskins, were reserved for women passengers.[75]

There was much discussion whether workmen's trains paid for themselves. The Cheap Trains Act of 1883 had given the Board of Trade extensive powers to oblige railway companies to increase their workmen's services if the need seemed to demand it.[76] The Great Eastern, therefore, was always at pains to insist that these 2d. services were not really remunerative. When in 1884, for instance, the general manager was challenged on this point, he would go no further than to say that 'it does not bring in the necessary profit', and went on to explain this observation by saying that the traffic paid its working expenses but no more.[77] Twenty years later, his successor advanced a more involved argument and even provided some figures of alleged costs. But he reached much the same conclusion: that the trains were not run at a loss but did not provide any return on the capital involved.[78] It would seem, therefore, that when the large and more profitable half-fare traffic was added, a modest return probably did result. The Great Eastern, of course, made much of the comparative absence of first class season ticket holders and the traffic which was lost by scaring away these valuable passengers:

'If a man takes a first-class season ticket,' declared the general manager, 'he probably is in such a position as enables his friends to come and visit him, and his children and wife to go to town . . .; while a workman, with his 2d. ticket, does not furnish any additional traffic.'[79]

Nevertheless, the carrying of large numbers at a small profit was not without its reward. It is significant that, however much the Great Eastern might lament the 'unprofitability' of its line, it still went out of its way to encourage the development of this working-class traffic. As an early L.C.C. inquiry pointed out:

This is essentially the workman's London Railway—the one, above all others, which appears to welcome him as a desirable customer whose requirements, accordingly, it makes the subject of special study and provision to an extent and in a variety of ways that no other London line seems to do.[80]

By building up its 'Poor Man's Line', the Great Eastern had helped to rescue itself from the financial distress which had confronted it in the later 1860s when no less a personage than Lord Cranborne—soon to be Lord Salisbury and later Prime Minister—as well as Sir Edward Watkin had been called in to re-establish the company's credit in order to raise capital so that these very suburban lines could be built. By creating a large suburban traffic the railway managed not only to perform a useful public service but also, it would seem, to reap a modest financial reward.

During the last quarter of the nineteenth century, then, both the Great Northern and the Great Eastern had built up a huge metropolitan passenger business, though rather different not only in social composition but also in scale; by the beginning of the present century the Great Northern's suburban traffic was of the order of 30,000,000 (calculated as single journeys) while the Great Eastern carried nearly 70,000,000 local passengers in and out of Liverpool Street and Fenchurch Street alone.[81] These services were reflected in—and a reflection of—the remarkable growth of population in the areas served by the two companies:

POPULATION OF DISTRICTS SERVED BY THE
GREAT EASTERN AND GREAT NORTHERN RAILWAYS,
1871–1901

	1871	*1881*	*1891*	*1901*
Tottenham	18,004	36,574	71,343	102,541
Edmonton	8,337	15,174	25,381	46,899
Essex within				
Metropolitan Police limits	127,910	236,254	413,679	672,214
Hornsey	11,746	22,486	44,523	72,056
Wood Green	4,865	9,882	25,831	34,233
Southgate	5,523	8,289	10,970	14,993

Source: Census returns summarized in R.C. on London Traffic, Vol. IV.

The North London Railway also managed to increase its traffic, despite the fact that for much of its length the building frontier had long passed beyond it. From about 30,000,000 journeys annually in the mid-1870s the total rose steadily year by year until it had reached 44,000,000 by the mid-1890s. In addition, the number of season tickets was also on the increase, from about 21,000 for each half-year of 1883 to some 34,000 for each half-year of 1895. By the early 1890s the railway was also providing about 7,000,000 journeys per year at workmen's fares. For a shilling a week users of these trains could travel from either Chalk Farm in one direction or Poplar in the other to Broad Street and back.[82] The North London no doubt benefited from, and helped to promote, the rapid growth of population in the Willesden district in this period—from 15,869 in 1871 to 27,453 (1881), 61,245 (1891) and 114,811 (1901). It was, however, its powerful protector, the London & North Western, which operated the very few workmen's trains which ran from there to Broad Street or Euston, as well as the ordinary third class return from Willesden Junction to Euston, which, at 8d. for 20 miles' travelling, was cheap but not cheap enough to invite a deluge which would interfere with its main-line traffic.[83] It did not wish to emulate the Great Northern. The effect of suburban railways, including the Metropolitan and the District, on the spread of London north of the Thames may be seen by comparing the growth of population within the Metropolitan Board of Works/London County Council limits (Hammersmith in the west, Hampstead and Finsbury Park in the north and Poplar in the east) with that beyond those limits but within the Metropolitan Police boundary. Most of those who lived in this outer London area and had to travel to the centre were really dependent on rail transport, for horse omnibuses took too long over the journey (and were more expensive) and horse trams, although offering cheaper fares than omnibuses, were equally slow and did not usually take passengers so near to their destination as did the trains.

NORTH OF THE THAMES
POPULATION OF METROPOLITAN BOARD OF WORKS/
LONDON COUNTY COUNCIL AREA AND OF
OUTER LONDON, 1871–1901

	1871	1881	1891	1901
M.B.W./L.C.C. area	2,530,521	2,845,848	2,982,238	3,088,480
Outer London	397,172	617,850	992,609	1,509,264
Total	2,927,693	3,463,698	3,974,847	4,597,744

Source: Census returns summarized in R.C. on London Traffic, Vol. IV.

The M.B.W./L.C.C. area figures conceal within them the fall in population in the centre, and to that extent there was a greater filling in of the gaps towards the boundary of that area than these totals would suggest. But this movement is trivial compared with the nearly fourfold increase in population beyond the boundary in what was then essentially 'railway' suburbia.

Suburban traffic south of the river

To the south of the river the numbers involved were much smaller and the contrast between the growth of the inner and outer areas much less marked:

SOUTH OF THE THAMES
POPULATION OF THE METROPOLITAN BOARD OF WORKS/
LONDON COUNTY COUNCIL AREA AND OF
OUTER LONDON, 1871–1901

	1871	*1881*	*1891*	*1901*
M.B.W./L.C.C. area	730,872	984,439	1,246,045	1,447,949
Outer London	226,076	318,524	412,914	535,709
Total	956,948	1,302,963	1,658,959	1,983,658

Source: Census returns summarized in R.C. on London Traffic, Vol. IV.

The boundary of the M.B.W./L.C.C. area in parts of south London, however, lay much farther from the City and West End than it did in the north. If the districts which were to compose the Metropolitan Borough of Woolwich and the remoter parts of those of Greenwich, Lewisham, Camberwell, Lambeth and Wandsworth may all be classed, on account of distance, as 'railway' suburbs, then the contrast between north and south London becomes much less marked, although the total potential railway traffic still remains appreciably smaller in the south.

These remoter areas south of the river were all districts which the main-line railways had sought to cultivate before the 1870s; by 1900 there was a spider's web of branches in the outer L.C.C. areas and extending into Kent and Surrey. The principal lines not already mentioned were opened to passengers as follows:

South Eastern Railway

Loop line, Hither Green via Sidcup to Dartford, 1 September 1866
Direct Tonbridge Line to Chislehurst, 1 July 1865; to Sevenoaks, 2 March 1868, throughout, 1 May 1868
New Cross, connections to East London Railway, 1876
Grove Park to Bromley, 1 January 1878
Elmers End to Hayes, 29 May 1882
Woodside and South Croydon (joint with London, Brighton & South Coast Railway), 10 August 1885
Bexleyheath line to Dartford, 1 May 1895
Chipstead Valley, Purley to Kingswood, 2 November 1897

London, Chatham & Dover Railway

Nunhead to Blackheath Hill, 18 September 1871; extended to Greenwich, 1 October 1888

Gravesend branch, 10 May 1886

Nunhead–Catford–Shortlands, 1 July 1892

London, Brighton & South Coast Railway

Sutton to Epsom Downs, 22 May 1865

Leatherhead to Dorking, 11 March 1867

South Croydon to Oxted (joint with South Eastern Railway), 10 March 1884

London & South Western Railway

Surbiton to Guildford via Effingham Junction and Leatherhead to Effingham Junction, 2 February 1885.[84]

As we have seen, the first of London's suburban services ran out to Greenwich, and by 1858 more than 13,500,000 passengers went in and out of the London Bridge stations via the various lines. The opening of stations across the river on its north bank during the 1860s undoubtedly added much to the attractiveness of these services, and the enlarging of the terminal accommodation is a clear indication that the traffic was growing heavier. During the later 1880s the bridges across the river to Charing Cross and Cannon Street were both widened, and this was followed by the widening of London Bridge station and the track from there to the Cannon Street bridge.[85] On 10 May 1886, the London, Chatham & Dover Railway opened a new terminal station, St. Paul's (now known as Blackfriars), with its own bridge over the river and easy access to the underground.[86] At Waterloo, extensions to the station were made in 1878 and 1885.[87] Only Victoria appears to have remained substantially unchanged during this period, and it was to be drastically altered and lengthened during the early years of the present century.[88]

Unfortunately, none of the main lines' records dealing with these suburban services appears to have survived, and any clues that may lie buried in the papers relating to the main-line systems as a whole have proved to be beyond disinterment. We do know, however, from another source[89] that there was a considerable workmen's traffic upon these lines. In 1892, for instance, the London & South Western ran 13 trains up to London every day from its various branches, the London, Brighton & South Coast 14, the Chatham 13 and the South Eastern (on its Dartford line) four. Workmen's tickets were available from so far afield as Weybridge (9d. return), Dartford (9d. return) and South Croydon (5d. return); but there were few 2d. returns south of the river, the Chatham's Ludgate Hill–Victoria service providing a notable exception. Most workmen's returns cost 3d. (London Bridge to Peckham Rye, Denmark Hill or Loughborough Park; Waterloo to Clapham Junction; Charing Cross to Spa Road) or 4d. (Waterloo to Wandsworth; Charing Cross to Deptford or New Cross; Ludgate Hill to Penge or Nunhead; London Bridge to Streatham, New Cross, Clapham Junction, Norbury, Crystal Palace or Victoria).

Some details collected for the Royal Commission on London Traffic provide an indication of the size to which the whole of this suburban traffic south of the river had grown by 1903:

PASSENGER JOURNEYS TO AND FROM
TERMINI SERVING SOUTH LONDON IN 1903,
TOGETHER WITH THE NUMBERS OF SUBURBAN AND
MAIN-LINE TRAINS ARRIVING AT THOSE TERMINI

	Passenger journeys during the year (millions)	Trains arriving on each weekday	
		suburban	main line
Charing Cross	10	152	35
Cannon Street	13½	59	3
London Bridge	30	243	50
City stations of the former L.C. & D. Rly. (Holborn Viaduct, Ludgate Hill, St. Paul's)	18	211	—
Waterloo	31	256	47
Victoria	29	306	64

Source: R.C. on London Traffic, Vol. I, 64–65; Vol. III, Appendix 6, Table 33.

The railways then were serving passengers who wanted to travel for a couple of miles or more, not for a couple of stations. References to the railways' 'omnibus' traffic, current in the 1860s, soon went out of fashion as the function of each form of transport came to be more clearly perceived. Capital was now spent on improving the railways' links with the suburbs and not upon new lines in the centre. Many such urban lines were in fact proposed, and a London Central Railway, from Euston and St. Pancras to Charing Cross, was authorized in 1871 with a capital of £2,000,000. It would have involved construction of new streets north and south of Leicester Square (on the pattern of Tothill Street, Westminster, and the Victoria Embankment with the District Railway beneath), and the Metropolitan Board of Works was prepared to contribute £200,000.[90] But this came to nothing; and, although another scheme (from Edgware Road to Westminster via Marble Arch and Hyde Park Corner) had the distinction of a Parliamentary committee's special report,[91] it was not proceeded with either. Significantly, the only new stretch of line which was built in the centre—the completion of the Inner Circle by the existing underground companies— was a resounding failure.

The completion of the Inner Circle

The extension of the underground to form a circle was first advocated, as we have seen, by the Lords' committee of 1863. Confronted by a vast number of railway schemes which were suddenly promoted as a result of the Metropolitan's initial success, the committee sought refuge in advocating a circular route, linking the main line termini, as the best solution of London's growing traffic problem. The Metropolitan, anxious to keep out competitors from a route which then had official backing, quickly secured Parliament's sanction to extend the City end of its line as far as Trinity Square (Tower Hill), and the District was

R

created to provide the southern part of the Circle. By 1876, the Metropolitan had built its line so far as Aldgate, quite near to Trinity Square, but the terminus of the District still remained at the corner of Queen Victoria Street and Cannon Street ('Mansion House'). It was upon the District, therefore, that the main burden of responsibility for the completion of the Circle rested. But the District was so loaded with debentures that it had difficulty even in paying the full dividend upon its 5 per cent. preference shares. It was in no position to embark unaided on the extension of its line through such extremely costly property.

At this juncture the underground again secured the collaboration of the Metropolitan Board of Works and the City authorities. Traffic congestion to the east of Cannon Street had become very severe. Stretches of Eastcheap and Tower Street, for instance, were only 15 feet wide, and carts going to and from the warehouses and docks were often involved in fearsome jams. To widen the roads in this part of London was very costly indeed, but if the work could be undertaken as part of a scheme to complete the Circle, then the burden on the local authorities would be considerably reduced. In 1873, therefore, when the Metropolitan made its by then annual submission to Parliament to abandon the building of its line beyond Aldgate, the Metropolitan Board of Works suggested the possibility of a joint street-widening and railway-building scheme.[92] The Metropolitan worked out such a scheme, but at about the same time George G. Newman, a member of the legal firm of Newman, Dale and Stretton, who boasted among their relatives influential members of the Metropolitan Board of Works,[93] came forward with a somewhat more adventurous plan which included, besides the completion of the Circle via Fenchurch Street, the linking of the underground with the Great Eastern and North London railways, and with the East London, which was then being built to Liverpool Street. Because it would link 'the extreme east end of

London with the west',[94] this line of the Inner Circle Completion Company, as the Newman concern was called, won the Metropolitan Board of Works' support, and in the following year, 1874, it secured Parliamentary sanction in preference to the Metropolitan's counter-proposal.[95] The Metropolitan Board of Works promised to pay £370,000 and the Commissioners of Sewers (the City authority) £130,000 when the building of a new road from Eastcheap to Fenchurch Street, together with the widening of Fenchurch Street itself, was completed.[96] £500,000, a very modest subsidy for an improvement on this scale, hardly set the Completion Company on its feet financially, particularly as, from the outset, the prosperous Metropolitan was its enemy and the poverty-stricken District its friend. No serious effort was made to raise capital until October 1877,[97] and then insufficient support was forthcoming.

The Metropolitan, having for some years refused to collaborate with the District in any scheme to complete the Circle, now changed its attitude and proposed that the two companies should finish the line themselves.[98] Sir John Hawkshaw was called in to advise on the most suitable route, and by the end of January 1878 he produced a report advocating a line under Cannon Street, Eastcheap and (Great) Tower Street (the last two being widened in the process) and then, with the aid of a new street (Byward Street) to Trinity Square, round to Aldgate.[99] The key to the whole venture, however, and the explanation of the Metropolitan's sudden change in attitude are to be found in the further proposal to build a branch from the Circle (with a junction on each side of Aldgate High Street) under Whitechapel High Street and Whitechapel Road to a point near the London Hospital where it would join the East London Railway. In this way the two underground companies would have the beginnings of an extension into the eastern suburbs and a link with the main-line railways south of the river.

The Metropolitan had been interested in obtaining such an outlet seven years earlier when the Great Eastern's extension to Liverpool Street was being planned. Indeed, the decision to build Liverpool Street at a low level had been taken so that when the Metropolitan and East London Railways were extended to it, as had already been authorized, they could both run trains into or through the station. The junction with the Metropolitan at Liverpool Street was agreed in the days when the cunning Parson and the grasping Fowler were still in control of the Metropolitan; but Swarbrick, the Great Eastern's general manager, soon realized that they were up to their old scheming:

... It is evident that Mr. Fowler wants under cover of the junction to have to do with the building of the station, and that Mr. Parson wants under the pretence of not wanting a station for themselves at present to effect a lodgement in ours with a view to the abandonment of their further extension to Tower Hill later on. ... My own view is that sooner or later, and as the best thing for both companies, we shall establish with them a local service from Stratford say, to Paddington ... but it will not do for us to provide them with a City terminus to the restriction of our own accommodation ...[100]

The junction was built, but, as we have already noticed (page 162), it was used by Metropolitan trains into Liverpool Street for only a short time until the Metropolitan's own station (Bishopsgate) was completed.[101] The junction was never used for regular traffic on to the Great Eastern system because the two companies could not agree on through fares,[102] but it is interesting to note that in August 1878—after the Whitechapel line had been approved in principle but before a formal application had been made to Parliament—Watkin, the chairman of the Metropolitan, wrote to suggest that the Great Eastern should reopen the junction and added:

There is no reason why a service of trains of an efficient character should not be put on between the Metropolitan system, the Great Eastern, the East London and railways south of the Thames.[103] The Great Eastern replied that they were willing to consider trains running between the Metropolitan and their own system but not on to the East London. The Metropolitan and the District thus secured written evidence which would help them to counter any Great Eastern opposition to their Whitechapel line.

It was almost certainly the East London's failing fortunes which had caused Watkin to become interested in it, and once his interest had been so aroused it became an essential part of his plan to link the East London with the Metropolitan. The East London, it will be recalled, had been opened through Brunel's Thames Tunnel from New Cross to Wapping at the end of 1869, and was later extended northwards. Trains worked by the Brighton Company started to reach Liverpool Street on 10 April 1876, some of them running through from Croydon; but they did not succeed in building up a profitable traffic. The East London claimed that the Great Eastern had strangled its prospects by only allowing it to have a single line into, and a single platform at, Liverpool Street. It could, therefore, run only about 70 trains in and out per day.[104] On the other hand, the Great Eastern also had grievances: the East London had paid no rent for the use of the platform and very few tolls for the use of the line into the station.[105] The Brighton Railway, as operators of the line, were also owed money. Both creditors put increasing pressure on the East London, and when its position became really desperate, Watkin appeared on the scene. In May 1878 he added it to the collection of railway companies of which he was chairman.[106] The stage was now set for the application to Parliament for authority to complete the Circle and to build the Whitechapel branch.

The importance of this link with the railways to the south soon became apparent at the committee hearing on the Bill. Samuel Laing, the chairman of the Brighton Railway, looked forward to his company's New Cross (Gate) station, which served both the Brighton and part of the South Eastern lines, becoming the Willesden Junction of the south; he added point to this by telling the committee that a move was afoot for the Brighton, South Eastern, Chatham, Metropolitan and District Railways to take a combined lease of the East London, which was by then in the hands of a receiver.[107] Forbes, the chairman of the District, had visions of trains starting at New Cross and, having reached Aldgate, running round the Circle in each direction alternately and then back to New Cross.[108] Eventually, in 1884, the joint lease of the East London (with the Great Eastern as sixth partner) was to come about, but New Cross (Gate) never became a terminus for Circle trains and was certainly never to be a second Willesden Junction. Indeed, when the two underground companies started to work trains along the East London Railway, only those of the District went to New Cross (Gate), the Metropolitan preferring to terminate its service at the other New Cross station several hundred yards away, owned by the South Eastern of which Watkin was also chairman. Nevertheless, that Laing could have advanced the suggestion that New Cross (Gate) might become an important transfer station shows that those who wished to put the finishing touch to the Circle really had another ultimate objective in mind.

The Metropolitan and District Railways (City Lines and Extensions) Act became law on 11 August 1879, but there were many delays before any work could be started. The former Completion Company had to be compensated for its expenses, and the Metropolitan Board of Works and Commissioners of Sewers had to be persuaded both to transfer their grants to the new route and to increase them (the Metropolitan Board of Works' contribution was raised to £500,000 and the Commissioners of Sewers' to £300,000).[109]

These negotiations were very protracted, and so the Metropolitan, having raised £1,250,000—its own half of the capital—and purchased some of the land between Aldgate and Trinity Square, promoted its own Act to build this stretch of the line.[110] It was opened for a limited number of trains to a temporary station just north of Trinity Square (known as Tower of London) on 25 September 1882.[111] By then all the obstacles to the completion of the rest of the line to Mansion House station had been removed and work on the remaining stretch had just started.[112] This involved the skilful underpinning of buildings and very careful attention to plans. As (Sir) John Wolfe Barry,* who, with Sir John Hawkshaw, was joint engineer, observed, 'It was often a question of a few inches whether an important and expensive building could or could not be avoided, the decision involving an expenditure or saving of many thousands of pounds'.[113] Much of the work had to be done by night, for the Act authorizing the line forbade any interference with the normal traffic of the streets between 6 a.m. and 6 p.m. This meant that the cutting had to be covered with planks of timber as it was excavated. Joseph Tomlinson, the Metropolitan's engineer, explained how the work was done:

The first thing that had to be ascertained was the length of the

*John Wolfe Barry, the youngest son of Sir Charles Barry, R.A., who designed the Houses of Parliament, was born on 7 December 1836. He was educated at Glenalmond College, Perthshire, and King's College, London. After practical training in the shops of Lucas Brothers, he became pupil and then assistant to (Sir) John Hawkshaw by whom he was employed as resident engineer for the Charing Cross and Cannon Street railway extensions. In 1867 he started in business on his own account and became consulting engineer for a number of railway schemes both at home and abroad. Among those in London were the District Railway's extensions to Ealing and Fulham, the Inner Circle completion (with Hawkshaw), and the Chatham's Blackfriars bridge and station. He is mainly remembered, however, for the building of Tower Bridge, and in recognition of this work he received a C.B. His firm was also engaged extensively in dock construction and he himself was concerned in three large oversea cable companies. He was much in demand as a witness before Parliamentary committees and as a member of royal commissions; and he devoted much of his time to the City & Guilds Institute, the University of London, and the two London colleges, Imperial and King's. He became a member of the Institution of Civil Engineers in 1868 and its president in the years 1896 and 1897. He also became vice-president of the Institution of Mechanical Engineers and an F.R.S. He died at Delahay House, Chelsea, on 22 January 1918. (*Proceedings of the Institution of Civil Engineers*, 206 (1920), 350–7; *D.N.B.*)

road that could be taken up, and the number of timber balks laid down and covered with the plank road within that time. The workmen had also to be trained and the work organized. The first night only two timbers, or 8 feet of road, were put in, and it was with the utmost difficulty that the road could be made good within the specified time. The next night two were put in much quicker, and as the men became drilled to the process, as many as five were placed and covered with the roadway planks in one night.[114]

Despite all these problems, the line was built at a little less than the estimated cost. Just to the east of the junction with the East London (St. Mary's Junction), the District built its own terminus at Whitechapel (Mile End).

The directors of the two underground companies and their party inspected the new lines on 17 September 1884, travelling from Cannon Street to New Cross and then back again round the Circle.[115] Regular public services were started on 6 October, being inaugurated appropriately by a train from New Cross (Gate).[116] Despite the four days of experimental working which preceded the opening, however, the underground services were thrown into chaos by the new schedules. Now that the horseshoe had become the Circle, an attempt was made to increase the frequency of trains from six to eight per hour in each direction and, at the same time, to feed into the system not only the existing trains from the branches (including those from the Middle and Outer Circles) but also two extra ones along the District's section and others from the East London. This meant that, while 280 trains per day were to be operated round the Circle (140 in each direction), a further 684, coming in from the branches via the junctions at Cromwell Road, Praed Street and Whitechapel, had to be fitted in amongst them. In fact, during the Inner Circle's disordered first few days, it was possible to work no more than 250 trains per day round the Circle and between 610 and 630 to and from the branches.[117] Dislocation was so severe that traffic some-times came to a complete standstill for hours on end, and there is at least one well-authenticated case of exasperated passengers having to get out of their train in the tunnel and walk to the nearest station—where, presumably, they caught an omnibus.[118]

The explanation of this chaotic state of affairs is to be found partly in the two companies' lack of confidence in each other. Each of them was keen to make the most of its own branch traffic even if this interfered with the timing of the Circle trains; and irregular running on the Circle, of course, was bound to disturb branch traffic on the rest of the system. Even while the new lines were being built, there was often strong disagreement between the Forbes and the Watkin factions, equally balanced on the joint committee, and the points of dispute had to be referred to a standing arbitrator. Only a few weeks before the Inner Circle was opened, an incident occurred at South Kensington which gives an indication of the intensity of ill-will which still prevailed on both sides:

CHAINED TO THE LINE AT SOUTH KENSINGTON
TWO RAILWAY COMPANIES AT LOGGERHEADS

. . . The right to a siding is disputed by the respective companies, the most vigorous contestant being the Metropolitan. The District, in order to enforce their right, have run an engine and train into a siding and have actually chained it to the spot, notwithstanding the fact that the engine fires are kept alight, steam kept up, and night and day a driver and stoker are in charge. A day or two ago the Metropolitan sent three engines to pull away the train and a tug of war ensued in which the chained train came off the victor . . .[119]

There were, however, serious difficulties inherent in the working of a circular service even if the two companies had managed to overcome their individual interest and old rivalry. (Sir) Myles Fenton, who as general manager of the Metropolitan had been responsible for the successful operation of that part of the underground from the outset, had

so early as 1874 expressed doubts about the merits of completing the Circle, and he probably left the Metropolitan for
the South Eastern in 1880 with some relief. He realized that
the Circle could never be worked 'as a continuous system
without trains being put away at some place where they
could be "gassed" and watered and examined . . .'[120] The
water in the condensing tanks had to be changed regularly
if the tunnels were not to be filled with steam and fumes—
enough escaped as it was—and the containers which supplied gas for the lighting of the carriages had to be constantly replenished. While the horseshoe system was in
operation, all this servicing could be done at the termini
with relative ease, but with the opening of the Circle, it
had to take place either on the through line or in a siding.
The solution was eventually found in a combination of the
two alternatives. Trains in each direction stopped at Aldgate to have the condensing water changed—a two minutes'
delay—and locomotives were taken off the trains at Kensington (the Metropolitan's at South Kensington and the
District's at High Street) for the fuller servicing. This
occupied about five minutes or so; the locomotive was,
therefore, ready to haul the next train round. The entire
circuit took 70 minutes, and by 1885 the frequency had
again been reduced to six per hour.[121] At first the two
companies seem to have continued the arrangement in force
in the former horseshoe and run alternate trains on both
outer and inner tracks;[122] but this was changed in due
course, the Metropolitan working all trains on the outer
track and two on the inner and the District, with its
smaller mileage, working the remainder.[123] Six trains per
hour eventually allowed more branch line trains to operate
than the total which had caused such confusion when the
Circle was opened. By 1897, as we noticed earlier in this
chapter, the Metropolitan ran 528 passenger and 14 goods
trains per day over the two tracks between King's Cross and
Edgware Road. It then operated 19 trains per hour in each

direction at the busiest times of the day on that part of its line, a considerable achievement in times of steam locomotives with a slow acceleration.[124]

From the beginning passengers had to travel round the Circle by the shortest route and for this purpose both tickets and platforms were plainly marked 'I' (for the inner track) and 'O' (for the outer).[125] A number of stations were more or less equidistant from others on the Circle, and this was later to prove a fruitful cause of further dispute between the two companies. And journeys remained smoky and unpleasant. The busy stretch between King's Cross and Baker Street, the oldest part of the Circle, was the worst-ventilated, despite the blow-holes of the early 1870s and the improvements which were made at Portland Road (Great Portland Street) and Baker Street stations at the end of the 1880s.[126] The gradient from east to west was uphill and the locomotives on the inner track therefore gave out fumes in plenty, not all of which were condensed. And it is hard to see how the change from coke to 'Welsh smokeless coal', of which each locomotive burnt three hundredweights every hour, improved matters,[127] although it was no doubt reassuring to passengers to hear from one of the engine drivers that the smoke was 'very seldom' thick enough to obscure his view of the signals.[128] Persistent complaints led eventually to a Board of Trade inquiry. At this the Metropolitan's general manager repeated the company's firmly (and long) held opinion that the fumes, far from being a cause of illness, were positively health-giving. Stations like Portland Road were 'actually used as sanatoriums for men who had been afflicted with asthma and bronchial complaints' and the sulphuric acid gas which, he conceded, was present in those tunnels was there in such small quantities that it acted merely as a disinfectant.[129] Perhaps the most appropriate comment on such an apologia is to be found in a *Times* leader printed the day after the Circle was opened:

A journey from King's Cross to Baker Street is a form of mild

torture which no person would undergo if he could conveniently
help it. Passengers have been consoled by the assurance that self-
asphyxiation by sulphurous fumes is not an injurious thing even
for the asthmatic; but this is a point on which coughing sufferers
cannot be expected to agree with railway directors.[130]

A journalist went round the Circle in 1893 on the footplate of a District locomotive, starting his journey at St.
James's Park. At first

the sensation altogether was much like the inhalation of gas
preparatory to having a tooth drawn. I would have given a good
deal to have waited just a minute or so longer. Visions of accidents,
collisions and crumbling tunnels floated through my mind; a
fierce wind took away my breath, and innumerable blacks filled
my eyes. I crouched low and held on like grim death to a little rail
near me. . . . Before and behind and on either side was blackness,
heavy, dense and impenetrable . . . Westminster Bridge, Charing
Cross, and the Temple were passed before I could think of anything but holding on to that rolling, rushing engine. . . . [At
Aldgate] the fireman at once jumped off the engine and made the
necessary arrangements for filling our water tanks. So quickly was
this done that probably none of the passengers noticed any difference in the length of the stoppage. . . . From Farringdon Street
to King's Cross is the longest stretch without a station, and the
driver here gave us an exhibition of full speed, and No. 18 came
into King's Cross at the rate of some 40 m.p.h. The average speed
of trains between one station and another is from 20 to 25 m.p.h.

The road now began to be uphill, and at the same time the air
grew more foul. From King's Cross to Edgware Road the ventilation is defective, and the atmosphere on a par with the "'tween
decks forrud' of a modern ironclad in bad weather, and this is
saying a good deal. By the time we reached Gower Street I was
coughing and spluttering like a boy with his first cigar. 'It is a
little unpleasant when you ain't used to it,' said the driver with
the composure born of long usage, 'but you ought to come on a
hot summer day to get the real thing!' Fog on the underground
appears to cause less inconvenience than do the sultry days of
July; then the atmosphere is killing. With the exception of this

one section (between King's Cross and Edgware Road) I found the air far purer than I had expected, and the bad air so much complained of by the 'sewer-rats'—as those who habitually use this circle are called in 'the City'—is due in a great measure to their almost universal habit of keeping all the windows and ventilators closed . . .

At High Street, Kensington, engines are changed so we jumped off. . . . Engine No. 18 went off into a shed to rest awhile, and No. 7, a precisely similar one, backed on to the train in her place. This resting of engines is rendered a frequent necessity from the strain caused by the numerous stoppages; incessant running in one direction has also been found bad for them as it wears the wheels on one side sooner than on the other. To remedy this, the engines half their time run 'backwards forwards'. . . . Off again, and this time down-hill. We dashed rapidly through the grass embankments outside Gloucester Road, past some men posting bills on the advertisement hoardings that border the line below South Kensington, now deep in a tunnel, now traversing a cutting open to the sky; until we shot once more into St. James's Park 70 min. after leaving it.[131]

Financially, the completion of the Circle was an utter failure. The capital, £2,500,000, of which each company raised half, constituted a separate guaranteed stock on which 4 per cent. had to be paid.[132] To meet this interest, a very large traffic was needed over the new lines, and this was never forthcoming. So the companies had to dip into such profits as their other activities yielded. The Metropolitan had a good income from its surplus lands,[133] but even so its dividend fell from what had become by then an almost traditional 5 per cent. to 4 per cent. for a year or two after the Circle's opening; and the District, which had been managing to pay 5 per cent. on its preference shares—and even an occasional 1 per cent. or so on its ordinaries—relapsed to 2¼ per cent. In 1886, Forbes confessed to the shareholders that the venture had been 'almost disastrous'; two years later he claimed that it was costing the company about £60,000 per year without any return.[134]

In such adversity the old hostility between the two companies flared up anew and in a much more violent form. There were long-drawn-out court hearings, notably about the amount which the District was due to pay the Metropolitan for its share of the Aldgate–Trinity Square section which the Metropolitan had built, and about the apportionment of the working loss between the two companies. The last trace of goodwill being now utterly dissipated, the two companies went to ridiculous lengths to steal each other's passengers. From May 1886, instead of being able to choose which way they were to travel round the Circle, passengers were invariably sent by the route which entailed the longer journey over the lines owned by the company issuing the tickets—and at the joint stations each company had its own separate booking office. At the same time the travelling public was subjected to a poster campaign aimed to attract traffic from the rival's trains.[135] In 1887 Forbes told the District's shareholders that he was applying to Parliament to end such 'disgraceful proceedings and litigations'. 'I am a pretty tough customer,' he added, 'but I assure you they begin to tear the heart out of me.'[136] He was Watkin's match, however. His disarming frankness was quite the equal of Watkin's feigned indignation, and in the end he outlived his old adversary.

How did two men so experienced in railway affairs and so well versed in the particular problems of London's traffic come to make such a grave miscalculation? That both Watkin and Forbes had real faith in the Inner Circle completion scheme, there can be no doubt. Forbes had been its constant advocate and, just before the opening, Watkin stated publicly that it would bring more than 50 per cent. more traffic to the underground.[137] That this was Watkin's honest opinion, was later confirmed by R. W. Perks, who was at that time the Metropolitan's legal adviser.[138]

The explanation of the experts' error, particularly Watkin's, is probably to be found, as has already been suggested,

in misplaced hopes of a large increase in traffic from railways south of the river via New Cross. This traffic never
materialized. Nor is its failure to do so very surprising.
Unlike the railways to the north, those to the south all had
termini which were well situated for passengers bound for
central London. While it is easy to see why passengers from
the north who wanted to get to the City should change
trains at Willesden Junction, it is difficult to understand
why those from the south should think of doing so at New
Cross, just to travel by a rather circuitous route on the
underground, stopping at every station. This applied
particularly to passengers bound for the southern part of the
Circle, along the newly-completed stretch of line, for it
would only take them to Cannon Street and Charing Cross
which South Eastern passengers could have reached any-
way without changing at New Cross. Brighton line passengers, however, who did not travel by trains to Victoria
ended their journey south of the river, at London Bridge.
Perhaps, in view of Laing's enthusiastic ideas about making
New Cross into another Willesden Junction, Watkin and
Forbes may have been given hopes that the Brighton company would encourage its passengers, by through—and
perhaps preferential—booking, to change at New Cross;
and maybe Watkin believed he could use his influence in
the South Eastern with similar results so far as passengers
bound for parts of London served by the Metropolitan
were concerned. Possibly it was expectations such as these
that led one of the experts at least to make the wrong
diagnosis.

The other main cause of miscalculation arose from the
over-estimation of the short-distance traffic which would
develop round the eastern part of the Circle. It was, as one
of the joint engineers aptly put it, 'rather the joining
together of two parallel lines than the completion of a
circle'.[139] The bulk of the traffic was along the parallel
lines and was unlikely to continue round the new eastern

connection. Perhaps, however, the Liverpool Street terminus was expected to furnish a large number of westbound passengers. This hope, if it were ever seriously held, was also to be dashed, for a high proportion of the users of Liverpool Street, as we have seen, were holders of 2d. and other cheap returns who were unlikely to patronize the underground. And—probably of greater importance in depriving the eastern part of the Circle of its growth prospects—cheaper omnibus services came upon the scene which charged fares with which the underground could not compete. This new competition coincided very nearly with the completion of the Circle and undoubtedly deprived the underground of much traffic not only between Liverpool Street and points to the west, but also on journeys such as that from King's Cross or Euston Square to Cannon Street or Charing Cross. Indeed, the new lease of life enjoyed by the horse omnibus, hard hit by railway competition in the later 1860s and only profitable in the early 1870s because of contracts for horsing tramways, is one of the most remarkable features of these years.

87. Opening the new Blackfriars Bridge, 1869

88. The Last Toll at Putney Bridge, 1880

89. Sir John Pound

90. John Howard Moore

91. Thomas Tilling

92. Samuel Birch

93. John Hopkinson

94. James Henry Greathead

95. Edward Hopkinson

96. Horse Trams on Pentonville Road: St Pancras in the background

97. Horse Tram at the Angel Junction, late 19th Century

98. Croydon Tramways Car at the 'Red Deer', 1875

99. North Metropolitan Tramways Car on the Clapton route

100. A Hansom Cab, photographed in 1877

101. Street Scene at Charing Cross, 1888, with Metropolitan Railway Three-Horse Omnibus and Umbrella

102. L.G.O.C. Knifeboard Omnibus at London Bridge Station, 1887

103. London Road Car Company's Garden Seat Omnibus at West Kensington, 1894, with Union Jack and Conductor's Bell Punch

104. Omnibus Driver and Conductor, 1877

CHAPTER EIGHT

LATE VICTORIAN LONDON

(II) THE ROADS

The last quarter of the nineteenth century saw the heyday of the horse omnibus. Benefiting from lower operating costs as a result of the removal of tolls and taxes and the cheapening of horse feed, the omnibus was able to make good profits, particularly from the growth of traffic in those central London streets where it was free of railway and tramway competition. The L.G.O.C.'s high dividends attracted newcomers into the omnibus business, notably the London Road Car Company which set a new standard by the comfort of its vehicles. The ensuing competition and cheaper fares won traffic from the hackney coaches, cabs and, to some extent, from the underground railways. The L.G.O.C. went through a critical phase in the early 1890s but its dividends soon recovered. Meanwhile on the main roads into the suburbs the horse trams were doing very good business. New tramway companies were formed and the older ones grew and prospered until the prospect of their purchase by the local authorities under the Tramways Act of 1870 cast a shadow over their affairs. But, in general, London's omnibus and tramway companies continued to pay higher dividends than its railways. The chief beneficiaries, however, were those Londoners, a growing proportion of the community, who could afford to travel by public transport.

ENCOURAGEMENTS FOR OMNIBUS OPERATORS

IN THE LAST quarter of the nineteenth century omnibuses were less burdened with tolls and taxes than they had ever been. The turnpike tolls had been swept away and so had the mileage duties, and the omnibus companies paid little in rates for their stables and depots. The railways, by contrast, still paid a passenger tax (although in 1883 this was removed from fares not exceeding 1d. a mile) and their stations and

s

other property were heavily rated. The railway companies contributed more towards the upkeep of the roads than did the omnibus proprietors who lived from them, and the underground railways, in the City if not elsewhere, had to pay a ransom towards road improvements in order to extend their lines. And the later 1870s and 1880s were years when a considerable amount of road improvement was being undertaken in central London—on a scale comparable, perhaps, with the Regency period. Many new and wide thoroughfares were opened: Northumberland Avenue, for instance (March 1876), Clerkenwell Road and Theobald's Road (1878), and, of much greater importance, Shaftesbury Avenue (January 1886) and Charing Cross Road (February 1887).[1] After the late 1870s omnibuses were also allowed to pass through the Bedford estate south of Euston Road, a district which had apparently been barred to all through traffic before then.[2] Many of the new roads were fine, broad highways, 60 feet wide; others, such as part of Gray's Inn Road, were widened to this new standard.[3]

The river crossings were also improved and increased in number. The Lambeth Suspension Bridge was opened in 1862 and the present Westminster and Blackfriars Bridges date from 1862 and 1869 respectively;[4] both the Albert Suspension Bridge and the original Wandsworth Bridge were opened in 1873.[5] New bridges were built at Putney in 1886 and at Hammersmith in 1887, and in 1890 the present Battersea Bridge took the place of the frail old timber structure which in 1883 had at long last been declared unsafe.[6] The opening of Tower Bridge in 1894 provided a much-needed crossing of the river below London Bridge itself.[7] And, by then, the tolls had for some time been removed from all the Thames bridges. To the toll-free London, Westminster, Blackfriars and Southwark Bridges[8] were added in 1878, Waterloo, and in 1879 Lambeth, Vauxhall, Chelsea, Albert and Battersea. Those at Wandsworth,

Putney and Hammersmith followed in 1880.[9] Both the range and the choice of river crossings were thus greatly extended for road users.

Omnibus proprietors were almost wholly exempt from irksome official regulations as well as from costly tolls. Although the police retained their long-established rights over the central termini of routes, this was no longer a major consideration as many services ran right through central London. The City authorities do not seem to have used the powers they had gained in 1863 to control routes, and the only nineteenth-century case of the omnibus proprietors assisting to ease traffic congestion—by going to Liverpool Street via Moorgate Street and London Wall and returning via Old Broad Street (the first known method of one-way omnibus working in London, introduced towards the end of the century)—was the result of persuasion rather than of direction.[10] The operator's freedom was almost unlimited. He could even pick up and set down wherever he pleased, although after 1867 he had to do this on the left of the road. The L.G.O.C. firmly resisted any attempt to introduce fixed stopping places.

'The reason why we carry so many passengers,' declared the L.G.O.C.'s chairman, 'is that they can get in and out at any point. They do not like to be taken a house or two beyond where they want to get out. They will jump in and pay their penny in order to be put down on the doorstep of the place where they want to get to.'[11]

Above all, the omnibus interests were helped at this time by considerable reductions in the price of horse feed. Imported maize, which, as we have already noticed, was used instead of oats from the later 1860s, became much cheaper in the 1880s than it had formerly been. The cost of feeding, together with that of bedding, for a stud of 12 horses fell from more than £170 per half year in the mid-1870s to between £140 and £150 in the later 1870s. From then onwards, it occasionally rose above £150, but some-times in good years it fell to so little as £130.[12] This was a most important development in an industry where, with comparatively little capital involved, a slight variation in the level of current expenditure (usually almost 90 per cent. of receipts) had a profound effect on the rate of dividend.

The L.G.O.C. and its associates settled down with all these advantages to enjoy the greatest advantage of all: their privileged position as operators in the streets of central London. From this traffic the trams were wholly, and the trains largely, excluded. It was the horse omnibus which was to have the real pickings of the traffic in the City and West End, a traffic which was growing particularly rapidly as people rode about more frequently on business or for pleasure. The omnibus could also attract passengers from the inner suburbs, even though a tram route might serve their area at lower fares, for it often ran nearer their homes and, at the other end of the journey, went right into the centre of London. The tram, on the other hand, set its passengers down on the outskirts and they had to walk the rest of the way—or catch an omnibus.

The extent and complexity of the omnibus services in central London in the later nineteenth century are clearly shown in the 20 or more pages devoted to them by Charles Dickens Jr. in the various editions of his *Dictionary of London*. In that of 1879, after listing all the routes, giving indications of their distinguishing marks—colour and fleet name—their starting and finishing times and fares, he attempted to show the Holborn and Strand routes by means of an elaborate table which, though typographically astonishing, could not have been of much use to anyone who did not know the answers already. The route number and the bus map had not yet been produced.

This profitable central traffic the omnibuses shared with the hackney carriages which also responded to the new demand. The number of licences issued rose from 7,818 in

1870 (3,295 of them for hansoms) to more than 10,500 in 1884 (hansoms then being in the majority).[13] So, by the early 1880s when there were probably fewer than 1,000 omnibuses altogether, the cabs and coaches—some ten times as numerous as the omnibuses and, therefore, of comparable total capacity—must have claimed a very considerable proportion of the central traffic. The fare within four miles of Charing Cross was 6d. per mile, and beyond that, 1s.; but, as there was a minimum fare of 1s.—and before the taximeter came in there was plenty of scope for charging more than the authorized rate[14]—these were not vehicles which many people could afford to travel in as a matter of course. But considerable numbers of people did use them occasionally when luggage had to be carried; the 'privileged' cabs—those which were allowed to pick up passengers at the arrival platforms of the main-line stations[15]— probably served quite a wide public.

The growing traffic soon brought upon the scene not only more hackney carriages but also more omnibuses. The L.G.O.C.'s own success, indeed, invited emulation. Until 1878 it continued to do well out of the horsing of many of London's tramcars. Profits of £82,000, £86,000 and £90,000 in 1876, 1877, and 1878 not only allowed a dividend of 12 or 12½ per cent. to be paid but also left large sums over to be put to reserve. By the end of 1878 this reserve fund stood at £95,000, £52,000 of which was invested abroad in Indian railways.

When the tramway horsing period was over, the L.G.O.C. increased its fleet of vehicles from 581 to 629 and transferred the most powerful of the former tramway horses to the additional omnibuses. Without the income from the tramway contracts, profits inevitably fell a little in 1879 (to £71,000), but by 1880 they were back again to more than £90,000. A 12½ per cent. dividend was again distributed and the reserve became even larger. But by then serious competition was already being contemplated. It was

fortunate for the L.G.O.C. that in 1879 the chairmanship
had been taken over by a very shrewd businessman, (Sir)
John Pound, the London leatherseller's son who had already
established the well-known leather goods firm. He was also
chairman of the Grand Hotel Company, Charing Cross,
and he was soon to develop many other business interests,
and ultimately to become in 1904–05 Lord Mayor. He
remained chairman of the L.G.O.C. until 1909. He was, in
short to be the L.G.O.C.'s champion, its Watkin (or
Forbes), during the coming contest.[16]

New Competition for the L.G.O.C.

The profitable possibilities of the London omnibus business
attracted the attention of the London Mercantile Association Ltd., a concern which specialized in company promo-
tions of all kinds and boasted a list of 200,000 investors
whom it could interest in any promising new undertaking.[17]
In May 1878 it started preliminary investigations. A traffic
survey was carried out to discover which routes were likely
to prove the most remunerative, and a representative was
sent to Paris and other European cities, and to some
English towns, to seek new ideas in omnibus design. For
various reasons, however, it was not possible to launch the
London & District Omnibus Company Ltd., as the venture was at first called, until the summer of 1880. It was
then proposed to raise £200,000 in £10 shares, but the
issue found little support and what there was came chiefly
from small investors. (They included a number of omnibus
conductors and drivers. The largest single holding (400
shares) was that of a Sauchiehall Street confectioner.) By
the end of 1880, with only £3 called up on under 4,000
shares, a mere £11,500 had been raised altogether.
    The promoters nevertheless went ahead with their plans,
and in March 1881 they were able to give a public showing
of four vehicles which were shortly to be put into service.[18]
One was merely an improved omnibus of traditional type,

but the other three were of quite novel design, the creation of Capt. Molesworth, R.N., of Northdown Hall, Bideford, who had taken out a provisional patent for his invention on 20 August 1880.[19] He had succeeded in building an omnibus which incorporated some of the most attractive features of the tramcar which was then proving so popular. His vehicle had small front wheels on a swivel axle and a platform over them—'like a tram car platform', to quote from the patent specification—on which passengers could climb with ease. From the platform they could either move along into the lower saloon, which was upholstered, or mount by steps to the upper deck, where there were a number of seats —'garden seats' as they came to be called, facing the direction of travel—instead of the two customary 'knifeboard' seats running along the whole length of the roof so that passengers faced sideways.[20] This design had later to be modified because passengers who missed their footing while getting on or off were liable to be run over by the rear wheels; the platform and steps were, therefore, moved to the back of the vehicle.[21] In this form the application of certain features of tramcar design was successful and was to prove a great asset in attracting passengers. The company, recognizing this fact, changed its name in April 1881 to the London Road Car Company Ltd.[22]

The Road Car Company, which did its best to mobilize patriotic feeling in its support—and against the 'foreign' L.G.O.C.—by flying a small Union Jack at the front of all its vehicles, began to work a route between Victoria and Sloane Square in that month, using three three-horse omnibuses. (The service was later extended to Hammersmith via Chelsea, predecessor to the modern route 11.) On the following 4 August the new company invaded one of London's busiest routes by running between Victoria and Broad Street. On this service six road cars were employed from the outset and 12 were at work a month later.[23] By the end of the year there were altogether 11 omnibuses and

16 road cars in service.[24] Early in the following year they started to run between Victoria and Oxford Circus. The company had been boldly launched but was still far from profitable. Indeed, the very heavy losses caused changes in its directors, H. S. Wilde being replaced as chairman by Capt. John Aylmer, M.P., a retired Army officer turned City merchant.[25] He found that 'those who were responsible for the starting of the company . . . had paid exorbitant prices for everything and handed over the stock . . . in a most inefficient condition'.[26] At the end of 1882 the original company, having lost £40,000—a large amount considering that only £57,000 of capital was then embarked in the business—was liquidated and the assets transferred to a new company of the same name.[27] Losses continued in 1883, although on a much smaller scale. The Road Car Company seems to have been rescued eventually from its unprofitable plight by Edward Hodson Bayley who, besides becoming chairman in August 1883, also acted as managing director. Born at Accrington in Lancashire, he had been trained as an engineer with John Brown's of Sheffield and had gone on to gain commercial experience in the City. After that he had acquired an old-established vehicle-building business in south London. He already possessed specialized knowledge of at least one important part of omnibus operation and undertook to keep the road cars in good repair.[28] In 1884 the previous year's loss of £5,625 was turned into a profit of £1,492,[29] and from then onwards the company continued to grow; by February 1887 it was operating 100 cars. But with growing prosperity came criticism of Bayley's contract for repairing vehicles; many shareholders believed that the concern was strong enough to undertake its own repairs. Bayley ceased to be chairman later in 1887, and Daniel Duff, formerly in charge of the Dundee Tramways, took over as manager, John Howard Moore becoming chairman. Moore, a successful tea merchant and head of a concern known as the British Tea

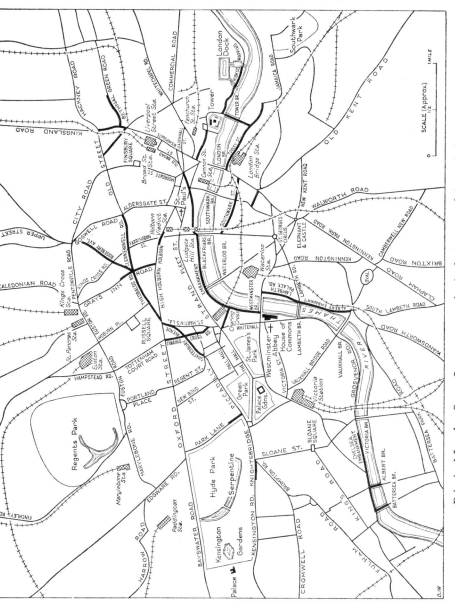

Principal London Street Improvements in the latter part of the 19th Century

SCALE (Approx.)

249

Trading Association, had been a supporter of the Road Car Company from the outset. He had become a director in Aylmer's time, and was apparently responsible for Bayley's introduction to the board in the first place.[30] Under the new regime the company continued to prosper. By the beginning of 1890, it owned 189 cars and its capital stood at just over £225,000.[31]

The competition from the road cars soon had, from the public's point of view, a salutary effect upon the L.G.O.C.'s fares and services. In February 1881, in anticipation of the new competition, the fare between Charing Cross and Bank was reduced from 3d. to 2d.[32] When the new cars started to run in the following August, the L.G.O.C. introduced 1d. fares between Ludgate Circus and Charing Cross or Broad Street, and 1d. stages were also introduced on the Victoria–Hammersmith route.[33] At the beginning of 1882, when the road cars began the service between Oxford Circus and Victoria, the fare on that route was also cut from 3d. to 2d., and later that year, when the new company started to operate from Clarendon Road, Notting Hill, to Victoria and to Charing Cross, the L.G.O.C.'s services on those routes were increased. As competition spread, more 1d. fares were introduced and existing 1d. stages were lengthened. By 1886, for instance, it was possible to ride from Liverpool Street to Charing Cross or from Charing Cross to Victoria for 1d.[34] The L.G.O.C.'s average fare per passenger fell steadily from $2\frac{1}{4}$d. in 1881 to 2d. in 1885 and to $1\frac{1}{2}$d. in 1889.

The newcomer had much less effect, however, in causing the L.G.O.C. to improve the design of its omnibuses. It is true that in 1883 the simple steps up to the roof began to be replaced by a safer mode of approach, and a few garden seats also made their appearance.[35] The entrance on the near side of the omnibus seems to have been introduced about this time or soon afterwards; now that omnibuses had to pick up and set down on the left of the road, this was obviously a much more convenient arrangement than an entrance at the back or (as with the early road cars) a platform which ran the whole width of the vehicle. But for the L.G.O.C. the process of adaptation was very slow. Even in 1891, 40 per cent. of its omnibuses still had knifeboards, and the very revealing reason given for this was that most of the vehicles were too old to be adapted.[36] Nevertheless, the fleet of 1891 was considerably larger than it had been ten years earlier, and this expansion was mainly the result of the new competition. The original quota of 600 vehicles, which dated from the company's formation, had not been exceeded for any length of time until the end of the 1870s when additional omnibuses were put on to make use of the surplus tram horses; even then the total was raised to only 629, and it did not become any greater until the appearance of the road cars. This, however, was the signal for a sudden increase to 649, and the number thereafter climbed steadily, exceeding 700 in 1884 and reaching 860 by 1891.[37]

Between them, the L.G.O.C. and the Road Car Company were then operating 1,135 vehicles, and there were many other omnibuses to be seen on the streets in addition to the 200 or so which the L.G.O.C.'s allies worked within the various associations, a total which had not been allowed to grow. There were, for instance, some 66 omnibuses operated by the tramway companies, serving chiefly as feeders across the bridges for their tram services.[38] The two underground railways ran more omnibuses in connection with their trains, on which through road and rail tickets were available. The Metropolitan's Portland Road (Great Portland Street)–Oxford Circus route, which had been extended to Piccadilly in 1874, was continued to Charing Cross in 1883.[39] In 1888 the Metropolitan also started to run omnibuses from Baker Street along Oxford Street and Bond Street to Piccadilly Circus, and in the following year the District, not to be outdone, sponsored a service between Baker Street and Charing Cross.[40] In 1892 the Metropolitan inaugurated an omnibus service between its Gower Street and Edgware Road stations via Tottenham Court Road, Oxford Street and Edgware Road, the distinguishing feature of which was a large red umbrella projecting from the front over the driver.[41] By that year the L.G.O.C. calculated that the two underground railways were running 28 omnibuses in competition with theirs. There were also many other competitors, ranging from the old-established firm of Thomas Tilling,[42] which operated 18 of its vehicles in opposition to the L.G.O.C., and certain substantial new-comers (The London Omnibus Carriage Company, 40 vehicles,[43] Andrews' Star Omnibus Company, 39,[44] Railways and Metropolitan Omnibus Company, 22[45]) to a whole host of small operators (each owning between one and eight vehicles) who between them ran a further 138. In all, by 1891 the L.G.O.C. and its associates operated 1,093 omnibuses; other concerns, including the Road Car Company with 244, ran 595—ten times as many opposition vehicles as there had been only 11 years before.[46] While the Road Car Company was by far the L.G.O.C.'s main competitor and had been responsible for ushering in a period of rivalry and fare-cutting, it was by no means the only source of opposition.

The L.G.O.C. holds its own—and then runs into difficulties

During the 1880s the L.G.O.C. withstood the growing attacks on its preserves virtually unscathed. In 1882 and 1883, during the initial assault, the dividend was cut only from 12½ to 10 per cent.; £10,000 had to be withdrawn from the reserve (of £105,000) in 1882, but it was replaced during the next year. The dividend was back to 12½ per cent. in 1884, 1885 and 1886, at the end of which year the reserve had been built up to the most impressive figure of £145,000. While the Road Car Company was struggling to make enough profit on its small capital to pay 5 per cent., the L.G.O.C. was making more money than ever. This very prosperous period came to an end, however, after 1886. In the second half of 1887 and during the following three years, the L.G.O.C.'s dividend fell to a rate of 10 per cent., and to pay this it was necessary to dip into the reserves. While both concerns steadily built up their traffic, the Road Car Company enjoyed a much faster rate of growth; indeed, between 1885 and 1886, 1887 and 1888, and 1889 and 1890 it gained as many new passengers as the L.G.O.C. did, even though in 1885 it had only been carrying one-tenth of the older company's total.

NUMBER OF PASSENGERS CARRIED BY THE L.G.O.C.
AND THE ROAD CAR COMPANY, 1885–1890[47]

Year	L.G.O.C.	Road Car Company
1885	76,550,042	7,333,126
1886	79,774,522	10,934,444
1887	90,415,516	17,908,123
1888	95,622,925	22,450,178
1889	104,476,937	29,245,202
1890	112,243,909	37,187,190

Source: R.C. on London Traffic, Vol. III, Appendix 40, Table H.

Despite its high dividend and large reserves, the L.G.O.C. was far from routing its Union Jack-flying rival. Even its own shareholders were now entertaining some doubts about the company's future prospects, as may be seen from their lukewarm response to the offer in 1890 of the 50,000 £4 shares, which had been authorized in 1855 and 1859 but still remained unissued. At £7 each, a seemingly attractive price, only just over 17,000 were taken up.[48]

The plain truth was that A. G. Church, who had been with the company from the start, first as its secretary and then from 1867 as its manager as well, was growing old and deaf and seems to have been losing his grip on affairs. Early in 1891, following an illness, he retired and was paid £5,000 in consideration of his long and loyal service.[49] He was succeeded by Robert Gresley Hall, the son of a member of the board. This *penchant* of the directors for promoting the interest of their near relations, although open to abuse and certainly inviting attack, on the whole served the company quite well. (Sir) John Pound himself had been introduced by his father-in-law, Thomas Lulham, a former chairman. (Sir) William Joynson Hicks, later Lord Brentford ('Jix', a member of various governments during the 1920s) was to be appointed the company's solicitor in 1892, no doubt at the suggestion of his father, Henry Hicks, a successful Smithfield meat salesman who had become vice-chairman the year before.[50] But the choice of R. G. Hall as managing director did not have such a fortunate outcome, largely because he had very soon to deal with an unprecedented crisis in the company's affairs.

This crisis resulted from the board's decision to introduce tickets as a means of checking the takings on each omnibus. It was an open secret that conductors kept back a proportion of their fares and shared the spoils with the drivers and horse keepers. The chairman himself even described to a shareholders' meeting what he had found on one occasion when he had travelled on an omnibus containing ten passengers:

The conductor had only two down on his list. After looking about, trying to get customers, I suppose, or to satisfy his own conscience as to what he should put down, he put down the figure four. I immediately said, 'Conductor, that won't do'. Without a word he put another four down. I said, 'Conductor, that won't do'. 'Won't it Sir?', he said. That was the first time he had spoken. Without another word he put down another two; so that he would have had six for himself and four for the Company.[51]

Previous attempts to keep a closer check on conductors had all failed. That of the L.G.O.C. in its early days was soon abandoned; another, tried out on the Hampstead service in 1879, was no more successful;[52] and a third, on the Hammersmith Road in 1882, resulted in a considerable fall in traffic, the conductors, it was alleged, being unable to issue tickets and keep a satisfactory look-out for passengers at the same time.[53] Church, who always held the opinion that tickets would cost more than they would yield in additional fares, was a staunch upholder of the long-established and well-tried method of relying on 'a staff of persons travelling continually in the omnibuses who are unknown to the conductors, who make their report of the number of passengers entering and leaving the omnibuses and this report is checked with the waybill'.[54] The Road Car Company, however, appears to have used tickets from the beginning. Indeed, its original promoters, the London Mercantile Association, secured the rights for an improved form of bell punch,[55] but it seems doubtful whether this type was ever used, for the Road Car Company was paying royalties to the Bell Punch Company in 1883. During the subsequent economy campaign under Bayley, however, it relied upon tickets alone, numbered but unpunched. This example and that of London's tramways, which had used tickets from the outset,[56] made the L.G.O.C.'s shareholders all the more eager to adopt a similar check. In fact, when tickets were at last introduced on the L.G.O.C.'s omnibuses on 31 May 1891 they led to a brief but costly strike, which lasted from the following 7 to 12 June. (It is discussed in the next chapter in connection with labour matters.) The L.G.O.C. lost over £26,000 on that half-year's working and made only £3,000 in the following one. The dividend fell to 5 per cent., paid out of the reserves. But the ticket system was firmly enforced, and early in 1892 the bell punch was also adopted.[57]

In 1890, the year before the strike, the L.G.O.C.'s earnings were £696,000; in 1892, the year after it, they were £805,000. While some of this large increase un-doubtedly came from the normal growth of traffic, most of it resulted from the closer check on the conductors. But the conductors had to be compensated by higher wages, more inspectors were needed, and there was also the bill to be paid for tickets and punches, part of which, however, could be offset by the advertising revenue from the tickets.[58] All this, together with an increase in the cost of horse feed in 1892 compared with 1890, caused expenditure to rise from £650,000 to £772,000, £13,000 more than revenue had done. The company was able to pay only 5 per cent. for the second year running and by the end of 1892 the reserve was down to £103,000. Shareholders were accustomed to better things, and the half-yearly meeting became very stormy. Pound's numerous 'outside' activities were the subject of critical observation. These by then included not only the Grand Hotel Company but also two other hotel concerns (the Hotel Metropole and Hatchetts), the Mount Kembla Coal and Oil Co. Ltd., and the South Metropolitan Cemetery Co. Ltd. He was also chairman of Charles Batey and Co. Ltd., McNamara and Co. Ltd., the London Tavern and Property Co. Ltd. and the New Asbestos Co. Ltd., not to mention his original leather goods interests.[59] But it was Hall and not Pound who was dismissed early in 1893 (after he had refused to resign) following a shareholders' inquiry, and the management was thereafter supervised by Pound himself and Henry Hicks, the vice-chairman, acting through various departmental heads. At the next shareholders' meeting Pound claimed that the company

under the old *régime* was slowly rotting from inherent decay, *laissez-faire* and approved dishonesty. It had gone too far to be patched up and your Directors had to pull it down and rebuild. It was on that work that they had been engaged during the past two years.[60]

Peaceful co-existence

The new management soon adopted a more conciliatory attitude towards the Road Car Company. There had already been several attempts to end price-cutting between the rivals, and the Road Car Company had joined the L.G.O.C. in talks with the strikers' representatives in 1891, but, except in that instance, without any positive result. In August 1893, however, the L.G.O.C. agreed to a suggestion from the Road Car Company that certain fares should be rearranged,[61] and in November the two concerns agreed to withdraw all competitive fares and to appoint joint time-keepers.[62] The latter arrangement did not work well, for, as the Road Car Company's chairman observed in the middle of the following year,

although the hostile spirit which had been engendered by so many years of rivalry between the two companies had completely passed away as concerning the members of the two boards, it still animated the men employed by the two companies, making the continuance of joint officials almost impracticable.[63]

Joint timekeeping was ended, but mutual consultation on fares continued. Two of the main independents—the London Omnibus Carriage Company and the Star Omnibus Company—also reached agreement with the associations on the routes where they operated.[64] Fares were advanced whenever possible, a rate of a 1d. per mile being aimed at; but fare increases tended to bring to the routes concerned new adventurers—Moore of the Road Car Company was already in 1894 calling them 'pirates'—and such competition limited the companies' freedom to raise fares.[65] Yet after 1892 the two larger companies became more profitable: the L.G.O.C.'s dividend rose first to 8 per cent. and then (in 1896) to $10\frac{1}{2}$ per cent., while that of the Road Car Company, usually less than 5 per cent., in 1896 jumped up to $7\frac{1}{2}$.

During these early years of peaceful co-existence, the L.G.O.C. increased the size of its omnibus fleet more rapidly than ever. In the middle of 1894, this stood at 882 vehicles, little more than the total of four years before, but by the end of 1896 it had grown to more than 1,050. The Road Car Company's fleet was also increasing fairly quickly, from 240 in the middle of 1892 to more than 300 at the end of 1896. By that year the L.G.O.C. carried

T

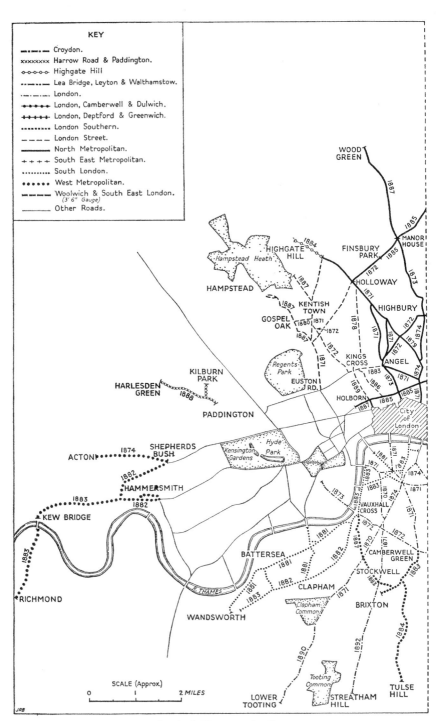

KEY

- ━·━·━ Croydon.
- xxxxxxxx Harrow Road & Paddington.
- ◦◦◦◦◦ Highgate Hill
- ━··━··━ Lea Bridge, Leyton & Walthamstow.
- ━·━··━ London.
- ━•━•━• London, Camberwell & Dulwich.
- ━+━+━+ London, Deptford & Greenwich.
- ·········· London Southern.
- ━ ━ ━ London Street.
- ━━━━ North Metropolitan.
- ++++ South East Metropolitan.
- ·········· South London.
- •••••• West Metropolitan.
- ━ ━ ━ Woolwich & South East London.
  (3' 6" Gauge)
- ━━━ Other Roads.

London's Tramways in 1895

258

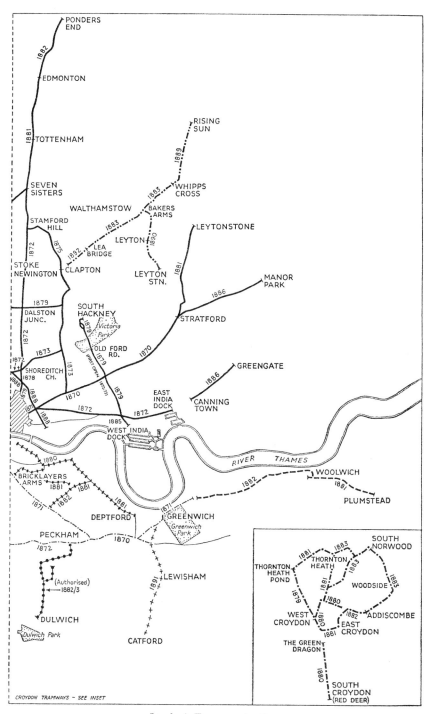

London's Tramways in 1895

259

159,000,000 passengers and the Road Car Company 54,000,000.[66] The Road Car Company had built up a traffic as large as the L.G.O.C.'s had been 15 years before when road cars had first come upon the scene, while the L.G.O.C.'s own traffic had nearly trebled during the same period. And, while the number of vehicles running in collaboration with the L.G.O.C. was not increased—although some proprietors no doubt gained a larger share of this limited total by purchasing vehicles from others within the various associations—new operators had entered the business, and a few of these newcomers were by the mid-1890s working in agreement with the larger companies. By then these smaller concerns were together carrying perhaps half as many passengers as the two larger ones; that is to say a total of about 100,000,000.[67]

The effect of omnibus competition on the underground and the hackney carriages

The omnibuses' great success in attracting new traffic, and, in particular, the shorter-distance passengers, by low fares, frequent services and more comfortable vehicles, took some of this class of traffic away from other forms of transport. Omnibus competition had been particularly severe along the great east–west route which ran between Chelsea, Victoria, Charing Cross and Liverpool Street. It not only reduced to negligible proportions all regular passenger traffic on the Thames, but it also hit particularly hard that part of the underground, the District Railway's, which served the neighbourhoods just north of the river. The final, unprofitable section of the Circle which had been opened in 1884 was, in fact, merely the eastern section of a much longer stretch of line which was already losing its short-distance traffic. From the end of 1881 onwards hardly a shareholders' meeting passed without Forbes, the District's chairman, bemoaning the injury done to them by the omnibus war. In 1887 he estimated that it was costing them

£30,000 per year; in 1888, £40,000; and in 1890, £50,000.[68] It was so much easier and more pleasant to jump on a passing omnibus in the Strand than to make one's way down to a smoky tunnel under the Embankment: only very bad weather would drive the short-distance passenger to such an extremity. By 1890, a prosperous year, the District carried 2,198,262 fewer passengers on intermediate journeys between the Monument and Sloane Square than it had taken between its Mansion House terminus and Sloane Square in 1882, just after the road cars had started to run.[69] Such increase in traffic as there was—from some 31,500,000 in 1882 to 35,725,000 in 1890 and 40,000,000 in 1896[70]— came from the growing western suburbs via the newly-built extensions of the line. By contrast, omnibus competition did not affect the Metropolitan Railway so severely. Its traffic grew from 69,350,000 in 1882 to 84,300,000 in 1890 and 91,000,000 in 1896.[71] Between 1886 and 1896, while the District had a struggle to pay 2 or 3 per cent. on its preference shares, the dividend on the Metropolitan's ordinaries was usually between 5 and 6 per cent.

The hackney coaches and hansom cabs also fell victim to the new omnibus competition. As we saw earlier in this chapter, their numbers grew rapidly during the 1870s, exceeding 10,500 by 1884. After a further but much slower increase to a peak of 11,400 in 1888, the total fell, and in 1893 it stood at 10,800, about the same figure as nine years before.[72] In 1894 the president of the cabmen's union explained this reversal in their fortunes partly in terms of the spread of the telephone—City men no longer had to take cabs to go and talk with their business contacts—and partly in terms of loss of fares to the omnibuses.[73] Some of the main-line terminal traffic had by then been lost to small, usually one-horse, vehicles which the railway companies either ran themselves or contracted with others to run for them. Another idea from Paris, they were apparently introduced to London by the North Western in or about

1880.[74] They were not licensed to ply for hire but ran to particular order, taking railway passengers and their luggage between their homes or hotels and the stations. In the mid-1890s the minimum fare seems to have been four shillings; at least, that was what the South Eastern and Great Western were then charging.[75] The railway companies were also the patrons of normal-sized omnibuses, licensed in the usual way, which ran between the main-line termini. The Great Northern, for instance, had four running to and from Waterloo via Charing Cross, and both the North Western and the Midland also had services to Charing Cross. On these omnibuses railway passengers who were booked through London travelled free.[76]

Of greater consequence to the coach and cab trade than the comparatively few special omnibuses which served the main-line termini was the greater attractiveness of the ordinary service vehicles which were plying for hire in increasing numbers in London's streets. The large glass windows, upholstered seats and less hazardous stairway to the roof (where garden seats were usually to be found) appealed to the more prosperous sections of the community, the cab trade's mainstay. In 1890, for instance, an article in the *Cornhill Magazine* drew attention to the effect of having the interior of omnibuses lined 'with Utrecht velvet or other handsome material suggesting the comfort, in some instances, of a first class railway carriage'. As a result, omnibuses were used by 'peeresses and others of high degree. . . . Ladies and gentlemen, officers, members of "first-class" clubs even, all patronize the once despised "bus".'[77] The same point was made four years later by Lord Aberdare in a letter to the Metropolitan Cab Inquiry. In his view 'the great changes affecting the use of cabs— especially hansoms—[were chiefly the result of] the almost universal use of omnibuses by whole classes who 20 years since were rarely seen in or on that now popular vehicle'.[78] The horse omnibuses had at last really come into their own.

The three horse tramway companies also prosper

The writer in the *Cornhill Magazine* who commented on the new *clientèle* which the more comfortable, upholstered omnibuses were attracting, went on to remark that

> the working man is rarely seen on the upholstered cushions; he feels himself uncomfortable and *de trop*. The tramcar is *his* familiar vehicle and he can ensconce himself there in his mortar-splashed clothes without restraint.

The tramcar, of course, catered for all sections of the community and served many middle-class neighbourhoods, but it certainly seems to have drawn its main strength from the inner, working-class suburbs. Tram fares were the cheapest of all, averaging just over 1¾d. in the early 1880s and falling to just over 1d. by 1896,[79] and the cars started sufficiently early in the morning to serve those who had to be at work between six and eight o'clock, unlike the omnibuses which were only just appearing on the streets by eight. Despite their slowness and their inconveniently situated 'central' termini, the tramways gained traffic at as fast a rate as the omnibuses. In 1875 the L.G.O.C. and the trams were carrying roughly the same number of passengers, just under 50,000,000. That is to say, when the L.G.O.C.'s 200 associates and the few rivals then in existence are added, the omnibuses probably carried about 70,000,000 to the tramcars' 50,000,000. By 1896, the comparable figures were about 300,000,000 and 280,000,000.[80]

Most of the traffic continued to be carried by the three companies which at the outset had successfully staked their claim to the most profitable districts. They subsequently opened new routes within those areas: the London Street Tramways, for instance, started to serve the hilly Caledonian Road in 1878 and the even steeper Pentonville Road in 1883; and the North Metropolitan opened a route along Canonbury Road and the New North Road in 1879.[81] And, more important, the three companies continued to push their lines farther out and so to enlarge their districts and keep pace with the growing suburbs. To the east, the North Metropolitan reached the 'Green Man' at Leytonstone in 1881, and a stretch of line separate from the main system was laid down in 1886 to serve the Barking Road, out at Canning Town. In the north, the London Street Tramways had by that year reached the southern fringes of Hampstead Heath. Its other northern limits were the foot of Highgate West Hill, Archway (approached via Junction Road) and Holloway Road (approached via Camden Road). And in the south the London Tramways Company started to run its Clapham Road cars to Totter-down Street, Tooting, at a 3d. fare, in February 1890, and in December 1892 it extended its other southern route to Telford Avenue, Streatham Hill, scaling Brixton Hill by means of cable traction.* Only one of the companies succeeded, however, in advancing its inner termini: this was the North Metropolitan which extended one of its routes from the Goswell Road end of Old Street to Holborn Town Hall (Gray's Inn Road) in October 1885, southwards down Gray's Inn Road in July 1887, and westwards along Theobald's Road in February 1887.[82]

Slow though the horse trams undoubtedly were, on the main routes the service was very frequent. Nobody had to wait long for a tramcar. From Clapham to Kennington, for instance, they ran every two minutes at peak hours and every three minutes at other times of the day, one tram being bound for Westminster Bridge, the next for Black-friars Bridge and the third for St. George's Church in Borough High Street. Each was painted a different colour according to its destination. The same arrangements operated on the other southern route, from Brixton to Kennington, thus giving a three-minute service from Ken-nington to each of the three termini at the busiest times and a 4½-minute service during the rest of the day. It is not

* See chapter ten.

surprising that, although it took half an hour or more to get from Clapham to the inner termini, the trams with their cheaper fares (2d. for those particular journeys) had driven most of the omnibuses from the roads concerned.[83] In Camberwell, another part of the London Tramways' network, the tramcar had also 'taken indisputed possession of long stretches of the main road', and in one of the busiest streets its passengers outnumbered those carried in omnibuses by nearly 15 to one.[84] The scale of operations was such that the company could, like the North Metropolitan, manufacture its own cars. Its works in Penrose Street, Walworth, came into use in 1884, a year after those of the North Metropolitan's at Leytonstone.[85] The London Tramways Company, having had its difficulties during the later 1870s, recovered to pay 5 or 6 per cent. in the 1880s and a higher rate in the 1890s. The London Street Tramways Company paid 8 or 9 per cent. in the 1880s and a little less than that in the early 1890s. And the North Metropolitan, the largest, was the most prosperous of all; its shareholders came to expect a return of at least 8 or 9 per cent. as a matter of course.

New tramway companies fill in the gaps and operate on the fringes

Other tramway companies formed later had to make the most of such main roads as were left. The most successful of them was the South London Tramways Company, formed in 1879. During the early 1880s it developed routes between Wandsworth and the southern end of Westminster Bridge, with a branch via Lambeth Road and St. George's Circus to Southwark Bridge Road and the Hop Exchange in Southwark Street. Serving York Road, Battersea Park Road, Queen's Road (Chelsea Bridge), St. John's Hill, Lavender Hill, Wandsworth Road and the Albert Embankment and having two convenient inner termini (one of them nearer to the Bank than that of any other tramway from the south), the company soon established itself as the fourth

largest in London. But it managed to pay only about 4 per
cent. This was rather better, however, than the dividend
distributed by its neighbour, the London Southern Tramways Company (1882), which edged its way between 1883
and 1887 into some vacant roads to the south-east. Its
services centered upon Coldharbour Lane, one route running from there to Vauxhall Cross via South Lambeth
Road, a second to Camberwell Green in one direction and
Brixton Church in the other, and a third to Norwood
Cemetery via Milkwood Road and Norwood Road. To the
north-east, and beyond the London Tramways' Old Kent
Road line, was the London, Deptford & Greenwich Tramways Company (more accurately described by its original
name of 1879, the Southwark & Deptford). In 1881 and
1882 it opened lines from Tooley Street, near Hay's Wharf,
to Deptford via Dockhead, Parker's Row, Jamaica Road,
Lower Road and Evelyn Street. It also had lines from the
Old Kent Road through Bermondsey Road, Grange Road,
Southwark Park Road, Rotherhithe New Road and, for a
time, a line in Spa Road. Most easterly of all the lines were
those of the Woolwich & South East London Tramways, a
narrow gauge (3 ft. 6 in.) track opened in 1881–82 from
Greenwich along the main road to Woolwich and on to
Plumstead High Street. Greenwich was also linked with
Catford via Lewisham by the South Eastern Metropolitan
Tramways (1888), the route being opened in October 1890.
To the south was the small system of the Croydon Tramways
Company (1878), opened between 1879 and 1883, and
amalgamated in the latter year with the Norwood &
District Tramways.[86] None of these smaller ventures was
very profitable, yet none sank to the ludicrous level of the
London, Camberwell & Dulwich Tramways. This com-
pany was formed (as the Peckham & East Dulwich) in
1882, to build a line south from Peckham High Street,
through Peckham Rye to 'The Plough' in Lordship Lane.
The track was laid by 1885, but a dispute with the local

vestry prevented any trams from running until 1895 or 1896—and then the service came to an end after five or six years.[87]

The smaller companies north of the river promoted to build tramways in the northern, eastern and western suburbs, while not so ridiculous as this, made nobody's fortune and often lost money. The North London Tramways Company, formed, in 1878, as the North London Suburban Tramways, opened a service from Ponders End to Stamford Hill in 1881–82 and built a branch along the Seven Sisters' Road to join the North Metropolitan at Finsbury Park in 1885. Two years later another line was opened from Manor House to Wood Green. Steam traction was used,* but the company slid into financial difficulties, and in 1891 passed into the hands of the North Metropolitan, which reverted to the use of horse power. Beyond the North Metropolitan's north-eastern boundary at Clapton, the Lea Bridge, Leyton & Walthamstow Tramways Company was formed in 1881 to run from Clapton along the Lea Bridge Road to Wood-ford. The first stretch, from the bridge over the Lea to Whipps Cross, was opened in 1883, but the company soon went into liquidation. In 1888 the tramway was revived by another company of the same name, and powers were gained to build a branch along High Road, Leyton, to a point near Leyton station and to extend the main line west-wards to the North Metropolitan's terminus, although there was to be no connection between the two systems. The track was repaired and trams started to run again in 1889. The extensions were opened at the beginning of the 1890s and thereafter the fortunes of the tramway began to improve.

The Highgate Hill Tramway, from Archway to Highgate Village, opened in May 1884, is remembered as the first such undertaking in Europe to employ Hallidie's patent system of cable traction, already operating successfully in San Francisco and other parts of the United States. It was

*See chapter ten.

not a great success, however, being liable to interruptions and accidents. Further details will be found in chapter ten in the course of an account of this new form of traction.

In west London, there were two tramway concerns. The first, the Harrow Road & Paddington Tramways Company (1886), opened 2½ miles of track from Amberley Road, Paddington, and along the Harrow Road to Harlesden in July 1888; a branch along Chippenham Road to Carlton Vale was given up in 1894, though the rails remained in place until 1912.[88] The second, the West Metropolitan Tramways Company, was formed in 1881 to take over the existing line running west from Shepherd's Bush along the Uxbridge Road and another one then being built along Goldhawk Road to King Street, Hammersmith; this was opened in March 1882. By early in the following year extensions had also been opened from Goldhawk Road to Kew Bridge in one direction and to Hammersmith Broadway in the other. The company was never at all profitable; having got into severe difficulties, it passed in 1894 to a newly formed concern, the London United Tramways Company. Under vigorous new management this dilapidated system was re-equipped, and in 1901 it was to become the pioneer of overground electric traction in the London area.

The L.C.C. and the tramways

None of the tramways, large or small, had security of tenure. The Tramways Act of 1870 laid down that local authorities had the right to purchase the various undertakings, usually after 21 years, without any compensation for goodwill. While the original companies of 1869—the North Metropolitan and the two concerns later merged to form the London Tramways—had in their 1870 extension Acts secured 28-year clauses,[89] the London Street Tramways, formed in 1870, could be purchased after 21 years should the local authority so decide.[90] By 1891, when the decision had to be taken whether to purchase or not, the

London Street Tramways had to deal with a new and vigorous local authority which was resolved to exercise its rights at the first opportunity. In 1889 the rather easy-going Metropolitan Board of Works was replaced by the much more determined London County Council, a directly elected body noted, particularly in its early years, for its radicalism. 'Its persistence in indulging in attacks upon privilege and vested interests', the official historians of the L.C.C. have observed, 'were uncompromising, almost ruthless.'[91] For the Progressives, the tramways represented an important means of social reform, and to have them available for municipal purchase on such reasonable terms was for them a stroke of fortune to be exploited to the full. Under municipal control the L.C.C. could not only secure additional profits to add to its rate income, but it could also provide cheap communication to its more distant housing schemes, and on the labour side give an example of how enlightened employers should behave. The Progressives started their campaign during 1891, and in October of that year it was agreed that the first $4\frac{1}{2}$-mile stretch belonging to the London Street Tramways should be purchased as soon as it became available.[92] There then followed a long legal tussle over the amount of compensation which was to be paid. The company, hoping to be taken over as a going concern, claimed £604,000 on the basis of 20 years' purchase. The arbitrator, however, interpreted the 1870 Act in the spirit in which it had been passed and awarded £102,000, plus a further £25,000 or so for rolling stock and horses—not an unfair figure when it is borne in mind that the whole of the company's paid-up capital for $13\frac{1}{2}$ miles of track was only £382,000. A number of appeals followed, but the arbitrator's award was finally upheld by the House of Lords in 1894.[93]

With the conditions of purchase firmly re-stated, the L.C.C. set about negotiating with the other companies, part of whose systems were then due, or becoming due, for purchase. At the election of 1895, however, the Progressives lost their majority on the Council, and the comprehensive agreement reached with the two northern undertakings in the following year was something of a compromise. By it the L.C.C. was to purchase that part of the London Street and North Metropolitan Tramways' systems which lay within the county boundary—48 miles in all—for £799,476, and to lease the whole of it back to the North Metropolitan which was to operate it until 1910 when the last of those lines would fall due for purchase. The company was to pay the L.C.C. £45,000 per year rent, plus interest on the purchase price of freehold and leasehold property, and $12\frac{1}{2}$ per cent. of any amount by which gross revenue should exceed the total for 1895.[94] Clauses were also included relating to employees' hours of labour and rates of pay, the running of workmen's cars and the fares to be charged.

In 1898 the Progressives were again returned. When in that year 48 miles of tramway south of the river belonging to the London Tramways Company fell into the L.C.C.'s hands, the Council decided not to lease the undertaking back to the company but to work the system itself as it was empowered to do by an Act obtained in 1896. With the take-over of these lines on 1 January 1899, the majority of London's horse tramways—the most profitable sections developed by the three main companies—had passed into municipal control. It was now the L.C.C.'s responsibility both to organize these lines into a unified system (and particularly to link the tramways north and south of the river) and to electrify them.

Private profit and social gain

Which of London's transport undertakings made the most of the growing traffic in the later nineteenth century? And did those concerns which carried the most passengers pay the best dividends?

The trend that was noticed in the third quarter of the

century—railways gaining passengers at a much more rapid rate than road transport—was clearly reversed after 1875. In 1875 perhaps somewhere between 150,000,000 and 170,000,000 journeys were made by train and perhaps a further 115,000,000 by omnibus and tramcar. By 1896 the comparable totals were of the order of 400,000,000 and 600,000,000.[95] The average journey by train, of course, was considerably longer (and more expensive) than that by tramcar or omnibus; the railways were still, therefore, responsible for greater movement of passengers than were the road services, and they continued to be the major force in the spread of population to the outer suburbs. Perhaps, too, the rise in the road transport figures would seem a little less rapid if we possessed details of the numbers of passengers who travelled by hackney carriage, for some of the omnibuses' gains were derived from this source. Nevertheless, there can be no doubt that if the third quarter of the nineteenth century saw London's railways developing their traffic most vigorously, the last quarter of the century found the road services reasserting themselves. Companies using horses were gaining traffic at a far faster rate than those using the most up-to-date locomotives.

The operators of horse omnibuses and horse trams—or at least the main companies, which were handling the bulk of the road traffic—continued to make good profits and could pay a high dividend upon the modest capitals involved, usually more than 5 per cent., sometimes 10 per cent. and on occasions even more than that. The railway companies, on the other hand, were rarely able to provide such rich returns upon the far larger amounts of capital which had had to be raised to build their costly urban lines. The North London, it is true, paid a very respectable $7\frac{1}{2}$ per cent., but much of it had been built by the mid-century before the urban frontier had advanced very far, and before land values only a few miles from central London had become very high. And it derived revenue from goods traffic as well as from passengers. The Metropolitan paid 5 per cent. or so, but half of this came from the surplus lands it owned. And, at the other end of the scale, shareholders in the District Railway (paying only 2½ per cent. even on its preference stock), the Great Eastern (probably making a profit on its suburban services but evidently not a large one) and the Great Northern (with its 'suburban incubus' and costly widening schemes) were, no doubt, somewhat envious when they saw how much more profitable the old-fashioned mode of traction could still be in London when adapted to later nineteenth-century needs.

It is tempting to argue that the railways bestowed the largest social benefit upon London by enabling it to continue to grow outwards, yet derived the smallest economic reward. Tramway and omnibus journeys of six miles or so, an hour's actual travelling time, were the maximum that people with a choice were willing to tolerate. Therefore the expansion of London beyond such a radius depended on steam trains capable of averaging at least twice the speed of horse-drawn vehicles. Yet such an argument presupposes that all housing development was taking place beyond the omnibuses' and tramways' six-mile limit; but that was not so. Within that limit many of the larger houses were being divided into apartments, their owners or previous occupiers having moved farther out. Some of the older property was being knocked down and new houses built on the site. Vacant spaces were being filled in. These processes are only too familiar to those who have lived in London in recent times. The inner suburbs, if they may be so called, depended upon the growth of tramway and omnibus (as well as upon railway) services for their development. The chairman of London Tramways was not exaggerating when he claimed, in 1884:

We have relieved London of an immense number of poor people by carrying them out to the suburbs . . . building has been going on very largely on our line of roads in south London. . . . The principal centre of our population is along the Old Kent Road and out by Walworth to Camberwell . . .[96]

And, if the Great Eastern, by means of cheap workmen's (and other reduced) fares enabled masses of people to escape from overcrowding in central London, so, too, did the North Metropolitan Tramways which not only provided cheap early-morning fares but also in 1891 introduced 1d. fares throughout the day on special, white-painted trams which ran from Aldgate to Poplar and to Stratford.[97]

Railways, omnibuses and trams between them contributed great, and to a large extent complementary, social benefits upon Londoners rich and poor. And on the poor, particularly. For them, this was at last the beginning of the age of improvement.

U

CHAPTER NINE

LABOUR

London's transport undertakings soon became important employers of labour. On the railways, wages generally represented total earnings, but on the omnibuses, and to a smaller extent on the trams, wages were considerably supplemented by privately-pocketed fares. The conditions under which tramway and omnibus men worked were, however, considerably inferior to those on the railways; in particular, hours were considerably longer and jobs were not so secure. Trade unionism among railwaymen was quiescent, but London's tramway and omnibus men, particularly the former, became organized for a short period during and after the Dock Strike of 1889. A strike of omnibus men took place in 1891 in an attempt to prevent the L.G.O.C. from introducing tickets as a check on conductors, but it failed.

AN IMPORTANT DISTINCTION BETWEEN ROAD AND RAILWAY WORKERS

IN THE MIDDLE of the 1820s, before the coming of the omnibus and the railway, probably not more than 5,000 men were employed in keeping London's 1,150 coaches and cabs and its 600 or so short-stages on the road and in manning the few early steamboats on the river.[1] In 1891, according to the census returns, the total had grown to 76,500, 48,200 of them in road transport and 28,300 on the railways.[2] Although the latter figure omits the carmen and carters engaged exclusively in the handling of goods, it inevitably includes many railwaymen who were concerned with the long-distance traffic to and from London, and to that extent it is not strictly comparable with the estimate for the 1820s which leaves out the long-distance stage coaches. Nevertheless, it seems probable that the labour force engaged in moving people into, out of, or across London grew perhaps tenfold during this period of nearly 70 years. Many new transport undertakings emerged, some, like the railway companies or the L.G.O.C. or the larger tramways, on a considerable scale. How did they treat their employees?

A broad distinction needs to be made at the outset between the men who worked on the railways, whether main-line or local, and those who were engaged in one or other form of road transport. The fundamental difference between the two arose from the way in which fares were handled. On the railways they were paid at a booking office and whoever was collecting them was under very close supervision. Tickets or turnstiles made personal gain almost impossible. On the roads, however, fares were collected by hundreds of men on hundreds of moving vehicles scattered throughout the length and breadth of the metropolis and any check was far more difficult. Consequently, while the men who worked on the railways had to rely on their wages, plus any gratuities which might come their way, those who worked in road transport were throughout most of the nineteenth century, to greater or less degree, in business on their own account, lessees of their employers' vehicles rather than mere wage earners.

The cabmen and their earnings

The drivers of cabs and coaches provide the best example of this bailee system. Those who operated in central London hired their vehicles and horses from the proprietors at a daily rate which varied with the time of year and the volume of traffic which might be expected. In May 1830, for instance—at the beginning of the busy season—cabs were hired at 25s. per day and it was thought that a driver's takings would then average about 30s.[3] Later in the century, when the price of horse feed was lower and the rate of taxation had been reduced, the maximum hiring rate was 19s. a day or, at most, a guinea, a figure to which it rose gradually from 10s. at the beginning of the season.[4] The extent to which the owners raised their rates in the season led to considerable resistance on the part of the drivers from about 1880 onwards when both omnibus competition and the coming of the telephone were making fares harder to earn. Drivers in the 1890s, who claimed they could take only 30s. a day, looked back longingly to the 1860s and 1870s when they were taking up to £2 or more.[5] In 1867 some of them had formed the Licensed Cabdrivers' Trade Union Society, but this had been short-lived.[6] In 1874 a stronger organization, the Amalgamated Society of Metropolitan Cabdrivers, was started; it lasted until the later 1880s but perished because of 'internal bickering and jealousies'.[7] It was eventually succeeded, in 1890, by the Metropolitan Cabdrivers' Trade Union and this, in its turn, was reconstituted four years later as the London Cabdrivers' Trade Union.[8] These associations were responsible for a number of strikes at the beginning of the busy season, the drivers refusing to take out cabs from certain yards until the rates of hiring were reduced. Having succeeded at these selected yards, the movement was then switched to others. These tactics, successful in 1882 but less so in 1888, were repeated at greater length (13 weeks), but apparently with even less success, in 1891.[9] The drivers were more fortunate three years later, however, when they staged their first general strike, which affected all the yards between 15 May and 11 June 1894. The dispute was referred to the Home Secretary, and a new scale of hiring charges, ranging from 10s. to 16s. per day, was agreed upon.[10] This was a considerable achievement in view of the large surplus of licensed drivers who wished to hire cabs and carriages. Anyone could then obtain a police licence to drive a hackney carriage without any test of his driving ability. All sorts of men—carpenters, house painters and decorators are among those particularly mentioned—took to the road for short spells between jobs. There was even one man who drove every Saturday afternoon and Sunday and worked as a compositor for the rest of the week.[11]

The extent of the hackney carriage drivers' earnings, therefore, depended upon their own resourcefulness in finding fares. By 1892, according to the general secretary of the London Cabdrivers' Union, they had to work on the average about 15 hours a day and be out on the road every other Sunday in order to earn a living wage.[12] A few years earlier, before omnibus competition was intensified, a working day of 13 hours seems to have been more usual, although in the season drivers had worked during (but not necessarily throughout) a 15-hour day, from 9 or 10 in the morning until midnight or 1 a.m.[13]

Employment on the omnibuses

Omnibus conductors, although paid a formal wage by their employers, also came to augment their wages by putting fares into their own pockets and so came to operate in much the same way as did the cabmen. These extra earnings were then shared with the drivers and horsekeepers as well as with watermen (not paid anything by the company) who looked after the omnibuses while their crews took a few minutes' rest. Already by the middle of the 1860s an L.G.O.C. official was claiming that something like £25,000 was being collected in fares every year over and above what was actually paid in.[14]

Earnings 'on the side' had been traditional in the coaching business, and the omnibus crews, who at first worked alongside and in competition with the short-stages, probably inherited the coachman's reluctance to live solely on his wages. On the long-stages the coachman and guard had kept the short-distance fares for themselves, and their level of wages took this extra income into account, together with the further earnings from tips for which there was a recognized scale according to mileage.[15] On the short-stages and the early omnibuses there were additional earnings from 'the box', passengers who travelled by the driver's side. According to Mayhew, writing in the middle of the century, drivers were paid either 34s. a week or 21s. plus the fares of their box-seat passengers, a sum which could often be supplemented by tips for the privilege of handling the reins.[16] This was a good income at a time when the unskilled earned £1 a week or less and the skilled man round about 30s. if he was fortunate. The conductor, too, making about 4s. a day in wages, plus whatever he could make privately, including the income from carrying parcels,[17] was also among the higher-paid groups of wage earner. When the L.G.O.C. was formed, conductors' wages on the various routes seem to have been standardized at 4s. a day and those of drivers at 5s. 6d. or 6s. Horsekeepers were paid 3s. 6d.[18] The new company's failure to introduce a ticket system in the later 1850s, however, seems a clear indication that these wages were already being heavily supplemented by privately-pocketed fares. The London *gérants* were all experienced proprietors who appear to have been quite content to let well alone and continue with the existing methods. These consisted of way-bills for each journey and periodical checks by men and women, known as 'spots', who mingled with the travelling public and subsequently sent in their confidential reports.[19]

The spoils system worked in this way: the proprietors knew approximately what the earnings of a given omnibus on a particular route should be. If a conductor was able to take more than that figure, nothing was said if he pocketed some of the difference. If, on the other hand, he had a run of bad luck or overdid things and persistently paid in less than the expected amount, he was dismissed for low earnings. From his extra takings, the conductor was expected to tip the driver, and the driver the horsekeeper. So all the company's wage earners had their cut. To this extent, even though the proprietors paid their men a formal wage, they were, in reality, hiring out their omnibuses to them. A fund for the repair of vehicles and other expenditure incurred through accidents, to which both drivers and conductors were obliged to contribute,[20] was in some respects a recognition of this relationship. So, too, was the failure of the owners to provide any uniforms,[21] each conductor and driver having to fit himself out with a hard-wearing black suit. The drivers sported top hats, but the conductors, having frequently to put their heads inside the door of the omnibus, preferred bowlers.

'The company', wrote Charles Booth in his great *Survey of Life and Labour in London*, 'encouraged the efforts of their men to serve and please the public, winking at, and allowing the men to profit by, a system which, but that it was tacitly acknowledged, could only be described as peculation. If the money received rose above a certain sum—which would vary a little according to circumstances —the conductor kept back the surplus. On the other hand, a certain amount was expected by the company, and if, one time with another, it was not forthcoming, the conductor was discharged. Whether he had failed to collect enough or had helped himself too freely was not inquired into.'[22]

How much the omnibus men were able to add to their wages, it is obviously impossible to say—and in any case the sum fluctuated with the traffic. Booth reported that conductors could earn so much as £4 or £5 in a good week.[23] It seems probable that 35s. to £2 would be a likely guess for the average. Such an income would put omnibus men among the highest-paid sections of the working classes, but the figure becomes less attractive when it is translated into an hourly rate, for the hours were extremely long.

The first omnibuses started to leave the depots at 7.30 in the morning, and their crews had to report for duty 20 minutes before that. They then worked 15 or 16 hours a day, the first men getting back between 10.30 and 11.30 and the later ones after midnight.[24] During the day's work, each omnibus made six return journeys. The length of the terminus breaks would depend on the nature of the route; they were occasionally as long as an hour but more usually only about 15 minutes.[25] During this time the crews had to snatch what refreshment they could at a nearby tavern while a waterman looked after their vehicle and horses; or perhaps they would eat the sandwiches they had brought with them or the basin of food which their wives had sent up. This was the omnibus men's life for seven days a week, Sundays and holidays being often busier than ordinary weekdays if the weather was fine. An unpaid day's leave could be obtained now and again—in which case 'odd' men came on as relief crews—but such days off were few and far between. 'Every horse in our stables', remarked a driver to Mayhew, 'has one day's rest in four, but it's no rest for the driver.'[26] For him, exposed to all weathers and liable to be fined for poor timekeeping, it was a hard life. And for the conductor, standing on his step at the back of the vehicle always on the look-out for passengers, helping them on and off and taking their fares, it was little less bleak and no less exacting. Nor did the 15 or 16 hours in the company's service constitute the whole of their working day, for many had some distance to walk between their homes or lodgings and the depot. The married men often saw their children only in the mornings before they set off for work.

Despite these very long hours, the lure of high weekly earnings never failed to produce a long queue of men eager to do omnibus work. This meant first of all securing a Metropolitan Police licence (under the Act of 1838),[27] for which the applicant had to be vouched for by two house-holders, and then, if accepted, doing relief work as an 'odd' man until a full-time vacancy came available. 'When we want six conductors', said the L.G.O.C.'s general manager in 1877, 'we probably have 60 or 80 candidates.'[28] With such a wide choice, the proprietors could pick their men carefully. Mayhew found conductors who had come from all walks of life: grocers, drapers, shopmen, barmen, printers, tailors, shoemakers, clerks, joiners, saddlers, coach builders, porters, town travellers, carriers, fishmongers and a lawyer's clerk turned picture dealer.[29] H. C. Moore, writing at the beginning of the present century, was even able to recall an Oxford graduate who had served as a London conductor at one time.[30] Neither the graduate nor his companions, Moore insisted, spoke with a cockney accent: the word 'lydy' was only used by conductors in novels. The drivers, however, were in his view intellectually inferior to the conductors, their often-quoted witticisms (for the benefit of roof passengers) were of the heavily rehearsed and often-repeated variety.[31]

The point is frequently made—and rightly—that those who worked in passenger transport did not have to suffer the effects of trade depressions in the same way as did working men in other occupations. Transport services kept running when the factories and workshops were idle or only working part-time, and when men in heavy labouring jobs could find no work at all. This, however, is by no means the whole story, for the evidence suggests that there was little continuous employment for quite a number of omnibus men, and particularly for conductors. The spoils system had its hazards as well as its prizes. The slightest cause of complaint, whether for low earnings or some other lapse, led to instant dismissal. Omnibus crews were hired by the day and fired on the spot. In 1879 Henry Hicks, not yet a director of the L.G.O.C. but already taking a close interest in its affairs, told a shareholders' meeting that he had been informed that upwards of three-quarters of the company's conductors left within the year and inquired whether this was true. The chairman, while agreeing that 'a large percentage' left, thought that the total drain was 'not to the extent mentioned'.[32] Clearly, the turnover of conductors, if not of drivers, was considerable, at least on the L.G.O.C. Unfortunately, however, we do not know whether the wastage was among trained men or was confined to recent recruits who had shown, after a few months' trial, that they were unsuited for this exacting form of work. Perhaps a very select few were able to show that they could work the spoils system to the company's satisfaction; there certainly does seem to have been a larger nucleus of seasoned veterans than the high turnover rate would suggest. It was this nucleus, no doubt, which gained for the omnibus crews such high popular esteem. Even some shareholders showed concern about their long hours of work, and the Rothschilds gave a Christmas box of a brace of pheasants to drivers and conductors of vehicles which passed their houses and, later, to other crews as well. By the end of the century, 3,000 brace were distributed every Christmas; in recognition of this generosity the Rothschilds' racing colours were attached to the drivers' whips and the conductors' bell-pulls at that time of the year.[33] In 1897 another private citizen, Morris Abrahams, was responsible for launching the Omnibus Men's Superannuation Fund. This was to provide any driver or conductor with an income of 15s. a week should he be incapacitated as a result of an accident during his work.[34]

Employment on the trams

The tramway companies used tickets from the outset and, no doubt because of this extra check, paid their conductors slightly higher wages than did the L.G.O.C.; in the 1870s pay on the North Metropolitan Tramways started at 5s. per day and rose to 6s. after six months.[35] Tram driving, however, which was not considered such a skilled task as omnibus driving, was paid at the same rate. It is evident, however, from an account written by George Lovett, a conductor who worked for the North Metropolitan in the middle of the 1870s, that tickets did not then prevent conductors from pocketing fares; and these winnings were shared with the driver. Short-distance passengers, particularly on a wet day, paid their fare just before jumping off and did not wait for a ticket. Conductors had a habit of picking up the last ticket to be punched from the seats or floor and issuing it again, preferably on the roof 'where the ring [of the ticket punch] is not confined'. And sometimes a sympathetic passenger would say, 'Well, I know you are not properly dealt with for this slavery, you needn't punch me a ticket'.

As with the omnibuses, the labour turnover was high. Lovett himself was employed for only five months; he believed that he was dismissed because his wages were due to go up to 6s. and the company preferred a new man at 5s. instead. This may well have been the case, but, from the company's point of view, perhaps he did not quite reach their exacting standard. At the same time, he asserted that no conductor lasted for more than a few years; he doubted whether the North Metropolitan had more than a dozen with two or three years' service. Unfortunately there is no means of checking this assertion. The hours were much the same as those on the omnibuses; Lovett usually started about 8 o'clock and went on until nearly midnight. Then he had to walk from the depot at Gillett Street (off Kingsland High Street) to his lodgings in Weymouth Terrace, a mile or so away. He was entitled to unpaid leave if he wished to take it, but, during his five months' service, he never had a day off. The company supported an annual outing to the country,[36] but he seems to have missed even this one brief moment of relaxation.

By the later 1880s the lot of the men who worked for the North Metropolitan Tramways seems to have improved a little. By 1887 a field was made available to them in which they could play cricket, and their wages were increased by a shilling a day on Bank Holidays.[37] In 1889, at the time of the Dock Strike when Thomas Sutherst, a barrister who had interested himself in the tramway and omnibus men's conditions,[38] organized between 2,000 and 3,000 tramway men and some from the omnibuses into their first trade union,[39] the North Metropolitan decided to allow three hours' rest in the middle of the day. It also stopped levying fines for most shortcomings.

'In 1889', testified a tramway man who later became a union official, 'most of the companies gave the men better conditions of labour and the inspectors . . . treated the men with more civility and altogether better than they did previous to any union being formed and furthermore the system that had been in vogue of fining the men excessive fines was practically abolished from the first agitation.'[40]

In 1889 the North Metropolitan also started a provident society, setting aside £1,000 for the purpose. The employee paid 6d. per week and for this he received 2s. 6d. per day in case of sickness, £15 in the event of death, and £10 (and four days' pay) if his wife died.[41] Wages, however, were somewhat less in money terms, though not in real terms, than they had been 15 years before. In 1892 the starting wage on the North Metropolitan, which had been 5s. in the 1870s, had been reduced, in response to the fall in prices, to 4s. 6d., and it took four months to reach 5s. and 12 months (instead of six) to reach 6s. And this was after a small rise had been granted in the previous year. Nevertheless, these rates were still very attractive. The following advertisement, which appeared twice weekly in the *Daily News*, never failed to produce plenty of keen recruits, particularly from the provinces:

THE NORTH METROPOLITAN TRAMWAYS COMPANY

Drivers and conductors wanted; none but respectable, intelligent, active men, of good character, employed; personal application indispensable; police licence required; wages 4s. 6d. per day to commence, 5s. per day after four months, and 6s. per day after 12 months service. Men over 40 years of age or under 5½ feet in height need not apply; drivers must be skilled coachmen and pass a pair-horse driving test before appointment; conductors must write a good hand and be fair arithmeticians; there is a provident society for the employés to which admission is gained after three months service by men of good health. Forms of application to be obtained on Tuesdays and Thursdays between 12 and 2 p.m., third floor, Ropemaker Street, Finsbury Pavement, E.C.[42]

By the middle of the 1890s, when Charles Booth was writing about London's tramway men, he put a driver's usual pay at 5s. 6d. a day—presumably the average based upon the higher rates paid by the various companies—a conductor's at 4s. 6d.—taking into account the large turnover of recent recruits at the lowest rate—an inspector's at 35s. a week and a horsekeeper's at 24s. As in the case of the omnibus men, no uniform was yet provided.[43] There was still a large turnover of labour. Throughout 1891, on the North Metropolitan, which employed 1,800 men altogether, conductors were dismissed at an average rate of five a week and drivers at the rate of two a week. How many found the work quite unendurable and resigned of their own accord was not stated.[44]

The ticket strike of 1891

The omnibus men's strike of 1891 was a direct outcome of the L.G.O.C.'s decision to limit, if not to end, the spoils system by the introduction of tickets on all its routes. On the trams and road cars tickets had so far discouraged, rather than prevented, conductors from putting fares into their own pockets, but the introduction of tickets by the L.G.O.C. and its associates meant that the ticket system became at last almost universal on London's road services.[45] Passengers got into the habit of expecting tickets wherever they went and this made it much more difficult for conductors to avoid issuing them.

The L.G.O.C. started seriously to consider the introduction of tickets towards the end of November 1890 when a Manchester concern, calling itself the Halfpenny Fare Company, approached it with an attractive proposition for advertising on the backs of tickets.[46] Discussion of this proposal went on for several weeks,[47] and at the half-yearly meeting in February 1891 A. G. Church, the managing director, who had always given any suggestion of introducing tickets a decidedly chilly reception, retired. On 2

March 1891, the board decided to adopt the Road Car Company's method of check, and the Bell Punch Company was asked to provide specimen tickets and boxes.[48] Bell Punch offered tickets at 5d. per 1,000 if the L.G.O.C. kept the advertising rights, and 4d. per 1,000 if they did not. The Hansard Publishing Union (Colley and Company), however, which was then in desperate financial straits and wanted the contract at all costs, put in a tender at 3d. and 2½d., which, having been cut to 2¼d., was accepted.[49] The ticket system was introduced on the L.G.O.C.'s omnibuses and those of its associates on 31 May 1891.

In making this important change, the L.G.O.C. recognized that the men's earnings would suffer and therefore made the gesture of increasing wages in an attempt to avoid a dispute. Drivers' wages were to be put up from 6s. to 7s. a day; those of conductors with more than three years' service from 4s. to 5s., but only to 4s. 6d. if less than three years had been served and not at all for the first year of service.[50] So a driver would receive 49s. a week instead of 42s.; but, in view of the apparent high turnover rate of conductors, it seems unlikely that very many of them would benefit from the 7s. advance while those in their first year would not be any better off at all.

The omnibus crews held a midnight meeting on Saturday, 6 June—very late at night was the only time when they had time to meet—and, with Thomas Sutherst, the creator of the union of 1889, playing a leading part, an immediate strike was determined on. Employees of the Road Car Company and other omnibus undertakings came out in sympathy, and there seem to have been very few omnibuses on the streets after midday on the following day, Sunday. On the Monday a deputation of drivers and conductors, together with Sutherst, met a joint gathering of L.G.O.C. and Road Car directors, and representatives of the other omnibus undertakings attended at a later stage to endorse the decisions that had been taken. The strikers could hardly base their claim upon the loss of illegal earnings, although everyone knew that these were the real cause of the dispute. Instead, they demanded a shorter working day. A 12-hour day was, in fact, conceded by the management, which also agreed to raise conductors' wages to 4s. 6d. a day during the first 12 months (and to 5s. after that instead of after three years), and horsekeepers' wages from 3s. 6d. to 4s. The maximum for drivers, however, was to be reduced from the 7s. recently offered to 6s. 6d. (and to 6s. during the first 12 months).[51] This was a considerable gain for the men in hours worked, and a modest financial gain for conductors, if not for drivers. The strikers held out for better terms for several days, but, on the following Saturday, 13 June, Sutherst agreed to the company's offer and the dispute ended. Those who had remained at work during the strike were each awarded a gratuity of two guineas;[52] and when the Lord Mayor later intervened on behalf of certain discharged employees, some of whom had served the company for more than 25 years, he received a sharp rebuke from the board:

The Directors regret that the Lord Mayor's sympathy should have been devoted to men in custody for breaking the law on the one hand and to those discharged for dishonesty or incapacity on the other.[53]

Of 1,047 conductors in the L.G.O.C.'s service on the day before the strike began, only 670 remained 11 months later. The trade union, which Sutherst himself confessed contained 'very few members' at the time of the strike, was replaced shortly afterwards by the Amalgamated Omnibus & Tram Workers' Union, but by October 1892 an omnibus driver—a hostile witness—claimed that it was 'completely broken up'.[54]

The various undertakings quickly introduced the 12-hour day, using relief crews to man the omnibuses for two of their journeys. But a strict 12-hour day did not last for long. First

of all, a 12-hour day was interpreted as meaning an average
of 12 hours: on 21 August 1891 the board of the L.G.O.C.
'allowed' the crews of the south-western district to work
alternate days of nine and 15 hours.[55] Then, by the autumn
of 1892, the old hours were restored for those who stated in
writing that they were willing to work them in return for an
additional shilling a day.[56] When Booth looked into this
matter in the middle of the 1890s, he found that omnibus
men were working 15 hours more often than 12, and when
they were doing 12 it was usually an alternating 15 and
nine.[57] The omnibus men had succeeded in making good
some of their lost earnings—their main concern—but only
to a limited extent in gaining a shorter working day.
Nevertheless the events of the later 1880s on the tramways
and of the early 1890s on the omnibuses did represent the
beginnings of a move away from a life which consisted
almost wholly of work.

Employment on the railways

The railway company's treatment of its employees was
much more enlightened. Railwaymen could often look
forward to promotion and face the future with a certain
amount of hope. In the locomotive department, for instance,
a youth would enter as a cleaner and graduate to fireman
and then, perhaps, to driver. Railway service usually
occupied a whole lifetime and was not, as so often on the
omnibuses and trams, merely incidental employment. When
the inquiry into the state of ventilation in the underground
was held in 1897, there was no difficulty in producing an
engine driver who had survived those smoky tunnels for 33
years (with only eight days' sick leave, and that to have a
tumour removed from his ear), and another who had
joined the company as a cleaner 24 years before.[58] There
were railwaymen's unions to which these men could belong
—the all-grades Amalgamated Society of Railway Servants
was formed in 1871 and the footplate men's union began as

111. The Tower Subway: the Waiting Room   112. Inside the Tower Subway Car

113. Tube Tunnellers and Shield

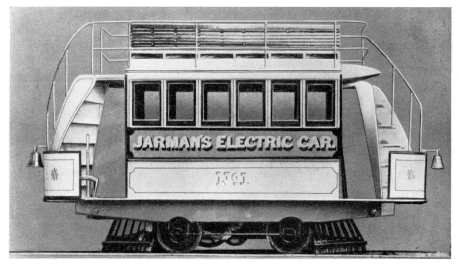

109. Jarman's Model Electric Battery Tram, 1886

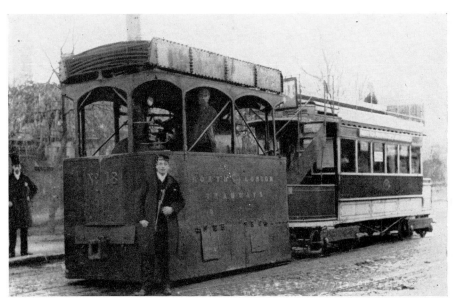

110. North London Tramways Steam Locomotive and Car on the Wood Green Line

107. The Highgate Hill Cable Tram

108. The Brixton Hill Cable Tram

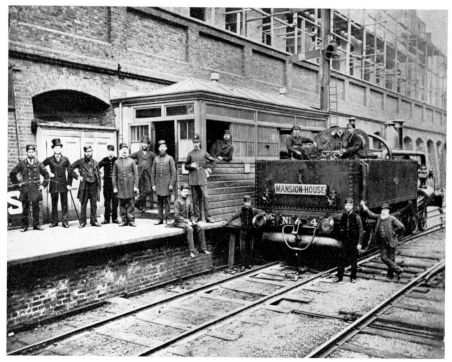

105. Metropolitan District Railway Staff at Earl's Court (Old Station), 1876

106. L.G.O.C. Stables at Rose Street, Hackney, 1901

a breakaway from it in 1879—but there is no evidence that either union gained much support from railwaymen on the underground and they were not involved in any serious disputes.

London's underground and suburban railways operated for much longer hours than did its road services; at the end of the 1870s, for example, the Metropolitan's first locomotive left the depot at 5.15 a.m. and the last one returned to it at 1.15 a.m., and by the end of the century the Great Eastern's all-night service to Walthamstow, started in June 1897, meant that Liverpool Street's suburban traffic went on right round the clock. (A porter, when asked when the last train left for Walthamstow, is alleged to have replied: 'Lor' bless you marm, there ain't no last train to Walthamstow.'[59]) Yet the railwaymen's hours were carefully spaced out in shifts so that none of them had to work for the whole of his waking hours. In 1871 the basic working week in the locomotive department of the Metropolitan Railway was reduced from $57\frac{1}{2}$ to 54 hours and it was still 54 hours in the 1890s, overtime then being paid at time and a quarter.[60] The crew of an underground train on the Circle usually worked for eight or nine hours at a stretch, taking their meals in the tunnel as they travelled along, for there was no time to eat at the longer stops when the locomotive itself had to be attended to.[61] Signalmen also worked an eight-hour day on the underground, and porters and ticket collectors $9\frac{1}{2}$ or ten.[62] It was very unusual indeed for any employee of the District or Metropolitan Railways to work more than 12 hours, but overtime was much more usual on the suburban services of the main-line companies than on the underground.[63]

The highest-paid railwaymen's earnings compared quite favourably with those of the tramway or omnibus men if the additional winnings of the latter are omitted. A driver on the Metropolitan was earning 6s. to 8s. per day in the 1890s and a fireman 3s. 6d. to 4s. 6d.[64] Moreover, when the

X

company's locomotive sheds were removed from Edgware Road to Neasden at the beginning of the 1880s, houses were built nearby and let to its employees at low rents. Watkin admitted that the company might lose 1 per cent. on the capital in this operation but claimed that it attracted 'a better class of workman . . . . My experience is that we gain indirectly a great benefit by practically improving the comfort of the people whom we employ.'[65] Signalmen and ticket collectors could earn 20s. to 30s. per week, guards 20s. to (in rare instances) 40s. and porters 15s. to 25s. (but most of them 20s. or less—and on an urban passenger line there was little luggage to be carried, and tips were scarce).[66] But all these men had the advantages of free uniform and free travel to and from their work. This enabled them to live outside central London, in districts where rents were lower. In the early 1890s, more than 80 per cent. of London's railwaymen lived in what Booth termed 'the outer ring of the metropolis' and enjoyed a higher standard of living than their wages alone would suggest.[67]

The railwaymen, wage earners though they were, were thus far better off than the road transport men in terms of hours of labour, security of employment, prospects of promotion and amenities. It is true that those who worked underground did not breathe so much fresh air as their opposite numbers on the surface, but—as in the case of the locomotive men already mentioned or the signalman at Gower Street who, in 1897, had served there for 28 years at a stretch[68]—they were said to be none the worse for the smoke, fumes and artificial lighting. It was at least dry in the tunnels and it was this protection from the elements which enabled the Metropolitan to boast that it had the healthiest railway staff in the country.[69] And the company took the wise precaution of appointing its own medical officer. Its first doctor started to diagnose and prescribe in September 1863, only a few months after the opening of the line. He was paid only £105 a year; but his successor, appointed six years later, received £200 a year, 'with a scale for special services'.[70]

Of the administrative staffs who controlled and developed London's passenger transport services at this time, very little is known. We do not know, for instance, the size of the staffs employed by the L.G.O.C. at its head office in Finsbury Square, by the Metropolitan Railway at Baker Street, or by the District Railway at Broadway, nor the conditions under which these men worked. Some idea of the range of their salaries, however, may be deduced from the isolated examples which have already been given in earlier chapters. Fenton came to the Metropolitan and Church to the L.G.O.C. at £500 a year. By 1869 Fenton was earning £1,200 and ten years later Church, then a director, was earning £2,500. Forbes, when he became managing director of the District in 1870, was paid £2,500 and Watkin received £2,000 at the beginning of his chairmanship of the Metropolitan in 1872. At the other end of the scale, when the L.G.O.C. was formed, its bookkeeper was paid £250 and a clerk £120.

CHAPTER TEN

THE SEARCH FOR
A NEW FORM OF TRACTION

During the later nineteenth century various new forms of traction were tried out, particularly on the tramways. These included specially-patented steam locomotives, battery-driven electric motors, and engines worked by various other means, including compressed air and even clockwork. The basic problem was to develop a source of power which added comparatively little dead weight to the vehicle. For this reason the cable system seemed to have possibilities. It was used successfully on two of London's tramways and was intended to be used on the City of London & Southwark Subway, a deep tube built during the later 1880s on the same principle as the Tower Subway of 1870. While the railway was under construction, however, the directors decided to employ electric power instead. In December 1890, when the City & South London Railway (as it had been renamed) was opened, it was the largest undertaking of its kind in the world. Like many pioneer ventures, however, other interested parties rather than the shareholders profited from the practical working information that it provided; but the necessary capital was not immediately forthcoming to take advantage of this knowledge.

TECHNICAL INERTIA

So long as horses continued to earn large profits for London's major omnibus and tramway undertakings, there was no particularly strong incentive to turn to any other method of traction. Costly though horse power undoubtedly was, such other methods, besides demanding much more fixed capital, might also lead to greater running costs, for they were still in an experimental stage of development, at least until the early 1890s. And touchy local authorities were likely to be even less favourably disposed to the idea of engines passing to and fro through the streets than they had been to horses. Clearly, there was much to be said for letting others shoulder the risks which these experiments were bound to incur, and waiting until trial and error had yielded an alternative source of power which was a proved commercial success.

The most obvious alternative to the horse was the steam engine. Hancock and others had tried to use it on London's roads in the 1830s and had failed. Now, after nearly half a century of technical improvement, others tried again. During the 1860s, Robert William Thomson, who in 1845 had become the first patentee of pneumatic tyres, used this invention to secure a better grip on the road when he tried to develop a satisfactory 'road steamer' in Edinburgh. Several such vehicles were built in the early 1870s under the direction of the future electrical engineer, R. E. Crompton, for use in India, and in 1871 and 1872 two steam omnibuses were carrying passengers in the Edinburgh area.[1] But interest soon switched to the application of steam to the newly-built tramways, where the track was better able to support the heavy engine. A design patented by John Grantham in 1871 was tried out on a stretch of the London Tramways' system in Vauxhall Bridge Road in November 1873.[2] The machinery was made by Merryweather & Sons, the London firm which had previously specialized in the manufacture of steam-driven fire pumps; it had just come under the control of James Crompton Merryweather, who had been trained at King's College, London.[3] A brisk, world-wide demand for steam trams soon developed. By the mid-1870s, 'many' Merryweather engines were said to be at work 'chiefly on the continent',[4] and other manufacturers, such as Kitsons of Leeds, the locomotive builders, were not slow to exploit this new market. Within a few years, steam trams were operating in various parts of Britain, subject after 1879 to legislation which limited their speed to ten miles per hour, forbade the emission of smoke or steam, and laid down that all the working parts of the engine were to be screened from public view. But although they were tried out on the North Metropolitan's Stratford–Leytonstone section as early as 1877 and on the Croydon system in 1884,[5] their only commercial use in the London area was on the poor and struggling North London Tramways which in 1883 had come under the control of a group headed by the redoubtable W. J. Carruthers-Wain.[6] From 1885 the North London Tramways ran 15 Merryweather locomotives both on their main route from Stamford Hill to Ponder's End and on the branch to Finsbury Park, and, in 1887, ten more were ordered from Dick, Kerr & Company in connection with a new line to Wood Green. But steam traction did not save the company. It was wound up in 1890, and in the following year the system passed to the North Metropolitan which reverted to the use of horses[7]— an apt comment on the endeavours of the previous years.

The great drawback of the steam tram was its weight; it was too heavy for use on tracks built for horse cars. Other, lighter types of prime mover were later tested, such as the Connelly oil engine which was tried out in the early 1890s on both the Croydon and the London, Deptford & Greenwich Tramways, and the Luhrig car, fitted with gas engines, which had a trial on the Croydon system in 1893.[8] Another solution to the weight problem was to use a stationary steam engine and devise some means of transmitting its power to a lighter form of machine on the vehicle. One way was to use the steam engine to wind clockwork springs fitted upon the tram. Experiments using this method, patented by E. H. Leveaux, a Belgian, took place in London in the mid-1870s.[9] Another idea, that of a Frenchman, Mekarski, was to drive the cars by compressed air, steam-driven compressor plants being situated at convenient points along the route. Trials of this system were carried out by the North Metropolitan in 1881 and by

London Street Tramways on several occasions later in the decade.[10] None of these ingenious devices, however, acquired any commercial importance in the London area. But there still remained two other ways of transmitting power from a stationary steam engine to a moving vehicle —cable traction and electricity. Both of these had a commercial future.

Cable traction

Cable traction was not new. It had been used, as we have seen, on the London & Blackwall Railway 40 years before; but its main advantage lay where steep gradients were involved. Its successful development in hilly San Francisco in the early 1870s by Andrew Smith Hallidie, a Londoner who had emigrated to the United States in 1853, had caught the public's imagination and ushered in the era of the cable car. By Hallidie's patent, the cable—a stout manilla rope bound by a number of lengths of stranded steel wire —moved in a conduit in the middle of the track. From the cab a 'gripper-man' could connect with the continuously moving cable by the turning of grooved grips, an operation which called for considerable physical strength. Cable lines were soon opened in Chicago and elsewhere in the United States, and the Hallidie Patent Cable Tramway Corporation Ltd. was subsequently formed to exploit the invention in England.[11] In 1882 a closely associated concern, the Steep Grade Tramways & Works Company Ltd., obtained a Board of Trade Provisional Order to build a 3 ft. 6 in. gauge line from the Archway Tavern up the hill to Southwood Lane, Highgate, a distance of nearly a mile. Construction began in October 1883, and the tramway was opened to the public on 29 May 1884. According to J. Bucknall Smith, the engineer responsible for its building, the route was chosen not because of the traffic which was to be expected, at least at the outset, but because it was the best situation close to the heart of London for exhibition purposes—an important consideration, for this was the first cable tramway in Europe.[12] That its cars were rarely filled surprised nobody, particularly in view of the occasional accidents and breakdowns which occurred.[13] The demonstration did not produce many orders; the Steep Grade Company was soon in financial difficulties, and in 1888 its parent company, the Patent Cable Tramways Corporation, went into liquidation.[14] The line was kept going, however, and in 1889 it passed to a new company which worked it until, in December 1892, it had to be closed by Board of Trade order after an accident.[15] It then lay derelict until 1897 when, with a new cable and cars provided with automatic brakes, it was reopened by yet a third concern, the Highgate Hill Tramway Company Ltd.[16]

Cable traction was applied more successfully to tramways elsewhere in Britain, notably in Edinburgh.[17] And at the beginning of the 1890s when the London Tramways wanted to extend their line from Brixton up the hill to Streatham, they chose this method of operation. Indeed, the whole section from Kennington to Streatham, which carried an eighth of the company's very considerable volume of traffic, was successfully worked by cable from December 1892.[18] By then, however, the superior advantages of electricity, the other promising method of transmitting power, were becoming apparent.

Early experiments with electricity

The principle of electric traction was simple but its application was difficult. Electricity used for this purpose was merely a means of transforming mechanical energy at one point into mechanical energy at another. A machine, known as a dynamo or electric generator, converted the mechanical energy of the steam engine, to which it was coupled, into electrical energy. This was then passed instantaneously by means of some form of electrical conductor to another machine on the vehicle—the motor—which re-converted the electrical energy into mechanical energy. The laws of electricity were known and the theory not difficult to master. The leading engineers of the day were able to make a very plausible case for electrification on purely theoretical grounds. And they were able to do so because an electric motor, or number of electric motors, was much lighter than a steam engine and fuel, and therefore encumbered the vehicle with much less 'dead' weight. But the practical development of electric traction was full of snags—how to transmit electricity to the moving vehicles, for instance, how to minimize losses in generation and transmission, how to calculate the load required by a number of vehicles all starting and stopping at different times, all traversing different gradients and negotiating different curves. While various primitive experiments had been conducted earlier in the nineteenth century—such as Robert Davidson's demonstration of a battery-driven electric locomotive on the Edinburgh & Glasgow Railway in 1842—it was only after 1866, when a greatly improved dynamo was designed, using electro- in place of permanent magnets, that electric traction became a commercial possibility.[19] In the 1870s dynamos were being sold in numbers on the continent and America by Siemens, by French firms manufacturing the product of Z. T. Gramme, and by several American companies, notably that dominated by C. F. Brush.

The first dynamos were used not for traction but to work arc lights, very bright sources of illumination suitable for streets, lighthouses, railway stations or large halls, and the French in particular took them up very quickly.[20] Watkin and Fenton went to Paris in 1878 to see a demonstration of this type of lighting, and in the following year it was tried out at Edgware Road and Aldersgate stations on the Metropolitan Railway, as well as at Charing Cross on the District.[21] In 1879 the American, Edison, and the Englishman, Swan, both working independently, developed incandescent filament lighting, using glass bulbs for the purpose, which was suitable for domestic as well as for public use. The Edison system, which allowed a large number of independently-operated bulbs to be supplied from a single source of power, was tried out on a wide scale in London even before it went into general service in America. This large-scale test—'for the purpose of determining definitely and exactly the cost', to quote Edison's engineer—took place at Holborn Viaduct. In April 1882 Edison's first 'Jumbo' dynamo started to supply 1,000 electric lamps in the road and on private premises between Holborn Circus and the Old Bailey; this was several months before the opening of the famous Pearl Street plant in New York.[22]

Lighting, in fact, commanded so much of the pioneers' attention that they had little time to spare for electric traction. Siemens and Halske, it is true, ran a model electric railway at the Berlin Trade Fair in 1879 and also had a demonstration line working at the Electrotechnical Exhibition in Paris in 1881. In that year, too, they took over a short length of tramway at Lichterfelde and, while continuing to operate a public service, used this for experimental purposes.[23] Meanwhile, at Menlo Park near Newark, New Jersey, Edison himself carried out a number of test runs between 1880 and 1883; but, as he later confessed, 'I could not go on with it because I had not the time. I had too many other things to attend to, especially in connection with electric lighting.'[24] It was left to others, notably the American, Frank J. Sprague, to develop the electric tramcar. Sprague, then an officer in the U.S. Navy engaged in experimental work on electricity, first became interested in the possibilities of its application to traction in 1882 while he was in London on a visit to the British Electrical Exhibition—as much, it would seem, because of his experiences on the steam-driven underground as because of what he saw at the exhibition. He resigned from the navy in the following year, and after a short spell with Edison, set up the Sprague Electric Railway & Motor Company and developed a satisfactory tramcar during the later 1880s.[25] The main problems were, particularly: how to feed the current to a moving vehicle and increase its flow to the motor as the motor started up and gathered speed (the answers were the trolley system and the series-parallel controller); how to reduce excessive brush and commutator wear caused by repeated starting (the remedy in this case was the introduction of carbon brushes); and how to position the motors so that they and the drive on to the wheels would not be too much disturbed by the car's jolting (here the solution was to mount the motors 'wheelbarrow fashion', supported partly by the axle and partly by springs from the frame).[26]

While large-scale tramway electrification proceeded apace in America in the later 1880s and early 1890s, most British tramway operators preferred to 'wait and see' for a few years longer. In London, the leading tramway companies, to whom horse traction still brought good profits, were certainly in no hurry to follow the American example. Their acquaintance with electric motors was confined to extended trials with battery cars, an inexpensive form of experiment involving no overhead wires or conduits, and undertaken only on limited stretches of their systems. The most important of these experiments was carried out by the Electric Traction Company (later known as the General Electric Power & Traction Company) on the North Metropolitan's Barking Road line between 1889 and 1893. In 1890 the company thought it worth while to secure powers to extend electric working to its other routes but never made use of them.[27] The Traction Company, a concern presided over by Lord Bury—which had interests in mining plant and launches as well as in tramways[28]—also applied, in January 1888, to conduct experiments on the Metropolitan Railway, the Metropolitan to have an option on the motor's use for five years if the trials should prove successful.

In the middle of the following year, however, Watkin told
the shareholders that the arrangements had ended because
the company had failed to carry out the experiments within the specified time. He then went on to reveal his ignorance
of the whole matter by adding that the Metropolitan was
instead considering an offer from another quarter to use a
direct current system 'which would do away with an engine
altogether'.[29]

But, although none of London's surface transport was
powered by wired electricity before 1900,[30] the new form
of power had by then been in use for several years to drive
trains underground. This first successful application of
electric traction is of twofold interest, for the electric trains
ran 50 feet or more below the surface, through iron tubes.

The first tube railway

The idea of building a tunnel by driving a circular iron tube
through London's clay was first successfully realized by
Peter William Barlow, F.R.S.,* a leading railway engineer
of Victorian times. In 1858 he had turned his attention to
reducing costs in the construction of large-span bridges. A
year or two later, while using cast-iron cylinders in building
the piers of Lambeth suspension bridge, he found that, so
long as these cylinders were being driven into clay, fine
gravel or sand, they went down without any difficulty. It
was only necessary to resort to compressed air when loose
rocks or coarse gravel were encountered.[31] Soon after this,
when a plan for a suspension bridge near the Tower had
been vetoed by the river authorities on the grounds that it
did not allow sufficient clearance for shipping, Barlow

*Peter William Barlow was born at Woolwich on 1 February 1809, the eldest son
of a teacher (later professor) of mathematics at the Royal Military Academy. He was
educated privately and became pupil of the engineer H. R. Palmer under whom he
was employed on the Birmingham & Liverpool Junction Canal and the London
Docks. He was subsequently resident engineer, under Sir William Cubitt, for the
building of the central division of the London & Dover Railway and later became
engineer-in-chief of its successor, the South Eastern Railway. He was also engaged
extensively in railway building elsewhere. He joined the Institution of Civil Engineers
in 1827 and became an F.R.S. in 1854. He died on 19 May 1885. (*Proceedings of the
Institution of Civil Engineers, 81*, 32–3; *D.N.B.*)

proposed that his iron cylinder technique should be used in a horizontal direction to drive a passenger subway under the river, and in 1864 he patented an excavating shield for this purpose.[32]

Barlow was not, however, to be the first to secure Parliamentary sanction to build a tube under the Thames. In 1865 the Waterloo & Whitehall Railway Company was authorized to construct a line under the river through a cylinder formed by riveting together 200-ft. lengths of cast-iron tube, 12 ft. 9 in. in diameter, which were to rest against four brick piers sunk into the bed of the river. This was, therefore, to be a dredging rather than a tunnelling operation. The railway was to run from the Whitehall end of Great Scotland Yard, across the site where the Embankment and the District Railway were about to be built, and over the river to a point adjacent to the arches of Waterloo station. It was to be operated by pneumatic pressure, T. W. Rammell, the patentee of a method of pneumatic propulsion, being its engineer. Work was started in October 1865, but the whole venture proved much more difficult and costly than its optimistic promoters had expected. After the crisis of 1866 the company found it almost impossible to raise additional capital, and construction ceased in 1868. The company itself was eventually wound up in 1882.[33]

Meanwhile Barlow was continuing to advocate a more modest scheme with a tunnel only 7 ft. in diameter. There were many delays because of opposition from riparian property owners, but in 1868 his proposals at last secured Parliamentary sanction.[34] Construction proved remarkably speedy and inexpensive. The tunnel itself, 1,430 ft. long, took only about five months to build and is said to have cost a mere £6 10s. 0d. per foot.[35] The method of construction which achieved these remarkable results has been most succinctly summarized by Mr. Charles E. Lee:

[The shield] was made of wrought and cast iron and weighed approximately 2⅛ tons. At the front end was a cast-iron cutting edge 7 ft. 2 in. in diameter, and behind this a wrought-iron face plate, in the centre of which was a doorway about 4 ft. square, closed with a water-tight iron sliding door. At the back of the shield were iron sockets, into which screw-jacks were fitted, and forced the shield forward. Through the water-tight door in the centre, sufficient clay was cut away by hand to make a chamber large enough for one man to enter. The first man worked single-handed until there was room for another to enter, and the two then completed the removal of the earth within the diameter of the shield for a distance of about 2 ft. The shield was then forced forward by means of screw-jacks into the space that had been cut.

The tunnel was lined with cast-iron rings 1 ft. 6 in. wide and $\frac{7}{8}$ in. thick. Each ring was built up in four segments, three of which were about 7 ft. wide and the remaining one 10 in. wide. Both segments and complete rings were bolted together with $\frac{3}{4}$-in. bolts through inside flanges 2 in. deep. The bottom segment was laid first, then the two side pieces and the small 10-in. section. . . . The joints were caulked with oakum and pointed with medina cement. The excess in diameter of the shield over that of the tube lining left a space of about 1 in. round the exterior of the latter. This was filled by pumping in blue lias lime, which, in addition to solidifying quickly, acted as a preservative to the iron.[36]

Each end of the tunnel was originally reached by lift through a shaft 10 ft. in diameter. The entrance kiosk at the northern end was situated at Tower Hill and the descent was 60 ft. The southern shaft, in Vine Street, not far from the junction with Pickle Herring Street, was 50 ft. deep. At first a railway track was laid along the tunnel and a single carriage, 10 ft. 6 in. long, big enough to carry a dozen passengers at a time, was hauled to and fro by wire rope, attached at each end to a four horse-power, single-cylinder engine. Numerous visitors were shown through the subway in February 1870; it functioned on an experimental basis from the following April and was formally opened on 2 August.[37]

Barlow designed the tunnel so that it dipped down towards the centre from each side. By so doing, he hoped not only to keep well within the clay but also to make the task of the stationary engines the easier, momentum gained by the carriage on the downward gradient being expected to help it part of the way up the other side.[38] This did not happen, however. The mechanical equipment was not a success and the promoters found it impossible to raise the capital for a second such tunnel, a little to the west of London Bridge, which had just gained Parliamentary approval.[39] A receiver was appointed for the Tower Subway Company in November 1870 and the railway was then removed. So, too, were the lifts. From 24 December 1870, users had to tramp up and down timber staircases and pass on foot through the tunnel which was then lit by open gas jets issuing at intervals from a pipe situated only a foot or so above the handrail. The tolls for this inferior service were reduced from 2d. (first class) and 1d. (second)—the underground carriage had known no class distinction, but first class passengers had been given priority for its places—to a uniform charge of $\frac{1}{2}$d. At this price more than a million people came to pass through the subway's turnstiles every year until, with the opening of Tower Bridge in 1894, it was no longer needed and was closed. (It is now used to carry hydraulic power and water mains under the river.[40])

The first tube railway failed because the cable system was not satisfactory. There could be no real future for tubes until some other alternative to the air-polluting steam locomotive could be developed. And even in the early days of the development of such an alternative, engineers were reluctant to depart from the shallow 'cut and cover' underground, despite the enormous expenditure involved; this, as the completion of the Circle showed, had become almost prohibitive.

Early schemes for electric underground railways

Apart from the completion of the Circle, there was little enthusiasm for the promotion of underground lines during the 1870s. The early 1880s, however, witnessed a re-kindling of interest. In addition to the lines projected from Charing Cross to Euston and from Edgware Road to Westminster, neither of which came to anything,[41] an underground railway was also authorized from Waterloo to Trafalgar Square.[42] This venture, promoted in 1882, was to be worked by electricity and had Siemens's backing. It was to be a shallow 'cut and cover' railway, to be carried under the river in two iron tubes. Not enough financial support was forthcoming, however, and the scheme did not get beyond the building of 20 yards of tunnel under Northumberland Avenue and the Embankment.[43] Two years later, in 1884, Siemens also gave their support to the London Central Electric Railway. This was to run from Charing Cross via Cranbourne Street (for Leicester Square) and New Oxford Street (with a branch to Piccadilly Circus), and then via stations near Lincoln's Inn Fields and Bedford Row to Gray's Inn Road, Holborn Circus, Farringdon Street and Cheapside. This, too, was to be a shallow underground railway. Siemens Brothers and Company (the British company, then enjoying huge profits from its submarine telegraph work[44]) was to provide all the operating staff and to work the line for five years for £28,000 per year. It was to be served by eight trains capable of speeds of about ten miles per hour and composed of up to five 27-passenger coaches, and it is particularly interesting to note that each coach was to have its own separate motive power. The current was to be supplied through a centre rail at a potential of some 400 volts.[45] At such an early stage in the history of electric traction, this line of over two miles in length was extremely daring in its conception. It was, however, rejected by Parliament not so much because of doubts about the possibilities of electric traction but apparently because the Metropolitan Board of Works, not without reason, objected to the disturbance of so many of its sewers. Officially, however, the Board's spokesman pointed out that it had

114. Arrival of the Prince of Wales at Stockwell Station, City & South London Railway,
4 November 1890

115. The Prince on the Tube Station Platform

116. Interior of 1890 C. & S.L.R. Trailer Car

117. L.G.O.C. Horse Omnibus Interior: a Reconstruction

118. Original C. & S.L.R. Locomotive and Carriages inside Stockwell Depot, 1890

supported the Waterloo–Trafalgar Square scheme of 1882 because of its 'distinct desire to further electrical experiment in London'. The 1884 scheme, in contrast, was merely 'speculative and experimental'.[46]

The City of London & Southwark Subway

Another underground railway, for which Parliament's sanction was also sought in 1884, did not interfere with any of the Metropolitan Board of Works' sewers, and the Bill managed to reach the Statute Book.[47] This was the City of London & Southwark Subway, a deep tube on the principle of the Tower Subway, but this time one conceived on a much larger scale than its predecessor. Two tubes, each 10 ft. (instead of 7 ft.) in diameter, were to be driven from a northern terminus in King William Street (near the Monument) to the Elephant & Castle, a distance of $1\frac{3}{8}$ miles. The cost was to be of the order of £300,000.

The origins of the undertaking are obscure, but perhaps the key is to be found in the type of traction to be used. The Waterloo–Trafalgar Square and Charing Cross–Cheapside projects were both to be worked by electricity; the City of London & Southwark, however, was to be operated by Hallidie's patent cable system. By this method ten separate cars, each carrying 50 passengers and travelling at ten miles per hour, were to provide a two-minute service.[48] James Clifton Robinson, soon to make his name as a pioneer in the field of electric tramways but then general manager of the Patent Cable Tramways Corporation, and Alfred Arnold, one of the Corporation's directors, both figured prominently before the Parliamentary committees, and in the course of the inquiry some of the members of these were taken to Highgate Hill to see a demonstration of the cable tramway at work just before its public opening.[49] No doubt, to the Cable Corporation the City of London & Southwark Subway was to be a means of showing that this kind of traction was preferable to electrical working on underground lines

Y

as well as on the surface. The pushing efforts of the rival electrical interests in the underground railway field made such a demonstration imperative.

Another of the subway's leading promoters was James Henry Greathead,* a South African who had been assistant to Barlow on the Tower Subway and in Barlow's later railway work. He was to be the civil engineer in charge of construction. Behind the scenes was the usual circle of professional company promoters; in this case Robert Alexander Meyer, public works contractor, Col. George Bruce Malleson, who already had quite a wide range of business interests to his name, and Arthur Stanley Felton.

Events moved very slowly at first, and the company's minutes reveal growing impatience with Meyer, the contractor. His agreement was cancelled in March 1885 and transferred to Edmund Gabbutt of Liverpool. Several months later, however, the Board was strengthened by the addition of Charles Grey Mott, Alexander Hubbard, Walter Robinson and C. Seymour Grenfell.[50] Mott, who became the company's chairman on 30 December 1885, was a successful Merseyside businessman who, having built up colliery interests in Lancashire and in Wirral, had in 1868 become a director of the Great Western Railway.[51] Robinson was another G.W.R. director. Mott was also at that time on the board of another underground line, the Mersey Railway which ran from Liverpool to Birkenhead and was then

*James Henry Greathead was born at Grahamstown, South Africa, on 6 August 1844. He came to England in 1859 for the completion of his education and in 1864 began a three-year pupilage with P. W. Barlow. He then became an assistant engineer on the construction of the Midland Railway's extension from Bedford to London. After the building of the Tower Subway, he set up in practice on his own (1871–73), but later became resident engineer on the District Railway's extension to Hammersmith. He became a member of the Institution of Civil Engineers in 1881. An interval of relative inactivity in the early 1880s was filled by making plans for a number of railways which were never built; during this time 'his inventive talent found employment in devising improvements in roller-skates, locking-nuts, hydraulic-apparatus and hydrants'. His fortune turned with the City & South London and he subsequently became joint engineer, with Sir Douglas Fox, for the Liverpool Overhead Railway, and, with W. R. Galbraith, for the Waterloo & City Railway. He was also associated with Fowler and Baker on the Central London Railway, but work on this had scarcely begun when, on 21 October 1896, he died. (*Proceedings of the Institution of Civil Engineers,* *127* (1897), 365–9.)

nearing completion. So too was Hubbard, yet another G.W.R. director. Together with Grenfell (of Pascoe Grenfell and Sons) and Sampson Hanbury, a member of an equally well-known family (who had been a director from the outset), the list of board members must have seemed quite imposing when it appeared on the prospectus—issued at last in February 1886—especially as Sir John Fowler's name was also included as consulting engineer.[52] (He had been engaged in December 1885 for a fee of 2,500 guineas[53]). The investing public, however, showed remarkable resistance to this resourceful attempt to impress it; the issue of shares—30,000 at £10 each—was not fully taken up, and Gabbutt had to take part of the payment for his work in stock.[54] In May 1886 he started to sink a temporary shaft just off the Old Swan Pier on the Middlesex side of the river, and on the following 28 October tunnelling began.[55]

The railway is extended and electric power adopted

The new board took an early opportunity to secure powers for the extension of its line from the Elephant & Castle to suburban Stockwell, thereby rather more than doubling its original length, to just over three miles. The diameter of the tubes on the extension was to be 10 ft. 6 in. instead of the 10 ft. of the original section. For this extension, an additional £300,000 in shares and £75,000 in debentures were authorized, making £600,000 plus borrowing powers of £175,000 for the entire line.[56] The Bill passed through Parliament in the session of 1887, and the extension contract was let to Walter Scott and Company of Newcastle upon Tyne. In 1887 it was still intended to use cable traction, the new section to be worked by a second cable.[57] But on 30 January 1888 the board heard that the Patent Cable Tramways Corporation had gone into liquidation, and counsel's opinion was sought on the matter. On 17 May a special meeting was called to consider proposals to work the line by electricity.

The board called in C. E. Spagnoletti to advise it. Spagnoletti was, no doubt, well known to Mott, Robinson and Hubbard as the G.W.R. telegraph superintendent. He had recently taken charge of the Paddington power station, a considerable undertaking promoted by the G.W.R. to light its London terminus, goods yard and the immediate vicinity.[58] From a wide range of tenders, that of Mather & Platt, the Manchester engineering firm, was accepted in January 1889. They were to be responsible for the electrification of the line and for the working of it for two years.[59] (Sir) William Mather had visited the U.S.A. in 1883 on behalf of the government, but at his own expense, to report on technical education in that country. While he was there, he secured the British rights for the manufacture of Edison's dynamo. Mather & Platt had as their electrical consultant John Hopkinson who was already consultant to the English Edison Company. He was a close friend of Sir Benjamin Baker who, as Fowler's partner, was particularly concerned, together with Spagnoletti and Greathead, with the awarding of the contract.[60]

Dr. John Hopkinson (b. 1849), the son of a Manchester engineer,[61] had had a brilliant academic career at Owens College and Trinity College, Cambridge, where he was Senior Wrangler in the Mathematical Tripos in 1870 and subsequently Smith's Prizeman and Fellow of the College. He then became superintendent of the lighthouse department of Chance Brothers' glassworks at Smethwick. Research on lighthouse development in the 1870s inevitably turned his interest to the subject of electricity just when electricity was starting to become commercially important. In 1878 he moved to London and set up as a consultant, and in the same year, at the age of 29, he was elected an F.R.S. There then followed a period in which he produced a notable series of learned papers in which he applied mathematical theory to a range of electrical problems— and an equally impressive series of patents in which he gave practical application to these ideas, including those for the three-wire system of direct current distribution and for a number of improvements in dynamo design.[62] Early in 1882 he was appointed consultant to the English Edison Company and soon set about improving the Edison dynamo, producing the far more efficient Edison-Hopkinson machine, 'of unique value because it was the first concrete expression of the correct principles of dynamo design'.[63] In this he had been helped by his younger brother, Edward (b. 1859), who also had a distinguished university career (10th Wrangler in the Mathematical Tripos at Cambridge in 1881) before working for a short time with Siemens. With this experience behind him, he went to the firm of Mather & Platt and soon became head of their electrical engineering department.[64] While still with Siemens, Edward Hopkinson had been in charge of the electrification of six miles of tramway between Portrush and Bushmills in Northern Ireland,[65] which the *Railway Times* at its public opening in September 1883 described as 'the first long electric tramway in the world'.[66] Two years later, after he had joined Mather & Platt, he was also given charge of another electrification scheme not many miles to the south, from Bessbrook to Newry. This line, equipped with Edison-Hopkinson dynamos, came into service in October 1885.[67] When the City of London & Southwark Subway gave the electrification contract to Mather & Platt, therefore, they hired two men who were extremely well informed by the standards of the day on the subject of electric traction.

Great resourcefulness was indeed required, for, as John Hopkinson himself pointed out early in 1890, nowhere had electric traction been undertaken on such a scale.

The largest in the United Kingdom is at Newry. There are some in America where I daresay the aggregate horse power may be as much as it is here but each car is lighter.[68]

The Engineer supported this view:

A number of small tramways, both on the Continent and in the United Kingdom, have been worked electrically, and in the United States many of the street tramways are worked in this way; but it has not hitherto been applied on any large scale to the working of a railway of the usual gauge for passengers.[69]

Confirmation also came from Sir Benjamin Baker. He went to the United States in 1890 to see what progress the Americans had made with the electrification of their railways, as distinct from their tramways. The only example he could find was an experiment on the Manhattan Railway in New York, and this had failed.[70]

Arrangements were made for Mather & Platt to start work on the line in June 1889,[71] and they were having trials on the northern part of it before the year was out, power being supplied from a temporary generating plant at Great Dover Street.[72] One of the decisions taken as a result of these trials was to use direct-action motors, with the armatures mounted on the axles so as to avoid gearing which caused a great amount of noise in the tunnels. These direct-action motors gave satisfactory service after they had been modified, but they inevitably limited the size of each motor.[73]

By 5 March 1890 the process of equipping had proceeded far enough to allow the Lord Mayor and a party of 70 guests to be taken in two carriages as far as the Elephant & Castle.[74] There was some delay in completing the Stockwell end of the line—an underground river had been encountered, running through a bed of shingle—and there were also delays in installing the lifts; but the official opening, by the Prince of Wales, took place on 4 November 1890, and regular public services on what had then been re-named the City & South London Railway started on 18 December.[75]

Apart from warehouses on the Hibernian Wharf, on the south bank of the river just to the west of London Bridge, the line ran under no buildings, the whole route having been planned to follow a number of roads. (Even so,

Greathead took the wise precaution of photographing beforehand any buildings which might become the subject of compensation claims.[76]) From the inner terminus, which lay at right angles under King William Street, the lines ran out westwards, curved sharply south—the two tubes being one over the other under the narrow Swan Lane—and then down a considerable gradient (1 in 40 in one tube and 1 in 14 in the other) under the river. At each station—King William Street, Borough, Elephant & Castle, Kennington, Oval and Stockwell—there were two hydraulically operated lifts each capable of carrying up to 50 passengers at a time to and from the trains. The car sheds and generating plant were situated at Stockwell.[77]

The railway started with 14 four-wheel locomotives, each a mere 14 ft. long, the frames of which were built by Beyer, Peacock. Each was driven by two series-wound motors coupled in series. Together the two motors were capable of developing 100 h.p. at a speed of 25 m.p.h. The current, at a pressure of 450 volts, was supplied via a centre rail mounted on glass insulators as on the Bessbrook Tramway.[78] It was produced by three—soon to be four—Edison-Hopkinson dynamos, two of which were in operation at a time. Each train consisted of three long bogie carriages which together could seat 96 passengers. The carriages were well upholstered and lit by electricity. They had only tiny windows high up at each side and came to earn the nickname of 'padded cells'. For a time, the two guards who worked on each train put up indicators to tell passengers which station they would reach next. A whole train weighed about 40 tons when filled with passengers and ran at an average speed, including stops, of about 11½ m.p.h. There was only one class—an innovation so far as London's railways were concerned—and originally only one fare, 2d. The idea of a uniform fare was copied from the New York Elevated Railroad. Passengers paid to pass through a turnstile.[79] No tickets were issued at the outset, but season tickets were introduced in 1891, and a 1d. fare was available from May 1891 between 6.45 and 8 a.m. and between 10 and 11 p.m.; the fare from Stockwell was raised to 3d. in the rush hour from October 1891. At first there was only a weekday service but from 5 April 1891 trains were run on Sundays from midday onwards.[80]

The City & South London Railway pays the penalty for being the pioneer

The world's first electric tube was a considerable technical achievement. In March 1891 John Hopkinson himself went so far as to declare it 'a complete success', but he made this statement while trying to impress a Parliamentary committee.[81] Perhaps *Herapath's* description of the line as 'a useful and promising novelty'[82] was nearer the mark. And, as with all new ventures, mistakes were made. The undertaking had, in fact, been promoted on too modest a scale both from a civil engineering and from an electrical point of view. The tunnels were too small and the arrangements at the King William Street terminus, built for cable traction, were unsatisfactory for electrical working. The station consisted of a single track flanked by a platform on each side and was a bad bottleneck. On the electrical side, the trains seem to have run well enough one by one, but when ten or so were in operation at the same time—when there was 1,000 horse-power on the line and not just 100—this posed practical problems which do not seem to have been fully anticipated by the Hopkinsons. To some extent this was not their fault because, having contracted to haul carriages weighing $4\frac{1}{4}$ tons each and having installed the equipment on this basis, they were presented with larger carriages each weighing more than seven tons. Each locomotive, therefore, had to haul about nine tons more than it had been built to haul.[83] This, no doubt, explains the earnest discussions which went on with Mather & Platt just before and after the line was opened, and the crop of burnt-out armatures in the early days.[84] But there were other, more fundamental, weaknesses. The total load depended on the number of trains starting off at the same time and the amount of uphill work on the line. While a theoretical maximum could be worked out, the maximum in practice could be learned only from experience when the railway was in full operation. Moreover, the worst gradient and curve, up from the river and round to the King William Street terminus, was the stretch of line farthest from the generating station which was more than three miles away at the other terminus. It is clear from the technical details of the feeding arrangements that there was a very heavy voltage drop on that part of the line and this limited the capacity of the whole railway. Instead of being able to run 20 trains an hour, as the company had originally planned, it could run only 14 or 16.[85] The stations, instead of being lit by electricity, were lit by gas,[86] and the electric lighting on the trains themselves gave only a feeble glimmer whenever a number of locomotives all accelerated at the same time.[87] 'We were the experimenters', confessed Mott in 1891, 'and made the City & South London Line a little too small.'[88]

Poor dividends discourage emulation

These technical limitations were inevitably reflected in the traffic returns. From the start the City & South London was chiefly a peak-hour line, crowded to its full capacity during the rush hour (*Punch* called it the 'sardine box' railway) and slack for the rest of the day. The number of passengers carried was quite small and increased very slowly. The total of 5,161,000 for 1891 had grown to only 6,980,000 by 1899[89]—a very poor showing compared with the large traffic handled, for instance, by the London Tramways, which served the roads immediately above the tube. In its first year the new tube handled little more than half the number of passengers that the Metropolitan Railway had carried during the first year of its existence nearly a third of a century earlier. While the City & South London made efforts to accommodate more traffic by improving the performance of its electric locomotives[90] and shortening the length of its signalling sections,[91] it could do nothing about the size of its tunnels or the very awkward gradient and curve into King William Street, although it did alter its terminus there in 1895, the two platforms being replaced by tracks and the original single line by an island platform.[92] There was really no solution to its difficulties, however, short of drastic alterations and extension. The company had in fact secured Parliamentary powers to extend to Clapham in 1890 even before the original section was opened. And in 1893 it was authorized to build a completely new and larger pair of tubes, each 11 ft. 6 in. diameter, northwards from the Borough to the Angel, cutting out the King William Street terminus altogether. But the dividends were so poor—nothing in 1891, rising to just under 2 per cent. in 1897—that for several years it was impossible to raise sufficient capital to press ahead with these plans even though Bank Rate was very low for much of the time. None of these extensions was opened to traffic until 1900.

Although it brought little financial reward to its share-holders, the City & South London pointed a very clear way to the future. Technical authorities, such as Lord Kelvin, were not slow to cite the example of this pioneer line as proof of the advantages of the electric train over the steam locomotive.[93] With the experience gained on the City & South London and further improvements in the standard of the electrical equipment, an electric tube railway capable of handling a heavy traffic and bringing a much more attractive return to investors became a definite possibility. But, while the engineers were radiating confidence in their own particular systems, businessmen held back. Their attitude of mind was very clearly expressed, even before the City & South London was opened, by J. S. Forbes. He was an authority on two counts for, in addition to his being chairman of the District Railway, he was also chairman of the London Electric Supply Corporation. This was then the largest electrical undertaking in the country and was also passing through a very difficult development phase.[94] Scientists, Forbes urged,

know very little that is certain—that I know of my own knowledge. . . . All these gentlemen mean well and they overcome great difficulties, but they only overcome them as they find them out; they cannot foresee them until they appear. . . . I think it is very material that before this thing [the City & South London] is extended in any direction, we should have some knowledge of it. . . . If I might take so great a liberty, I would suggest caution to those eminent gentlemen.[95]

There was much to be said for this point of view. It certainly appealed to the investing public, the more so after the City & South London came to show such poor returns. Of a number of tubes which were authorized in the early 1890s, only one, the Waterloo & City, was opened before 1900. Fuller consideration of the delay in building a successor to the City & South London must await discussion of the problems confronting these first really full-scale electric tubes. Their opening, and road transport's even more effective response in the form of the electric tramcar and the motor bus, provide the second climax in our story. This new clash between road and rail will be the subject of the opening chapters of the next volume.

NOTES

INTRODUCTION

1. These are figures for the City and Metropolitan Police areas and are taken from M. L. Moore, *A Century's Extension of Passenger Transport Facilities (1830–1930) Within the London Transport Board's Area and Its Relation to Population Spread* (London Ph.D. thesis 1948).
2. Richard Kelsey, surveyor to the City of London, to R.C. on Metropolitan Termini, 1846 [91] XVII, q. 2279.
3. H. J. Dyos, *Victorian Suburb: A Study of the Growth of Camberwell* (Leicester 1961), 62.
4. P. G. Hall, *The Industries of London Since 1861* (1962) *passim.*
5. Charles Pearson to R.C. on Metropolitan Termini, 1846 [91] XVII, q. 2355.
6. Thomas Waring to S.C. on Metropolis Improvements, 1836 [517] XX, q. 375
7. Report of the R.C. on the Housing of the Working Classes, 1884–85 (C. 4402) XXX, 18.
8. J. A. R. Pimlott, *The Englishman's Holiday* (1947), 161.
9. William Haywood, *Report to the Special Committee upon Improvements of the Commissioners of Sewers on Traffic and Improvements in the Public Ways of the City of London* (1866), 43.

CHAPTER ONE

THE ORIGINS OF THE OMNIBUS

1. *The Letters of Horace Walpole* (ed. Mrs. Paget Toynbee), XIV (Oxford 1905), 447. Daniel Lysons, *The Environs of London* (4 vols. 1792–96) and the supplement to this work (1811) for the increase in number of houses in these places between 1790 and 1810.
2. John Summerson, *Georgian London* (1945), 93. Unless otherwise stated, this paragraph is based upon this source.
3. F. W. H. Sheppard, *Local Government in St. Marylebone* (1958), 94–99.

4. Sir Pelham Warner, *Lord's 1787–1945* (1947), 18.

5. *London and its Environs; or the General Ambulator* (12th ed. 1820), 32.

6. Summerson, *op. cit.*, 159.

7. 'Vehicular Statistics of London: I Omnibuses', *Chambers's Edinburgh Journal*, 14 June 1845. After the coming of omnibuses, private coaches were occasionally still hired to collect a number of people at their own homes and take them to the omnibus route. In 1860, for instance, such a coach collected residents living round Clapham Common. They booked their seats in it by the year. (House of Lords Record Office, evidence of Henry Doxat to Commons' Committee to the London, Chatham and Dover (Metropolitan Extensions) Bill, 20 April 1860.)

8. *Journal of a Tour and Residence in Great Britain during the Years 1810 and 1811.* By a French Traveller [L. Simond] (2 vols. Edinburgh 1815), I, 17–18.

9. A Statement of the Number of Short-Stage Coaches standing in the Streets of the City of London and the daily Number of Journeys performed by them (Corporation of London Records Office, B.12.V).

10. According to Edwin A. Pratt, *A History of Inland Transport and Communication in England* (1912), 325, in the heyday of coaches, between 1820 and 1835, there were more than 3,000 coaches on the road.

11. House of Lords Record Office, Arthur Geddes to the committee of the House of Commons on the London & Blackwall Railway Bill, 1836.

12. P.R.O., T1/2616. Memorial from the principal proprietors of public cabriolets to the Lords Commissioners of H.M. Treasury, 1 January 1829.

13. G. A. Thrupp, *The History of Coaches* (1877), 121; George Shillibeer to S.C. on the Hackney Coach Office, 1830 [515] X, 63; William Harnett Blanch, *Ye Parish of Camerwell* (1877), 82; 50 Geo. III cap. xlviii.

14. Francis Roe to S.C. on the Hackney Coach Office, 1830 [515] X, 51.

15. Stanley Harris, *Old Coaching Days* (1882), 36; E. Vale, *The Mail-Coach Men of the Eighteenth Century* (1960), 41.

16. Stephen Dowell, *A History of Taxation and Taxes in England* (2nd ed. 4 vols. 1888), III, 40–45; 44 Geo. III cap. xcviii.

17. 55 Geo. III cap. clxxxv.

18. 1 Geo. I stat. 2 cap. 57; 3 Geo. IV cap. 95. For the limits of the Bills of Mortality, see the introduction to the census report of 1861 (Parliamentary Papers, 1863 [3221] LIII (Pt. 1), 13) and John Angus, 'Old and New Bills of Mortality', *Journal of the Statistical Society of London*, XVII (1854), 117.

19. 54 Geo. III cap. 147; 55 Geo. III cap. 159; Henry Charles Moore, *Omnibuses and Cabs: Their Origin and History* (1902), 195. For the earlier history of the hackney coach monopoly, see W. T. Jackman, *The Development of Transportation in Modern England* (2nd ed. 1962), 125–31.

20. Moore, *op. cit.*, 205 *seq.*; 'Vehicular Statistics of London: II Hackney Coaches and Cabs', *Chambers's Edinburgh Journal*, 28 June 1845; Francis Roe, William Bulnois and Richard Box to S.C. on the Hackney Coach Office, 1830 [515] X.

21. Return of the numbers of hackney coaches, chariots and cabriolets licensed, 1830 [687] XXX; William Powell to S.C. on the Hackney Coach Office, 1830 [515] X, 8.

22. Stephen Dowell, *op. cit.*, III, 37 *seq.*; 48 Geo. III cap. 87.

23. *The Times*, 19 May 1828. Letter from J.T.

24. William Powell to S.C. on the Hackney Coach Office, 1830 [515] X, 8–9. This was permitted by 55 Geo. III cap. 159.

25. *The Times*, 23 May 1828.

26. William Hill to S.C. on the Hackney Coach Office, 1830 [515] X, 24–25.

27. P.R.O., T1/2617. Memorial of Thomas Henman, Clerk to the Committee of Hackney Coach and Chariot Owners, 29 December 1828; Henry Clement, William James, George Peerless and George Green to S.C. on the Hackney Coach Office, 1830 [515] X.

28. P.R.O., T1/2616. Memorial of the Principal Proprietors of Public Cabriolets, 1 Jan. 1829.

29. Summerson, *op. cit.*, ch. 13; H. J. Dyos, 'Urban Transformation: A Note on the Objects of Street Improvement in Regency and Early Victorian London', *International Review of Social History*, II (1957) pt. 2, 259–65.

30. *Pigot and Co's London and Provincial New Commercial Directory for 1822/23*, 11; S.C. on London Coal Trade, 1837–38 [475] XV, appendix 5.

31. Charles Pearson to S.C. on Metropolitan Communications, 1854–55 [415] X, q. 1337.

32. *L.C.C. Survey of London*, XXIV, 5; XXV ch. 5. For London bridges, see *Knight's Cyclopaedia of London* (1851), ch. 22 and John Timbs, *Curiosities of London* (1855), 57 *seq.*

33. *L.C.C. Survey of London*, XXIV, 5.

34. *Ibid.*, XXV, 45–46.

35. *Ibid.*, 46.

36. For the Metropolitan Turnpike Commission, see T. F. Ordish, 'History of Metropolitan Roads', Report of the London Traffic Branch of the Board of Trade for 1910, 1911 [Cd. 5472] XXVII, 184–6, 188 (appendix H); R. H. Spiro, Jr., 'John Loudon McAdam and the Metropolitan Turnpike Trust', *Journal of Transport History*, II (1956), 207–13.

37. *The Perambulator or Book of Reference to Every Street, Square, Court, Passage and Public Building in the Cities of London and Westminster* (c. 1832), 61.

38. *Mirror of Parliament*, 31 March 1829 (II, 938).

39. 10 Geo. IV cap. 59.

40. Fourth Report from the Commissioners of Turnpike Roads North of the Thames, 1830 [362] XV. (For an illustration of the Seven Sisters, see Edward Walford, *Old and New London* (6 vols. n.d.), V, 373.) Ordish, *op. cit.*, 186, 188. In their Fifth Report, 1831 [41] XII, the Commissioners stated that City Road from Islington to Finsbury Square was still under their control, 'kept in order notwithstanding the immense thoroughfare of omnibuses, stage coaches etc. to which it is exposed'.

41. P.R.O., T.22/21. Treasury to Hackney Coach Commission, 15 October 1828.

42. Report from S.C. on the Hackney Coach Office, 1830 [515] X, 3–4.

43. 1 & 2 Wm. IV cap. 22; Corporation of London Records Office, Police Committee Correspondence. Letter from Sir Francis Roe, 22 January 1834.

44. Henry Charles Moore, *op. cit.*, 216 *seq.*

45. 'Vehicular Statistics of London: II Hackney Coaches and Cabs', *Chambers's Edinburgh Journal*, 28 June 1845.

46. *Mechanics' Magazine*, 8 August 1829.

47. 'View of the City from Albion Place' by Black at the London Museum, dated 1798; a copy of Rowlandson drawing (reproduced from *The Field* in 1911) is in the London Transport Photograph Library, M1/6. See also *Public Advertiser*, 19 January 1772, for what may be possibly an earlier example (Charles White, 'The London Omnibus', *Notes & Queries* CLXIII (1932), 348).

48. *Journal of a Tour and Residence in Great Britain during the Years 1810 and 1811*. By a French Traveller [L. Simond] (2 vols. Edinburgh 1815), I, 19–20.

49. London Transport Photograph Library, M1/6; John Timbs, *Curiosities of London* (1855), 559.

50. London Transport Photograph Library, M1/6.

51. Louis Lagarrigue, *Cent Ans de Transport en Commun dans la Région Parisienne* (2 vols. Paris 1956), I, 29–31.

52. George Shillibeer to the S.C. on the Hackney Coach Office, 1830 [515] X, 64.

53. *The Times*, 13 July 1829. For Laffitte, see Rondo E. Cameron, *France and the Economic Development of Europe, 1800–1914* (Princeton 1961), 112–14.

54. George Shillibeer to the S.C. on the Hackney Coach Office, 1830 [515] X, 64, 101–3.

55. P.R.O., T1/2585.

56. We owe this point to Mrs. Saunders, the St. Marylebone Borough Archivist.

57. *D.N.B. sub* Shillibeer.

58. *The British Traveller*, 4 July 1829. (Copy in the Ashbridge Collection at St. Marylebone Public Library.)

59. 3 Geo. IV cap. xcv, sec. 1 and 2; H.M. Inland Revenue (Hayes Repository), Board of Stamps and Taxes Letters and Memorials. Memorial from Shillibeer 29 February 1832. According to Moore (*op. cit.*, 12, and *D.N.B.* article on Shillibeer), Shillibeer's original omnibus had 22 seats. This figure has often been repeated. It is clear from the description published in the *Mechanics' Magazine* on 8 August 1829, however, that the vehicle was a 20-seater.

60. Moore, *op. cit.*, 12.
61. George Shillibeer to S.C. on the Hackney Coach Office, 1830 [515] X, 63.
62. *The Times*, 13 July 1829.
63. *Ibid.*
64. George Cloud to S.C. on the Hackney Coach Office, 1830 [515] X, 66. The *Morning Herald*, 6 & 10 October 1829, advertised an omnibus running from Somerset House to Hammersmith. It included a library of books for the benefit of passengers (Charles White, *loc. cit.*).
65. George Shillibeer, *ibid.*, 63. The Police Committee of the Court of Aldermen estimated in May 1830 that forty omnibuses came into the City, each making four journeys (Corporation of London Records Office, Minutes of the Police Committee, 5 May 1830).
66. H.M. Inland Revenue (Hayes Repository) Minutes of Board of Stamps and Taxes, 5 January, 11 January 1831.
67. *London Gazette*, 29 April, 13 May, 23 August 1831.
68. *The Times*, 29 June 1831.
69. *Hansard*, V, (3rd ser.), col. 77; *The Times*, 22 August 1831.
70. *Journals of the House of Commons*, LXXVI, 16 August 1831. Our italics.
71. *The Times*, 13 September 1831.
72. House of Lords Record Office, Petition of proprietors of hackney coaches and cabriolets against the Hackney Coach Amendment Bill, 14 September 1831.

CHAPTER TWO

THE ASCENDANCY OF THE
OMNIBUS AND THE FIRST LONDON RAILWAYS

1. *Gentleman's Magazine*, *102*, Pt. 2, 76, 7 January 1832.
2. *The Times*, 17 February 1832.
3. *The Times*, 27 February 1832.
4. Corporation of London Records Office, Minutes of the Police Committee of the Court of Aldermen, 31 January 1834.

5. *The Penny Magazine*, 31 March 1837.
6. 'Vehicular Statistics of London: I Omnibuses', *Chambers's Edinburgh Journal*, 14 June 1845.
7. In 1830 Shillibeer described the use of three horses as 'my distinguishing feature' (S.C. on the Hackney Coach Office, 1830 [515] X, 63).
8. 2 & 3 Wm. IV cap. 120.
9. 'One description of passengers only' in the 1822 Act which allowed omnibuses to be taxed by the number of seats (see above, p. 21) had been interpreted to mean inside passengers only. See cases reported in the *Weekly Dispatch*, 24 June 1832 (copy in B.T.C. Records, L.G.O.C. 4/3).
10. H.M. Inland Revenue (Hayes Repository) Board of Stamps and Taxes: Letters and Memorials, 29 February, 24 March 1832.
11. *Robson's London Directory for 1833.*
12. H.M. Inland Revenue (Hayes Repository) Minutes of Board of Stamps and Taxes, 25 January 1832.
13. *Ibid.*; and Letter Book, 29 September 1832; *London Gazette*, 17 March 1837.
14. Guildhall Library, Noble Collection, C.48/61. See also William C. A. Blew, *Brighton and Its Coaches* (1894), 208.
15. *London Gazette*, 17 January 1834. Morton is mentioned as having been associated with Shillibeer in the Minutes of the Board of Stamps and Taxes, 10 October 1832.
16. *D.N.B. sub* Shillibeer; *The Times*, 23 March 1836; P.R.O., T1/4215.
17. P.R.O., T1/4215, Shillibeer and Noldwrit's Case. The rest of this paragraph is based upon this bundle of papers. Details of the debt to Cave will be found in *The Times*, 10, 26 May 1837 and of steamboat competition in evidence of John Wheatley to S.C. on Internal Communication Taxation 1837 [456] XX, qq. 290 *seq.* and 'Early Days of the London and Greenwich Railway', *Railway Magazine, 78* (1936), 82.
18. Louis Lagarrigue, *Cent Ans de Transport en Commun dans la Région Parisienne* (2 vols. Paris 1956), I, 30.
19. George Shillibeer to S.C. on a General Scheme of Extramural Sepulture, 1850 [1158] XXI, 124 *seq.*; Guildhall Library,

Noble Collection, 48/1; *The Times*, 7 November 1856; 23 August 1866.

20. 2 & 3 Vict. cap. 66; *The Times*, 14 October, 4 November 1839.

21. *Scenes*, chapter XVI, 'Omnibuses'.

22. *The Times*, 16 April 1842.

23. *Mechanics' Magazine*, 9, 30 March 1839; *The Times*, January 1841 quoted in Henry Charles Moore, *Omnibuses and Cabs* (1902), 55–56.

24. *The Penny Magazine*, 31 March 1837.

25. *The Times*, 7 April 1832.

26. *The Times*, 17 October 1832.

27. *The Times*, 14 July 1834, 3 October 1838.

28. *The Times*, 24 July 1835, 6, 10, 26 February, 14, 28 July 1836.

29. 1 & 2 Vict. cap. 79.

30. Appendix 2; *The Penny Magazine*, 31 March 1837.

31. *The Times*, 15 January 1834.

32. Sir Walter Gilbey, *Modern Carriages* (1905), 29.

33. 'Vehicular Statistics of London: I Omnibuses', *Chambers's Edinburgh Journal*, 14 June 1845.

34. *The Times*, 20 August 1838. The Secretary of this body was Thomas Haydon (*ibid.*). It seems to have been responsible for negotiating with the City authorities, in May 1840, regulations for preventing obstructions. Haydon then attended as secretary, together with Heard, Collingwood, Chancellor and Hudson. (Corporation of London Records Office, A.108.J, Report to the Court of Mayor and Aldermen from the Police Committee.)

35. *The Penny Magazine*, 31 March 1837.

36. *New Monthly Magazine*, 1833 (Part 2), 194–5.

37. *The Times*, 30 January 1836.

38. 'Vehicular Statistics of London: I Omnibuses', *Chambers's Edinburgh Journal*, 14 June 1845; *The Times*, 16 April 1842.

39. *The Times*, 20 August 1838.

40. *Post Office Directory*, 1844. The address was given as 13 St. Alban's Place, Edgware Road. There was also another concern called the London Omnibus Conveyance Co., 4 Portman Place, Edgware Road, which made its appearance in the directories from 1842.

41. London Transport Photograph Library, H/7775, Wilson's Omnibus Procession, 1 May 1845; 'Silverpen', 'The History and Present Condition of the Metropolitan Omnibus Drivers and Conductors', *The Working Man's Friend and Family Instructor*, 3 August 1850.

42. London Transport Photograph Library; John Tilling, *Kings of the Highway* (1957), 35.

43. Stanley Harris, *Old Coaching Days* (1882), 193; *The Coaching Age* (1885), 107 *seq.*; Benjamin Worthy Horne to R.C. on Railway Termini, 1846 [91] XVII.

44. *D.N.B. sub* Sherman; Harris, *Old Coaching Days*, 194.

45. Harris, *The Coaching Age*, 162 *seq.*; 'Silverpen', *loc. cit.*

46. Henry Humpherus, *History of the Origin and Progress of the Company of Watermen and Lightermen of the River Thames, 1514–1859* (3 vols, n.d.), III, 123–5; Frank Burtt, *Steamers of the Thames and Medway* (1949), 8–9.

47. Humpherus, *op. cit.*, 119; Burtt, *op. cit.*, 11–12; newscutting from the *Monthly Chronicle c.* 1838–39 (Guildhall Library, Noble Collection, C48/33); report from the S.C. appointed to inquire into the state of the Port of London, 1836 [557] XIV, appendix 22.

48. *Hansard*, II (3rd ser.), col. 647, 17 February 1831.

49. Guildhall Library, Noble Collection, C48/3; advertisement of Margate New Steam Packet Company, 26 June 1834.

50. For a collision when two steamboats tried to pick up passengers from the same wherry at Isleworth, see *The Times*, 13 July 1831.

51. Report from the S.C. appointed to inquire into the state of the Port of London, 1836 [557] XIV, appendix 17 and 22.

52. *Ibid.*, evidence of John Matthews, q. 3482.

53. Report on Steam Vessel Accidents, 1839 [273] XLVII, appendix, pp. 13–17. For steamboat racing, see, for instance, *The Times*, 16 June 1831.

54. *The Times*, 11 June 1830; House of Lords Record Office, John Taylor to the Commons' committee on the London & Blackwall Railway Bill, 23 March 1836.

55. *Ibid.*

56. *Ibid.*, evidence of Capt. John Fisher, 25 March 1836; William Nokes to Lords' committee on the carriage of passengers for hire upon the river Thames, 1837 [245] XX, 16, 17.

57. Capt. Cunningham and Daniel Halsey to S.C. appointed to inquire into the state of the Port of London, 1836 [557] XIV. qq. 3305, 3425.

58. William Nokes to Lords' committee on the carriage of passengers for hire upon the river Thames, 1837 [245] XX, 17; B.T.C. Records, Minutes of London & Blackwall Railway, 5 December 1842.

59. House of Lords Record Office, George William Clifton to Commons' Committee on London & Blackwall Railway Bill, 26 March 1836; Capt. Cunningham to S.C. appointed to inquire into the state of the Port of London, 1836 [557] XIV, q. 3278.

60. John Eggar Cooper, solicitor of the Watermen's Company, to the Lords' committee on the carriage of passengers for hire upon the river Thames, 1837 [245] XX, 12.

61. House of Lords Record Office, Alexander Coombe, Town Clerk of Gravesend, to Commons' committee on London & Blackwall Railway Bill, 28 March 1836.

62. William Nokes to Lords' committee on the carriage of passengers for hire upon the river Thames, 1837 [245] XX, 16.

63. Andrew Leighton Leith, *ibid.*, 21 *seq.*; Guildhall Library, Noble Collection, C48/33, *Monthly Chronicle*, c. 1838–39; Humpherus, *op. cit.*, III, 325, 342.

64. Abraham Howard and Thomas Cundy to R.C. on Metropolitan Improvement, 2nd Report, 1845 [348] XVII, qq. 24–25.

65. Burtt, *op. cit.*, 56.

66. *Illustrated London News*, 21 November 1846.

67. Burtt, *op. cit.*, 55–56.

68. *Monthly Chronicle, loc. cit.*

69. Charles E. Lee, 'Centenary of the London Motor Omnibus', *Transactions of the Newcomen Society*, XIII (1932–33), 132. The information in this paragraph is derived from this source, Walter Hancock, *Narrative of Twelve Years' Experiments . . . of Employing Steam Carriages on Common Roads* (1838), C. St.

C. B. Davison, *History of Steam Road Vehicles* (1959) and R. W. Kidner, *First Hundred Road Motors* (1950). For some later observations by Hancock's nephew and pupil, see Walter Hancock's contribution to the discussion following Robinson Souttar's paper to the Institution of Civil Engineers on 'Street Tramways', *Proceedings, 50* (1876–77), 47.

70. Alfred Rosling Bennett, *The First Railway in London* (1912), 4. This and the next paragraph are based upon this source.

71. *Ibid.*, 15; House of Lords Record Office, William Cubitt to Lords' committee on London & Croydon Railway Bill, 7 May 1838.

72. B. Reed and C. E. Lee, 'London Bridge', *Railway Magazine, 79* (1936), 435–42; R. B. Fellows, 'The Failure of Bricklayers' Arms as a Passenger Station', *ibid., 90* (1944), 209–12, 272–4. The rest of this paragraph and the following one are based on these sources.

73. J. Simmons, 'Railway History in English Local Records', *Journal of Transport History,* I (1953–54), 163–4, quoting Common Council Minutes, 1, 3 March 1836; 19 January, 27 February 1837.

74. B.T.C. Records, LBW 1/1–3, London & Blackwall Railway, Shareholders' and Directors' Minutes; T. Rowland Powel, 'London's Loneliest Line', *Railway Magazine, 79* (1936), 47–51; Charles E. Lee, 'The London & Blackwall Cable Railway', *ibid., 87* (1941), 424–5.

75. Report of the commissioners on railway termini within or in the immediate vicinity of the Metropolis, 1846 [91] XVII 5–7.

76. House of Lords Record Office, Joseph Locke and John Duncan to Commons' committee on London & Blackwall Railway Bill, 23, 25 April 1850; G. H. Lake, *The Railways of Tottenham* (1945), 10–12; Cecil J. Allen, *The Great Eastern Railway* (1955), ch. 1 & 2; *Herapath's Railway Journal,* 19 June 1847; *Illustrated London News,* 3 March 1849. The branch from Stratford to Woodford and Loughton was opened on 22 August 1856 and extended to Ongar on 24 April 1865 (Allen, *op. cit.,* 20, 55).

77. B.T.C. Archives, NL 1/1, East and West India Docks and Birmingham Junction Railway, Minutes of General Meetings.

78. *Ibid.*, 9 June 1851; London & Blackwall, half-yearly meeting, 29 August 1851.

79. Michael Robbins, *The North London Railway* (4th ed. 1953), 4–5.

80. H. D. Welch, *The London, Tilbury & Southend Railway* (1951), 4–5.

81. William James Chaplin to R.C. on Metropolitan Termini, 1846 [91] XVII, qq. 1546, 1605–8.

82. House of Lords Record Office, Cornelius Stovin to Commons' committee on London and South Western Railway (London Bridge) Extension, 21 July 1846; Sam Fay, *A Royal Road* (1883), 69.

83. *Ibid.*, 60, 70.

84. Report of the R.C. on Metropolitan Termini, 1846 [91] XVII, 5.

85. *Railway Times*, 23 May 1857; Edwin Course, *London Railways* (1962), 199. The London & Croydon offered seasons at reduced price when taken by more than one member of the same family (Guildhall Library, Noble Collection, C.48/5). The London & South Western offered a similar concession (Course, *op. cit.*, 199).

86. *Railway Times*, 29 June 1850.

87. Charles Pearson to R.C. on Metropolitan Termini, 1846 [91] XVII, qq. 2811 *seq.*

88. *The Times*, 28 November 1851; the *London Journal* printed a drawing of Pearson's proposed central terminus (Guildhall Library, Noble Collection, C.48/5).

89. Charles Pearson to the S.C. on Metropolitan Communications, 1854–55 [415] X, q. 1356.

90. J. Butler Williams, 'On the Principles of Railway Management and on the Profitable Increase in the Traffic Produced by Great Reductions in the Charges', *Journal of the Statistical Society of London*, IX (June 1846), 122–3.

91. *Illustrated London News*, 22 April 1843.

92. *Ibid.*, 15 July 1843.

93. William James Chaplin to R.C. on Metropolitan Termini, 1846 [91] XVII, q. 1596.

94. C. F. Dendy Marshall, *A History of the Southern Railway* (1936), 46; advertisement Guildhall Library, Noble Collection, C.48/5; Edgar Browne, *Phiz and Dickens* (1913), 26.

95. Dendy Marshall, *op. cit.*, 270–1.
96. *Ibid.*, 81–82; *Economist*, 10 August 1844; Ald. J. Humphery to R.C. on Metropolitan Termini, 1846 [91] XVII, q. 2123.
97. Samuel Norwood to S.C. on Sale of Beer Act, 1854–55 [407] X, qq. 1850, 1894.
98. *Ibid.*, evidence of George Hawkins, q. 2185; Dendy Marshall, *op. cit.*, 283–4; Samuel Phillips, *Guide to the Crystal Palace and Neville Park* (1854), introductory note and 15. See also Edmund W. Gilbert, *Brighton, Old Ocean's Bauble* (1954), 148–9, 204–5.
99. John Hammill to S.C. on Sale of Beer Act, 1854–55 [407] X, q. 759.
100. *Ibid.*, evidence of Arthur Wightman, q. 2207.
101. *Railway Times*, 19 June 1852.
102. Lloyd Saunders, *Old Kew, Chiswick and Kensington* (1910), 234; W. Robins, *Paddington Past and Present* (1853), vii; Francis Bennoch to S.C. on Metropolitan Communications, 1854–55 [415] X, q. 226.
103. For the effect of railway competition in this direction, see *ibid.*, evidence of Charles Pearson, q. 1345.
104. *Ibid.*, qq. 1340 *seq.*
105. *Bradshaw's Monthly General Railway and Steam Navigation Guide*, January 1855; Samuel Laing to S.C. on Metropolitan Bridges, 1854 [370] XIV, q. 23.
106. Return of the number of licences granted for stage carriages 1862 [350] XXXI. The estimate of 3,000 omnibuses which was made by the *Morning Chronicle*'s reporter (cited in *Household Narratives*, October 1850 and repeated by the *Illustrated London News*, 1 November 1851) does not accord with this or other official licence or mileage returns of the period nor with totals given at the time of the London General's formation. There were, however, about 3,000 cabs and perhaps this was the cause of confusion. The figure of 1,472 for 1844, given in 'Vehicular Statistics of London: I Omnibuses', *Chambers's Edinburgh Journal*, 14 June 1845 also seems far too high.
107. 5 & 6 Vict. cap. 79.
108. Painting by Pollard at the London Museum.
109. *Morning Chronicle* cited in *Household Narratives*, October 1850.

110. *The Times*, 28 February 1851.

111. Lagarrigue, *op. cit.*, I, 32.

112. Henry Charles Moore, *Omnibuses and Cabs* (1902), 62; *Illustrated London News*, 21 November 1846.

113. *Ibid.*, 12 December 1846. See also Thackeray on 'disgusting' 2d. omnibuses in *Punch*, 25 March 1848.

114. *Illustrated London News*, 17 July 1847; *Knight's Cyclopaedia of London* (1851), 528; Charles Manby Smith, *Curiosities of London Life* (1853), 222–6. For the sixpenny fare, see Gladstone's recollections as reported by Sir Henry Lucy, *The Diary of a Journalist* (1920), 101.

115. *The Times*, 18 October 1851; Return of mileage duty 1852–53 [952] LVII.

116. *Illustrated London News*, 25 October 1851.

117. *The Times*, 11 November 1851.

118. *The Times*, 4 December 1851; 17 March 1852.

119. *The Builder*, quoted in *The Times*, 18 October 1851.

120. Charles Manby Smith, *op. cit.*, 227–33.

121. *The Times*, 4 December 1851.

122. G. A. Sekon, *Locomotion in Victorian London* (1938), 27–28.

123. Return of mileage duty 1852–53 [952] LVII.

124. 16 & 17 Vict. cap. 33; *The Times*, 21 September 1853; 19 August 1854.

125. J. E. Bradfield, *Stage Carriage Duty, Observations on the Injustice, Inequalities and Anomalies of the Present System of Taxation of Stage Coaches* (1853), 15–16.

126. Return of mileage duty 1852–53 [952] LVII; Return of taxes and duties 1857 (Sess. 2) [301] XXV; J. E. Bradfield, *The Public Carriages of Great Britain* (1855), 41.

127. M. L. Moore, *A Century's Extension of Passenger Transport Facilities (1830–1930) within the London Transport Board's Area and Its Relation to Population Spread* (London Ph.D. thesis 1948), 71.

128. John Hargrave Stevens, surveyor to the western division of the City, to S.C. on Metropolitan Communications, 1854–55 [415] X, 1249.

129. Reports of S.C. on Metropolitan Improvements, 1836 [517] XX; 1837–38 [418] [661] XVI; 1840 [410] [485] XII; 1841 [398] IX; reports of R.C. on Metropolitan Improvements,

1844 [15] XV; 1845 [348] [619] [627] XVII; 1846 [682] XXIV; 1847 [861] XVI; 1851 [1356] XXIX. See also report of the S.C. on the London Coal Trade, 1837–38 [475] XV.

130. First report of the R.C. on Metropolitan Improvement, 1844 [15] XV, 6.

131. William Chadwick to R.C. on Metropolitan Termini, 1846 [91] XVII, q. 2759.

132. John Coope Haddan to S.C. on Metropolitan Communications, 1854–55 [415] X, q. 161.

133. John Timbs, *Curiosities of London* (1855), 60; Francis Bennoch to S.C. on Metropolitan Bridges, 1854 [370] XIV, q. 341.

134. *Knight's Cyclopaedia of London* (1851), 512; half-yearly report of the Charing Cross Bridge Company (Guildhall Library, Noble Collection, C.48/4.)

135. William Hosking to R.C. on Metropolitan Termini, 1846 [91] XVII, qq. 2585–7.

136. Samuel Laing to S.C. on Metropolitan Bridges, 1854 [370] XIV, qq. 14–15.

137. Sir Joseph Paxton to S.C. on Metropolitan Communications, 1854–55 [415] X, q. 714.

138. *Ibid.*, Paxton, q. 850; the Rev. Walter Blount, q. 1165.

139. *Ibid.*, William Moseley, qq. 423 *seq.*

140. *Ibid.*, Paxton, qq. 716 *seq.*

CHAPTER THREE

THE EARLY YEARS OF THE
LONDON GENERAL OMNIBUS COMPANY

1. J. R. T. Hughes, *Fluctuations in Trade, Industry and Finance* (Oxford 1960), 29; Michael G. Mulhall, *History of Prices Since the Year 1850* (1885), 184; Thomas Tooke and William Newmarch, *A History of Prices* (1857), V, 33–37.

2. J. E. Bradfield, *Stage Carriage Duty, Observations on the Injustice, Inequalities and Anomalies of the Present System of Taxation of Stage Coaches* (three editions in 1853 and a fourth

in 1854). The Acting Committee (formed on 26 September 1853) consisted of M. Balls (Brixton), W. Cranfield (Black-friars Road), R. Carpenter (Paddington), J. Clark (Pimlico), H. Edmonds (Maida Hill), J. R. Elliott (King's Cross) C. Gamble (Westminster), H. Gray (Earl Street, Blackfriars, who had been chairman of the meeting at which the committee was formed), R. Glover (Stratford), R. Hartley (Walham Green), J. Hardwick (Hammersmith), J. Hands (New Road), John Johnson (Thistle Grove, Brompton), A. Lines (St. John's Wood), A. McNamara (Finsbury), R. Render (Clapham), J. Roads (Paddington), J. Trevett (Paddington), Willan (Kingsland), James Willing (Walworth Gate), John Wilson (Holloway). The committee's office was at 19 Strand.

3. Sir Henry Lucy, *The Diary of a Journalist* (1920), 101.

4. *The Morning Post*, 22 November 1854. (Copy in B.T.C. Archives, L.G.O.C. 4/3.)

5. 18 & 19 Vict. cap. 78.

6. *Illustrated London News*, 3 February 1855, 107; Tooke and Newmarch, *op. cit.*, 43–45, Mulhall, *op. cit.*, 184.

7. *Illustrated London News*, 9 June 1855, 558.

8. Rondo E. Cameron, 'The Crédit Mobilier and the Economic Development of Europe', *The Journal of Political Economy*, December 1953, 464; *France and the Economic Development of Europe 1800–1914* (Princeton 1961), chapters 6 and 7; David S. Landes, *Bankers and Pashas* (1958), chapter 1; M. Aycard, *Histoire du Crédit Mobilier, 1852–1867* (Paris 1867). The transport aspects of this paragraph are based upon Louis Lagarrigue, *Cent Ans de Transports en Commun dans la Région Parisienne* (Paris 1956), I, 32–39.

9. Archives Nationales, F12 67.60, Moreau-Chaslon to Isaac Pereire, 28 November 1854.

10. Royal Society of Arts, Minutes of Committee, 21 November 1854, 12 April, 27 August 1855; *Journal of the Society of Arts*, 5, 12 September 1856.

11. University College, London, Chadwick Papers, draft of letter from Chadwick to an unspecified newspaper editor, 27 November 1858 in unnumbered box labelled 'Letters and Notes from Chadwick to Unknown Persons'. Chadwick

subsequently published some of the contents of this letter as a paper to the London Statistical Society under the title of 'Results of Different Principles of Legislation and Administration in Europe; of Competition for the Field as compared with Competition within the Field', *Journal of the Statistical Society of London*, XXII (1859), 381–420.

12. *Ibid.*

13. Count Orsi, *Recollections of the Last Half-Century* (1881); Lagarrigue, *op. cit.*, I, 39; British Patent 10,890/23 October 1845; P.O. London Directories.

14. *Illustrated London News*, 20 October 1855; *Economist*, 12 July 1856, 759.

15. Report by the Registrar of Joint Stock Companies, 1856 [60] [77] LV; B.T.C. Records, PROS 3/1/5, Preliminary Announcement of the London Omnibus Company Limited.

16. *Morning Post*, 16, 17 November 1855. (Copy in B.T.C. Records, L.G.O.C. 4/3.)

17. *Morning Post*, 16 November 1855.

18. *Ibid.*

19. B.T.C. Records, L.G.O.C. 4/4, Prospectus of the L.G.O.C. (Another copy may be found in Guildhall Library, Noble Collection, C.48/61.)

20. Archives Nationales, F84, *Compagnie Générale des Omnibus de Londres: Statuts*.

21. B.T.C. Records, L.G.O.C. 1/1, Minutes of *Gérants*. This and later paragraphs are based upon this source unless otherwise stated.

22. *Morning Post*, 16 November 1855.

23. B.T.C. Records, L.G.O.C. 4/4.

24. B.T.C. Records, L.G.O.C. 1/41, Index to *Conseil de Surveillance* [London Section].

25. *Illustrated London News*, 30 August 1851, 258, for presentation to Roney on his leaving the Eastern Counties Railway.

26. See *Report of Sir Cusack P. Roney to the London Board of Directors of the Grand Trunk Railway of Canada* (May 1855).

27. B.T.C. Records, EC 1/61, Report of Committee of Investigation; EC 1/12, Board Minutes, 10 January 1856.

28. B.T.C. Records, L.G.O.C. 1/39, Minutes of the *Conseil de Surveillance* [Paris section], 14 October.

29. *Ibid.*, 24 December 1857; 25 March 1858.

30. B.T.C. Records, L.G.O.C. 1/46, Report of *Gérants*, 25 April 1857. (French version in Archives Nationales, F84.)

31. *The Times*, 8 January 1856; *Illustrated Times*, 12 January 1856.

32. *Ibid.*

33. B.T.C. Records, L.G.O.C. 1/41, Index of *Conseil de Surveillance* [London section] *sub* Appointments.

34. B.T.C. Records, L.G.O.C. 1/46, Report of *Gérants* and arbitration award 10 November 1857.

35. Post Office Records, Agreement between the Postmaster General and Thomas John Bolton, 8 September 1847 with endorsement (Bolton and McNamara) 30 December 1851; F. E. Baines, *On the Track of the Mail Coach* (1895), 167, 314; Post Office Records, Minutes, *182*, 255.

36. *Illustrated London News*, 9 February 1856; B.T.C. Records, L.G.O.C. 1/42, General Meeting, 31 March 1862; L.G.O.C. 1/3, Minutes, 28, 29, 31 March, 4 April 1862; House of Lords Record Office, James Willing to Commons' committee on Metropolitan Railway (Trinity Square Extension) Bill, 31 May 1864. In December 1869 James Willing junior received the contract for lighting the L.G.O.C.'s omnibuses (L.G.O.C. 1/8, Minutes, 2, 9, 16 December 1869).

37. B.T.C. Records, L.G.O.C. 1/41, Index *sub* Hartley and Trevett; L.G.O.C. 1/2, Minutes of Directors, 19 April, 22 August, 28 October 1859.

38. Report of *Gérants*, 25 April 1857. (French version in Archives Nationales, F84.)

39. Highbury had 'all the advantages of steam power for bruising and chaffcutting' at the time it became the property of the Company (Minutes of *Gérants*, 18 February 1856).

40. Report of *Gérants*, 21 April 1858. (French version in Archives Nationales, F84.)

41. J. Ewing Ritchie, *Here and There in London* (1859), 187–99; Report of *Gérants*, 13 October 1858; Third Annual General Meeting, 27 April 1859.

42. *Morning Post*, 18 February 1856. (Copy in B.T.C. Archives, L.G.O.C. 4/3.)

43. Report of *Gérants*, 25 April 1857.

44. *The Times*, 25 February 1856.
45. Report of *Gérants*, 25 April 1857.
46. B.T.C. Records, L.G.O.C. 1/1, Minutes of *Gérants*, 16 February 1857; L.G.O.C. 1/2, Minutes of Directors, 24 June 1859.
47. *Ibid.*, 16 February, 20 July 1857; *The Times*, 6 December 1856.
48. Minutes of *Gérants*, 21 April 1856.
49. *Ibid.*, 10, 17 November, 1 December 1856.
50. Report of *Gérants*, 25 April 1857, 21 April 1858, 27 April 1859.
51. B.T.C. Records, L.G.O.C. 1/41, Index to *Conseil de Surveillance* [London Section] *sub* McNamara. For a drawing and description of a Manchester omnibus, see *Illustrated London News*, 8 March 1856.
52. *The Times*, 16 May 1856.
53. Report of *Gérants*, 10 November 1857.
54. *Ibid.*, 25 April 1857, 21 April 1858, 27 April 1859.
55. Minutes of *Gérants*, 16 August 1858.
56. *The Times*, 18 April 1856.
57. Report of *Gérants*, 25 April 1857; Minutes of *Gérants*, 13 April 1857.
58. *The Times*, 10 March 1858.
59. *The Times*, 29 August 1857.
60. B.T.C. Records, L.G.O.C. 1/46, Report of Third Annual General Meeting, 27 April 1859; Minutes of *Gérants*, 13 December 1858.
61. This section is based upon B.T.C. Records, L.G.O.C. 1/39, Minutes of the *Conseil de Surveillance* [Paris Section] which began on 13 September 1856. The earlier minutes do not appear to have survived.
62. Report of *Gérants*, 25 April 1857; *Herapath's Railway Journal*, 23 May 1857.
63. B.T.C. Records, L.G.O.C. 1/1, Minutes, 13 July, 21 September 1857; 22 March 1858; interview with W. S. Birch, then aged 94, *Daily Mail*, 23 February 1934; 'Some Recollections of Mr. William Samuel Birch', *Motor Transport*, 1 July 1929. We owe the last reference to Mr. C. E. Lee.
64. Report of *Gérants*, 13 October 1858.

2A

65. Minutes of the *Conseil de Surveillance*, 13 September 1856.
66. *Railway Record*, 7 February 1857.
67. Minutes of the *Conseil de Surveillance*, 19 April 1858.
68. W. Bridges Adams, 'On the Application of Rails for Horse Transit in the Streets and Environs of London and also for Railway branches', *Journal of the Society of Arts*, VI, 190, 13 February 1857; Charles Klapper, *The Golden Age of Tramways* (1961), 10–12; *Hansard's Parliamentary Debates*, 3rd ser., CXLIX, 173, 15 March 1858.
69. *Illustrated London News*, 19 November 1853; Louis Lagarrigue, *Cent Ans de Transports en Commun dans la Région Parisienne* (2 vols. Paris n.d.), I, 40–41; Klapper, *op. cit.*, 12–13. The line was extended to Versailles but there was no further tramway development in Paris until the 1870s.
70. B.T.C. Records, PROS 3/1/11.
71. Minutes of the *Conseil de Surveillance*, 6 October 1857.
72. *The Times*, 16 March 1858; Klapper, *op cit.*, 14; University College, London, draft of letter from Chadwick to an unspecified newspaper editor, 27 November 1858 (see note 11). The Company was re-registered on 6 October 1860 at the time of Train's activities (Return of Joint-Stock Companies, 1862 [58] LV).
73. Minutes of *Gérants*, 5 October 1857.
74. *Ibid.*, 16 May 1859; L.G.O.C. 1/2, Minutes of Directors, 13, 20 May 1859; *The Times*, 3 January 1857.
75. University College London, draft of letter from Chadwick to an unspecified newspaper editor, 27 November 1858 (see note 11).
76. *Ibid.*; Return of Joint-Stock Companies, 1857–58 [324] LIII; *The Times*, 7, 8 November 1856. Shillibeer was named as one of the directors.
77. *The Times*, 15 November 1856.
78. *The Times*, 21 February 1857.
79. *The Times*, 26 September 1857; 8 November 1858.
80. Minutes of *Gérants*, 9 November 1857.
81. *The Times*, 8, 12, 19, 22 December 1858; PRO B.T. 31/24/122.
82. Report of *Gérants*, 25 April, 10 November 1857.
83. *Illustrated London News*, 9 February 1856.

84. Minutes of the *Conseil de Surveillance*, 30 January 1857.
85. University College, London, Chadwick Papers, *sub* Foucaud, draft of letter, 2 January 1857.
86. Report of *Gérants*, 13 October 1858.
87. Archives Nationales, F84, *Bases Principales de la Compagnie Générale des Omnibus de Londres (Anglaise) qui doit remplacer la Compagnie actuelle (Française).*
88. Archives Nationales, F84, leaflet to French shareholders of the L.G.O.C., March 1862.
89. *Herapath's Railway Journal*, 9 March 1867.
90. B.T.C. Records, L.G.O.C. 1/42, General Meeting, 3 March 1868.
91. See report and accounts, dated September 1911, in the Archives Nationales, F84. It is not known whether there are any later examples.
92. B.T.C. Records, L.G.O.C. 1/2, Minutes of Directors, 31 December 1858.
93. *Herapath's Railway Journal*, 13 September 1863. For a brief history of this debt, see *ibid.*, 11 March 1865.
94. Minutes of Directors, 22 August, 23 September 1859.
95. *Ibid.*, 14 October, 11 November 1859.
96. *Ibid.*, 17 January 1860.
97. B.T.C. Records, L.G.O.C. 1/1, Minutes of the Managers' Committee, 12 December 1859, 2 April 1860.
98. *Herapath's Railway Journal*, 18 May 1861.
99. *Ibid.*, 31 May, 13 September 1862; 25 March, 29 August, 13 September 1863; 19 March 1864.

CHAPTER FOUR

THE FIRST CLIMAX

(1) THE COMING OF THE UNDERGROUND RAILWAY

1. Evidence of Robert Stephenson to R.C. on Metropolitan Termini, 1846 [91] XVII, q. 237.
2. Evidence of John Hargrave Stevens to S.C. on Metropolitan Communications, 1854–55 [415] X, q. 1177–8; House of

Lords Record Office, William Tite to Commons' committee on North Metropolitan Railway Bill, 1854. The underground scheme was replaced by one for a viaduct, but only a few arches were actually built.

3. Evidence of John Hargrave Stevens to S.C. on Metropolitan Communications, 1854–55, q. 1177.

4. *The Times*, 19 August 1830.

5. 1 & 2 Vict. cap. lxxxiii; 3 & 4 Vict. cap. cxii; 5 & 6 Vict. cap. ci; 8 & 9 Vict. cap. xvii; 11 & 12 cap. clxii; William J. Pinks, *The History of Clerkenwell* (1881), 351–2.

6. *Letter from Charles Pearson to W. H. Ashurst, Esq.* (1845) (Copy at Guildhall Library).

7. Corporation of London Records Office, Pearson's historical survey, 13 January 1852 (Papers relating to Central Terminus Co.); 14 & 15 Vict. cap. cxx; Pinks, *op. cit.*, 352–3.

8. Corporation of London Records Office, MS. 142.5, Mr. Walker's Report on the City Central Railway Terminus and Fleet Valley Improvement, 15 December 1851; P.D.70.18, letter from Sidney Smith, secretary of the City Terminus Company, to Thomas Hall, chairman of the Improvement Committee, 7 February 1853; drawing of central terminus in *The London Journal* (Guildhall Library, Noble Collection, C.48.5).

9. *The Times*, 28 November 1851.

10. Corporation of London Records Office, Pearson to Improvement Committee, 19 December 1851 (Papers Relating to Central Terminus Co.).

11. B.T.C. Records, MET 1/1, Directors' Report to First General Meeting, 31 August 1853.

12. E. T. MacDermot, *History of the Great Western Railway* (1927), I, 476 *seq.*; P.O. Directories.

13. House of Lords Record Office, subscription contract with deposited plans of the Bayswater, Paddington & Holborn Bridge Railway.

14. B.T.C. Records, MET 1/1, Minutes, 10 January 1853; Thomas Mackay, *The Life of Sir John Fowler* (1900), 148 *seq.*; *D.N.B. sub* Fowler.

15. House of Lords Record Office, William Malins to Commons' committee on North Metropolitan Railway Bill, 26 May 1854.

Inquiries through the press have failed to add anything to the little that is known about William Malins. It is just possible that he may have been the elder brother of (Sir) Richard Malins, a judge and for a time M.P. for Wallingford, who is mentioned in accounts of the opening of the railway. Richard Malins was born at Evesham and in 1868 a member of the family owned property at Pershore (Robert P. Dod, *The Parliamentary Companion*, editions after 1852; *V. C. H. Worcestershire*, IV, 156).

16. B.T.C. Records, MET 1/2, Minutes, 8 April, 29 July, 18 November 1863; 11 January 1865.

17. See, for instance, the chairman's statement at the General meeting reported in *Herapath's Railway Journal*, 14 February 1863.

18. *Herapath's Railway Journal*, 3 September 1853.

19. MET 1/1, Minutes, 10 January 1853. Those named in the subscription contract were: George Bernard Townsend, gentleman, Salisbury (£5,000); William Burchell, gentleman, Upper Harley Street (£20,000); Alexander John Kinloch, Esq., Park in the County of Aberdeen and 17 St. John's Wood Road (£10,000); Robert Russell Notman, Esq., 8 Waverley Place, St. John's Wood (£5,000); John Rankine Davidson, engineer, 12 Bishopsgate Street and Elm Villa, Finchley (£5,000); Edward Ladd Betts, contractor (£20,000); Thomas Brassey, contractor (£20,000); Samuel Morton Peto, Esq. (£20,000); Thomas Edward Dicey, Esq., 2 Princes Terrace, Hyde Park (£20,000); Bonamy Price, Esq., 11 Princes Terrace, Hyde Park (£20,000); Patrick Kilgour, Esq., J.P., 69 Hamilton Terrace, St. John's Wood (£10,000); Thomas Earle, Esq., 4 Warwick Gardens, Kensington (£20,000); Thomas Webster Harby, gentleman, 25 Gloucester Road, Regent's Park (£20,000); William Malins, Esq., 16 Savile Row, St. James's (£15,000); Henry Earle, Esq., 44 Parliament Street (£15,000) (House of Lords Record Office, list with deposited plans, 1 November 1852).

20. House of Lords Record Office, evidence of William Malins to Commons' committee on Bayswater, Paddington & Holborn Bridge Railway, 2 June 1853 and deposited plans dated 1 November 1852.

21. MET 1/1, Minutes, 31 August 1853; 17 & 18 Vict. cap. clxxxvi.
22. *Minutes of Common Council*, 22, 24 February 1853.
23. House of Lords Record Office, evidence of Sidney Smith to Commons' committee on North Metropolitan Railway Bill, 26 May 1854, and of William Tite, 1 June 1854; *Railway Times*, 7 May 1853.
24. *Railway Times*, 11 June 1853.
25. MET 1/1, Minutes, 31 August, 7 November 1853. For Ayrton, see *Dictionary of National Biography*, Supplement.
26. MET 1/1, Minutes, 10 November 1853.
27. Charles H. Grinling, *The History of the Great Northern Railway 1845–1902* (1903), 89.
28. MET 1/1, Minutes, 27, 29 December; House of Lords Record Office, subscription contract with plans for North Metropolitan Bill, 1854.
29. House of Lords Record Office, evidence of Fowler to Commons' committee on North Metropolitan Railway, 29 May 1854.
30. *Ibid.*, Brunel, 30 May 1854.
31. 17 & 18 Vict. cap. ccxxi. Powers to form a junction with the Great Northern were obtained in 1856 by 19 & 20 Vict. cap. cix.
32. 18 & 19 Vict. cap. cii. For the monetary situation at this time, see Sir John Clapham, *The Bank of England* (1944), II, 222 *seq*.
33. MET 1/1, Minutes, 27 February 1856. Malins later explained his resignation on the grounds of his connection with the Railway Reform Association (*Herapath's Railway Journal*, 17 May 1856). He was, in fact, chairman of that body which was then engaged in criticism of Great Western policy. See Malins's letter to the chairman of that railway, printed in the *Railway Times*, 9 August 1856.
34. *Herapath's Railway Journal*, 29 August 1863.
35. MET 1/1, Minutes, 30 July, 1, 8 August 1856.
36. *Ibid.*, 16 December 1853; Sir John Clapham, *An Economic History of Modern Britain*, II, 208.
37. MET 1/1, Minutes, 13 September, 7 November 1856; 24 February 1857.

38. W. T. Passingham, *London's Markets* (n.d.), 23–24; Pinks, *op. cit.*, 353.

39. *Herapath's Railway Journal*, 14 March 1857.

40. MET 1/1, Minutes, 26 August 1857.

41. *The Economist*, 5 January 1858, quoted by Clapham, *Bank of England*, II, 238.

42. MET 1/1, Minutes, 26 February 1858.

43. MET 1/1, Minutes, 7 April 1858; *Herapath's Railway Magazine*, 27 March, 3 April 1858.

44. MET 1/1, Minutes, 23 April 1858.

45. *Ibid.*, 26 August 1857; Robert P. Dod, *The Parliamentary Companion* (1855 edition). Wilkinson had been M.P. for Lambeth between 1852 and 1855.

46. MacDermot, *op. cit.*, 511–12, 517. According to the Post Office Directories, the partnership between Burchell and Parson was ended in the mid-1850s. Parson thereafter appears as a member of the firm of Baker and Parson.

47. *Herapath's Railway Journal*, 23 October 1858.

48. See the transcript 'carefully revised and extended' by Pearson, a copy of which is at the Corporation of London Records Office, P.D.46.9.

49. Minutes of Common Council, 3, 24 March, 1 April 1859; *Herapath's Railway Journal*, 25 April 1863.

50. MET 1/1, Minutes, 22 May 1860; Pinks, *op. cit.*, 353; House of Lords Record Office, Fowler to Commons' committee on Metropolitan Railway Bill, 5 July 1859; 22 & 23 Vict. cap. xcvii. The share capital was reduced to £850,000, with powers to raise one-third of that amount by loan.

51. MET 1/2, Minutes, 26 November 1862.

52. MET 1/47, Sub-Committee Minutes, 20 June 1859; House of Lords Record Office, evidence of Charles Pearson to Commons committee on London, Chatham & Dover (Metropolitan Extensions) Bill, 23 April 1860; 'Fowler's Ghost', 'Railway Connections at King's Cross', *Railway Magazine*, *108* (1962), 297–304.

53. MET 1/1, Minutes, 21 October, 6, 8, 13 December 1859. Smith and Knight later became involved in railway building abroad. The partnership was turned into a limited company but this had to be wound up after the Royal Sardinian

Railway had defaulted on 'a very large sum' (*Herapath's Railway Journal*, 23 December 1865).

54. Benjamin Baker, 'The Metropolitan and Metropolitan District Railways', *Proceedings of the Institution of Civil Engineers*, lxxxi (1884-85).

55. 24 & 25 Vict. cap. cxxxiii; 25 & 26 Vict. cap. lviii; MET 1/2, Minutes, 6 August 1862. Calls were to be made in four instalments of £2 10s. od. in August 1862 and January, May and September 1863.

56. House of Lords Record Office, evidence of Charles Pearson to Commons' committee on London, Chatham & Dover (Metropolitan Extension) Bill, 23 April 1860.

57. MET 1/2, Minutes, 25 March, 23 April, 21 May 1862. Myles Fenton was later appointed general manager on a five-year contract beginning 30 June 1863 at a salary of £800 per year plus a bonus on receipts in place of his original salary of £500 (*ibid.*, 7 October 1863). From 1869 it was raised to £1,200 (*ibid.*, 29 June 1870). For summary of his career, see G. A. Sekon, *The History of the South Eastern Railway* (1895), 29-30.

58. Pink, *op. cit.*, 361-2.

59. *The Times*, 6 August 1862; *Herapath's Railway Journal*, 16 August 1862; *Illustrated London News*, 6, 13 September 1862. See Mackay, *op. cit.*, 172, for the names of the other members of the party. The first trip on the railway, to try out Fowler's smoke-consuming locomotive, was from Edgware Road to Paddington on 28 November 1861. The first through journey took place on the following 5 April in a train composed of wagons alone (*The Times*, 30 November 1861; 7 April 1862).

60. MET 1/2, Minutes, 12 November, 10 December, *Herapath's Railway Journal*, 17 January, 14 February 1863. There had been a ceremonial tour of the line on the day before it was opened to the public (*ibid.*, 10 January 1863).

61. House of Lords Record Office, evidence of Charles Pearson to Commons' committee on London, Chatham & Dover (Metropolitan Extension) Bill, 23 April 1860.

62. *Ibid.*

63. Charles E. Lee, *Passenger Class Distinctions* (1946), 50-51.

64. *Herapath's Railway Journal*, 27 August 1864; Lee, *op. cit.*, 51. House of Lords Record Office, evidence of Myles Fenton to

Commons' committee on Metropolitan Railway (Trinity Square Extension) Bill, 31 May 1864.

65. MET 1/2, Minutes, 24 September 1862.

66. *Ibid.*, 11 February 1863. The annuity was £250.

67. *Herapath's Railway Journal*, 17 January 1863; House of Lords Record Office, evidence of Myles Fenton to Commons' committee on Metropolitan Railway (Trinity Square Extension) Bill, 7 June 1864.

68. *Herapath's Railway Journal*, 27 August 1864.

69. *A Mid-Victorian Pepys*, ed. S. M. Ellis (1923), 246–7, 283.

70. *The Times*, 30 November 1861.

71. MacDermot, *op. cit.*, I, 607, 624–5. A Cooke and Wheatstone instrument supplied to the London & Blackwall Railway is to be seen at the Science Museum.

72. T. S. Lascelles, 'Underground Signalling in Steam Days', *Railway Magazine*, *93* (1947), 102–3; Charles E. Lee, *The Metropolitan District Railway* (1956), 39. By 1873 some of the signals were only 400–500 ft. apart and speeds of up to 35 m.p.h. were obtained (Evidence of Myles Fenton to S.C. on Regulation of Railways (Prevention of Accidents) Bill, 1873 [148] xiv, qq. 1236, 1241.)

73. MET 1/2, Minutes, 25 February 1863; Benjamin Baker, *op. cit.*, 8–9; A. R. Bennett, 'The Early Locomotive History of the Metropolitan Railway', *Railway Magazine*, *22* (1908), 317, and *id.*, *The Chronicles of Boulton's Siding* (1927), 190–209. The engine actually built was a 2–4–0; drawings of a 2–2–2 tank (*Railway Magazine*, *8* (1901), 63; C. Baker, *The Metropolitan Railway* (1951), 41) appear to relate to an earlier project that was not pursued. On the genesis of the bogie, C. Hamilton Ellis, *British Railway History*, I (1954), 353–7.

74. MacDermot, *op. cit.*, I, 787–9, 880; B. Baker, *op. cit.*, 9; Bennett, 'Early Locomotive History'; *Diaries of Sir Daniel Gooch, Baronet* (1892), 80–81.

75. MacDermot, *op. cit.*, I, 841–2, 844–5; a three-carriage G. W. train on the Metropolitan illustrated *ibid.*, I, 441; C. Hamilton Ellis, *Nineteenth-Century Railway Carriages* (1949), 47–48, 53.

76. MET 1/2, Minutes, 25 March 1863.

77. MET 1/2, Minutes, 28 February, 11 April 1866; MET 1/3, Minutes, 26 September, 21 November 1866.

78. MET 1/2, Minutes, 19 October 1864, 11 January 1865; *The Times*, 12 December 1961; *Men Who Have Earned Success* (booklet published by Spiers and Pond Ltd., 1961).

79. Evidence of John Parson to S.C. on Metropolitan Railway Communication, 1863 [500] VIII, qq. 727–30. See also Parson's comments on the G.W. locomotives at the half-yearly meetings of shareholders reported in *Herapath's Railway Journal*, 5 March 1864.

80. MET 1/2, Minutes, 14 January 1863.

81. *Herapath's Railway Journal*, 28 March, 18 April 1863.

82. MET 1/2, Minutes, 15 April, 6 May 1863.

83. *Ibid.*, 15 July 1863. The junction had been authorized by 24 & 25 Vict. cap. cxxxiii.

84. MET 1/2, Minutes, 21, 31 July 1863.

85. *Ibid.*, 29 July 1863; *Herapath's Railway Journal*, 8 August 1863; Charles H. Grinling, *History of the Great Northern Railway* (1898), 202. For details of the Great Northern engines, see Benjamin Baker, *op. cit.*, 10; G. F. Bird, *The Locomotives of the Great Northern Railway, 1847–1910* (1910), 32–34; A. R. Bennett, 'Early Locomotive History', 317.

86. MET 1/2, Minutes, 7 October 1863. The locomotives were to cost £2,600 each.

87. *Herapath's Railway Journal*, 3 October 1863. For the Ashbury Railway Carriage & Iron Company, see *Railway Magazine*, 2 (1898), 78–84.

88. *Ibid.*, 5 March 1864.

89. *Ibid.*, 27 August 1864; House of Lords Record Office, evidence of John Fowler to Commons' committee on Metropolitan District Railways (No. 2) Bill, 8 July 1864.

90. Benjamin Baker, *op. cit.*, 10; A. R. Bennett, 'The Early Locomotive History of the Metropolitan Railway', *Railway Magazine*, 22 (1908), 497–503; *id.*, *Boulton's Siding*, 195–8; E. L. Ahrons, *Locomotive and Train Working in the Latter Part of the Nineteenth Century*, V (1953), 121–6; C. Hamilton Ellis, *British Railway History*, I (1954), 356–7; 'Staffordshire Knot', 'British 4–4–0 Tank Engines', *Railway Magazine*, 94 (1948), 153–6; C. Baker, *op. cit.*, 41–43.

91. K. R. Benest, 'The Coaching Stock of the Metropolitan Railway', *Underground*, Nos. 4, 6, 8, 10 (1962); C. Hamilton

Ellis, *Nineteenth-Century Railway Carriages* (1949), 53–55; C. Baker, *op. cit.*, 47–48; *Herapath's Railway Journal*, 28 March 1868, reporting speech by Fowler.

92. *Herapath's Railway Journal*, 3 October 1863; 5 August 1871; 17 February 1872; MET 1/2, Minutes, 4 October 1865; MET 1/3, Minutes, 28 August 1867; Benjamin Baker, *op. cit.*, 10. On the condensing of water, A. R. Bennett, 'Early Locomotive History', 319–20.

93. Metropolitan Railway (Finsbury Circus Extension) Act 1861, 24 & 25 Vict. cap. ccxxxiii; *Railway Times*, 2 March 1861.

94. B.T.C. Records, MET 1/2 Minutes, 11 February 1863.

95. MET 1/2, Minutes, 25 February, 4 November 1863; 23 March 1864.

96. *Herapath's Railway Journal*, 3 February, 28 July 1866.

97. *Railway Times*, 20 June, 25 July, 15 August 1863; 5 March 1864.

98. *Herapath's Railway Journal*, 9 July 1864. The Hammersmith & City also tried in 1864 to extend their line to Richmond, but Parliament preferred the London & South Western's Bill (*Herapath's Railway Journal*, 3 September 1864).

99. Quoted in D. V. Levien, *A Short History of the Birmingham, Bristol and Thames Junction Railway* (1933) (typescript at B.T.C. Records). This gives an admirable account of both the West London and West London Extension Railways.

100. B.T.C. Records, H & C 1/4, Copy of Inspector's Report, 30 June 1864; *Herapath's Railway Journal*, 14 May, 9 July 1864; Bradshaw, January 1865.

101. *Herapath's Railway Journal*, 4 February 1865.

102. B.T.C. Records, MET 1/3, 22 May 1867; HCJ 1/1, Minutes of Joint Committee, 18 January 1866.

103. MET 1/2, Minutes, 5 April 1865, HCJ 1/1, Minutes, 9 June 1865.

104. 27 & 28 Vict. cap. cciii; Anon., 'The Metropolitan and Saint John's Wood Railway', *Journal of the Railway and Canal Historical Society*, November 1958.

105. 28 & 29 Vict. cap. xxxi.

106. *Railway News*, 11 April 1868, which gives a good account of the railway. Although a single line, it had double-line track

at the two stations at St. John's Wood and Marlborough Road. The tokens on the two trains were men who changed at St. John's Wood (W. J. Passingham, *The Romance of London's Underground* (1932), 28–29). When it was opened to Swiss Cottage, the railway was described as 'continued and nearly finished to within a few yards of the North London Station at Finchley Road' (*Railway News*, 11 April 1868). The Metropolitan agreed to allow the St. John's Wood a rebate of 12½ per cent. on through bookings to and from all stations on the Metropolitan until the St. John's Wood's dividend reached 6 per cent. The St. John's Wood was not to divide more than 6 per cent. until the rebate had been repaid with interest (MET 1/2, Board Minutes, 8 March 1865). In 1866 the Metropolitan offered further help and was considering subscribing £100,000 of the £250,000 preference capital which was then required (MSTJ 1/1, Board Minutes, 31 October, 3 November 1866).

107. *Railway Times*, 27 February 1869; MSTJ 1/1, Board Minutes, 17 February 1869.

108. Bennett, 'Early Locomotive History', 204.

109. Charles H. Grinling, *The History of the Great Northern Railway, 1845–1902* (1903), 202.

110. *Ibid.*, 203.

111. *Railway Times*, 24 August 1867; *Herapath's Railway Journal*, 31 August 1867; G. F. A. Wilmot, *The Railway in Finchley* (Finchley 1962). When the railway was originally opened, it was only a double-line track as far as Highgate but the line was doubled to East End, Finchley at the end of 1867 and to Church End, Finchley in June 1869. The Barnet section was a double line from the outset.

112. Grinling, *op. cit.*, 293.

113. *Herapath's Railway Journal*, 26 August 1871.

114. Grinling, *op. cit.*, 257–8, 301.

115. MET 1/2, 11 January 1865, letter from Kelk.

116. 27 & 28 Vict. cap. cclx; *Herapath's Railway Journal*, 29 July 1865; Benjamin Baker, *op. cit.*, 23.

117. *Herapath's Railway Journal*, 8 August 1868.

118. Metropolitan Meat and Poultry Market Act, 23 & 24 Vict. cap. cxciii; *Herapath's Railway Journal*, 7, 28 November 1868.

119. *Herapath's Railway Journal*, 18 July 1868.

120. *Herapath's Railway Journal*, 3 October 1868.

121. G. H. Lake, *The Railways of Tottenham* (1945), 16–18. From 1868 until 1870 the Great Eastern had operated a suburban service from Fenchurch Street to Highgate Road via Tottenham but this was a roundabout and difficult route. The decision to allow the line to be worked by Midland trains from the other end of the Tottenham & Hampstead Junction Railway was part of the general agreement between the Great Eastern and Midland which allowed Great Eastern trains to run into St. Pancras; and, of course, the Great Eastern's own suburban line to Tottenham was being built.

122. Michael Robbins, *The North London Railway* (4th ed., 1953), 18–19.

123. *Ibid.*, 3; *Herapath's Railway Journal*, 24 February 1866; *Illustrated London News*, 3 February 1866.

124. George P. Neele, *Railway Reminiscences* (1904), 141–4. The two sets of high level platforms were replaced by one island upper platform in 1894 ('Willesden Old Station', *The Home Counties Magazine*, I (1899), 198–200).

125. H. V. Borley, 'North London Railway Expresses from Fenchurch Street', *Journal of the Railway and Canal Historical Society*, May 1956.

126. Robbins, *op. cit.*, 13, 17.

127. Grinling, *op. cit.*, 301–3; Robbins, *op. cit.*, 7.

128. 27 & 28 Vict. cap. cccxiii. The Great Eastern had been unsuccessful in its attempts to get permission to use the terminus which the North London planned at Broad Street (1862) and to promote its own terminus at Finsbury Circus (1863). See evidence of G. P. Bidder to Commons' committee on Great Eastern (Metropolitan Station and Railways) Bill, 20 July 1864 (House of Lords Record Office).

129. Bethnal Green to Stoke Newington 27 May, to Edmonton 22 July, to Walthamstow by the end of September 1872; and to Chingford on 17 November 1873. (*Herapath's Railway Journal*, 1 June, 27 July 1872; *Railway News*, 25 May 1872; *The Times*, 23 July, 25 September 1872; Cecil J. Allen, *The Great Eastern Railway* (1955), 58; P.R.O., MT 6/66/987, authority for opening Walthamstow branch, 21 April 1870.)

130. *Railway Times*, 14 February 1874; 9 October, 6 November 1875.
131. R. K. Kirkland, 'The East London Railway', *Railway Magazine*, 99 (1953), 413-18.
132. L. T. C. Rolt, *Isambard Kingdom Brunel* (1957), 20-37, 143-4, 313; *Knight's Cyclopaedia of London* (1851), 543-52.
133. Kirkland, *loc. cit.*
134. *Herapath's Railway Journal*, 28 March 1868.
135. *Herapath's Railway Journal*, 14 February 1863; 11 February 1865; *A Peep into the Future of the Metropolitan Railway* (1865), 3-7.

CHAPTER FIVE

THE FIRST CLIMAX

(II) RAILWAYS OVER THE RIVER AND THE
EXTENSION OF THE UNDERGROUND

1. Report from the S.C. on Metropolitan Communications, 1854-55 [415] X, iii.
2. The Mid-Kent had been opened on 1 January 1857 (C. F. Dendy Marshall, *A History of the Southern Railway* (1936), 401) and the Caterham—from Caterham Junction (Purley)—on 4 August 1856 (Jeoffry Spence, *The Caterham Railway* (1952), 27). The Mid-Kent was later extended to Addiscombe Road, Croydon (Act 1862; opened 1 April 1864).
3. House of Lords Record Office, Cornelius Wills Eborall to Commons' committee on London Bridge & Charing Cross Railway Bill, 22 March 1859; George Frederick Holroyd to Commons' committee on the London, Chatham & Dover (Metropolitan Extension) Bill, 18 April 1860.
4. *Ibid.* (Eborall).
5. *Ibid.* Report from the S.C. (Lords) on Metropolitan Communication 1863 [500] VIII, appendix A. There were counted during the 24 hours ended 6 p.m. on 17 March 1859, 4,483 carts, wagons etc.; 4,286 cabs; 9,245 omnibuses; and 2,430 other vehicles.

6. House of Lords Record Office, evidence of Henry Doxat, a Clapham resident, to Commons' committee on the London, Chatham & Dover (Metropolitan Extension) Bill, 23 April 1860.

7. Report of R.C. on Metropolitan Termini, 1846 [91] XVII, 4.

8. The best account will be found in Charles E. Lee's two articles 'The West End of London Railway' and 'The First West End Terminus', *Railway Magazine*, *102* (1956), 649–55, *104* (1958), 162–4. For the new Chelsea suspension bridge, see *Illustrated London News*, 10 April 1858.

9. *Railway Times*, 4, 11 November 1854; 17 & 18 Vict. cap. ccv; 18 & 19 Vict. cap. cxcviii.

10. *Illustrated London News*, 6 September 1851.

11. Charles E. Lee, 'Victoria Station, London, in the Nineteenth Century', *Railway Magazine*, *106* (1960), 614–20; *Illustrated London News*, 6 October 1860; *Railway Times*, 23 February 1861. The Grosvenor Hotel was already being built at the time of the station's opening. The station itself was still far from finished when trains started to arrive in October 1860.

12. The best account of the early history of the East Kent Railway is that given by its secretary, George Frederick Holroyd, to the Commons' committee on the London, Chatham & Dover (Metropolitan Extensions) Bill, 18 April 1860 (House of Lords Record Office). See also R. W. Kidner, *The London, Chatham & Dover Railway* (1952).

13. Holroyd's account; *Railway Times*, 26 February 1859.

14. Samuel Smiles, John Charles Rees and Edward Ryde, *Statement in Support of the Proposed London Bridge and Charing Cross Railway* (February 1858).

15. C. E. Lee, 'Victoria Station'.

16. *Railway Times*, 26 February 1859.

17. *D.N.B. sub* Peto; *Knight's Cyclopaedia of London* (1851), 802.

18. F. G. Parsons, *The History of St. Thomas's Hospital* (3 vols. 1932–36), III, 149–50, 152–3, 173, 176.

19. *Illustrated London News*, 11 June 1864. The hotel was not opened until May 1865 (*ibid.*, 20 May 1865).

20. *Herapath's Railway Journal*, 16 January 1864. The station at Charing Cross was still then under construction. The extension was built by an independent company (the London

Bridge & Charing Cross Railway) with financial support from the South Eastern and was subsequently bought by the South Eastern.

21. E. A. Course, *The Evolution of the Railway Network of South-East England* (London Ph.D. thesis 1958), I, 224, This geographical study is a most valuable guide to the complicated railway developments in south London at this time.

22. R. W. Kidner, *op. cit.*, 5, 14; *Illustrated London News*, 10 June 1865. Battersea–Herne Hill was opened on 25 August 1862; Herne Hill–Beckenham Junction on 1 July 1863; City branch to Elephant & Castle, in October 1862. There is a good description of the building of the Holborn Viaduct in *The Architect*, 6 November 1869 (copy at Guildhall Library, Noble Collection, 48/4).

23. *Illustrated London News*, 8 September 1866.

24. *Illustrated London News*, 5 August 1865.

25. *Herapath's Railway Journal*, 18 August 1866; 19 October 1867.

26. 25 & 26 Vict. cap. cxliv.

27. *Herapath's Railway Journal*, 7 March, 19 September 1863. E. T. MacDermot, *History of the Great Western Railway*, I (1927), 444-5.

28. Lee, 'Victoria Station'; *Railway Times*, 4 August 1860; 24 & 25 Vict. cap. lxxxi; *Herapath's Railway Journal*, 16 August 1862.

29. Lee, 'Victoria Station'.

30. *Herapath's Railway Journal*, 24 January 1863; Dendy Marshall, *op. cit.*, 295.

31. *Ibid.*, 150; *Herapath's Railway Journal*, 7 April, 11 August 1866.

32. *Railway News*, 3 October 1868; *Herapath's Railway Journal*, 13 February 1869; Dendy Marshall, *op. cit.*, 306.

33. *Herapath's Railway Journal*, 2 January 1869.

34. *Herapath's Railway Journal*, 4 July 1863; 2 January, 13 February 1869.

35. *Ibid.*, 27 & 28 Vict. cap. clxvi. North London Trains were diverted via this route through Kew Gardens station to Richmond. (Michael Robbins, *The North London Railway*, 4th ed. 1953, 5.)

36. *Herapath's Railway Journal*, 2 January 1869; Metropolitan Railway, *Official Record of Events*.

37. Report from the Joint Select Committee on Railway Schemes (Metropolis), 1864 [87] XI, iii; *The Letters and Memoirs of Sir William Hardman* (ed. S. M. Ellis) (1925), 105, 142.

38. Report from the S.C. (Lords) on Metropolitan Communication, 1863 [500] VIII, iv–v.

39. S.C. on Thames Embankment, 1860 [494] XX; R.C. on Thames Embankment 1861 [2872] XXXI.

40. 25 & 26 Vict. cap. 93; 26 & 27 Vict. cap. 45.

41. John Fowler to S.C. (1860), qq. 1689–92, 1801; Robert Baxter to R.C. (1861), p. 3.

42. John Fowler to S.C. (Lords) 1863, q. 941.

43. Report of S.C. (Lords) 1863, iv.

44. 27 & 28 Vict. cap. cccxii; 28 & 29 Vict. cap. cli; Charles E. Lee, *The Metropolitan District Railway* (1956), 2–4.

45. MET 1/2, Minutes, 16 December 1863.

46. *Herapath's Railway Journal*, 5 March 1864.

47. John Fowler to Joint Select Committee, 1864, qq. 290–2.

48. B.T.C. Records, MDR 1/1, Minutes, 11 July 1864; MET 1/2, Minutes, 29 June 1864.

49. See the *Railway Gazette*, *83* (1945), 593–4, for a contemporary photograph of the building of this section of the line.

50. *Herapath's Railway Journal*, 20 February 1869.

51. *The Times*, 24 August 1866.

52. Reproduced in the *Railway Gazette*, *83* (1945), 617–18.

53. *The Times*, 24 August 1866.

54. *Herapath's Railway Journal*, 6 March 1869.

55. MET 1/3, Minutes, 13 July 1870; Lee, *op. cit.*, 3–4.

56. *Herapath's Railway Journal*, 6 March 1869.

57. Gladstone quoted by Sir John Clapham, *The Bank of England* (2 vols. 1944), II, 265.

58. *Ibid.*, II, 266.

59. *Herapath's Railway Journal*, 17 March, 6 October 1866; Annual Report of the Metropolitan Board of Works, 1867–68, 22–24.

60. Annual Report of the Metropolitan Board of Works, 1869–70, 21.

61. *Ibid.*, 1867–68, 21. There were also a few wharves between Westminster Bridge and Temple Gardens but, as these were

used mainly for the coal trade, the Royal Commission on the Thames Embankment had seen no objection to their removal (1861 [2872] XXXI, iii).

62. *Ibid.*, iv.

63. Annual Report of the Metropolitan Board of Works, 1867–68, appendix 3; Award of Mr. Hawkshaw, 1867–68 [172] LXII.

64. Annual Report of the Metropolitan Board of Works, 1868–69, 21.

65. 32 & 33 Vict. cap. lxii.

66. *Herapath's Railway Journal*, 6 August 1870; Annual Report of the Metropolitan Board of Works, 1870–71, 18.

67. *Herapath's Railway Journal*, 6 August 1870.

68. *Herapath's Railway Journal*, 5 August 1871. For a detailed description of the District Railway and its stations, see A. Edmonds, *History of the Metropolitan District Railway to June 1908* (typescript at L.T.E. Library).

69. *Herapath's Railway Journal*, 6 October 1866.

70. *Herapath's Railway Journal*, 23 March 1872.

71. *Herapath's Railway Journal*, 5 August 1871; *Railway Times*, 5 August 1871; Edmonds, *op. cit.*, 75.

72. Lee, *op. cit.*, 34–36, 39; E. L. Ahrons, *Locomotives and Train Working in the Latter Parts of the Nineteenth Century*, V (1953), 126–8.

73. MDR 1/1, Minutes, 19 July 1866.

74. Neele, *op. cit.*, 142.

75. Wilfred L. Steel, *The History of the London and North Western Railway* (1914), 326–8.

76. Neele, *op. cit.*, 143; *Herapath's Railway Journal*, 23 March 1872; Lee, *Met. Dist.*, 3–4.

77. *Herapath's Railway Journal*, 10 August 1872.

78. C. Hamilton Ellis, *British Railway History*, I (1954), 300.

79. *Herapath's Railway Journal*, 6 February 1875.

80. See, for instance, the District's chairman's insistence that, after amalgamation, preference shareholders should receive 3 per cent at first and then 5 per cent after a few years. The preference shareholders were then lucky if they received 1 or 2 per cent.

81. *Herapath's Railway Journal*, 6 August 1870; *D.N.B.* (2nd Supplement) *sub* Forbes.

82. *D.N.B.* (2nd Supplement) *sub* Watkin.

83. *Railway Times*, 8 February 1868, 27 February, 13 March, 28 August 1869, 26 February, 2 July 1870.
84. *Herapath's Railway Journal*, 17 February 1872.
85. MET 1/4, Minutes, 15 May, 12 June 1872; *Herapath's Railway Journal*, 17 August 1872.
86. MET 1/4, Minutes, 24 July, 7, 9 August 1872.
87. Roger Fulford, *Votes for Women* (1957), 73. Pochin's country seat was at Bodnant in Denbighshire. His only daughter married Charles Benjamin Bright M'Laren who was to be created the first Baron Aberconway in 1911 and became chairman of the Metropolitan Railway.
88. Sir Allan Grant, *Steel and Ships: The History of John Brown's* (1950), 26–28; Sir John Clapham, *An Economic History of Modern Britain*, II, 138.
89. Norman McCord, *The Anti-Corn Law League* (1958), 97–103.
90. *Herapath's Railway Journal*, 19 October 1872. In the later 1870s Nasmyth was said to be the largest shareholder in the Metropolitan Railway with £100,000 of stock (*ibid.*, 27 January 1877; 19 January 1878).
91. *Herapath's Railway Journal*, 19 October 1872; George Dow, *Great Central*, I (1959), 196, 260. There was one other director, George Morphett.
92. *Herapath's Railway Journal*, 12 October 1872.
93. *Ibid.*
94. MET 1/4, Minutes, 23 October 1872.
95. *Herapath's Railway Journal*, 19 October 1872.
96. *Ibid.; Dod's Parliamentary Companion*; William E. A. Axon, *The Annals of Manchester* (1886), 397.
97. *Herapath's Railway Journal*, 24 July 1875.
98. *Herapath's Railway Journal*, 9 December 1876; 20 January 1877.
99. *Herapath's Railway Journal*, 2 March 1867.
100. *Herapath's Railway Journal*, 22 June 1867.
101. *Illustrated London News*, 3 February 1866.
102. Evidence of John Hawkshaw to the S.C. (Lords) on Metropolitan Communication, 1863 [500] VIII, q. 1104.
103. Cecil J. Allen, *The Great Eastern Railway* (1955), 58.
104. Michael G. Mulhall, *The History of Prices Since the Year 1850* (1885), 48.

105. A fuller account of some of these services will be found in J. F. Gairns, 'London Local Train Services of Thirty-Five Years Ago', *Railway Magazine*, *21* (1907), 416–22; *22* (1908), 215–18.

106. *Herapath's Railway Journal*, 12 February, 15 July 1876.

107. *Herapath's Railway Journal*, 1 August 1863.

108. *Herapath's Railway Journal*, 2 March 1867; 29 February, 22 August 1868.

109. Royal Commission on London Traffic, 1906 [Cd. 2752] XLI, vol. III, appendix 6, table 5.

110. Charles Capper, *The Port and Trade of London* (1862), 179.

111. G. A. Sekon, *Locomotion in Victorian London* (1938), 69, 71–72; Frank Burtt, *Steamers of the Thames and Medway* (1949), 61–62; *Herapath's Railway Journal*, 6 May 1882.

112. Based on half-yearly returns. In January 1869 the L.G.O.C. was confronted by only 22 rival omnibuses and in May 1870 by 33 (L.G.O.C. 1/8, Minutes, 19 May 1870).

113. House of Lords Record Office, Myles Fenton to Commons' committee on Metropolitan Railway (Trinity Square, Extension) Bill, 31 May 1864.

114. *Herapath's Railway Journal*, 1 September 1866.

115. *Herapath's Railway Journal*, 12 September 1874.

116. B.T.C. Records., L.G.O.C. 1/6, Minutes, 19 January 1867. McNamara died on the morning of 18 January. Church was given a seat on the board in 1879 (*Herapath's Railway Journal*, 1 March 1879).

117. *Herapath's Railway Journal*, 26 February 1870.

118. Metropolitan Streets Act 1867, 30 & 31 Vict. cap. 134, secs. 4 and 8. The radius was extended to six miles in 1885 (Charles E. Lee, *The Horse Bus as a Vehicle*, British Transport Museum, 1963).

119. The City of London Traffic Regulation Act 1863, 26 & 27 Vict. cap. 206, sec. 3.

120. House of Lords Record Office, Forbes to Commons' committee on Metropolitan and Metropolitan District Railway Bill, 25 March 1879.

121. L.G.O.C. 1/3, Minutes, 17 January 1862; L.G.O.C. 1/4 Minutes, 13 February 1863; MET 1/2, Minutes, 29 August 1866; MET 1/4, Minutes, 12 September, 23 October 1872;

P. A. Keen, 'Metropolitan Railway Road Services', *Journal of Transport History*, I (1954), 216–22. The Camden Town route was worked by the L.G.O.C. from 1874.

122. The figures refer to the City and Metropolitan Police areas.
123. G. F. A. Wilmot, *The Railway in Finchley* (Finchley 1962), 7, 16, 19, 22; *Bradshaw's Railway Guide*.
124. *Herapath's Railway Journal*, 20 January 1866; 6 February 1875.
125. *Herapath's Railway Journal*, 25 August 1866; 31 August 1867; 29 August 1868.
126. Robbins, *op. cit.*, 8.
127. *Ibid.*, 7.
128. *Herapath's Railway Journal*, 25 August, 15 September 1866.
129. *Herapath's Railway Journal*, 25 August 1866; HCJ 1/1, Minutes, 5 October 1865.
130. James Forbes to Joint S.C. on Railway Schemes (Metropolis), 1864 [87] XI, q. 279. Forbes later confessed that he found the fixing of fares a baffling problem. He told the District's shareholders in 1875 that 'he had thirty years experience of passenger fares about London and the longer he lived the less he appeared to know about the exact fare to charge, as the amounts were so sensitive from month to month. . . . He had endeavoured to learn all he could about them and was at times nonplussed' (*Herapath's Railway Journal*, 6 February 1875).
131. *Ibid.*, Fowler, q. 400.
132. MET 1/2, Minutes, 5 April 1865; *Herapath's Railway Journal*, 5 August 1865.
133. *Herapath's Railway Journal*, 6 February 1875.
134. James Forbes to Joint S.C. on Railway Schemes (Metropolis), 1864 [87] XI, q. 283.
135. *Herapath's Railway Journal*, 28 July 1866.
136. Charles E. Lee, *Passenger Class Distinctions* (1946), 50–55. The rest of this paragraph is based upon this source unless otherwise stated.
137. By January 1869, according to *Bradshaw's Railway Guide*, workmen's trains left Victoria at 4 a.m., 5 a.m., and 5.5 a.m. and Ludgate Hill at 5 a.m. and 6 a.m.
138. *Herapath's Railway Journal*, 29 August 1868.

139. See, for instance, extract from the Brighton's report for July–December 1867 printed in Dendy Marshall, *op. cit.*, 302–3.
140. *Herapath's Railway Journal*, 5 April 1862.
141. *Herapath's Railway Journal*, 7 September 1867; Church to S.C. (Lords) on Horses, 1873 [325] XIV, qq. 798 *seq.*
142. S.C. on Metropolis Turnpike Roads, 1856 [333] XIV, Henry Browse, qq. 706–7 and Earl of Lonsdale, q. 1658; *The Times*, 14 December 1859.
143. S.C. on Metropolis Turnpike Roads, 1856 [333] XIV, Henry Browse, q. 82; Augustus Lines, q. 896.
144. *Illustrated London News*, 2 July 1864; Mark Searle, *Turnpikes and Toll Bars* (n.d.), II, 638–9; 690 *seq.*
145. Tenth Report of Commissioners of Inland Revenue, 1866 [3724] XXVI, 13.
146. *Herapath's Railway Journal*, 7 September 1867.
147. Stephen Dowell, *A History of Taxation and Taxes in England*, 2nd ed. (4 vols. 1888), III, 50.

CHAPTER SIX

HORSE TRAMWAYS

1. Bradfield, the omnibus operators' spokesman, later suggested that so much as £1,000 had been paid to road authorities (J. E. Bradfield, *Tramways or Railways on Metropolitan Streets will be Mischievous and Dangerous Obstructions and Nuisances* (1867), 13) but we have come across no evidence to support this assertion.
2. See C. Greene and G. P. Rippon, *Street Railways in London. Special Reports of the Debates in the Representative Council of St. Marylebone* (1860).
3. Charles Klapper, *The Golden Age of Tramways* (1961), 20–23. The Bayswater Road line 'quietly disappeared' in September 1861, that in Victoria Street ceased operation on 6 March 1862 and the Kennington line, apparently, on 21 June 1862 (*ibid.*, 22–23). See also Charles E. Lee, 'The English Street Tramways of George Francis Train', *Journal of Transport*

History, I (1953–54), 98–103, and Antonia Bunch, 'George Francis Train and Street Railways in London', *Tramway Review*, No. 31 (1961), 186–94.

4. William Newton to Jt. S.C. on Tramways (Metropolis), 1872 [252] XII, q. 452.

5. Klapper, *op. cit.*, 16–17.

6. House of Lords Record Office, Henry Gore and Morton Fisher to S.C. on North Metropolitan Tramways Bill, 7 April 1869. For a diagram of the step rail, see George Francis Train, *Observations on Street Railways* (1860), 46, and Charles Burn, *On the Construction of Horse Railways for Branch Lines and for Street Traffic* (1860), 55. Burn notes that in America a rail was often laid down 'which forms a railway for flanged vehicles and a tramway for ordinary vehicles . . .' (p. 37). See also the comments of Philadelphia's mayor, printed in Charles Mackay, *Street Railways for London* (1868), 9.

7. Herbert Bright, *Remarks on Street Tramways Applied to London and Its Suburbs* (1868), 8.

8. *Tramways as a Means of Facilitating Street Traffic of the Metropolis* (1865), 10.

9. *Parliamentary Debates* (3rd ser.), clxii, cols. 639–41, 16 April 1861; clxviii, col. 701, 23 July 1862; *Herapath's Railway Journal*, 28 June 1862; Lee, *op. cit.*, 103.

10. House of Lords Record Office, George Hopkins to S.C. on North Metropolitan Tramways Bill, 8 April 1869.

11. *Standing Orders of the House of Commons*, 1867 [553] LVI, No. 16. The company remained in being until 1883 but built no tramways (P.R.O., B.T. 31/1194/2659C).

12. Much of this paragraph is based on the committee minutes at the House of Lords Record Office.

13. P.R.O., B.T. 31/1581/5198, papers relating to London Tramways Co. Ltd.; B.T.C. Records, NMT 1/1, Minutes of North Metropolitan Tramways, 16 September 1869 (the only set of early tramway minutes which has, apparently, survived); Klapper, *op. cit.*, 86; *Herapath's Railway Journal*, 15 January, 14 May 1870. By 1872 most of the Danes had withdrawn from what was then the London Tramways Co. and the shares were in the hands of a large number of small investors living in various parts of Britain (P.R.O., B.T. 31/1581/5198).

Stephenson of New York continued to supply tramcars for some time. Between 1879 and 1883, for instance, the London Tramways bought 221 from them and the North Metropolitan 75 (R. W. Kidner, *The London Tramcar, 1861-1951* (1951), 4).

14. For the powers originally sought by the companies, see Board of Trade return on Railway and Tramway Bills, 1868-69 [7] LIV.

15. The company was registered on 6 October 1860 with a capital of £50,000 (Return of Joint Stock Companies 1862 [58] LV).

16. L.G.O.C. 1/3, Minutes, 2 November 1860.

17. L.G.O.C. 1/3, Minutes, 16, 30 November, 7, 28 December 1860.

18. L.G.O.C. 1/3, Minutes, 19 April, 3 May 1861. There was also an application from another American by the name of Beers (*ibid.*, 22 March 1861).

19. L.G.O.C. 1/6, Minutes, 14 February 1867; Bradfield, *op. cit.*; id., *Street-Railways or Street-Tramways will be Mischievous and Dangerous Obstructions in the Crowded Streets of London* (1868).

20. L.G.O.C. 1/8, Minutes, 27 May 1869.

21. NMT 1/1, Minutes, 16 September 1869. No details are given.

22. L.G.O.C. 1/8, Minutes, 15 July, 30 December 1869; 26 May 1870; 16 March 1871; 26 June 1873; 11 July 1878.

23. 32 & 33 Vict. cap. xciv. The promoters named in the Act were: William Evans, John Humphreys, Charles Oppenheim and William White the Younger. Possibly William Evans may be identified with the man of the same name who was a director of Train's Bayswater line (Lee, *op. cit.*, 98).

24. *Herapath's Railway Journal*, 7 May 1870.

25. *Herapath's Railway Journal*, 4 February 1871

26. 32 & 33 Vict. cap. xvc. The promoters named in the Act were: William Morris, William Sheldon and John William Thomas.

27. 32 & 33 Vict. cap. ci; *Herapath's Railway Journal*, 14 May 1870. The promoters named in the Act were: James Fraser, John Thomson Pagan and Charles Francis Macdonald. At the board's meeting on 30 September 1869, John Weston of The Cedars, Putney, Benjamin Broughton of Bradford and

J. I. Corrigan of 27 King Street, E.C., became directors, Weston becoming chairman. (NMT 1/1). The company was authorized to build its line out to Stratford Church.

28. *Herapath's Railway Journal*, 14 May 1870; Thomas Kenworthy Rowbotham to Jt. S.C. on Tramways (Metropolis), 1872 [252] XII, qq. 299, 303.

29. London Tramways Co., Ltd. was registered on 14 December 1870 to take over the Pimlico, Peckham & Greenwich company.

30. The promoters were John Humphreys and William White of the Metropolitan Street Tramways and William Morris and William Sheldon of the Pimlico, Peckham & Greenwich. Elias de Pass was named as fifth promoter. In 1872 it was stated that there were 'substantially' only two tramway companies in London but 'more in form' (John Morris to Jt. S.C. on Tramways (Metropolis), q. 439).

31. London Street Tramways Act, 33 & 34 Vict. cap. clxxi; North Metropolitan Tramways Act, cap. clxxii; Metropolitan Street Tramways Act, cap. clxxiii; Pimlico, Peckham & Greenwich Street Tramways (Extensions) Act, cap. clxxiv. The Pimlico, Peckham & Greenwich also had a second Act (cap. clxvii) to empower it to double the line already authorized, to make more passing places, etc.

32. L.G.O.C. 1/8, Minutes, 16 June 1870.

33. *Herapath's Railway Journal*, 17 December 1870.

34. George Hopkins to Jt. S.C. on Tramways (Metropolis), 1872, q. 14. The tramway companies were responsible for the section of road through which their rails passed and eighteen inches on each side of them.

35. 33 & 34 Vict. cap. 78, sec. 43. This applied to tramways promoted by Provisional Order or by private Act and became part of the Acts authorizing the four schemes of 1870. In the case of the three other tramways, however, the time-limit was extended from 21 to 28 years.

36. Thomas Coates to S.C. on Tramways Bill, 1870 [205] X, q. 22.

37. P.R.O., M.T. 6/65, 66 and 67. The relevant boxes contain nothing on tramways.

38. George Macaulay Trevelyan, *The Life of John Bright* (1925), 411.

39. 33 & 34 Vict. cap. 78, sec. 9.

40. 33 & 34 Vict. cap. 78, sec. 3.

41. *Minutes of the Proceedings of the Metropolitan Board of Works* (January–June 1870), 340; Report from S.C. on Tramways Bill, 1870, xi.

42. Letter from Tyler to Secretary (Railway Dept.) Board of Trade, 28 March 1871 [211] LX, 22–25.

43. *Minutes of the Proceedings of the Metropolitan Board of Works* (January–June 1871), 51–58.

44. Report of Jt. S.C. on Tramways (Metropolis), 1872, iv.

45. *Hansard's Parliamentary Debates*, 3rd ser., ccvii, cols. 639–40. For Beresford-Hope, M.P. for Cambridge University, see *D.N.B.* and Klapper, *op cit.*, 21.

46. Report of Jt. S.C. on Tramways (Metropolis), 1872, vi.

47. Klapper, *op. cit.*, 99.

48. 34 & 35 Vict. cap. clxxix; *Herapath's Railway Journal*, 28 February 1874; Klapper, *op. cit.*, 100–1.

49. *Herapath's Railway Journal*, 13 June 1874.

50. George Hopkins to Jt. S.C. on Tramways (Metropolis), 1872, q. 11.

51. Thomas Kenworthy Rowbotham, *ibid.*, q. 242.

52. Robinson Souttar, 'Street Tramways', *Minutes of Proceedings of the Institution of Civil Engineers*, *50* (1876–77), 24–26. The remainder of the paragraph is based upon this source.

CHAPTER SEVEN

LATE VICTORIAN LONDON

(I) THE RAILWAYS

1. J. A. Banks, *Prosperity and Parenthood* (1954), 103–12; G. D. H. Cole, *Studies in Class Structure* (1955), 55–58.

2. P. G. Hall, *The Industries of London Since 1861* (1962), 10.

3. William Ashworth, *The Genesis of Modern British Town Planning* (1954), 11–12. In the 1880s the four suburbs were: Leyton (133·3 per cent), Willesden (121·9 per cent), Tottenham (95·1 per cent), and West Ham (58·9 per cent). In the

1890s the places of most rapid growth included East Ham, Walthamstow, Leyton, West Ham, Willesden, Hornsey, Tottenham and Croydon.

4. The census returns for the London area are conveniently summarized in vol. IV of R.C. on London Traffic, 1906 [Cd. 2987] XLII, 728–38.

5. Banks, *op. cit.*, 130–2.

6. William Ashworth, *An Economic History of England, 1870–1939* (1960), 240.

7. *Ten Years' Growth of the City of London* (Report of the Corporation's Local Government and Taxation Committee, 1891), 14; Report of R.C. on London Traffic, 1905 [Cd. 2597] XXV, 6.

8. Quoted in Richard S. Lambert, *The Universal Provider* (1938), 45.

9. Asa Briggs, *Friends of the People* (1956), 20; Phyllis Heathcote, 'Le Bon Marché de Paris', *The Guardian*, 24 October 1960.

10. Julia Hood and B. S. Yamey, 'The Middle-Class Co-operative Retailing Societies in London, 1864–1900', *Oxford Economic Papers*, October 1957, 309–22.

11. *Ibid.*, 318 n.; *1849–1949: A Story of Achievement* (centenary volume privately printed by Harrods, 1949); Nikolaus Pevsner, *London* (1952), 251; *Economist*, 25 February 1911.

12. Lambert, *op. cit.*, 62, 68, 73, 75, 239.

13. *Ibid.*, 107.

14. *Ibid.*, 186, 220.

15. Letter to the editor of *Herapath's Railway Journal*, 1 May 1869.

16. *Ibid.*, 20 February 1892.

17. James B. Jefferys, *Retail Trading in Britain, 1850–1950* (Cambridge 1954) 21–25.

18. The original shop, a few doors to the north of the Winter Garden Theatre, was closed a few years ago on the opening of a new supermarket on the other side of the road. A commemorative plaque used to hang on the wall. A reference to the beginnings of Sainsbury's is to be found in Mrs. David Greig's autobiography, H. S. Greig, *My Life and Times* (privately printed *c.* 1939), 24. She herself set up in business with her fiancé, David Greig, in Brixton in 1888. (*Ibid.*, 50 *seq.*)

19. *City Men at Home* (1892), 83. See also Alec Waugh, *The Lipton Story* (1951).

20. Henry Leach, 'Football London', in George R. Sims, *Living London* (3 vols., 1901), I, 296; *The History of the Football Association* (1953), 57, 172–3.

21. J. A. R. Pimlott, *The Englishman's Holiday* (1947), 144–9.

22. B.T.C. Records, MET 4/11, G.W.R. handbill Easter 1877; MET 4/8, handbill May 1892.

23. Pimlott, *op. cit.*, 162 *n*.

24. *Ibid.*, 163.

25. B.T.C. Records, MTCC 1/2. Figures cited in prospectus of the Metropolitan Tower Construction Co. Ltd., 21 October 1891.

26. Charles E. Lee, *The Metropolitan District Railway* (1956), 50. The toll was removed at the end of 1908.

27. *Ibid.*; B.T.C. Records, MET 4/9.

28. Brooke Alder, 'London's Pleasure Gardens' in Sims, *op. cit.*, III, 341–7; *Herapath's Railway Journal*, 3 August 1894, 8 February 1895; Claud Langdon, *Earls Court* (1953).

29. B.T.C. Records, MET 4/9, advertisement for Olympia, 1888; *Herapath's Railway Journal*, 14 February 1891.

30. Charles Dudley, 'Some London Shows', in Sims, *op. cit.*, III, 223. The British Museum possesses annual catalogues from 1864.

31. W. Macqueen-Pope, *Shirtfronts and Sables* (1953), ch. 11.

32. B.T.C. Records, WTE 1/1, Minutes of the Tower Company, 9 January 1890, 22 April 1891; B. Wilson and J. R. Day, 'A London Rival to the Eiffel Tower', *Country Life*, 19 May 1955, 1298.

33. B.T.C. Records, MTCC 1/2, Minutes of Metropolitan Tower Construction Company Ltd., 21 September 1892; Report, 7 December 1896.

34. B.T.C. Records, WTE 1/1, Reports of the Tower Company, 3 December 1898.

35. A useful summary is contained in the statement submitted on behalf of the London Music Hall Proprietors' Protection Association to the S.C. on Theatrical Licences and Regulations and printed as appendix 3 to its Report, 1866 [373] XVI. A fuller, and more popular, account is contained in W. Macqueen-Pope, *The Melodies Linger On* (n.d.).

36. S.C. on Theatres and Places of Entertainment, 1892 [240] XVIII, appendix 15.
37. *Ibid.*, Report, iv.
38. Lee, *op. cit.*, 50.
39. R.C. London Traffic, Vol. III, 1906 [Cd. 2752] XLI, Table 5, p. 127. For 1875 the tramway totals have been added from the tramway companies' returns, and the traffic on the main-line companies estimated at half that of the two underground companies and the North London. For 1895, the number for main-line suburban passengers is based upon D. Kinnear Clark's estimate for 1891 (cited in *London Statistics*, XI (1901–2), 95) and for omnibuses other than those operated by the L.G.O.C. and the Road Car Company upon a list of competing omnibuses given in the L.G.O.C. Minutes, 20 November 1891 (B.T.C. Records, L.G.O.C., 1/21).
40. *Herapath's Railway Journal*, 28 July 1877, 5 July 1879, 13 March, 14 August 1880. In 1883 a junction was put in with the Great Western just east of Ealing Broadway and District trains ran from Mansion House to Windsor from 1 March 1883. The service was not financially successful, however, and was withdrawn on 30 September 1885 (*Herapath's Railway Journal*, 4 August 1883; Lee, *op. cit.*, 9).
41. *Ibid.*, 7 February, 13 March 1880; B. Weber, 'A New Index of Residential Construction, 1838–1950', *Scottish Journal of Political Economy*, June 1955.
42. *Herapath's Railway Journal*, 4 August 1883. The original terminus was on the site of the present bus garage at Hounslow Town. For details of the railway in the Hounslow area, see C. E. Lee, *The Metropolitan District Railway* (1956), 48.
43. *Herapath's Railway Journal*, 8 June 1889.
44. S. Fay, *A Royal Road* (1883), 112–13; J. S. Gilks, 'Railway Development at Kingston on Thames', *Railway Magazine*, *104* (1958), 566–7.
45. *Railway Magazine*, *104* (1958), 513–14.
46. *Herapath's Railway Journal*, 12 July 1879; 10 January, 31 July, 7 August 1880.
47. *Ibid.*, 26 March 1881; 14 July 1883.
48. *Ibid.*, 18 July 1885; 21 January 1888; 18 May 1889; 3 September 1892; *Dickens's Dictionary of London* (1879), 175.

49. Board of Trade Committee on Ventilation of Tunnels of the Metropolitan Railway, 1898 [C. 8684] XLV, appendix 18; K. R. Benest, 'The Coaching Stock of the Metropolitan Railway', Pt. 4, *UndergrounD*, October 1962. For the locomotive history of the railway in the 1890s, see A. R. Bennett, 'Early Locomotive History of the Metropolitan Railway', *Railway Magazine*, *23* (1908), 204; *24* (1909), 46; P. Densham, *London Transport: Its Locomotives* (1947). For the Metropolitan's acquisition of lines running north of Aylesbury as far as Verney Junction (on the London & North Western Oxford and Bletchley line) and a small place called Brill, in Oxfordshire, see W. E. Edwards, 'The Aylesbury & Buckingham Railway', *Railway Magazine*, *23* (1908), 185, 303; Charles E. Lee, 'The Duke of Buckingham's Railways, with Special Reference to the Brill Line', *ib.*, *77* (1935), 235; G. Machell, 'Railway Development at Aylesbury', *ib.*, *101* (1955), 739, 863; R. G. M. Baker, 'The Metropolitan & Great Central Joint Line', *ib.*, *106* (1960), 390, 501; E. J. S. Gadsden, *Duke of Buckingham's Railways* (1962).

50. *Herapath's Railway Journal*, 21 July 1887.

51. Harold Pollins, 'The Last Main Line to London', *Journal of Transport History*, IV (1959–60), 85–95; R. M. Robbins, 'Baker Street for the Midlands? Or How the Metropolitan Tried to Become a Main-Line Railway' (1961) (typescript at L.T.E. Library).

52. Board of Trade Committee on Ventilation of the Metropolitan Railway, 1898 [C. 8684] XLV, vi.

53. In 1884 a 5½-mile branch from West Hampstead to Hendon was authorized by Parliament; but this was not proceeded with. It would have run directly parallel with the Midland's existing line, which offered a shorter route to the City. (*Bradshaw's Railway Manual*.)

54. Charles H. Grinling, *The History of the Great Northern Railway* (1903), 349.

55. Evidence of Henry Calcraft to R.C. on Housing, 1884–85 [C. 4402] XXX, q. 10,029.

56. *Ibid.*, q. 9,965; Lord Lymington, qq. 12,048, 12,050.

57. G. F. A. Wilmot, *The Railway in Finchley* (Finchley Public Libraries Committee, 1962), 30.

58. *Ibid.*, 28.
59. Grinling, *op. cit.*, 304, 349, 374, 376, 380–1, 398–400, 406–8, 415.
60. Wilmot, *op. cit.*, 31.
61. For the accidents in Canonbury Tunnel (1881), at Hornsey (1882) and at Finsbury Park (1886), see Grinling, *op. cit.*, 350–2, 353–4, 373.
62. *Ibid.*, 407.
63. Sir Henry Oakley to R.C. on London Traffic, vol. II, 1905 [Cd. 2751] XL, q. 18,587. In 1903 the figure was 33 millions and was stated to have grown by a million per year 'for years'.
64. L.C.C. Report on Workmen's Trains, *London Statistics*, II (1891–92), 320–4.
65. *Herapath's Railway Journal*, 12 January, 3 August 1878; 25 January 1879; Cecil J. Allen, *The Great Eastern Railway* (1955), 210. There was also a short extension from the original station at Chingford to the present one.
66. 27 & 28 Vict. cap. cccxiii, sec. 80.
67. William Birt to R.C. on Housing, 1884–85 [C. 4402] XXX, q. 10,217.
68. *Ibid.*, Henry Calcraft, qq. 9,963, 9,965.
69. *Ibid.*, William Birt, q. 10, 279.
70. Edgar Harper to R.C. on London Traffic, vol. II, 1905 [Cd. 2751] XL, q. 5,057; Scott Damant, 'Notable Stations— 1. Liverpool Street', *Railway Magazine*, 5 (1899), 401–9.
71. William Birt to R.C. on Housing, q. 10,180.
72. *Ibid.*, q. 10,179.
73. John Francis Sykes Gooday to R.C. on London Traffic, qq. 18,566–18,568.
74. *Ibid.*, Edgar Harper, q. 5,057; Gooday, q. 18,566.
75. *Ibid.*, Gooday, q. 19,134.
76. 46 & 47 Vict. cap. 34.
77. William Birt to R.C. on Housing, qq. 10,214, 10,216.
78. Gooday to R.C. on London Traffic, q. 18, 517.
79. *Ibid.*, q. 18,557.
80. *L.C.C.* Report on Workmen's Trains, *London Statistics*, II (1891–92), 325.
81. R.C. on London Traffic, vol. I, 64–65.

82. L.C.C. Report on Workmen's Trains, *London Statistics* (1891–92), 339–42; *Herapath's Railway Journal*, 10 August 1894. The previous figures in this paragraph are from half-yearly reports.

83. L.C.C. Report on Workmen's Trains, *London Statistics* (1891–92), 343–4; George P. Neele, *Railway Reminiscences* (1904), 309–10.

84. C. F. Dendy Marshall, *History of the Southern Railway* (1936); R. W. Kidner, *The London, Chatham & Dover Railway* (1952); id., *The South Eastern Railway* (1953).

85. *Herapath's Railway Journal*, 16 July 1887, 21 July 1888. 17 January 1891.

86. *Herapath's Railway Journal*, 15 May, 31 July 1886.

87. See centenary articles in *Railway Gazette*, 18 June 1948, and *Modern Transport*, 19 June 1948.

88. Charles E. Lee, 'Victoria Station in the Twentieth Century', *Railway Magazine, 106* (1960), 684.

89. L.C.C. Report on Workmen's Trains, *London Statistics* (1891–92), 299–317.

90. *Bradshaw's Railway Manual* (1872), 148, appendix 10–14.

91. Special Report from the S.C. on the Metropolitan Railway (Park Railway and Parliament Street Improvement) Bill, 1884 [194] XV. For a list of railways proposed within central London, see R.C. on London Traffic, vol. III, appendix 57, Statements M and N.

92. B.T.C. Records, MET 1/5, Minutes, 26 March, 23 7 May, 22 October 1873.

93. B.T.C. Records, M. & D.J. 1/19, Minutes of the Metropolitan and District Joint Committee, 30 April 1879.

94. *Minutes of the Proceedings of the Metropolitan Board of Works*, January–June 1874, p. 412, 27 March 1874.

95. 37 & 38 Vict. cap. cxcix.

96. *Minutes of the Proceedings of the Metropolitan Board of Works* January–June, 1874, 624, 22 May 1874; *Herapath's Railway Journal*, 16 May 1874.

97. *Herapath's Railway Journal*, 10 November 1877 for prospectus.

98. House of Lords Record Office, J. S. Forbes to Commons' committee on Metropolitan and Metropolitan District Railway Bill, 25 March 1879.

99. *Herapath's Railway Journal*, 26 January 1878.
100. Christ Church, Oxford, Salisbury Papers, Swarbrick to Salisbury, 1 July 1870.
101. *Herapath's Railway Journal*, 24 July 1875.
102. House of Lords Record Office, Sir Edward Watkin to Lords' committee on Metropolitan and Metropolitan District Railway Bill, 24 June 1879. The Great Eastern insisted upon the through fares being the sum of the individual fares on each line and the Metropolitan wanted them to be less than that.
103. *Ibid.*
104. House of Lords Record Office, Sir Henry Watley Tyler to Commons' committee on Metropolitan and Metropolitan District Railway Bill, 28 March 1879.
105. *Ibid.*
106. House of Lords Record Office, Sir Edward Watkin to Lords' committee on Metropolitan and Metropolitan District Railways Bill, 24 June 1879; B.T.C. Records, ELR 1/1, letter from Watkin to shareholders of East London Railway, 29 June 1878.
107. House of Lords Record Office, Samuel Laing to Commons' committee on Metropolitan and Metropolitan District Railway Bill, 21 March 1879.
108. *Ibid.*, Forbes, 25 March 1879.
109. *Minutes of the Proceedings of the Metropolitan Board of Works*, January–June 1880, 37; 9 January 1880; B.T.C. Records, M. & D.J., 1/21, Minutes, 15 June, 2 August 1881; 1/22, Minutes, 10 May 1882.
110. 44 & 45 Vict. cap. xxv.
111. *Herapath's Railway Journal*, 20 January 1883.
112. B.T.C. Records, M. & D.J. 1/22, Minutes, 6, 27 September 1883.
113. John Wolfe Barry, 'The City Lines and Extensions (Inner Circle Completion) of the Metropolitan and District Railways', *Proceedings of the Institution of Civil Engineers*, LXXXI (1884–85), 41.
114. *Ibid.*, 55. Tomlinson in discussion on Wolfe Barry's paper.
115. *Herapath's Railway Journal*, 20 September 1884.
116. *The Times*, 7 October 1884.
117. B.T.C. Records, M. & D.J. 1/23, Minutes, 20 August, 15 October, 1884; *Herapath's Railway Journal*, 24 January 1885.

2C

118. *Railway Times*, 18 October 1884.

119. *West London Advertiser*, 30 August 1884, quoted in Minutes of Metropolitan and District Joint Board (B.T.C. Records, MDR 1/138, 3 September 1884).

120. House of Lords Record Office, Fenton's evidence given in 1874 quoted by Forbes to Commons' committee on Metropolitan and Metropolitan District Railway Bill, 26 March 1879.

121. B.T.C. Records, M. & D.J. 1/23, Minutes, 5 November 1884; evidence of A. Langford to Board of Trade Committee on Ventilation of Tunnels on the Metropolitan Railway, 1898 [C. 8684] XLV, qq. 2,286–2,289, 2,292, 2,308, 2,317, 2,320; *Herapath's Railway Journal*, 25 July 1885; A. Edmonds, *History of the Metropolitan District Railway to June 1906* (typescript at L.T.E. Library), 71.

122. Charles E. Lee, *The Metropolitan District Railway* (1956), 30.

123. *Ibid.*; evidence of A. Langford to Board of Trade Committee on Ventilation, 1898, q. 2,314.

124. *Ibid.*, Report, vi.

125. B.T.C. Records, M. & D.J. 1/23, Minutes, 6 August 1884; *The Times*, 7 October 1884.

126. *Herapath's Railway Journal*, 5 August 1871; 17 February 1872; 15 September 1888; 26 January, 20 July 1889; evidence of John Bell to Board of Trade committee on Ventilation, 1898, qq. 404, 406, 426.

127. *Ibid.*, Report, vi. A driver in 1897 stated that coke had not been used for 'many years' (*ibid.*, Langford, q. 2,271).

128. *Ibid.*, Langford, q. 2,256.

129. *Ibid.*, John Bell, qq. 429, 430.

130. *The Times*, 7 October 1884.

131. One of a series of articles entitled 'The Romance of Modern London' published in *The English Illustrated Magazine*, August 1893 and reprinted in the *Railway Magazine*, 90 (1944), 133–7, 150.

132. For the District's delays in raising its share of the capital, see B.T.C. Records, M. & D.J. 1/21, Minutes, 24 November 1881, 15, 29 March 1882; 1/22, 10 May, 19 July 1882.

133. From 1887, when the railway and the surplus lands accounts were divided, the latter usually paid 2½ per cent. interest and

the former the same amount or a little more. (See, for instance, *Herapath's Railway Journal*, 21 January 1888.)

134. *Herapath's Railway Journal*, 20 February 1886; 3 March 1888.
135. G. A. Sekon, *Locomotion in Victorian London* (1938), 190; *Herapath's Railway Journal*, 31 July 1886; 19 February 1887. For an illustration of a Metropolitan Railway poster, see Michael Robbins, *The Railway Age* (1962).
136. *Herapath's Railway Journal*, 19 February 1887.
137. *Herapath's Railway Journal*, 2 September 1884.
138. Evidence of R. W. Perks to R.C. on London Traffic, vol. II, 1906 [Cd. 2751] XL, q. 19,586.
139. Wolfe Barry, *op. cit.*, 39.

CHAPTER EIGHT

LATE VICTORIAN LONDON

(II) THE ROADS

1. Percy J. Edwards, *History of London Street Improvements, 1855–1897* (1898), 51, 57–60; G. Laurence Gomme, *London in the Reign of Victoria* (1898), ch. 8.
2. G. A. Sekon, *Locomotion in Victorian London* (1938), 49–50.
3. Edwards, *op. cit.*, 63.
4. Mark Searle, *Turnpikes and Toll Bars* (n.d.), I, 55. Blackfriars Bridge was widened between 1907 and 1909 (Harold P. Clunn, *The Face of London* (n.d.), 54). Lambeth Suspension Bridge was demolished in 1929; in its later years it was used by pedestrians only.
5. Searle, *op. cit.*, I, 61; Sekon, *op. cit.*, 23. The first Wandsworth Bridge was demolished in 1934 and replaced by the present one (Clunn, *op. cit.*, 425).
6. Clunn, *op. cit.*, 421, 426–7; Sekon, *op. cit.*, 23–24. Putney Bridge was extensively widened in 1934.
7. Clunn, *op. cit.*, 46. Further down the river the Woolwich Free Ferry had been started by the L.C.C. in 1889. The Blackwall

Tunnel was opened in 1897 and the Greenwich Tunnel (for pedestrians only) in 1902 (R.C. London Traffic, vol. III, 271). The Rotherhithe Tunnel followed in 1908.

8. Searle, *op. cit.*, II, 638. The present Southwark Bridge dates from 1921.

9. *Ibid.*, II, 657–9, 660–1. Waterloo Bridge was pulled down in 1934 and the present bridge took its place during the Second World War.

10. R.C. London Traffic, vol. I, 82; vol. II, Alderman Sir Edmund Knight, q. 14,450, John Lulham Pound, qq. 17,652, 17,673.

11. Pound, q. 17,698.

12. These figures are given in the L.G.O.C.'s half-yearly reports.

13. Report of the Home Office Committee of Enquiry on the Cab Service of the Metropolis, 1895 [C. 7607] XXXV, 1, 300; Sekon, *op. cit.*, 81.

14. For the success of the taximeter in Germany and hostility to it in London, see the evidence of Bruhn, Westendorp, Junge and Max to Enquiry on Metropolitan Cab Service, qq. 667 *seq.*, and Bruce, q. 755. The fare of 6d. per mile had been introduced in 1853 and the minimum fare of 1s. in 1867.

15. Sekon, *op. cit.*, 82–86.

16. *Herapath's Railway Journal*, 23 August 1879. The details in this and the previous paragraph are based upon the L.G.O.C.'s half-yearly reports. For Pound, see *The Times*'s obituary, 20 September 1915 and the appropriate volumes of *The Directory of Directors*.

17. P.R.O., B.T. 31/2680/14350, London Mercantile Association Limited to London and District Omnibus Company Limited, 20 August 1880. The remainder of the paragraph is also based upon this source.

18. *The Times*, 14 March 1881.

19. British Patent number 3,381 of 1880. According to the *Directory of Directors* for 1880, Capt. Molesworth was chairman of the Royal Aquarium and Summer and Winter Garden Society Ltd.—presumably the company which ran the recently-opened Westminster Aquarium which stood on the site now occupied by Central Hall, Westminster.

20. *The Times* (14 March 1881) reported that 'the traveller on the roof has a most pleasant seat in a chair fronting the horses'. The illustrations in Henry Charles Moore, *Omnibuses and Cabs* (1902), 103 and Sekon, *op. cit.*, 45, however, show knifeboard seats. For the upholstered interior of road cars, see 'The Bus', *Cornhill Magazine* (March 1890), 303.

21. Moore, *op. cit.*, 102; *Railway Times*, 5 May 1883.

22. P.R.O., B.T. 31/2680/14350.

23. *Railway Times*, 17 December 1881; 25 February 1882; B.T.C. Records, L.G.O.C. 1/15, Minutes, 25 August, 1 September 1881. For the Union Jack, see Moore, *op. cit.*, 105–8.

24. *Railway Times*, 17 December 1881.

25. *Ibid.*; *Dod's Parliamentary Companion* (eds. 1880 to 1885); Post Office Directory, 1879.

26. *Railway Times*, 16 December 1882.

27. P.R.O., B.T. 31/2680/14350; *Herapath's Railway Journal*, 25 August 1883.

28. Post Office Directory, 1879; *The Times*, 8 March 1938; *Leading Men of London* (1895), 207.

29. *Railway Times*, 7 March 1885.

30. *Railway Times*, 27 August 1887; 17 March 1888; *City Men at Home* (*c.* 1892), 103–9.

31. *Railway Times*, 1 March 1890.

32. B.T.C. Records, L.G.O.C. 1/15, Minutes, 24 February 1881.

33. B.T.C. Records, L.G.O.C. 1/15, Minutes, 1, 8 September 1881.

34. B.T.C. Records, L.G.O.C. 1/15, Minutes, 5 January 1882; L.G.O.C. 1/16, Minutes, 16 November 1882; 18 January 1883; *Herapath's Railway Journal*, 20 February 1886.

35. B.T.C. Records, L.G.O.C. 1/16, Minutes, 23 November 1882; *Herapath's Railway Journal*, 24 February 1883.

36. B.T.C. Records, L.G.O.C. 1/21, Minutes, 24 July 1891.

37. Figure for 1891 in B.T.C. Records, L.G.O.C. 1/21, Minutes, 20 November 1891; other figures from half-yearly reports.

38. L.G.O.C. Minutes, 20 November 1891.

39. P. A. Keen, 'Metropolitan Railway Road Services', *Journal of Transport History*, I (1953–54), 231; B.T.C. Records MET 4/12.

40. Keen, *op. cit.*, 233, 239; *Herapath's Railway Journal*, 20 July 1889. In 1892 the Charing Cross–Baker Street service was cut back to Piccadilly Circus.

41. B.T.C. Records, L.G.O.C. 1/21, Minutes, 5 March 1892; Keen, *op. cit.*, 233; Moore, *op. cit.*, 109 (photograph). The earlier Metropolitan Railway omnibuses had been of the large, three-horse type and divided into compartments, but by 1892 the two underground railway companies together were operating only eight such vehicles and fifteen pair-horse ones (L.G.O.C. 1/21, Minutes, 20 November 1891).

42. According to John Tilling, *Kings of the Highway* (1957), 69, Tillings had 220 horse omnibuses in continuous operation in 1901. In addition to the 18 vehicles running against the L.G.O.C., Tillings also ran others in association with it. In 1887, for instance, Benjamin Thomas Baxter, Tilling's manager, mentioned eight such omnibuses on the roads between Brixton or Clapham and the City (House of Lords Record Office, evidence to Commons' committee on City of London and Southwark Subway Bill, 10 March 1887).

43. The London Omnibus Carriage Company, formed in 1886, occupied a yard at Baker Street and had a depot at York Road. It ran services between Victoria and King's Cross, Victoria and Baker Street, and Baker Street and Charing Cross. (R.C. Labour, vol. II, Thomas Sutherst, q. 15,756; vol. III, Henry A. Jones, qq. 18,427, 18,429.)

44. Solomon Andrews, born at Trowbridge in 1835, started business as a street vendor of home-made confectionery in Cardiff in the 1850s. He invested his savings in a cab business and was also involved in carriage building. In the 1870s he started to run omnibuses in Cardiff, in 1882 patenting a new kind of omnibus (British Patent 2511 of 1882) and in 1887 patenting inside seats which faced forwards (British Patent 16,800 of 1887). He was soon operating omnibuses in various provincial towns as well as in London and tramways in North Wales. He owned a number of retail businesses and transformed Pwllheli into a seaside resort (*Railway Times*, 2 July, 3 December 1887; *The Times*, 9 November 1888; *Reynolds Newspaper*, 15 November 1908; Charles Klapper, *The Golden Age of Tramways* (1961), 166).

45. The Railways and Metropolitan Omnibus Company operated a service between Waterloo station and the City via Stamford Street and Blackfriars Bridge (Report of Home Office Committee of Enquiry on the Cab Service of the Metropolis, 1895 [C. 7607] XXXV, Scotter, q. 6,797).

46. B.T.C. Records, L.G.O.C. 1/16, Minutes, 18 January 1883; L.G.O.C. 1/21, Minutes, 20 November 1891.

47. In making these comparisons, it should be borne in mind that the Road Car Company employed a ticket check while the L.G.O.C. did not do so.

48. *Herapath's Railway Journal*, 22 February 1890.

49. *Herapath's Railway Journal*, 21 February 1891.

50. For Joynson-Hicks, who was later to play a notable part in the company's history, see H. A. Taylor, *Jix, Viscount Brentford* (1933).

51. *Herapath's Railway Journal*, 21 February 1880.

52. *Herapath's Railway Journal*, 1 March 1879.

53. B.T.C. Records, L.G.O.C. 1/15, Minutes, 8 December 1881; L.G.O.C. 1/16, Minutes, 9 March, 18 May 1882. The system had been invented by the celebrated J. N. Maskelyne.

54. *Herapath's Railway Journal*, 3 March 1877.

55. P.R.O., B.T. 31/2680/14350.

56. The Road Car's Annual Report for the year ended 31 December 1884 includes payment for bell punches during the previous year. For the subsequent use of numbered tickets only, see *The Cornhill Magazine*, March 1890, 305. For the use of tickets on the first stretch of permanent tramway from Brixton to Kennington, *Herapath's Railway Journal*, 7 May 1870. For the Bell Punch Company, formed in 1878 to acquire the patent rights of an American hand registering ticket punch which had already been adopted by the North Metropolitan and London Tramways, *Modern Transport*, 26 June 1948.

57. B.T.C. Records, L.G.O.C. 1/21, Minutes, 8, 22 January, 5 February 1892.

58. These advertising rights on tickets were raised when the L.G.O.C. first opened negotiations with the various ticket concerns (L.G.O.C. 1/21, Minutes, 27 November, 4, 18 December 1890; 19 March 1891). The L.G.O.C. took over

all its own advertising in the following year (*ibid.*, 11 March 1892).

59. *Herapath's Railway Journal*, 3 September 1892; *Directory of Directors*, 1891.

60. *Herapath's Railway Journal*, 25 March 1893.

61. B.T.C. Records, L.G.O.C. 1/23, Minutes, 31 August 1893.

62. B.T.C. Records, L.G.O.C. 1/23, Minutes, 9, 16 November 1893; *Herapath's Railway Journal*, 3 March 1894.

63. *Herapath's Railway Journal*, 25 August 1894.

64. B.T.C. Records, L.G.O.C. 1/22, Minutes, 11, 25 November 1892; L.G.O.C. 1/23, Minutes, 19, 26 October, 2, 9, 16, 23 November 1893; 21 June 1894.

65. *Herapath's Railway Journal*, 3 March 1894. According to the *Oxford English Dictionary*, the word pirate was first used in this context in the *Daily News*, 12 December 1889.

66. R.C. London Traffic, vol. III, appendix 40, table H.

67. In 1891 the L.G.O.C. and Road Car Company operated 1,135 vehicles and their associates and competitors 553 (L.G.O.C. Minutes, 20 November 1891).

68. *Herapath's Railway Journal*, 3 March, 25 August 1888; evidence of Forbes to Commons' committee on City of London and Southwark Subway Bill, 20 March 1890 (House of Lords Record Office).

69. *Herapath's Railway Journal*, 14 February 1891.

70. R.C. London Traffic, vol. III, appendix 40, table H.

71. *Ibid.*

72. Report of Home Office Committee of Enquiry on the Cab Service of the Metropolis, 1895 [C. 7607] XXXV, 300.

73. *Ibid.*, evidence of Frederick White, q. 4,633–4,634.

74. 'The Bus', *Cornhill Magazine*, March 1890, 301; George P. Neele, *Railway Reminiscences* (1904), 233.

75. Cttee. Metropolitan Cab Service, Lambert, q. 7,734; appendix IV.

76. *Ibid.*, Oakley, q. 9,074, 9,076; appendix IV.

77. 'The Bus', *Cornhill Magazine*, March 1890, 303–4.

78. Cttee. Metropolitan Cab Service, quoted by Bruce, q. 634.

79. R.C. London Traffic, vol. III, appendix 77, table B.

80. R.C. London Traffic, vol. III, appendix 40, table H. For the omnibus total, see above, p. 260.

81. Much of this and subsequent paragraphs is based upon Charles Klapper, *The Golden Age of Tramways* (1961), chapter 9, and the map of London's tramways in 1896 (R.C. London Traffic, vol. V).

82. *Herapath's Railway Journal*, 30 January 1886; 30 July 1887; 28 January 1888.

83. Evidence of Robert James Wylie, traffic manager of the London Tramways Company to Commons' committees on City of London and Southwark Subway Bills, 10 March 1887, 19 March 1890 (House of Lords Record Office).

84. H. J. Dyos, *Victorian Suburb* (Leicester 1961), 78–79.

85. *Railway and Tramway Express*, 22 November 1884; 14 February 1885; *Railway Times*, 9 February 1884. A long, illustrated account of the Leytonstone works is to be found in the *Tramway and Railway World*, February 1892.

86. For a detailed survey of developments in Croydon, see 'SouthmeT', *The Tramways of Croydon* (1960), chap. 1.

87. Dyos, *op. cit.*, 74–75.

88. Information from Mr. Charles E. Lee.

89. 33 & 34 Vict. cap. clxxii, clxxiii, clxxiv.

90. 33 & 34 Vict. cap. clxxi, sec. 44.

91. Sir Gwilym Gibbon and Reginald W. Bell, *History of the London County Council, 1889–1939* (1939), 79.

92. *Ibid.*, 615–16.

93. *The Economist*, 1 April 1893, 4 August 1894.

94. J. W. Benn's memorandum to the R.C. London Traffic (vol. III, 240). The rest of this paragraph is based upon this source. The tramway companies' offer was preferred to that of the County of London Tramways Syndicate which proposed to acquire all the undertakings on behalf of the L.C.C. and then work them (*Minutes of the Proceedings of the L.C.C.* (1896), 30 April 1896, pp. 554–9).

95. R.C. London Traffic, vol. III, table 5, p. 127; estimate for omnibuses other than those operated by L.G.O.C. based upon list in L.G.O.C. Minutes, 20 November 1891 (L.G.O.C. 1/21), and estimate for main-line suburban traffic on D. Kinnear Clark cited in *London Statistics*, XI (1901–02), 95.

96. *Herapath's Railway Journal*, 19 January 1884.

97. *Railway Times*, 4, 25 April 1891.

CHAPTER NINE

LABOUR

1. Return of hackney coaches, chariots and cabriolets, 1830 [687] XXX; above, p. 4.
2. Figures quoted in Charles Booth, *Life and Labour of the People in London*, VII (1896), 287.
3. Report from the S.C. on the Hackney Coach Office, 1830 [515] X, evidence of Francis Rose (p. 25) and Richard Box (p. 59).
4. R.C. Labour, vol. II, 1892 [C.6795] XXXVI, evidence of Edwin Dyke, qq. 16,608, 16,609.
5. R.C. Labour, vol. III, 1893–94 [C. 6894] XXXIII, evidence of John Beasley, qq. 17,406, 17,410; Report of Home Office committee of Enquiry on the Cab Service of the Metropolis, 1895 [C. 7607] XXXV, evidence of Frederick White, qq. 4,624–4,625.
6. Booth, *op. cit.*, VII, 302.
7. *The Cab Trade Gazette*, 1 February, 1 March 1884; R.C. Labour, vol. II, evidence of Edwin Dyke, q. 16,599.
8. Booth, *op. cit.*, VII, 302–3.
9. R.C. Labour, vol. III, evidence of Robert Jenkins, q. 17,817; William Robert Levick, qq. 17,884, 17,860, 17,861.
10. Booth, *op. cit.*, VII, 291, 303.
11. R.C. Labour, vol. II, evidence of Edwin Dyke, qq. 16,599, 16,600.
12. R.C. Labour, vol. III, evidence of John Beasley, q. 17,364, 17,366.
13. Home Office committee on Metropolitan Cab Service, evidence of Frederick White, qq. 4,624–4,625; Edmund Yates, *The Business of Pleasure* (2 vols. 1865), I, 61.
14. Yates, *op. cit.*, I, 54.
15. Stanley Harris, *The Coaching Age* (1885), 120–1; E. W. Bovill, *The England of Nimrod and Surtees* (1959), 143–4.
16. Henry Mayhew, *London Labour and the London Poor* (4 vols. 1861), III, 344; John Pound to shareholders' meeting reported in *Herapath's Railway Journal*, 22 August 1891.
17. B.T.C. Records, L.G.O.C. 1/1, Minutes, 13 October 1856.

18. L.G.O.C. 1/2, Minutes, 13 May 1859; L.G.O.C. 1/46, Report, 25 April 1857; *Herapath's Railway Journal*, 3 March 1877. For an attempted strike of horsekeepers in the Paddington and St. John's Wood districts, following an effort to stop drivers' tips to them, see L.G.O.C. 1/1, Minutes, 13 October 1856, 11 May 1857.

19. 'Vehicular Statistics of London—1. Omnibuses', *Chambers's Edinburgh Journal*, 14 June 1845; *Herapath's Railway Journal*, 3 March 1877.

20. L.G.O.C. 1/1, Minutes, 29 March 1858; 20 February 1860.

21. Edmund Yates, however (*op. cit.*, I, 37), recalled that the drivers and conductors of Wilson's Favourites at one time wore 'green liveries, always renewed . . . on the occasion of the Queen's birthday'; but this was the exception that was worth recording.

22. Booth, *op. cit.*, VII, 311.

23. *Ibid.*, VII, 314.

24. L.G.O.C. 1/1, Minutes, 23 November 1857; J. Ewing Ritchie, *Here and There in London* (1859), 191; 'Silverpen' (Eliza Meteyard), 'The History and Present Condition of the Metropolitan Omnibus Drivers and Conductors', *The Working Man's Friend and Family Instructor*, 3 August 1850; R.C. Labour, vol. III, evidence of R. T. Kingham, q. 18,105.

25. R.C. Labour, vol. III, evidence of R. T. Kingham, q. 18,133; Booth, *op. cit.*, VII, 315–16.

26. Mayhew, *op. cit.*, III, 345.

27. See above, pp. 34–5.

28. *Herapath's Railway Journal*, 3 March 1877.

29. Mayhew, *op. cit.*, III, 345.

30. Henry Charles Moore, *Omnibuses and Cabs* (1902), 148.

31. *Ibid.*, 149–50.

32. *Herapath's Railway Journal*, 23 August 1879.

33. Moore, *op. cit.*, 150–3.

34. *Ibid.*, 153–7.

35. George Lovett, *Modern Slavery. Life on the London Tramway Cars* (1877). The rest of this paragraph is based upon this source.

36. B.T.C. Records, NMT 1/3, Minutes, 28 June 1876.

37. *Herapath's Railway Journal*, 6 August 1887.

38. For Sutherst, see *City Men at Home* (*c.* 1892), 136 *seq.*

39. R.C. Labour, vol. II, evidence of John Atkinson, q. 16,457; vol. III, evidence of Robert Lawrence Adamson, qq. 18,244, 18,245.

40. R.C. Labour, vol. II, evidence of John Atkinson, q. 16,457.

41. *Railway Times*, 20 June 1891.

42. R.C. Labour, vol. II, quoted by John Atkinson, q. 16,504.

43. Booth, *op. cit.*, VII, 317–18.

44. R.C. Labour, vol. III, evidence of Robert Lawrence Adamson, q. 18,260.

45. Balls Brothers appear to have been the last to introduce tickets, in August 1901. (Information from Mr. Charles E. Lee.)

46. B.T.C. Records, L.G.O.C. 1/21, Minutes, 27 November 1890.

47. *Ibid.*, 4, 18 December 1890.

48. *Ibid.*, 2 March 1891.

49. *Ibid.*, 19, 26 March 1891. The Hansard Publishing Union was unable to supply the tickets quickly enough, however, and, at the beginning of 1892, the contract was transferred to Bell Punch at 5d. per 1,000 (Minutes, 22 January 1892).

50. *Ibid.*, 8, 26 May 1891.

51. *Ibid.*, 8 June 1891.

52. *Ibid.*, 12 June 1891.

53. *Ibid.*, 22 June 1891.

54. R.C. Labour, vol. II, evidence of Thomas Sutherst, qq. 15,859, 15,861; vol. III, evidence of Richard Thomas Kingham, q. 18,009; note by Harry Peirce to Frederick Hammill, q. 22,690.

55. B.T.C. Records, L.G.O.C. 1/21, Minutes, 21 August 1891.

56. *Herapath's Railway Journal*, 3 September 1892.

57. Booth, *op. cit.*, VII, 314.

58. Board of Trade committee on Ventilation of Tunnels on the Metropolitan Railway, 1898 [C. 8684] XLV, evidence of A. Langford, qq. 2,249, 2,278; and of E. Adams, qq. 2,326–2,328.

59. *Herapath's Railway Journal*, 19 January 1878; Scott Damant, 'Liverpool Street', *Railway Magazine*, 5 (1899), 401–9.

60. B.T.C. Records, MET 1/4, Minutes, 29 November 1871; R.C. Labour, 1892 [C.6795] XXXVI, replies from employers, no. 408.

61. Board of Trade Committee on Ventilation of Tunnels on the Metropolitan Railway, evidence of A. Langford, q. 2,301 and Thomas Stonebanks, qq. 2,427, 2,428.
62. Booth, *op. cit.*, VII, 337. Signalmen were working a 12-hour day on Sundays in 1891, however, with one Sunday off in three. Guards, inspectors, porters, ticket collectors and ticket examiners worked about 14 or 15 hours on Sundays (Edward Harford to S.C. on Railway Servants (Hours of Labour)), 1890–91 [342] qq. 2,511–2,518).
63. Booth, *op. cit.*, VII, 338.
64. R.C. Labour, 1892 [C. 6795] XXXVI, replies from employers, no. 408. For a useful summary of railwaymen's wages in the middle years of the nineteenth century, see P. W. Kingsford, 'Railway Labour, 1830–1870' (London Ph.D. 1951), 148 *seq.*
65. R.C. Housing, 1884–85 [C. 4402] XXX, evidence of Sir Edward Watkin, qq. 10,423, 10,424.
66. Booth, *op. cit.*, VII, 340.
67. *Ibid.*, VII, 349.
68. Board of Trade committee on Ventilation of Tunnels on the Metropolitan Railway, evidence of John Bell, q. 432.
69. *Ibid.*, q. 429.
70. B.T.C. Records, MET 1/2, Minutes, 23 September 1863; MET 1/3, Minutes, 17 November 1869.

CHAPTER TEN

THE SEARCH FOR
A NEW FORM OF TRACTION

1. Charles E. Lee, 'Rise and Decline of the Steam-Driven Omnibus', *Transactions of the Newcomen Society*, XXVII (1949–50; 1950–51), 181–2; R. E. Crompton, *Reminiscences* (1928), 46 *seq.*; William Woodruff, *The Rise of the British Rubber Industry* (Liverpool 1958), 73; R. W. Kidner, *The First Hundred Road Motors* (1950), 49 and plate XIX. For Thomson, see the *Dictionary of National Biography.*

2. Charles Klapper, *The Golden Age of Tramways* (1961), 40–41.

3. For Merryweather, see *Leading Men of London* (1895), 326.

4. Robinson Souttar, 'Street Tramways', *Minutes of the Proceedings of the Institution of Civil Engineers, 50* (1876–77), 15. This paper includes a critical and, on the whole, pessimistic appraisal of steam tramways at that time. For Merryweather's export trade, see also Klapper, *op. cit.*, 43.

5. *Ibid.*; *Railway and Tramway Express*, 25 October 1884.

6. Carruthers-Wain, assistant secretary of the London, Brighton & South Coast Railway until 1885, was, at one time or another, on the board of the Manchester, Bury, Rochdale & Oldham Steam Tramways; the North Staffordshire; South Staffordshire; Birmingham Central; Croydon; Stockton & Darlington; North London; and Southwark & Deptford. He was also chairman of Swan & Edgar.

7. Klapper, *op. cit.*, 102. For photographs of the Merryweather and Dick, Kerr locomotives, see H. A. Whitcombe, *History of the Steam Tram* (ed. with introduction by Charles E. Lee) (1954), 14, 32.

8. *Ibid.*, 52. For illustrations of the Connelly tractor and Luhrig car, see 'SouthmeT', *The Tramways of Croydon* (1960) 22, 26.

9. Klapper, *op. cit.*, 47–48.

10. *Ibid.*, 51.

11. *The Engineer*, 12 January 1883. For Hallidie see the *Dictionary of American Biography*.

12. *Railway Times*, 29 November 1884. For a detailed technical description of the Highgate Hill Cable Tramway, see J. Bucknall Smith, *A Treatise upon Cable or Rope Traction* (1887), 94 *seq.*

13. Klapper, *op. cit.*, 48; *Railway Times*, 29 November, 6 December 1884; 10, 24 January 1885.

14. *Railway Times*, 29 May 1886; B.T.C. Records, CSL 1/1, Minutes of the City of London and Southwark Subway Co., 30 January 1888.

15. *Railway Times*, 24 August 1889; *Tramways Institute Quarterly Journal*, March 1893. The company was called the Highgate and Hampstead Cable Tramways Ltd.

16. *Railway World*, April 1897.

17. D. L. G. Hunter, 'The Edinburgh Cable Tramways', *Journal of Transport History*, I (1954), 170–84.

18. Klapper, *op. cit.*, 49–50; *Railway World*, January 1893; August 1895. The contractors were Dick, Kerr and Co. and the consulting engineer W. N. Colam who had previously been connected with the Hallidie concern and with Edinburgh Tramways.

19. Percy Dunsheath, *A History of Electrical Engineering* (1962), chap. 7; Georg Siemens, *History of the House of Siemens* (Munich 1957), I, 78–79.

20. J. D. Scott, *Siemens Brothers, 1858–1958* (1958), 45; Harold C. Passer, *The Electrical Manufacturers, 1875–1900* (Cambridge, Mass. 1953), 15–20. For the Gramme and Lontin dynamos, see S.C. on Lighting by Electricity, 1878–79 [224] XI, 226–30.

21. B.T.C. Records, MET 1/9, Minutes, 20 November 1878; *Herapath's Railway Journal*, 14 June, 11 October 1879; 6 November 1880.

22. C. Mackechnie Jarvis, 'The Distribution and Utilization of Electricity', *A History of Technology* (ed. Charles Singer and others) (Oxford 1958), V, 213–28; evidence of Edward H. Johnson to S.C. on Electric Lighting Bill, 1882 [227] X, qq. 3,010–3,011; R. H. Parsons, *Early History of the Power Station Industry* (Cambridge 1940), 10–12. For Swan, see Kenneth R. Swan, *Sir Joseph Swan* (1946).

23. Siemens, *op. cit.*, I, 85, 86, 89. According to Alexander Siemens, in 1883 the Lichterfelde line, 'the real experimental line—the real pioneer', only had two carriages running upon it and only ran twelve times per day (House of Lords Record Office, evidence to S.C. on London Central Electric Railway Bill, 29 April 1884).

24. *Electrical World*, 9 August 1884, cited in Passer, *op. cit.*, 221.

25. George W. Hilton and John F. Due, *The Electric Interurban Railways in America* (Stanford 1960), 6.

26. Passer, *op. cit.*, 216–18; 237 *seq.*; Klapper, *op. cit.*, 62–64.

27. Klapper, *op. cit.*, 69–72.

28. *Herapath's Railway Journal*, 27 September 1890.

29. *Herapath's Railway Journal*, 21 January, 21, 28 July 1888; 26 January, 20 July 1889; 19 July 1890.

30. This excludes the short pleasure line built from the Wood Green gate of Alexandra Park up to Alexandra Palace and opened on 13 May 1898. It was removed in the autumn of the following year. For this fiasco, see J. H. Price, 'London's First Electric Tramway', *Journal of Transport History*, III (1958), 205–11.

31. House of Lords Record Office, Peter William Barlow to Lords' committee on Tower Subway Bill, 24 March 1868.

32. Peter W. Barlow, *On the Relief of London Street Traffic* (1867), 6–7; British Patent 2207 of 1864, amended by British Patent 813 of 1868.

33. R. K. Kirkland, 'The Waterloo & Whitehall Railway', *Railway Magazine, 101* (1955), 636–8, 648. See also letter from Mr. J. Foster Petree, *ibid.*, 872.

34. 31 & 32 Vict. cap. viii.

35. P.R.O., MT 6/67/1869, Report of (Sir) Henry W. Tyler, 20 April 1870.

36. Charles E. Lee, 'The First Tube Railway', *The Railway Magazine, 89* (1943), 332–3.

37. *Ibid.*, 333, 335; *Illustrated London News*, 9 April 1870.

38. Barlow, *op. cit.*, 8.

39. 33 & 34 Vict. cap. cxxiv. Southwark and City Subway Act, 1870.

40. Lee, *op. cit.*, 335.

41. See above, p. 225

42. 45 & 46 Vict. cap. cclv. No committee minutes can be traced at the House of Lords Record Office.

43. House of Lords Record Office, Henry Law to Commons' committee on London Central Electric Railway Bill, 29 April 1884; T. S. Lascelles, *The City and South London Railway* (1955), 3.

44. Scott, *op. cit.*, 64–65.

45. House of Lords Record Office, Henry Law and Alexander Siemens to Commons' committee on London Central Electric Railway Bill, 29 April 1884.

46. *Ibid.*, William Robins Selway, 30 April 1884.

47. 45 & 46 Vict. cap. clxvii.

48. House of Lords Record Office, James Henry Greathead to Commons' committee on London (City) and Southwark Subway Bill, 9 May 1884.

49. *Ibid.*, James Clifton Robinson, 13, 14 May; Alfred Arnold, 14 May. According to his evidence, Arnold, a barrister, lived at Clare Hall near Halifax and was a director of the Halifax Union Bank. He spent about two months of the year in London.

50. B.T.C. Records, CSL 1/1, Minutes, 30 December 1885; 5 February 1886.

51. *Leading Men of London* (1895), 96.

52. *Herapath's Railway Journal*, 13 February 1886.

53. Minutes, 18 December 1885.

54. Minutes, 26 February 1886.

55. House of Lords Record Office, Charles Grey Mott to Commons' committee on City of London and Southwark Subway Bill, 9 March 1887.

56. *Herapath's Railway Journal*, 14 June 1888; Mott to Commons' committee, 9 March 1887.

57. J. H. Greathead, 'The City & South London Railway; With Some Remarks Upon Subsequent Tunnelling by Shield and Compressed Air', *Proceedings of the Institution of Civil Engineers*, *123* (1896), 39–123.

58. Parsons, *op. cit.*, 51. For the termination of the agreement with Spagnoletti, see CSL 1/3, Minutes, 2, 16 January 1894.

59. Minutes, 15 January 1889; C. G. Mott to Commons' committee on City and South London Railway Bill, 16 March 1891.

60. *Ibid.*; Evelyn Hopkinson, *The Story of a Mid-Victorian Girl* (privately printed 1928), 57.

61. For John Hopkinson senior, a partner in the firm of Wren and Hopkinson, who became mayor of Manchester in 1882–83, see *John and Alice Hopkinson (1824–1910)* (ed. Mary Hopkinson and Lady Ewing) (n.d.). Glimpses of the home background are to be found in the autobiography of another son who gained distinction, Sir Alfred Hopkinson, *Penultima* (1930).

62. For Hopkinson's papers to learned societies, see *Original Papers of the Late John Hopkinson* (ed. with a memoir by B. Hopkinson) (Cambridge University Press, 2 vols. 1901). For a recent assessment of him, see James Grieg, *John Hopkinson, 1848–1898* (lecture at King's College, London, 14 November 1949, reprinted from *Engineering*, 13, 20 January 1950).

63. Memoir by B. Hopkinson (*op. cit.*), liv.

64. See the excellent essay in social history by his daughter, Katharine Chorley, *Manchester Made Them* (1950), particularly chapter 6.

65. House of Lords Record Office, Edward Hopkinson, John Hopkinson, Alexander Siemens to Commons' committee on London Central Electric Railway Bill, 29 April 1884; Klapper, *op. cit.*, 57–59.

66. *Railway Times*, 22 September 1883 cited in Klapper, *op. cit.*, 58.

67. *Ibid.*, 59–60; Edward Hopkinson, 'Electrical Tramways: The Bessbrook & Newry Tramway', *Proceedings of the Institution of Civil Engineers, 91* (1888), 193–281.

68. House of Lords Record Office, John Hopkinson to Commons' committee on City of London and Southwark Subway Bill, 19 March 1890.

69. *The Engineer*, 7 November 1890.

70. Sir Benjamin Baker's written contribution to the discussion published at the end of Edward Hopkinson's paper, 'Electrical Railways: The City & South London Railway', *Proceedings of the Institution of Civil Engineers, 112* (1893), 281–2.

71. Minutes, 18 June 1889.

72. House of Lords Record Office, J. H. Greathead, C. G. Mott and John Hopkinson to Commons' committee on City of London and Southwark Subway Bill, 18, 19 March 1890.

73. E. Hopkinson, *op. cit.*, contributions of Greathead, John Hopkinson and Edward Hopkinson, 218, 221, 245, 248, 251, 279.

74. *Herapath's Railway Journal*, 8 March 1890.

75. *Railway Times* and *Herapath's Railway Journal*, 8 November 1890, 11 April 1891. For a passenger's description of the opening journey, see W. J. Passingham, *The Romance of London's Underground* (1932), 52–53.

76. *The Engineer*, 7 June 1889.

77. Lascelles, *op. cit.*, 6–7; 12–13.

78. *The Engineer*, 7 November 1890.

79. *Railway Times* and *Herapath's Railway Journal*, 8 November 1890.

80. *Railway Times*, 4 April, 16, 22 May 1891; Lascelles, *op. cit.*, 17; CSL 1/2, Minutes, 13 October 1891.

81. House of Lords Record Office, Dr. John Hopkinson to Commons' committee on City and South London Railway Bill, 13 March 1891.
82. *Herapath's Railway Journal*, 8 November 1890.
83. E. Hopkinson, *op. cit.*, 227, 279.
84. CSL 1/2, Minutes, 23 October 1890; 24 March, 12 May, 20 July 1891; Lascelles, *op. cit.*, 17; E. Hopkinson, *op. cit.*, 279.
85. E. Hopkinson, *op. cit.*, 227.
86. CSL 1/2, Minutes, 6 May 1890.
87. Lascelles, *op. cit.*, 17.
88. House of Lords Record Office, C. G. Mott to Commons' committee on City and South London Railway Bill, 16 March 1891.
89. For details of traffic, receipts and dividends, see R.C. London Traffic, vol. III, appendix 50, table 1.
90. CSL 1/2, Minutes, 5 May 1891; Lascelles, *op. cit.*, 17, 22–23.
91. Lascelles, *op. cit.*, 18–19.
92. *Ibid.*, 20; 'Jubilee of the City Tube', *Railway Magazine*, 87 (1941), 221, 224.
93. Michael Robbins, 'Lord Kelvin on Electric Railways', *Journal of Transport History*, III (1958), 235–8.
94. Parsons, *op. cit.*, 35–36.
95. House of Lords Record Office, J. S. Forbes to Commons' committee on City and South London Railway Bill, 20 March 1890.

APPENDICES

APPENDIX 1

Termini of short-stage routes from the City in 1825
and the traffic on each route

Destination	Number of coaches	Number of return journeys per day
Acton	1	4
Battersea	1	3
Blackheath	8	22
Blackwall	29	72
Bow and Bromley	2	5
Brentford	11	14
Brixton	7	24
Bromley (Kent)	1	1
Brompton	1	2
Camberwell	23	104
Carshalton	1	1
Chelsea	10	25
Cheshunt	1	1
Clapham	21	57
Clapton	12	44
Cockfosters	1	2
Croydon	5	10
Deptford	2	3
Dulwich	5	11
Ealing	2	3
Edmonton	17	39
Eltham	1	1
Enfield	2	3
Finchley	1	1
Fulham	12	28
Greenwich	10	28
Hackney	7	39
Ham	3	3
Hammersmith	12	30
Hampstead	10	17
Hendon	1	1
Highgate	4	10
Homerton	5	32
Hornsey	4	8
Isleworth	1	2
Islington	11	53
Kennington	6	24

Destination	Number of coaches	Number of return journeys per day
Kensington	5	14
Kentish Town	7	50
Kew Bridge	1	2
Kilburn	2	5
Kingsland	5	20
Lewisham	2	2
Merstham	1	1
Mitcham and Tooting	7	12
Newington	6	27
Norwood	5	13
Paddington	54	158
Peckham	10	40
Plaistow	2	4
Pimlico	1	3
Ponders End	5	8
Richmond	6	12
Roehampton	1	1
Rotherhithe	3	9
Southgate	1	1
Stamford Hill	2	11
Stratford	2	2
Streatham	4	8
Sydenham	5	9
Turnham Green	1	2
Walthamstow	9	9
Waltham Abbey	1	1
Wandsworth	10	23
Wanstead	3	5
Wimbledon	1	2
Woodford	4	6
Woolwich	1	1

Source: A Statement of the Number of Short-Stage Coaches standing in the Streets of the City of London and the daily Number of Journeys performed by them (Corporation of London Records Office, B.12.V).

APPENDIX 2

Board of Stamps' list of omnibuses and short-stages
licensed to operate in the London area 1838–39

Route	Owner	Vehicles	
Balham Hill–Gracechurch Street	Geo. Heathcote	2 o.	1 s.s.
	W. Riches	1 o.	2 s.s.
	R. Render	1 s.s.	
	J. Naylor	1 o.	
	W. Hilton	1 o.	1 s.s.
–Red Lion, Strand	J. Porter	1 s.s.	
–Charing Cross	W. Sheldrick	1 o.	1 s.s.
Battersea–Leadenhall Street	W. Jones	1 o.	
Belgrave Square–Bank	S. Wimbush and Co.	1 o.	
Bexley Heath–Fleet Street	R. Davis	1 s.s.	
Blackheath–Charing Cross	W. Plummer	2 s.s.	
–Catharine Street, Strand	J. Smith	1 s.s.	
–Gracechurch Street	H. and J. Simmons	3 s.s.	
	C. Collins	2 s.s.	
	E. Clarke	2 s.s.	
Blackwall–Leadenhall Street	R. Lambert	1 s.s.	
–Bank	R. Lambert	1 o.	3 s.s.
–Gloster Coffee House, Piccadilly	R. Lambert	3 o.	
	A. Scott	3 o.	
	T. Fardell	9 o.	
	J. Hendricks	2 o.	
	S. Underwood	2 o.	
	T. Allard	1 o.	
	J. Cobb	1 o.	
	Sarah Nelson	2 o.	
–Sloane Street	T. Fardell	7 o.	
	W. Spyers	1 o.	
	S. Underwood	1 o.	
	S. Underwood and Co.	1 o.	
–Edgware Road	T. Wilson	5 o.	
Bow–Green Man and Still, Oxford Street	T. H. Giles	6 o.	
–Hyde Park Corner	T. H. Giles	1 o.	

Route	*Owner*	*Vehicles*	
Brixton Road–Gracechurch Street	M. Balls	1 o.	
	T. Griffiths	1 s.s.	
	T. F. Balls	1 o.	
Brixton Church–Gracechurch Street	M. Balls Junr	3 o.	1 s.s.
	W. Martin	1 o.	
Brixton Hill–Gracechurch Street	M. Balls	4 o.	3 s.s.
	W. Martin	3 o.	2 s.s.
–High Holborn	William Walters	1 s.s.	
–Green Man and Still, Oxford Street	William Walters	2 o.	
	William Martin	1 o.	
–Bow Church	W. Blane	1 s.s.	
	M. Balls	1 s.s.	
Bromley, Mx.–Chelsea	J. Alexander	2 o.	
Brompton, Mx.–Royal Exchange	J. & H. Liley	1 o.	
Camberwell–Fleet Street	T. J. Clifford	1 o.	
	Thomas Walters	1 o.	
–Green Man and Still	W. Stevens	1 o.	
–Gracechurch Street	J. Grayson	1 o.	1 s.s.
	R. Wright	2 o.	
	J. Langley	1 o.	
	J. Shepherd	5 o.	1 s.s.
	J. Wear	1 o.	
	J. Bullock	1 o.	
	W. Jones	1 o.	
	J. Proudfoot	1 o.	
Chelsea–Bank	J. Cripps	1 o.	
–Leadenhall Street	W. Williams	1 o.	
–Whitechapel Church	J. Gomb	1 o.	
–Mile End Gate	W. Bennett	3 o.	
	George Chancellor	9 o.	
	P. Long	4 o.	
	J. Child	1 o.	
	G. Childs	2 o.	
	J. Brown	1 o.	
	H. Wood	1 o.	
	J. Thorogood	1 o.	
	W. Edwick	2 o.	
	W. J. Haydon	1 o.	
	J. Watson	1 o.	
	J. Gomb	1 o.	
Chigwell Row–Royal Exchange	P. Barnard & Co.	4 s.s.	
	W. Powling	1 s.s.	

Route	Owner	Vehicles	
Chingford–Royal Exchange	J. Pitt & Co.	1 s.s.	
Clapham–Gracechurch Street	W. Hilton	1 s.s.	
	F. Harris	1 o.	
–Coach and Horses, Strand	S. Fownes	1 o.	
–Regent's Circus, Piccadilly	S. Fownes	1 o.	
–Green Man and Still,			
Oxford Street	R. Render	1 o.	1 s.s.
–Blue Posts, Holborn	R. Render	1 o.	
Clapham (Plough)–Gracechurch			
Street	W. Dale	2 o.	
	G. Heathcote	1 o.	
	W. Harris	3 o.	
	G. J. Saltwell	1 o.	
	R. Render	1 o.	
	J. Nayler	1 o.	
	W. Riches	1 o.	
	W. Stemp	1 o.	
Clapham Rise–Gracechurch Street	R. Boxall	1 s.s.	
–Green Man and Still,			
Oxford Street	G. Kerrison & Co.	1 o.	
	J. Kerrison & Co.	1 o.	
Clapton–Bishopsgate Street	J. Kerrison	1 o.	1 s.s.
	J. Newman	2 o.	
	J. Breach	1 o.	
	T. Bryan	1 o.	2 s.s.
Clapton Gate–Bishopsgate Street	G. Whitbread	1 o.	
	W. Clarke	1 o.	
	J. Handy	1 o.	
	Thomas Martin	1 o.	
Croydon–Gracechurch Street	J. Moseley	1 s.s.	
	Charles Morton	2 s.s.	
	W. Inkpen	2 o.	3 s.s.
	G. Matthew	1 s.s.	
	Robt. Marshall	1 o.	
	C. Harber	3 s.s.	
	T. Leighton and Co.	1 o.	
–Elephant and Castle	W. Gilham	1 s.s.	
–Green Man and Still,			
Oxford Street	W. Inkpen & Co.	1 s.s.	
–Charing Cross	W. Inkpen & Co.	2 s.s.	
Dalston–Bank	R. Oddy	1 s.s.	

Route	Owner	Vehicles	
Deptford–Fleet Street	J. J. Lucas	1 o.	
	M. Brooks	1 o.	
–Charing Cross	T. Kemiss	1 o.	
–Gloster Coffee House, Piccadilly	A. Courthope	1 o.	
–Gracechurch Street	A. Courthope	1 o.	
Deptford Road–Bank	W. Beenbrook	1 s.s.	
Deptford Lane–Gracechurch Street	R. Webling	1 o.	
	J. Smith	1 o.	
Dulwich–Fleet Street	E. Hogan and Co.	1 s.s.	
	E. Wheels	2 s.s.	
Dulwich–Charing Cross	E. Wheels	1 s.s.	
Dulwich East–Gracechurch Street	J. Glover	1 s.s.	
Ealing–Bank	T. Ives Junr.	2 o.	
	James Ives	1 o.	
East India Docks–Bank	R. Lambert	3 s.s.	
Edgware Road–Bank	R. Goulsborough	1 o.	
	J. Till	2 o.	
	P. Sellick	1 o.	
	S. Taylor	2 o.	
	Thomas Bird	2 o.	
	R. Morgan	2 o.	
	W. Cowderoy	3 o.	
	W. Gilbert	2 o.	
	R. Trevett	2 o.	
	S. Pierce	1 o.	
	J. Newell	1 o.	
	J. Johnson	2 o.	
	W. Waterlow	2 o.	
	M. Sanderson	1 o.	
	S. Gaywood	1 o.	
	T. J. Bolton	4 o.	
	Joseph Bardell	3 o.	
	J. J. Bardell	2 o.	
	R. Blore and Co.	31 o.	
Edmonton–Bishopsgate Street	J. Willis	2 o.	1 s.s.
	S. and J. Isaac	3 o.	2 s.s.
	Joseph St. John	3 o.	1 s.s.
	W. Matthews Junr.	1 s.s.	
–Snow Hill	W. Matthews Junr.	1 o.	
	R. Winder	1 s.s.	
	W. Matthews Senr.	1 o.	2 s.s.
–Bank	E. Gibbons	1 o.	1 s.s.

Route	Owner	Vehicles	
Elephant and Castle–Gracechurch Street	M. Sanderson	1 s.s.	
–Charing Cross	–. Bristow	1 s.s.	
–Tottenham Court Road	N. F. Okey	2 o.	
Enfield–Bishopsgate Street	J. Glover	2 o.	1 s.s.
	W. Glover	1 o.	1 s.s.
Enfield Wash–Bishopsgate Street	W. Wright	1 s.s.	
Euston Square–Regent Circus, Piccadilly	W. Chaplin	1 o.	
–Spread Eagle, Gracechurch Street	W. Chaplin	1 o.	
–Lad Lane	W. Chaplin	1 o.	
–Charing Cross	B. W. Horne	1 o.	
–Cross Keys, Wood Street	B. W. Horne	1 o.	
–George and Blue Boar, Holborn	B. W. Horne	1 o.	
Finchley–Charing Cross	P. Smith	1 o.	
–Bank	D. Ellis	1 s.s.	
Forest Hill–Gracechurch Street	J. Prince	1 s.s.	
Fulham–Bank	J. S. Pickard	1 o.	
	Geo. Webb	4 o.	
	W. Blanch	1 o.	
	T. Coggan & Co.	1 o.	
	J. Patey	1 o.	
	J. Bartlett	1 o.	
	W. King	2 o.	
	J. Kempshall & Co.	3 o.	
Fulham North End–Mile End Gate	J. Williams	1 o.	
Great Western Railway–Bank	E. Sherman & Co.	1 o.	2 s.s.
	H. Edwards	1 o.	
	W. Gilbert	2 o.	1 s.s.
	J. Crawford	1 o.	
	W. Chaplin	2 o.	
	B. W. Horne	1 o.	
Greenwich–Somerset House	J. Matson	1 o.	
–Green Man and Still, Oxford Street	J. Matson	4 o.	
	J. Wheatley	2 o.	
–Charing Cross	J. Wheatley	4 o.	4 s.s.
–King William Street	J. Wheatley	6 s.s.	
Hackney–Royal Exchange	J. Barber Junr.	4 o.	
	M. Fulham	3 o.	

Route	Owner	Vehicles	
Hadley–Blue Posts, Holborn	J. Salmon	1 s.s.	
–Three Nuns, Aldgate	T. Ellwood	1 s.s.	
–Old Bell, Holborn	B. Godden	1 s.s.	
–Blue Posts, Tottenham Court Road	G. Wild	1 s.s.	
Hammersmith Broadway– Leadenhall Street	C. Chesterton	5 o.	
	Thomas Chancellor	1 o.	
–Mile End Gate	J. Williams	1 o.	
	T. Ashton	1 o.	
Hammersmith–Bank	J. Buckmaster	1 o.	
Hammersmith Gate–Whitechapel Church	H. Sibley	3 o.	
Hampstead–Bank	W. Woolley	1 o.	
	A. Hamilton	1 o.	7 s.s.
–Blue Posts, Tottenham Court Road	A. Hamilton	2 o.	
–Blue Posts, Holborn	A. Hamilton	1 o.	
–Charing Cross	A. Hamilton	4 s.s.	
	W. Woolley	1 o.	2 s.s.
Herne Hill–St. Paul's	G. Grayson & Co.	1 o.	
–Gracechurch Street	J. Langley	1 s.s.	
–Bow Church	R. Wright	1 s.s.	
–Camberwell	J. Langley & Co.	1 s.s.	
Highbury Barn–Royal Exchange	E. Wilson and Co.	1 o.	
Highgate–Bank	J. Wiber and Co.	1 o.	
	S. Hickinbottom	1 o.	1 s.s.
Holloway Gate–Bank	M. Spain	1 o.	
Holloway–Charing Cross	T. Shorter and Co.	1 o.	
	E. Wilson and Co.	1 o.	
–Bank	D. Ellis	3 o.	
	W. Whittle	1 o.	
	E. and J. Wilson	1 o.	
–Moorgate Street	E. and J. Wilson	10 o.	
	J. and J. Balls	2 o.	
	J. Barton	1 o.	
Homerton–Bank	R. Steel	2 o.	
	H. Hawkins	1 o.	
Hornsey–Royal Exchange	E. Vass	1 o.	
	D. Ellis	1 o.	
	R. Baker	1 o.	

Route	Owner	Vehicles
Hounslow–Bank	J. Kidd	1 o.
	J. Swait	1 o.
–Coventry Street	Jos. Limpus	1 o.
Isleworth Gate–Bank	T. Powell	4 o.
	J. Swait	1 o.
	J. Kidd	2 o.
	J. Attfield	2 o.
Islington–Elephant and Castle	W. Coleman	1 o.
	J. C. Paul and Co.	1 o.
–Albany Road	E. Morrison	1 o.
Kennington Gate–Islington	W. Hughes	3 o.
	J. Wells	2 o.
	W. E. Coleman	2 o.
	T. Cowling and Co.	2 o.
	J. Lawrence	1 o.
	E. Morrison	2 o.
	W. Chinn	1 o.
	J. C. Paul	1 o.
	C. L. Baker	1 o.
–Tottenham Court Road	T. Howell	1 o.
–King's Cross	R. Hedges	3 o.
	C. L. Baker	2 o.
	T. Cowling and Co.	2 o.
	W. E. Coleman	1 o.
Kensington–Bank	J. Hardiman	1 o.
Kentish Town–Leadenhall Street	Jos. Bardell	3 o.
	Geo. Moore	1 o.
	G. Moore and Co.	1 o.
	J. J. Bardell	2 o.
	J. Wiber and Co.	1 o.
	J. Swift	1 o.
	E. H. King	1 o.
Kent Road–Gracechurch Street	J. Smith	2 o.
Kew Bridge–Bank	Thomas Fitkin	2 o.
	A. Mitchell	1 o.
	T. Powell	3 o.
	George Cloud	4 o.
	H. Mitchell	1 o.
Kilburn–Bank	R. Trevett	1 o.
Kingsland–Bishopsgate Street	Wm. Spinks	2 o.
Lewisham–Gracechurch Street	W. Herring	1 s.s
–Charing Cross	F. Bryant	2 s.s.

Route	Owner	Vehicles
Lisson Grove–Elephant and Castle	Richard Carpenter	3 o.
	J. Till	6 o.
	J. Clarke and Co.	3 o.
	H. Fisher	4 o.
	J. Hill and Co.	3 o.
	James Waterlow	2 o.
	S. Hill	1 o.
	R. Blore and Co.	5 o.
	A. Ward and Co.	2 o.
Mile End Gate—Bond Street, Oxford Street	W. Bennett and Co.	4 o.
	J. Hendricks	2 o.
	J. J. Bardell	2 o.
	W. Hattersley & Co.	1 o.
	J. and R. Bonnor	1 o.
Mill Hill—Blue Posts, Holborn	Wm. Woolley	1 s.s.
Morden–Gracechurch Street	T. and S. Holden	4 s.s.
–Fleet Street	T. and S. Holden	1 s.s.
–Somerset House	T. and S. Holden	2 s.s.
Nine Elms–Lad Lane	W. Chaplin	1 o.
–Spread Eagle, Gracechurch Street	W. Chaplin	1 o.
–Regent Circus, Piccadilly	W. Chaplin	1 o.
–Green Man and Still, Oxford Street	R. Nelson and Co.	1 s.s.
–Old Bell, Holborn	B. W. Horne	1 o.
–George and Blue Boar, Holborn	B. W. Horne	1 o.
Norwood–Gracechurch Street	G. Glover	4 s.s.
–Fleet Street	G. Glover	1 s.s.
–Green Man and Still, Oxford Street	W. Moseley and Co.	1 o. 2 s.s.
Notting Hill–Mile End Gate	J. Dearle	1 o.
	C. Horwood and Co.	6 o.
	R. Blore and Co.	1 o.
Oxford Street–Ludgate Hill	J. Nelson	1 s.s.
Paddington–Bank	G. Smith	2 o.
	D. Hone	1 o.
	J. Hands	1 o.
	R. Carpenter	5 o.
	T. Bull	4 o.
	J. Boissonade	1 o.

Route	Owner	Vehicles	
Paddington–Bank (*contd.*)	R. Trevett	2 o.	
	J. Trevett.	1 o.	
	J. Price and Co.	1 o.	
	J. Hands	3 o.	
	C. Salmon	3 o.	
	S. Pierce	7 o.	
	T. S. Wall	3 o.	
	S. Taylor	2 o.	
	H. Cook	1 o.	
	H. Edmonds and Co.	3 o.	
	H. Edmunds [*sic*]	5 o.	
	S. Gaywood	1 o.	
	T. Purday	1 o.	
	J. Roads	2 o.	
	H. Knapp	2 o.	
	T. Meredith	1 o.	
	F. Meredith	1 o.	
	P. Sellick	2 o.	
Peckham–Gracechurch Street	H. Drew	6 o.	1 s.s.
	J. Prince and Co.	6 o.	1 s.s.
–Charing Cross	E. Tanner	2 o.	
–Fleet Street	George Creed	2 o.	
Peckham (Adam and Eve)–Gracechurch Street	G. Ross	1 o.	
	James Smith	2 o.	
	R. Hodgson	1 o.	
Piccadilly–Elephant and Castle	J. Nelson	1 s.s.	
Pimlico–Leadenhall Street	J. Clark	2 o.	
	H. Tapps	2 o.	
	W. H. Miller	3 o.	
Pine Apple Gate–Bank	R. Blore and Co.	9 o.	
	S. Pierce	1 o.	
	T. Bird	1 o.	
	J. Johnson	1 o.	
	P. Sellick	1 o.	
Pinner–Bull, Holborn	F. Meredith and Co.	1 o.	
Plaistow–Leadenhall Street	S. Covell	1 s.s.	
Putney–Bank	C. Wemsley	1 o.	
Richmond–Bank	T. Harris	1 o.	
	S. Taylor	2 o.	
	R. Ayling	1 o.	
	J. and H. Costelow	1 o.	

2E

Route	*Owner*	*Vehicles*
Richmond–St. Paul's	S. Taylor	4 o.
	J. and H. Costelow	1 o.
Romford–Saracen's Head, Aldgate	E. Boyce	1 s.s.
–Belle Sauvage, Ludgate Hill	E. Boyce	1 s.s.
	T. Collett	1 s.s.
St. John's Wood–Bank	J. Bartlett and Co.	1 o.
	R. Blore and Co.	2 o.
Southgate–Snow Hill	W. Pickard	1 s.s.
	W. Matthews Senr	1 s.s.
Stoke Newington–Kings and Key, Fleet Street	J. Ranson	1 s.s.
–Green Man and Still, Oxford Street	L. Willan	1 o.
–Bank	L. Willan	5 o.
	E. Lapwood	1 o.
	J. Eldridge	1 s.s.
–Bishopsgate Street	T. Hunt	1 o.
	W. Spinks	3 o.
Streatham–Gracechurch Street	G. Newman	2 s.s.
Sydenham–Fleet Street	H. Doo	2 s.s.
–Bow Church	H. Doo	1 s.s.
Teddington–Black Lion, Water Lane	J. Tapps	2 s.s.
Tottenham–Green Man and Still, Oxford Street	L. Willan	1 o.
Tottenham Green–Bishopsgate Street	G. Sumpter	2 o.
Tooting–Gracechurch Street	G. Nightingale & Co.	1 s.s.
	T. and S. Holden	1 o.
–St. Paul's	G. Nightingale & Co.	1 o.
Totteridge–Blue Posts, Holborn	R. Davis and Co.	1 o.
Turnham Green–Bank	J. Hardwick & Co.	2 o.
	T. Powell	1 o.
	G. Cloud	8 o.
Twickenham–Bank	J. Ford	1 o.
	J. Littlewood	2 o.
	W. J. Haynes	1 o.
Uxbridge–New Inn, Old Bailey	R. Nash	1 s.s.
–Bell, Holborn	W. Tollit	1 s.s.
	J. Tollit	2 s.s.
	W. Tollit Junr.	1 s.s.

Route	Owner	Vehicles	
Uxbridge–West Drayton	W. Tollit Junr.	1 o.	
Vassall Road–Gracechurch Street	T. F. Balls	1 o.	
Vauxhall–Gracechurch Street	J. Wheatley	1 o.	
—Oxford Street	J. Wheatley	1 o.	
	W. H. Balls	3 o.	
—Charing Cross	J. Richardson	1 o.	
Walthamstow–Bishopsgate Street	R. Wragg and Co.	2 s.s.	
—Royal Exchange	R. Wragg and Co.	1 s.s.	
Wandsworth–Gracechurch Street	E. Emmett	1 s.s.	
	T. S. Taylor	1 s.s.	
	G. Chaundy	3 s.s.	
—Green Man and Still, Oxford Street	H. Hardingham	1 o.	1 s.s.
—Leadenhall Street	W. Jones	1 o.	1 s.s.
Wandsworth Road–Gracechurch Street	T. Spratley	1 o.	
	G. Reeve	3 o.	
Wanstead–Royal Exchange	T. Green and Co.	2 s.s.	
West Ham–Leadenhall Street	G. Spray	1 s.s.	
	W. Mock	1 s.s.	
	W. Schooling	1 s.s.	
	G. Crump	1 o.	2 s.s.
	W. H. Neale	4 s.s.	
	S. Levy	1 s.s.	
	H. Bish	2 o.	2 s.s.
	G. Woods	1 s.s.	
—Bank	J. Alexander	1 o.	
—Sloane Street	J. Alexander	1 o.	
West India Docks–Billiter Square	R. Lambert	6 s.s.	
Wimbledon–St. Paul's	E. Dawney and Co.	1 o.	
Woolwich–Charing Cross	J. Wheatley	8 o.	
—Deptford	J. Wheatley	6 s.s.	
	C. Melton	1 s.s.	
	—. Connolly	1 s.s.	
	William Pershouse	2 s.s.	
	J. Brooks	1 s.s.	
—Greenwich	J. Mungahl	1 s.s.	
	W. Graves	1 s.s.	

Source: Robson's London Directory for 1839.

APPENDIX 3

List of Omnibuses delivered by Messrs. Orsi and Foucaud
to the London General Omnibus Co. 1856

Date of Payment 1856	Route	No. of omnibuses and name of owner
7 Jan.	Stoke Newington–Bank	2 Forge
		3 McNamara
		1 George Willan
		2 Leonard Willan
		2 Hunt
		1 Woodford
	Kingsland–Bank	3 Forge
		3 McNamara
		2 Woodford
	Kingsland Gate	2 Leonard Willan
	Hackney	5 Barber
	Dalston–Bank	1 Forge
		1 Woodford
13 Jan.	Highbury	48 Wilson
		1 Whittle
		2 Stainton
14 Jan.	Putney Bridge–London Bridge	1 Weaver/Hartley
		6 Roads and Johnson
		2 Webb
		6 Hartley
		3 Hawtrey
	Wimbledon–St. Paul's	1 Hartley
	Brompton–London Bridge	5 Hartley
		1 Hawtrey
		10 Roads and Johnson
		3 Bennett (on 24 Feb.)
	Chelsea–Hoxton	2 Roads and Johnson
		4 McNamara (on 21 Jan.)
		6 Chancellor (on 28 Jan.)
		2 Williams (on 30 Jan.)
		3 Bennett (on 24 Feb.)
	Chelsea–Bethnal Green	2 Roads and Johnson
		2 Smith (on 21 Jan.)

Date of Payment	*Route*	*No. of omnibuses and name of owner*
14 Jan. (*contd.*)	Chelsea–Bethnal Green	6 Chancellor (on 28 Jan.) 2 Williams (30 Jan.) 4 Bennett (on 24 Feb.) 2 Martin (on 24 March)
	Chelsea–Islington	6 Roads and Johnson 2 Joshua Hands 1 Farmer (on 25 Jan.) 2 Kerstian (on 25 Jan.) 2 Wall (on 27 Jan.) 2 Trevett (on 27 Jan.) 2 Rickards (on 28 Jan.) 1 Edmonds (on 10 Feb.) 1 Cook (on 1 April)
18 Jan.	Kent Road and Hoxton	4 Proom 4 McNamara (on 21 Jan.) 1 Hudson (on 21 Jan.) 1 Page (on 23 Jan.) 1 Martin (on 24 March)
	Shoreditch and Elephant and Castle	4 Proom 5 McNamara (on 21 Jan.) 4 John Howes (on 25 Jan.) 1 Westrup (on 25 Jan.)
19 Jan.	Clapton	1 Kerrison 3 Hinkley 1 Mayston 2 H. E. Breach 2 Marden (on 24 March)
21 Jan.	Woodford and Post Office Epping and Post Office Woodford and Lea Bridge Barnet and Post Office Great Western Rly. and London Bridge	4 McNamara 1 McNamara 1 McNamara 2 McNamara 1 Willing 3 Trevett 1 Meredith (on 29 Feb.) 1 Bird (on 9 Dec.)

Date of Payment	Route	No. of omnibuses and name of owner
21 Jan. (contd.)	Royal Oak and Fenchurch St.	1 Trevett
		1 Roads (on 28 Jan.)
		1 Melliship (on 28 Jan.)
		1 Meredith (on 29 Feb.)
	Kilburn Gate and Whitechapel	2 Trevett
		1 Stanbrook (on 1 Feb.)
		1 Seaburn (on 11 Feb.)
	Kilburn Gate and London Bridge	1 Trevett
		1 Melliship (on 28 Jan.)
		1 Stanbrook (on 7 Feb.)
		1 Seaburn (on 11 Feb.)
		1 Unite (on 11 Feb.)
		1 Nettlefold (on 16 Feb.)
	Royal Oak and London Bridge	1 Trevett
		1 Wall (on 23 Jan.)
		1 Roads (on 28 Jan.)
		1 Bird (on 9 Dec.)
		1 Edwards (on 9 Dec.)
	Royal Oak and Whitechapel	1 Trevett
		1 Unite (on 11 Feb.)
		1 Edwards (9 Dec.)
	Whitechapel and Notting Hill	12 Nelson
		1 Bennett (on 22 March)
	Whitechapel and Edgware Rd.	1 Nelson
	Eastern Counties Rly. and Notting Hill	2 Nelson
22 Jan.	New Road	4 Mrs. Bull
		3 Carpenter
		2 Warboys (on 23 Jan.)
		1 Surbey (on 28 Jan.)
		2 Price (on 28 Jan.)
		1 Edmonds (on 10 Feb.)
		1 Nettlefold (on 16 March)
		3 Cook (on 6 July)

Date of Payment	Route	No. of omnibuses and name of owner
22 Jan. (*contd.*)	New Road	4 Steakman (on 24 Aug.) 3 Parker (on 19 Oct.)
23 Jan.	Edgware Road and London Bridge	1 Wall 3 Roads (on 28 Jan.)
	Oxford Street	4 Wall
28 Jan.	Swiss Cottage and London Bridge	1 Roads 1 Melliship
	Clapton Arms and London Bridge	1 Roads
	Marble Arch and Farringdon St.	1 Cotton (on 10 Feb.) 2 Seaburn (on 11 Feb.) 1 Forge (on 11 March)
	Paddington and Oxford Street	2 Melliship
	Brixton and Gracechurch Street	3 Willing
	Camden Town and Camberwell	2 Willing
	Camden Town and Hungerford	1 Willing 2 H. Aste (on 9 March)
	Camden Town and Hungerford Market	1 Willing
	Camden Town, Swiss Cottage and St. John's Wood	1 Willing
4 Feb.	Atlas	2 Henton 1 Augustus Lines (on 1 Sept.)
	City Atlas	1 Henton 3 Augustus Lines (on 1 Sept.) 1 Kempshall (on 1 Dec.) 1 Ashton (on 2 Dec.)
	Kilburn Gate	1 Henton
	New Road–Royal Oak	1 Hone [*sic*]
	Paddington–Holborn	1 Hone [*sic*]
7 Feb.	Royal Oak and London Bridge via Oxford Street	1 Luckeak

Date of Payment	Route	No. of omnibuses and name of owner
10 Feb.	Atlas, St. John's Wood and Camberwell Gate	1 Edmonds
	Great Northern Rly. and London Bridge	1 Edmonds
	Atlas, Swiss Cottage and London Bridge	1 Edmonds
	Pimlico and Blackwall Rly.	15 Clarke
		2 Ingram
11 Feb.	Tottenham to Oxford Street (Green Man and Still) via Balls Pond, Islington, New Road, and Portland Place	1 French
	Camberwell Gate and Swiss Cottage	1 Rickards
	Camberwell Gate and St. John's Wood	1 Rickards
	Notting Hill and Whitechapel	1 Seaburn
15 Feb.	Harlesden Green and London Bridge	1 Andrews
	Kensal Green and London Bridge	2 Andrews
17 Feb.	Edmonton, Southgate and London	1 Catchfield
	Southgate and London	1 Winder
19 Feb.	Edmonton and London	1 Hepper
24 Feb.	Euston Square and London Bridge	1 Adderson
	Swiss Cottage and Camberwell Gate	1 Kershaw
		1 Brown
		2 Green (on 6 July)
		2 Arnell (on 6 July)
26 Feb.	Royal Oak, Westbourne Grove, and London Bridge	1 Hammond
		1 Edward Ellis (on 26 Oct.)
29 Feb.	Wheatsheaf and London Bridge	1 Meredith
	Marlborough Arms	1 Meredith
	Great Western Rly. and Hungerford	1 Meredith
		2 Welch (on 30 March)

Date of Payment	Route	No. of omnibuses and name of owner
29 Feb. (*contd.*)	Notting Hill Gate and Mile End Gate	1 Meredith 9 Herman Hendricks (on 13 April)
	Clarendon Road, Notting Hill and Mile End Gate	1 Meredith
3 March	Old Kent Road and St. John's Wood	1 Broad
	Edmonton and City	1 Petit & 1 James Webb (17 March)
	Wheatsheaf, Edgware Road and London Bridge	1 Bergen 1 William Williams
	Royal Oak, Whitechapel, Oxford Street	1 William Williams
4 March	Ledborough Road and London Bridge	1 T. J. Bolton 8 James Gough (on 6 July)
	Royal Oak and Whitechapel	2 T. J. Bolton
	Royal Oak and Eastern Counties Rly.	1 T. J. Bolton
9 March	Bayswater	2 E. H. Roads 2 Harper Roads 1 Robert Wilson (on 20 March) 2 Bird (on 6 July) 3 Morgan (on 19 Oct.)
	Bayswater and Whitechapel	3 H. Aste 3 Thomas Grant (on 9 March) 1 Forge (on 11 March) 7 Parker (on 19 Oct.)
	Westminster and Bank	3 Langley 5 Gamble
	Hampstead and Bank	5 H. Aste 1 Miller 1 Lowe 1 Rhodes and Pye (on 15 March)
	Kentish Town and Bank	2 H. Aste
	York and Albany and Camberwell Gate	4 H. Aste

Date of Payment	*Route*	*No. of omnibuses and name of owner*
10 March	St. John's Wood and London Bridge	1 Brooks
		1 Cook
16 March	Hungerford and Camden Town	1 William Rhodes
	Mailcoach, Starch Green, and Mile End Gate	1 Boissenade
	Great Northern Rly. and Hungerford	1 Nettlefold
		4 Hedges (on 7 July)
22 March	Notting Hill and Mile End Gate	1 J. Bennett
24 March	Green Gate, Hackney, and Elephant and Castle	2 Martin
31 March	Stratford and Piccadilly	2 Peck
		1 Paul
		2 Ellis
		3 J. E. North
		1 James Smith
		1 Mrs. Scheyer
		1 Pound
		3 E. Smith (on 1 April)
		1 E. Gibbon (on 1 April)
		1 Charles Wenden (on 4 April)
		3 Thomas Wenden (on 6 April)
	Plaistow and Post Office	1 Mann
1 April	Kensington and London Bridge	3 Gard
13 April	Bayswater and Mile End Gate	1 Pickman
	Kilburn Gate and Commercial Street, Whitechapel	1 Herman Hendricks
	Notting Hill Gate and Commercial Street, Whitechapel	5 Herman Hendricks
	Shepherd's Bush and Mile End Gate	1 Herman Hendricks
	Victoria, Acton Bottom and London Bridge	1 Herman Hendricks
	Blackwall and Knightsbridge (Sloane Street)	4 Herman Hendricks
		1 Emmerson
		1 Albon
		2 Elijah Spinks

Date of Payment	Route	No. of omnibuses and name of owners
13 April (*contd.*)	Blackwall and Knightsbridge	2 V. Jones 1 Denchfield 1 Horsman 1 Scott 1 Simmons
19 May	City Atlas, Marlborough and London Bridge	1 Edmonds
	Camden Town and Hungerford	1 Wooley
	City Atlas, Swiss Cottage and London Bridge	1 Edmunds 1 Cook (6 July)
26 May	Eagle, Camden Town, and Kennington Gate	3 Elliott
2 June	Clapton and London	1 Hinckley
8 June	Gracechurch Street and New Cross Gate	3 Joshua Ware
22 June	Peckham Rye and Fleet Street	1 George Creed
29 June	Barnsbury Park and Kennington	5 Hughes 5 Hall (on 6 Oct.)
30 June	Peckham Rye and Oxford Street	2 George Creed 1 Willing (on 13 July)
6 July	Marble Arch	1 Cook 1 Bardell (on 2 Nov.) 1 Bird (on 9 Dec.)
7 July	Cattle Market and Pimlico	2 Isaacs
18 July	Gracechurch Street and Deptford	1 Field 1 Bliss
27 July	Kennington and Islington	2 Cranfield
1 Aug.	Hungerford and Paddington	2 Allen and Weeks 2 Augustus Lines (on 1 Sept.)
	Camden and Kennington	4 Warboys
4 Aug.	Hammersmith and London Bridge	3 Douglas 6 Bardell and Cowderoy 2 Alfred Cloud 3 Hardwick (on 18 Aug.)

Date of Payment	Route	No. of omnibuses and name of owner
24 Aug.	Paddington and Oxford Street	4 Spearman
1 Sept.	Paddington and Hungerford	2 Lines
14 Sept.	Hammersmith	4 Standly
		4 Ayres (on 29 Sept.)
	Kew Bridge	3 Standly
		2 George Cloud (on 6 Oct.)
	Brentford	3 Standly
20 Sept.	King's Cross and Kennington	5 T. J. Bolton
6 Oct.	Clapham and City	2 Howes
	Merton and City	1 Howes
13 Oct.	Finchley and Bank	1 George Bolton
	Wood Green and London Bridge	1 Palmer
19 Oct.	Isleworth and St. Paul's	1 Blackwell
2 Nov.	Kentish Town and Bank	4 Bardell
	Norwood and Gracechurch Street	1 Matthews
10 Nov.	Croydon	1 Hill
1 Dec.	Kilburn Gate, Whitechapel and London Bridge	5 Kempshall
	Kilburn Gate	1 Garton
		2 Ashton (on 2 Dec.)
9 Dec.	Kilburn Gate and London Bridge	2 Bird

Source: B.T.C. Records, L.G.O.C. 4/1.

APPENDIX 4

A History of London Transport
Volume One

Corrigenda

Page

44	Last line	for 'the opening of London's earliest railway' read 'the opening of London's earliest passenger railway'
48	3rd line from bottom	for 'temporary station at the Minories on 8 July 1840' read 'temporary terminus at the Minories on 6 July 1840'.
130	Lines 29–30	for 'and to provide . . . Burton beer' read 'and as events worked out to provide storage space underneath for Burton beer'
130 131	Last 2 lines Lines 1–7	for passage 'From 1 July 1870 . . .' to 'on the High Road.¹²¹' substitute: 'From 1870 suburban passengers also started to reach the Midland line from the Tottenham & Hampstead Junction Railway. Midland trains first ran from Moorgate to Crouch Hill on 1 October 1870, and they were extended to South Tottenham (a station originally called 'West Tottenham & Stamford Hill') when it was opened on 1 May 1871.¹²¹'
133	Lines 24 and 25	the public opening of the East London line was 7 December 1869, giving connection to the Brighton line only at New Cross; the S.E. connection was opened for regular traffic in 1880
207	Line 17	for 'Victoria Palace' read 'Royal Standard (later Victoria Palace)'
210	Line 14	for 'West End Lane, Hampstead' read 'West Hampstead'
210	Line 24	Chesham extension was opened for public traffic on 8 July 1889 (official inauguration 15 May 1889).
220	2nd line from bottom	A workman's return of 6d. from Willesden junction to Euston or Broad Street was introduced in February 1885. In the following June the fare for the return journey of 10 (not 20) miles to Euston was cut to 4d.
231	Line 12 and note	add to end of note on Sir John Wolfe Barry 'He was created K.C.B. in 1897 and assumed the additional surname of Wolfe in 1898.'
266	Line 18	for 'Bermondsey Road' read 'Bermondsey New Road'

267	9th, 10th and 11th lines from bottom	for 'to extend the main line . . . systems' read 'to extend the main line westwards to the North Metropolitan at Clapton although there was to be no connection between the two systems'
291	Line 2	add 'A provident society for Metropolitan Railway staff was set up in 1877 by the company; members paid 3d. or 6d. a week and the company contributed £200 a year, increased to £300 in 1883.'
291	Line 7	for 'Baker Street' read 'Westbourne Terrace'
345	Add at end of Note 73	M. Robbins, 'Fowler's Ghosts', *Railway Magazine*, 109 (1963), 390
348	Note 111, Line 6	for 'Church End, Finchley in June 1869' read 'Finchley and Hendon (renamed Finchley in 1872 and Finchley, Church End in 1894) in November 1869'
349	Note 121, Lines 1–2	Delete 'G. H. Lake, . . . From 1868' and read '*Railway News*, 8 October 1870; *Engineer*, 5 May 1871. From 21 July 1868 . . . '
366	Note 49, lines 11–12	for 'small place called Brill, in Oxfordshire' read 'a small place called Brill on the border of Oxfordshire'